THE
100
BEST
STOCKS
TO BUY IN
2014

PETER SANDER
AND
SCOTT BOBO

Aadamsmedia

AVON, MASSACHUSETTS

Published by
Adams Media, a division of F+W Media, Inc.
57 Littlefield Street, Avon, MA 02322. U.S.A.
www.adamsmedia.com

ISBN 10: 1-4405-6628-3
ISBN 13: 978-1-4405-6628-8
eISBN 10: 1-4405-6629-1
eISBN 13: 978-1-4405-6629-5

Printed in the United States of America.

10 9 8 7 6 5 4 3 2 1

This book is available at quantity discounts for bulk purchases.
For information, please call 1-800-289-0963.

Contents

Dedication

We continue to dedicate this book to all of you active investors who have the sense of purpose and independence of thought to make your own investing decisions, or at least to ask the right questions. You continue to be wise enough—and inquisitive enough—to realize that not all the answers can be found in one place, and smart enough to seek the convenience of a good place to start.

Acknowledgments

Peter continues to be thrilled to have research partner and life friend Scott Bobo on board as an official coauthor of this book. Only Lincoln, Churchill, and Buffett can begin to match his use of humor to make complex matters simple, interesting, and fun. Peter also recognizes the good work of Value Line Inc. and their Investment Survey, which does more than any other known source to turn piles of facts and figures into a simple, readable page. Next, no book happens without the added value of exercise to keep a body in shape and a mind clear, and to that end he offers his thanks to his exercise companions. And of course his boys Julian and Jonathan and new life partner Marjorie inspire him to do this book year after year.

Scott would like to acknowledge the tireless efforts of his friend and coauthor Peter Sander in setting and keeping a high standard in the research and writing of this series. His diligence is what makes these books and our readers successful. Scott's wife Lorie continues to train Scott in the fine art of dissecting financial statements and has yet to complain about the bread crumbs on the keyboard. Scott's brother and sister, in spite of everything, still pick up the phone when he calls. Finally, Scott would like to acknowledge his mother's fearless spirit as a source of inspiration.

PART I

THE ART AND SCIENCE OF INVESTING IN STOCKS

By Peter Sander

The Art and Science of Investing in Stocks

We get two major complaints from you about our annual *100 Best Stocks* books. (Yes, we *do* read your reviews.) But isn't it a bit strange to start off a book by discussing reader complaints? Perhaps, but it also helps us make a couple of key points.

The two complaints are:

- "The book is outdated." (*I won't buy it again as it is not worth it. The data is too far out of date to be helpful.*—Ronald Kudla, January 2013)
- "There aren't enough new companies to look at." ("While I wasn't expecting a huge overhaul, paying for another book to read about 12 new companies on the list doesn't seem like a bargain at all."—D. Ng, November 2011)

As conscientious authors dedicated to serving our reading customers—individual investors and perhaps a few professionals in the community—we read your reviews daily and strive to take your feedback into account as we put together new editions. Your reviews are concise, thoughtful, and helpful (except perhaps for one that cited data inaccuracy based on the price of Coca-Cola, which apparently unbeknownst to that reader had undergone a two-for-one split between the time we wrote it and the time he read it and researched the stock. Our bad, again, I suppose, for the time lag). We encourage the feedback, so much so that I am offering my personal e-mail address for the first time for those reviews: *ginsander@hotmail.com*.

First, about that time lag. Yes, we do the research for our stock list 8–10 months before the year actually starts (for 2014, during March through May of 2013). We know that's a big lag, especially in today's cyberworld. But as I'll explain in the next section, the book is intended as a place to start your research—not to finish it—and the kinds of companies we choose "have legs"—that is, they'll be as good a year or two from now as they are today, or we wouldn't choose them. We know you'd like more current information, and we encourage you to get it from a multitude of more current sources. We couldn't deliver everything you need even if we could deliver this research the day after we completed it.

Second, about the number of companies replaced. Mr. Ng made his comment in a year where we replaced 12 companies. Last year, we replaced 14 out of the 100. This year, we're replacing 8. Why so low? Simply because we've had a great year (more on that in a minute), and we feel that the best horses to get us another win are the same ones we're running now. Remember, our adage is,

"Sell when there's something better to buy." We did a lot of research and didn't come up with much that was better to buy. Importantly, we feel that the stocks we've chosen are not only well positioned to win a stretch drive, but we think they will also do better on a sloppy track—a market downturn or correction. That *too* is part of the selection criteria for a *100 Best Stock*.

Into the Winner's Circle—Almost

It was a terrific finish for last year's *100 Best Stocks* list; in fact, we beat the field handily, finishing ahead of 47 of the 48 Lipper mutual fund benchmarks in our 2013 test period. We got nipped in the stretch by the Lipper Health/Biotech fund benchmark but beat the rest. Upshot: If you had invested with us, you would have done better with us than in all but one fund category—and that category probably brings more risk than our more diversified list. Table 0.1 shows this happy result.

▼ **Table 0.1: Performance Compared to Major Benchmarks**

100 BEST STOCKS 2013 COMPARED TO LIPPER MUTUAL FUND INDEX BENCHMARKS, ONE-YEAR PERFORMANCE, APRIL 1, 2012–APRIL 1, 2013

Fund Benchmark	1-year return	Fund Benchmark	1-year return
Health/Biotech	23.3%	International	9.3%
100 Best Stocks to Buy 2013	19.2%	Pacific Region	9.1%
Mid-Cap Value	18.4%	Balanced	9.0%
Small-Cap Value	16.7%	Multi-Cap Growth	8.6%
Multi-Cap Value	15.7%	International Equity Income	8.3%
Utility	15.3%	Stock/Bond Blend	8.2%
Large-Cap Value	15.0%	General U.S. Taxable	8.0%
Mid-Cap Core	14.9%	Large-Cap Growth	7.4%
Small-Cap Core	14.8%	Long-Term Taxable Bond	7.2%
Equity Income	14.2%	General and Insured Muni	6.3%
Real Estate	13.9%	World Bond	5.6%
S&P 500 Funds	13.3%	Intermediate Bond	5.5%
Multi-Cap Core	13.1%	Short-Term U.S. Bond	5.5%
Large-Cap Core	12.9%	Intermediate U.S. Bond	4.2%
Avg. U.S. Stock Fund	11.8%	Intermediate Muni	4.0%
High-Yield U.S. Taxable	11.8%	Emerging Markets	3.5%
Small-Cap Growth	11.4%	Long-Term U.S. Bond	3.3%
European Region	11.2%	Science and Tech	2.9%
Telecommunications	11.2%	Mortgage Bond Funds	2.9%
Global Equity Income	11.0%	Short-Term Taxable Bond	2.7%
High-Yield Muni	10.1%	Short-Term Muni	0.8%
Global	9.9%	Specialty Diversified Equity	0.1%
Mid-Cap Growth	9.7%	Latin American	-2.2%
Natural Resources	9.7%	Gold Oriented	-23.6%

It's (Even More) about the Individual Investor

If you bought this book, you're probably an astute and experienced individual investor who invests in individual stocks in individual companies. Are you alone? Heck no. In fact, more and more investors are putting themselves in the driver's seat. Why? It's simple: "Nobody cares about your money more than you do."

The trend towards self-directed investing was highlighted in a recent *Wall Street Journal* article entitled "A New Era for Do-It-Yourself Investing." In the study central to the article, they asked mostly middle-tier investors whether they were relying more or relying less on advisers since the 2008–09 financial crisis. Some 50 percent of respondents said "less"; only 21 percent said "more." (The rest said "no change.") They cited a trend toward "investors wanting to be more involved" and toward brokerages offering do-it-yourself services with only occasional help from professional advisers when requested.

Does this mean that everyone is picking their own stocks? No, not necessarily, and not entirely. They may still be using any of among the 14,000 mutual funds or 1,500 exchange-traded fund (ETF) "products" (or hedge funds, if they're wealthy enough) that do the driving for them.

What's emerging today is actually a hybrid model. Do most of the decision-making and work yourself, and get an adviser when you need one. It's in that spirit we provide this book.

Every edition of *The 100 Best Stocks to Buy* is intended as a core tool for the individual investor. Sure, it's hardly the only tool available. Today's explosion of Internet-based investing tools has made this book one of hundreds of choices for acquiring investing information. With the speed of cyberspace, our book will hardly be the most current source.

So does the delay built into the publishing cycle make our book a poor information source? Not at all. As we previously said, it works because the companies we choose don't change so much and because they avoid the temptation to manage short-term, quarter-to-quarter performance. We chose these companies *because* they have sustainable performance, so who cares if the latest details or news releases are included? In *100 Best Stocks to Buy in 2014*, as with all of our previous editions, we focus on the *story*—the story of each company—not just the latest facts and figures.

As such, *100 Best Stocks* is intended as a handy guide and core reference for your investing, not as a be-all end-all investing source. Thus, as much as a source of facts and numbers itself, *100 Best Stocks* is intended to present the story for each company and to serve as a model for selecting the best companies and stocks to invest in. By narrowing the universe to the best and the brightest companies out there, *100 Best Stocks* is designed to serve as a place to start, not finish, your investment analysis.

To that same point, *100 Best Stocks* goes well beyond just being a stock screen or a study of stocks to invest in. Analysis forms the base of *100 Best Stocks*, but it isn't the rigid, strictly numbers-based selection and analysis so often found in published "best stocks" lists. Sure, we look at earnings, cash flow, balance sheet strength, and so forth, but we'll also look far beyond those things. We'll look at the intangible and often subtle factors that make truly great businesses—that is, companies—great. That is, once again, the *story*.

We feel that the 100 companies listed and analyzed in the pages that follow are the best companies to own for 2014. That said, the word "own" has become a more active concept these days. Gone are the days of "own forever." Today, there is no forever; the economy, technology, and consumer tastes simply change too fast, and the businesses that participate in the economy by necessity change with it.

So going forward, we offer the 100 best companies to own now and in 2014, those that have the best chances of not only surviving but evolving with—or even ahead of—the economy based on their current market position and approach to doing business. We think these are the best companies to (1) stay with or perhaps stay slightly ahead of business change, (2) provide short- and long-term returns in the form of cash and modest appreciation, and (3) do so with a measure of safety or at least reduced volatility so that you can burn your energy doing other things besides staring at stock quote screens and CNBC day and night.

What this all means is simple and straightforward: You'll have to take the information presented, do your own assessment, reach your own conclusions, and take your own actions. Anything else would go beyond our intentions, and more importantly, stop short of the mark for you.

With that in mind, make the most of what follows, and good luck with your investing!

What's New for 2014

For 2014, we've charted the same course. Continuing forward is our emphasis on sustainable value, strong market position and other intangibles, and sustainable and growing cash returns to investors, in the form of dividends and share buybacks as well as share appreciation. We continue to take interest in the persistency of dividend increases above and beyond the yield itself, and we continue to stay focused on total shareholder returns.

That all said, there are a few minor points of evolution to disclose. That is, they are slight tweaks in our approach and thought process in selecting companies:

- *Low-volatility bias.* We have always reported the figure *beta*, a slightly imperfect but widely available measure of a stock's performance relative to the market (a beta less than 1.00 means a stock tends to fluctuate less than the overall market as measured by the S&P 500 index). But this year, a new emphasis on getting decent returns *with minimal risk* has become a new investing theme, demonstrated by the advent of new exchange-traded funds tied to specially crafted low-volatility indexes, and perhaps brought home even more by Peter's research and compilation of a new book, *All about Low Volatility Investing* (McGraw-Hill, 2014). With the right approach to investing, you can get decent, slightly better than average returns, while still being able to sleep at night. In this year's edition, we brought that idea more to the forefront, taking beta more into consideration and making more mention of it in our narratives.

- *A little more defense.* The markets blew through the records in early 2013, and we're naturally cautious animals anyway. As we go to press, many of our picks—and most of the alternatives—are at 52-week or even all-time highs. We think the coming year may be a good time to get a little more defensive. We're already heavy in so-called defensive stocks—food, consumer nondurables, energy—but we upped that just a bit and took a couple of companies that had just seemed to outgrow reasonable expectations, such as Caterpillar, off the list. As we move forward we wouldn't be surprised to see our list lose ground in the coming year, but we'd still expect to "win the race" by losing less than the overall market and comparative benchmarks.

- *Our first investment "product"—a REIT.* Up to now, we have stuck exclusively with ordinary stocks in individual companies (with a handful of "ADRs" for foreign companies sprinkled in; these are essentially stocks). This year, we added a REIT—a real estate investment trust—to the mix to get a good yield and some safe and income-oriented exposure to the real estate market. It is the Health Care REIT (that's the name of the investment company), specializing in medical and senior care facilities throughout the U.S. We are also *de facto* taking on a second REIT as long-time *100 Best* pick Iron Mountain Inc. is currently converting itself to a REIT. For all intents and purposes it acts like a stock, but it is structured differently, paying out 90 percent of income. (As such, it may have different tax consequences for you as an investor. For this and more about investing in REITs, see our Iron Mountain entry.) We don't expect to make this a book about funds but may sprinkle a few such investments going forward in the interest of returns and diversification. In that spirit, we introduce a new section about ETFs at the end of Part I and offer a list of ETFs that follow many of the same principles that guide our *100 Best Stocks* selections.

About Your Authors

PETER SANDER

Peter is an independent professional researcher, writer, and journalist specializing in personal finance, investing, and location reference, as well as other general business topics. He has written 39 books on these topics, as well as numerous financial columns, and performed independent, privately contracted research and studies. He came from a background in the corporate world, having experienced a 21-year career with a major West Coast technology firm.

He is, most emphatically, an individual investor, and has been since the age of 12, when his curiosity at the family breakfast table got the better of him. He started reading the stock pages with his parents.

Yes, he has an MBA from Indiana University in Bloomington, but it isn't an MBA in finance. He also took the coursework and certification exam to become a certified financial planner (CFP). By design and choice, he has never held a job in the financial profession. His goal has always been to share his knowledge and experience in an educational way, a way helpful for the individual as an investor and a personal financier to make his or her own decisions.

He has never earned a living giving direct investment advice or managing money for others, nor does he intend to.

Peter began his investment writing career with *Value Investing for Dummies* and has been writing on value-oriented investing ever since.

SCOTT BOBO

Peter and Scott have been friends and colleagues since, roughly, tenth grade (a long time!). Scott has been part of the team for 3 years, and has been huge not only in identifying the *100 Best Stocks* but also analyzing them and explaining their pros and cons crisply and in plain English so that you can make the best use of the list. Having Scott on the team allows you to get the combined wisdom and observations of 2 people, not just 1, in an arena where 1 plus 1 almost always equals something greater than 2.

Scott has been an investor since age 14, when he made the switch from analyzing baseball box scores to looking at the numbers and charts in the business section. In his 20-plus years in engineering and technology management, he's learned that a unique product value proposition is important to the success of any company. He has also learned (the hard way) that proper financial fundamentals are critical. From a development manager's perspective, comprehending a new product's risk/reward proposition is one of the keys to a company's success. From an investor's perspective, it's also one of the keys to successful value investing in a dynamic, innovation-driven market.

Scott adds a strong analytical touch. But he is most at home as an applications engineer, explaining how a company's products work and how they apply to a customer's needs. Consequently, and in addition to analytical legwork, Scott really adds an extraordinary and very real-world sense of how a company's products "fit" in the marketplace. Determining whether a company's products are relevant, best-in-class, and have a competitive advantage over others is an oft-overlooked core skill for a value investor. Scott brings this skill to the table in a big way.

Scott is the co-creator and the driving force behind our *100 Best Aggressive Stocks* and *100 Best Technology Stocks* books published in 2012.

A "Low-Volatility" Investing Book

You've heard about—and just read about—the new trend toward low-volatility investing. That is, investing to minimize risk and volatility—to be able to sleep at night and count on your otherwise unpredictable retirement—and achieve decent investing returns all the same. That's the subject of Peter's new aforementioned book, and some of the "DNA" from that book has leaked into this one.

What we're getting at here is the low-volatility nature of the sequential editions of this book. We try to keep the analysis the same, and for the most part we keep the presentation the same. Each year we make a few adjustments, pruning away a few stocks and adding a few others. We do that adhering to our core principles without having any particular number of changes in mind. This year, in a tip of our caps to the "horses we rode in on," we are only changing 8 stocks. Tables 3, 4, and 5 detail the 8 deletions and additions to the 2013 list.

The methodology used for analysis and selection of the *100 Best Stocks* remains largely unchanged. We continue to place more focus on dividends. More and more, especially in today's volatile markets, we feel that investors should get paid something to commit their precious capital to a company; it's a sign of good faith to investors and provides at least some return while waiting for a larger return in the future—or if things happen to go south later on. So, as it turns out, some 98 of this year's *100 Best* pay at least some dividends—that's up from 96 last year, 95 in 2012, and 91 on the 2011 list. Apple fell out of that tree in a big way, declaring a dividend exceeding $10 and recently raised to $12.20 annually. That leaves only CarMax and Itron. These stocks are included because of other excellence factors; we can turn our heads the other way on the dividend for a while but would expect some dividends eventually as the business models mature. Additionally, for dividend-paying stocks, we continue our preference for companies with a track record for regular dividend *increases*. We have started tracking, for each company, the number of dividend increases or *raises* (yes, you can think of them as comparable to a raise in your own wage or salary) in the past 10 years. We are proud to report that of the 98 *100 Best* stocks paying dividends, fully *88* of them raised their dividend from 2012 to 2013. Of those 98, *53* of them have raised their dividends in each of the past 10 years, and 13 more have raised them each of the past 9 years (most took a year off during the Great Recession) adding up to 66, or almost two-thirds of our stocks able and willing to give you annual raises. Pretty good stuff, in our view.

As in all editions, we will give you a performance report on our 2013 picks, which as noted earlier, were pretty successful. Finally, we will continue with our "stars" lists identifying the best stocks in 6 different categories, with one small tweak:

1. Yield Stars (stocks with solid dividend yields—Table 6)
2. Dividend Aggressors (companies with strong and persistent records and policies toward dividend *growth*—Table 6.1)
3. Safety Stars (solid performers in any market—Table 7)
4. Growth Stars (companies positioned for above-average growth—Table 8)
5. Prosperity Stars (formerly Recovery Stars—companies poised to emerge rapidly from the recovery. Now that the recovery seems to be in full swing, these are companies expected to do particularly well in a strong economy—Table 9)
6. Moat Stars (companies with significant sustainable competitive advantage—Table 10)

So, if you're an investor partial to any of these factors, like safety, these lists are for you.

Oh, What an Amazing Year!

The strong market performance in 2012 and especially the early months of 2013 doesn't require much explanation—if you were watching the news or watching your stocks at all, you saw it. Stocks went up—almost all stocks—in a persistent march quite unlike the more "bubbly" advances of the dot-com era. Fears—some left over from the 2008–2009 crisis itself—subsided, while at the same time, companies had been whipped into shape by that crisis to restructure and fine-tune their operations toward greater efficiency. All the while, the Fed pumped billions of stimulus dollars into the economy through their quantitative easing bond-buying program. Europe, while still a problem, sent smaller shockwaves into the markets as it appeared that local authorities were willing to take more action to deal with the recession. As we feel the "Europe problem" is really a euphemism for excessive debt and fragility of the banking system, we're not sure everyone's out of the woods yet, but the declining fears of an immediate Europe (or Europe-triggered) calamity did help.

Companies eked out higher profits, but not so much higher as *share price* growth would indicate. Most companies grew earnings in the single digits, while their share prices advanced in double digits. Why? First, many companies with a strong international presence (admittedly, one of our stronger preferences) faced currency headwinds—many lost as much as 5 percent off the top and bottom line to currency exchange. The market, as it probably should, seemed to forgive that. Many companies were also in the final stages of restructuring programs induced by the recession, and commodity prices ran high during the period.

All that said, the pace of share repurchases continued to run very high, as companies, regardless of earnings performance, continued to act as cash-generating machines despite the attenuated earnings. Some $274 billion in share buybacks (in excess of share issuance) was achieved by U.S. companies through September 2012, and another $286 billion is in the pipeline through 2013. More than half the companies on our *100 Best Stocks* list could be classified as "buyback aggressors," retiring 10–20 percent and sometimes more of their outstanding shares since 2004—all of which, of course, serves to increase returns, both to the shareholders that sell and those who remain to enjoy a higher rate of return on the remaining shares.

Going forward—and as indicated by stock prices as we go forward in mid-2013—business trends will continue favorably. Still greater efficiencies, the apparent winding down of commodity prices, solid energy supply, a still-accommodative Fed, and a shrinking fear of global calamity all seem to be propelling things forward. Currency headwinds may linger as other economies, notably Japan, make aggressive moves towards devaluing their currencies and stimulating their economies. We think it's rather like one of those fair-weather days after a storm passes, with beautiful, bright, clear sunshine and those puffy white clouds, which don't pose so much as a threat with all of the stable, high-pressure air around them. But they're still there, and a change in atmospheric pressure, humidity, or a host of other factors can cause those clouds to grow skyward into threatening cumulonimbus clouds once again.

What are some of those "other factors" that could change the stable weather pattern? We remain concerned about debt levels and continued complexity (and fragility) of the financial system. Although we've gotten used to most of this, and have learned how to handle some of the smaller shocks, like Cyprus, there are still elephants in the room. We are also concerned about the eventual transition of Fed chair Bernanke and the gathering clouds of reduced Fed stimulus flows (translation: higher interest rates) —how fast that might happen and what the impacts might be. The Fed has gotten a lot better about reducing the surprise factor, but there's still a substance factor—a change—to contend with. We also have political gridlock and a president who continues to move toward lame duck status. Big problems won't get solved quickly.

For businesses, we do see continued plusses in lower commodity prices, greater efficiencies, and what we see as an eroding China factor—that is, China and other low-cost manufacturing "havens" aren't the havens they were once thought to be. We've cited this before, and still think there will be a continuing trend toward locating high-value-add manufacturing activities back in the United States, along with a continuation of foreign companies locating here. The Japanese situation is a wild card, with the recent yen devaluation moving a lot of high-value-add manufacturing that way, too, but a stronger Japanese market also bodes well for U.S. markets. In sum, we think 2014 will be a good year for stocks but are more cautious in light of recent gains. We feel we are in good position to capture the year's gains, but also to weather any storm that might arise from those puffy white clouds. Our mantra remains: Buy stocks in companies that make or do things people want and can make or deliver them efficiently.

Report Card: Recapping Our 2013 Picks

Who would ever have thought that Apple would be our biggest loser on the 2013 list? It was, and fellow tech titan Intel was Loser #2.

First, however, just a short reminder of how we evaluate our gains. There are many ways to evaluate the performance of a group of stocks over time. Some are simplistic, such as simply averaging the percent gain in each share price. But such a method may not weight a portfolio very realistically, for it assumes you buy the same number of shares of Apple at $450 as you would Southwest Airlines at $14. We continue to feel it's better to take the approach of an investor with $100,000 to invest—who invested $1,000 in each of the *100 Best Stocks* across the board, regardless of share price. Sure, you end up with some weird quantities of shares in your portfolio, but the portfolio, and thus the performance metrics, isn't weighted in favor of more expensive stocks.

The Bottom Line

We already gave you the bottom line of our "grade A" 2013 performance—up a full 19.2 percent for the year. This means that if you had invested $100,000 in our *100 Best Stocks 2013* list—$1,000 in each of the 100 stocks, on April 1, 2012—you would have ended up with $116,652 on April 1, 2013, not including dividends paid during that period. That's a 16.7 percent gain. Including dividends of some $2,684 (up from $2,327 last year), you would have ended up with $119,246. The S&P, as measured by the buyable SPDR S&P 500 ETF Trust, was ahead just 11.4 percent ($114,110) during that period—a clear victory for us by several lengths.

Winners and Losers

The full list of the *100 Best Stocks 2013* and how they did through the comparison period can be found in Appendix A. At this point, we'll give a short overview of what worked and what didn't. First, the winners:

▼ Table 1: Performance Analysis: *100 Best Stocks 2013*
TOP WINNERS, 1-YEAR GAIN/LOSS,
APRIL 1, 2012–APRIL 1, 2013; * = NEW FOR 2013

Company	Symbol	Price 4/1/2012	Price 4/1/2013	% change	Dollar gain, per $1,000 invested* = New for 2013
Valero*	VLO	$25.77	$45.49	76.5%	$765.23
Southwest Airlines	LUV	$8.24	$13.48	63.6%	$635.92
Visa	V	$78.12	$123.16	57.7%	$576.55
Whirlpool*	WHR	$76.86	$118.46	54.1%	$541.24
Time Warner Inc.*	TWX	$37.75	$57.62	52.6%	$526.36
Amgen	AMGN	$67.87	$102.51	51.0%	$510.39
Otter Tail	OTTR	$21.70	$31.14	43.5%	$435.02
Comcast	CMCSA	$30.01	$41.98	39.9%	$398.87
Cincinnati Financial	CINF	$34.51	$47.22	36.8%	$368.30
Seagate Technology*	STX	$26.96	$36.56	35.6%	$356.08
Eastman Chemical*	EMN	$51.69	$69.87	35.2%	$351.71
McCormick	MKC	$54.43	$73.55	35.1%	$351.28
Heinz	HNZ	$53.55	$72.27	35.0%	$349.58
Campbell Soup	CPB	$33.85	$45.36	34.0%	$340.03
International Paper	IP	$35.10	$46.58	32.7%	$327.07
Kimberly-Clark	KMB	$73.89	$97.98	32.6%	$326.03
Union Pacific	UNP	$107.48	$142.41	32.5%	$324.99
Monsanto	MON	$79.76	$105.63	32.4%	$324.35
Church & Dwight	CHD	$49.19	$64.63	31.4%	$313.88
Clorox	CLX	$68.75	$88.53	28.8%	$287.71

Our overall winning percentage was better than ever as mentioned earlier, with some 87 of our *100 Best* picks finishing ahead of last year even before dividends. The good were good and the better were better: This was the year for recent picks and for excellent companies that took a little while longer to recover from the recession. Three of the 5 top winners—Valero,

Whirlpool, and Time Warner—were new picks for the year, and all but one of the top 10 winners were added in the past 3 years. We caught the resurgence in the refining business (translation: lower-cost domestic crude) and a stepping forward of stocks that generally perform well with a solid economy—Southwest, Visa, and Whirlpool. Previously undiscovered value was discovered in Otter Tail, Comcast, Cincinnati Financial, Seagate, and Eastman. Then we get to our list of solid and steady food and staples stocks such as Campbell Soup and Kimberly-Clark. It didn't hurt that Warren Buffett's Berkshire Hathaway took Heinz off our hands at a nice premium—the second year in a row this has happened (following Lubrizol in 2012).

Now, for the losers:

▼ **Table 2: Performance Analysis:** *100 Best Stocks 2013*

TOP LOSERS, 1-YEAR GAIN/LOSS,
APRIL 1, 2012–APRIL 1, 2013; * = NEW FOR 2013

Company	Symbol	Price 4/1/2012	Price 4/1/2013	% change	Gain/loss per $1,000 invested
Suburban Propane	SPH	$43.00	$44.50	3.5%	$34.88
IBM	IBM	$208.65	$213.30	2.2%	$22.29
Itron*	ITRI	$45.41	$46.40	2.2%	$21.80
Aetna	AET	$50.16	$51.13	1.9%	$19.34
Starbucks	SBUX	$55.89	$56.95	1.9%	$18.97
McDonald's	MCD	$98.10	$99.69	1.6%	$16.21
Tiffany*	TIF	$69.13	$69.54	0.6%	$5.93
Verizon	VZ	$37.78	$37.26	-1.4%	$(13.76)
Bed Bath & Beyond	BBBY	$65.77	$64.42	-2.1%	$(20.53)
Praxair	PX	$114.64	$111.54	-2.7%	$(27.04)
UnitedHealth Group	UNH	$58.94	$57.21	-2.9%	$(29.35)
Harman International*	HAR	$46.81	$44.63	-4.7%	$(46.57)
Total S.A.	TOT	$51.12	$47.98	-6.1%	$(61.42)
DuPont	DD	$52.90	$49.16	-7.1%	$(70.70)
St. Jude Medical	STJ	$44.31	$40.44	-8.7%	$(87.34)
United Technologies	UTX	$89.58	$79.80	-10.9%	$(109.18)

Teva Pharmaceuticals	TEVA	$45.06	$39.68	-11.9%	$(119.40)
Caterpillar	CAT	$106.52	$86.97	-18.4%	$(183.53)
Intel*	INTC	$28.12	$21.84	-22.3%	$(223.33)
Apple	AAPL	$599.55	$442.66	-26.2%	$(261.68)

While we would have liked to have all *100 Best* stocks turn out to be winners, the odds are stacked pretty highly against that. That said, only 13 losers out of 100 ain't bad.

As we already pointed out, Apple and Intel improbably topped our losers' list. We think Apple overcorrected in its transition from a growth to a value stock and has a few other unanswered questions, but a 26.2 percent drop was a bit much. The rest of the list has a few highfliers like Starbucks, Teva, and Bed Bath & Beyond that just didn't fly, and a few such as Total S.A., Caterpillar, McDonald's, IBM, and perhaps DuPont that were hurt a bit more by European jitters than some. DuPont had that problem and was hit a little more by investments in alternative energy. Realize that the first 7 stocks on this list were gainers, though they were just small gains and were bested by the rest of our list.

Sustainable Investing

With the recent volatility and the speed of change becoming an increasingly permanent characteristic of today's markets, many financial journalists and pundits have recently announced the demise of long-term investing, specifically the so-called "buy-and-hold" strategy. The speed of change—change in technology and consumer tastes (think tablets and the PC industry), news-driven change (think BP or JP Morgan Chase), or change in market structure and business models (think Netflix or Blockbuster)—does indeed bring some concern to the idea of buying shares and locking them away in your safe deposit box. More than ever, you need to stay on your toes and watch for change.

What it really means is that you need to select companies that understand their markets, adapt well to change, and stay in front it. It also means that a periodic review of your investments—*all* of your investments—is more important than ever. You should evaluate from scratch every stock you own, as though you were going to buy it again, at least once a year. That's what we do when compiling a *100 Best Stocks* list.

That doesn't mean that long-term investing is dead. Great companies respond to change and find ways to continue to satisfy customers and make money, regardless of the mood and change of the day. Companies such as Procter & Gamble reinvent themselves constantly, not with a big house-cleaning (pardon the pun) and restructuring every few years. Southwest Airlines tweaked their offering a bit to attract more revenue from business customers without upsetting their traditional consumer base with baggage fees and the like. Coca-Cola and PepsiCo are both innovating new ways to custom mix and dispense beverages at restaurants and fountains. Starbucks is rapidly evolving their single-serve and K-Cup businesses. You get the idea.

Value—Now More Than Ever

The bottom line is this: For intelligent investors, chasing the latest fad doesn't work; neither does buying something and locking it away forever. Investors must make intelligent choices based on true value and follow those choices through time and change. It all points to taking a value-oriented approach to investing and to staying modestly active with your investments.

The next obvious task is to define what we mean by a "value" approach. Essentially, it is to think of buying shares in a company as buying the company itself; it is about putting yourself in an entrepreneurial frame of mind, not just an investment frame of mind. Would you want to own that business? Why or why not?

Fundamentally, whether or not you want to own the business depends on two factors: first, the returns you expect to receive on your investment in the near- and long-term future, and second, the risk you'll take in generating those returns. Fortunately, the third factor the prospective entrepreneur must consider—"Do I have the time for this?"—is less of a consideration for the investor.

You are looking for tangible value—tangible worth—for your precious, scarce, and hard-earned investment capital. That return doesn't have to be immediate in the form of dividends or a share of the assets, as many in the traditional "value school" suggest. It can come as growth for the longer term. If you realize your return in the form of owning a share of a larger company eventually, that's still a legitimate return. Cash flow received later in the form of a higher share price or a takeover is still cash return; it is just less certain because of the forces of change that may take place in the interim. It is also theoretically worth less because of the nature of discounting—a dollar received tomorrow is worth more than a dollar received 20 years in the future.

The point: Many investment experts distinguish between "value" and "growth" investing; in fact, mutual funds are often classified as being one or the other. We dismiss this separation; growth can be an essential component of a firm's value.

Value also implies safety. The safety comes in three forms. First is the fundamental quality and soundness of the firm's financial fundamentals—that is, income, cash flow, and the balance sheet. Value companies have plenty of reserves, a large enough *margin of safety*, to weather downturns and unforeseen events in the marketplace. Second, they have strong enough intangibles (brands, market position, supply-chain strength, etc.) to maintain their position in that marketplace and generate future returns.

Thirdly, if you're really practicing value-investing principles, you buy these companies at reduced prices, when the markets are down, when the company is out of favor. You're looking for situations where the price is less than what you perceive to be the value, although calculating the value that precisely is elusive. When you "buy cheap" you provide another margin of safety; that margin makes it less likely that the stock will drop further. It gives you room for error if you turn out to be wrong about a choice. Again, it's much like buying a business of your own—you want to pay as little as possible in case things don't turn out as you'd expect.

So taking a value approach provides greater confidence and safety and is more likely to get you through today's volatile business and investing cycles.

Stay Active

What do we mean by "stay active"? Staying active means that you should remain abreast of your investment and, like any business you own, keep an eye on its performance. Periodically review it as you would your own finances to see if it is making money and generally doing what you think it should be doing. You may watch the stock price daily, and you may also watch for news bulletins about the company, and you should keep track of earnings announcements.

Time permitting, you should listen in on investor conference calls (usually at earnings announcements) to see what management has to say about the business. In addition, you should watch your business in the marketplace. See how many people are going to your local Starbucks and whether they are enjoying the experience, and look for other signs of excellence. We're not talking about constantly monitoring the stock price. Instead, we're suggesting a remote oversight of the business as though it were one of a portfolio of businesses you happen to own that, while professionally managed, requires an occasional glance to make sure everything is still acting according to your best interests. We also recommend a periodic review—at least annually—of whether your investments are still your best investments.

Evaluate each investment against its alternatives. If you still perceive it to be the best value out there, keep it. If not, consider a swap for something new.

YOU DON'T NEED TO BE A MATH GENIUS

Calculating value can be a daunting task, especially if one goes into the nuances of compounding, discounting, and all that business school stuff. Today's value investor doesn't ignore the numbers but shuns complex mathematical formulas, which in the recent bust, tended not to work anyway; greater forces overtook almost all statistical and mathematical models for stock analysis, leaving many a "quant" scratching his or her head.

Buying companies is not a math-driven process, just as you can't evaluate a school based on its test scores alone. Warren Buffett and Charlie Munger have made this clear over the years and came back to the point with emphasis in the 2009 Berkshire Hathaway shareholders meeting. Buffett mused: "If you need to use a computer or a calculator to make the calculation, you shouldn't buy it." Reading between the lines: the story should be simple and straightforward enough to be obvious without detailed calculations.

Munger, Buffett's relatively more intrepid sidekick, added: "Some of the worst business decisions I've ever seen are those with future projections and discounts back. It seems like the higher mathematics with more false precision should help you, but it doesn't. They teach that in business school because, well, they've got to do something."

No need to read between the lines there.

Indeed, while the numbers are important, savvy value investors try to see where the puck is going. And that means a clear-eyed assessment of the intangible things that make companies great.

The *100 Best Stocks* for 2014: A Few Comments

Although not every indicator points up at the present time, America and many other parts of the world seem to be in a gradual recovery. At least things are better than they were in the depths of the Great Recession.

At the moment, we do foresee a continued rebound in U.S. manufacturing and value-add economic activity. Many companies have found out
that moving stuff overseas isn't the good-times panacea they had all anticipated. Foreign companies continue to invest in the United States because of
good supply chains and skills for building things like automotive transmissions and electronics here, although that trend may slow a bit with the weakening of the Japanese yen and the competitive pressure that might lead to.

We continue to believe—and hope—that we are undergoing a long-
term, semisubconscious adjustment away from financial services and other
low-value-add industries to a back-to-basics, let's-make-things-that-people-
need mentality. We are slowly moving back toward the thinking that factories and research labs are better places to put capital than housing and real
estate; that should bode well for the longer term.

For 2014, as always, we think that companies will do well that have
good business models, produce high-value-add things that people (or companies) need, do it efficiently, and generate a lot of cash. First, though, the
companies removed from the 2013 list:

▼ Table 3: Companies Removed from 2013 List

Company	Symbol	Category	Sector
Bed Bath & Beyond	BBBY	Aggressive Growth	Retail
Caterpillar	CAT	Aggressive Growth	Industrials
ExxonMobil	XOM	Growth and Income	Energy
Heinz	HNZ	Growth and Income	Consumer Staples
Intel	INTC	Conservative Growth	Information Technology
Marathon Oil	MRO	Growth and Income	Energy
Nucor	NUE	Aggressive Growth	Materials
Teva Pharmaceuticals	TEVA	Aggressive Growth	Health Care
Harris	HRS	Aggressive Growth	Information Technology
Hewlett-Packard	HPQ	Aggressive Growth	Information Technology
Lubrizol	LZ	Growth and Income	Materials
Northern Trust	NTRS	Conservative Growth	Financials
Oracle	ORCL	Aggressive Growth	Technology
Staples	SPLS	Aggressive Growth	Retail

With one exception, it wasn't easy to cut anybody from the 2013 list! The one exception was easy—Heinz—because it was acquired by Buffett's Berkshire Hathaway and private equity firm 3G Capital.

The rest of the story starts with the fact that we only had 13 losers to begin with, but of course, we don't just look at last year's performance. We did develop some longer-term strategic concerns about the remaining 7 deletions; hence, their removal from the list. Bed Bath & Beyond was doing okay, but not as well as we would have hoped given the housing and recession recovery; we feel the concept may be facing competitive headwinds from the likes of more traditional outlets such as Target, Macy's, home improvement warehouses, and others.

We felt a bit overexposed to energy exploration and production, and particularly became concerned as ExxonMobil continued to turn in poor reserve replacement performances in a new era of increased domestic production. Chevron, ConocoPhillips, and Total S.A. will continue to carry the energy E&P torch. Caterpillar has been a champ, but we feel they are too exposed to mining and the volatility of the construction industry and may face considerable competition especially from resurgent Japanese firms like Kubota and others in the wake of the yen's devaluation. Intel, likewise, faces bigger strategic issues with the transition to mobile devices, an arena in which they lag behind. Additionally, they have huge physical plant investments that are hard to turn in another direction—we don't like taking a company off the list after one year but felt it prudent in this case. Nucor was a tough call—an excellent company with an excellent track record but in an industry brimming with overcapacity and soft prices; we feel they may eventually win the struggle, but it will take time. Finally, Teva seemed to lose their direction and are in restructuring mode in an industry already facing headwinds because of patent expirations and health cost management headwinds.

Next, we'll move on to their replacements:

▼ **Table 4: New Companies for 2014**

Company	Symbol	Category	Sector
Aqua America	WTR	Growth and Income	Utilities
Bemis	BMS	Conservative Growth	Consumer Staples
Corning	GLW	Aggressive Growth	Information Technology

Health Care REIT	HCN	Growth and Income	Health Care
Kroger	KR	Conservative Growth	Retail
Quest Diagnostics	DGX	Aggressive Growth	Health Care
State Street	STT	Conservative Growth	Financials
Walmart	WMT	Conservative Growth	Retail

We only have 8 new companies, so there's space here to add at least 1 sentence about each. Aqua America satisfies our more conservative bent at this juncture, gives exposure to the oft-forgotten water industry, and we like their strategy of plying numerous small water works into a bigger, more efficient company. Bemis, the food packaging giant, gives exposure to what we see as a growing trend toward prepackaged, prepared foods for a millennial generation that no longer accepts bones in its fried chicken. Corning is a solid play in tablets, smartphones, and other "smart" displays—no matter which way the technology tide turns, they should benefit (and they pay a nice dividend besides). Health Care REIT is our first foray into packaged investments, and we think it's a good place to start; it gives real estate exposure and follows the healthcare and aging bandwagons as well. Kroger is a rock-solid retail grocer with intriguing new retail concepts; Quest Diagnostics replaces Teva as a less-risky, cash-effusive health-care play. State Street gives us a little more exposure to the financial sector (our third entry) and is a specialist in those packaged investments and in "wholesale" products for the financial industry—again, whoever wins, State Street will benefit. Finally, although admittedly it isn't our favorite place to shop, we couldn't ignore the excellence of Walmart any longer (if it makes you feel any better, Warren Buffett couldn't either, raising his stake to almost 50 million shares in early 2013).

To give a bit of a big-picture view of our changes, Table 5 gives our annual summary of what changed by sector. The shifts reflect minor tweaks, not wholesale change in any one sector. A little more Financials, a little less Energy, and a diverse balance tilted toward the relative safety of Consumer Staples and Health Care with a slight emphasis in the Industrials and Retail sectors to run a little with economic strength.

▼ **Table 5: Sector Analysis and 2014 Change by Sector**

NUMBER OF COMPANIES:

Sector	On 2013 List	Added for 2014	Cut from 2013	On 2014 List
Business Services	2			2
Consumer Discretionary	4	1		5
Consumer Durables	1			1
Consumer Staples	14		1	13
Energy	8		2	6
Entertainment	1			1
Financials	2	1		3
Health Care	15	2	1	16
Heavy Construction	1			1
Industrials	13		1	12
Information Technology	8	1	1	8
Materials	7		1	6
Restaurant	2			2
Retail	9	2	1	10
Telecommunications Services	3			3
Transportation	5			5
Utilities	5	1		6

Yield Signs

In late 2011, we hit an unusual milestone in the annals of investing. The average dividend yield of the S&P 500 exceeded the yield of the 10-year T-note for the first time since 1958. In fact, the S&P 500 yield hit 3.3 percent, some 0.6 percent higher than the T-note's yield of 2.7 percent. Most recently, because of the rapid rise in stock prices into mid-2013, both yields were recently about the same, just over 1.9 percent. We believe much of the market's recent rise came from investors chasing these higher yields, which has driven stock prices to parity with bonds. This is why we've gone a bit conservative with this issue of *100 Best Stocks*—if interest rates start to rise, and the Fed has indicated it may pursue such a policy, the relationship will reverse and stocks may appear less attractive. That said, we still prefer dividend-paying stocks where the dividend is likely to grow. You'll enjoy these gains while bond prices could fall; we think you will still come out ahead in the long run with stocks like the ones chosen.

Sure, dividends and dividend-paying stocks are riskier, for the stock price can go up and down with the fortunes of the economy, not to mention the fortunes of individual companies. But, as mentioned, the price of bonds can go down too if policy intervention brings interest rate increases or if inflation rears its ugly head. With dividend-paying stocks, especially those inclined to raise their dividends, you get an attractive yield from the day you buy the stock, but you'll also get handsome raises over time. And as we reported earlier, some 88 of the 98 dividend-paying stocks on the 2013 *100 Best* list raised their dividends in 2012, and some 53 of those have raised their dividends in each of the past 10 years. We like this. We like it a lot. A company that raises its dividend 10 percent will roughly double the payout in just 7 years. (Calculation? Rule of 72—divide the percent increase into 72 and you'll get the number of years it takes to double: 72/10 equals 7.2 years.) You could end up with twice the income in addition to any gains or growth in the price of the stock.

We continue to focus on those healthy companies willing to not only share a portion of their profits but also to give you, the investor, a periodic raise to recognize the value of your commitment of precious investment capital. In that spirit, in our presentation format we make permanent our showing of the number of dividend increases in the past 10 years in the header right after Current Yield. We also make permanent the Dividend Aggressors list in our Stars lists presented shortly. Dividend aggressors are companies with substantial payouts that are also growing those payouts at a persistent and substantial rate. They have indicated through both words and performance that they continue to do so and have the resources to do it. So it isn't enough to raise the dividend each year by just a penny; it must be substantial. It also isn't enough to raise the dividend each year but still only be yielding 0.5 percent. There are lists of "dividend achievers" floating around on the Internet, and there are even a few funds constructed around a dividend achievers index. Our Aggressors are—well—a bit more aggressive.

The climate for dividend growth continues to be favorable. Standard & Poor's estimates that some 402 of the S&P 500 companies pay a dividend, the highest in over a decade, and that 2013 dividends will be fully 17.4 percent for the year ahead, up from 16 percent projected last year for the year 2012. Companies are swimming in cash, and rather than commit to expensive wages or business investments that might not pan out, they are simply returning cash to previously starved shareholders. Lower commodity input prices will help further. Finally, companies whipped themselves into shape during the Great Recession and now have enough to invest in their businesses *and* return cash to shareholders. The risks in the bond markets and the persistence of favorable dividend tax treatment for investments (not as good as before, but still good) continue to contribute to this story.

The growing-dividend-plus-growing-stock scenario continues to be one of our favored retirement-planning and retirement-investing scenarios. While we do expect markets overall, and our selected stocks in particular, to appreciate over time as good businesses capture more markets, become more efficient, and get better in general, stock price growth has become less dependable than in the past. The decades-long record of 10–11 percent annual growth, we think, will become more difficult to match. As a result, we think the more solid play is to invest for dividends, and particularly for dividend growth—and hey, if the stock price happens to grow, too, so much the better.

Appendix B shows dividend yields for all *100 Best Stocks* for 2014, which includes the number of dividend raises in the past 10 years. Appendix C shows all *100 Best* companies, sorted by percentage yield, with the highest yielders at the top of the list.

Dancing with the Stars

We continue developing and sharing our "star" categories—groups of stocks, essentially the "best of the best" in categories we chose to highlight—yield stars, dividend aggressors, safety and stability stars, growth stars, and moat stars. This year, we replace recovery stars with prosperity stars—same idea but perhaps more tuned to a growing instead of recovering economy. We provide these stars lists because we know that every investor has his or her own preferences, and thus there are no "best" stocks within our "best" list, that is, there is no number one, two, and so on within the list.

Table 6 shows the top 20 stocks on our *100 Best* list by percentage yield as of mid-2013.

▼ **Table 6: Top 20 Dividend-Paying Stocks**

Company	Symbol	Projected 2013 Dividend	Yield %	Dividend raises, past 10 years
Total S.A.	TOT	$3.15	7.4%	5
Suburban Propane	SPH	$3.50	7.3%	9
AT&T	T	$1.80	4.7%	9
Southern Company	SO	$2.02	4.3%	10
ConocoPhillips	COP	$2.64	4.2%	9
Duke Energy	DUK	$3.09	4.2%	6
Health Care REIT	HCN	$3.06	4.1%	10
Otter Tail	OTTR	$1.30	3.9%	5
Verizon	VZ	$20.60	3.9%	7
Dominion Resources	D	$2.25	3.7%	10
Paychex	PAYX	$1.27	3.6%	8
Seagate Technology	STX	$1.40	3.6%	7
Waste Management	WM	$1.46	3.5%	9
DuPont	DD	$1.76	3.3%	4
Molex	MOLX	$0.88	3.3%	10
Sysco	SYY	$1.12	3.3%	10
Chevron	CVX	$3.76	3.2%	10
NextEra Energy	NEE	$2.60	3.2%	10
Cincinnati Financial	CINF	$1.64	3.1%	10
Johnson & Johnson	JNJ	$2.56	3.1%	10

Table 6.1 shows our list of Dividend Aggressors for 2014:

▼ **Table 6.1: Dividend Aggressors**

COMPANIES WITH STRONG DIVIDEND TRACK RECORDS

Company	Symbol	Dividend	Yield %	Dividend raises, past 10 years
3M Company	MMM	$2.54	1.8%	10
Automatic Data Processing	ADP	$1.70	2.5%	10
Baxter	BAX	$1.80	2.9%	10
Chevron	CVX	$3.76	3.2%	10
Clorox	CLX	$2.61	3.0%	9
Coca-Cola	KO	$1.12	2.6%	10
Iron Mountain	IRM	$1.20	2.8%	4
J. M. Smucker	SJM	$2.08	2.0%	10
Johnson & Johnson	JNJ	$2.56	3.1%	10
Kimberly-Clark	KMB	$3.08	3.1%	10
McDonald's	MCD	$3.15	3.0%	10
NextEra Energy	NEE	$2.60	3.2%	10
Norfolk Southern	NSC	$2.00	2.6%	10
Procter & Gamble	PG	$2.29	3.1%	10
Seagate Technology	STX	$1.40	3.6%	7
Southern Company	SO	$2.02	4.3%	10
Sysco	SYY	$1.12	3.3%	10
United Parcel Service	UPS	$2.48	2.8%	10
Waste Management	WM	$1.46	3.5%	9
Wells Fargo	WFC	$1.00	3.1%	7

REMEMBER, THERE ARE NO GUARANTEES

While dividends and especially high yields are attractive, investors must remember that corporations are under no contractual or legal obligation to pay them! Interest payments on time deposits and bonds are much more clearly defined, and failure to pay can represent default. But with dividends, there is no such safety net. Companies can—and do—reduce or eliminate dividends in bad times, as most strikingly observed with BP in the wake of the Deepwater Horizon Gulf spill disaster and most bank stocks after the 2008 dive. Dividend investors should therefore keep an eye out for changes in a company's business prospects and shouldn't put too many eggs in a single high-yielding basket. On the flip side, as investors become more conscious of returns, and as corporate management teams become more conscious of such investor consciousness, we've seen a lot of companies trumpet their recent dividend increases rather loudly to their investors and the investing public. It's a nice sound that we hope to continue to hear.

Safety Stars

Safety stars are companies we think will hold up well in volatile and negative stock markets as well as recessionary economies. They have stable products and customer bases, and long traditions of being able to manage well in downturns. This list is mostly unchanged from last year—the Heinz acquisition led to the rather obvious add of Aqua America. It wouldn't have been hard to pick a few more candidates like Colgate-Palmolive or Southern Company from the remainder of the *100 Best* list.

▼ **Table 7: Safety Stars**

TOP 10 STOCKS FOR SAFETY AND STABILITY

Company	Symbol	Dividend	Yield%
Aqua America	WTR	$0.70	2.2%
Becton, Dickinson	BDX	$1.98	2.0%
Campbell Soup	CPB	$1.16	2.5%
Clorox	CLX	$2.61	3.0%
General Mills	GIS	$1.32	3.0%
J. M. Smucker	SJM	$2.08	2.0%
Johnson & Johnson	JNJ	$0.76	2.1%
Kimberly-Clark	KMB	$3.08	3.1%

TOP 10 STOCKS FOR SAFETY AND STABILITY

McCormick	MKC	$1.36	1.9%
Sysco	SYY	$1.12	3.3%

Growth Stars

Looking at the other side of the coin, we picked 10 stocks we feel are especially well positioned to grow, even in a negative economy and especially in a positive one. We had to take Nucor off the list (and the *100 Best* list) due to steel industry weakness, and replaced St. Jude with the still more promising Visa and Seagate because of their dominance in their industries, the improving economy, and in the case of Seagate, prospects in the cloud computing and solid state memory arenas.

▼ **Table 8: Growth Stars**

TOP 10 STOCKS FOR GROWTH

Company	Symbol	Dividend	Yield%
Apple	AAPL	$11.65	2.6%
CarMax	KMX	—	—
Harman International	HAR	$0.60	1.2%
Itron	ITRI	—	—
Mosaic	MOS	$1.00	1.6%
Nike	NKE	$0.81	1.3%
Perrigo	PRGO	$0.34	0.3%
Seagate Technology	STX	$1.40	3.6%
Tractor Supply Company	TSCO	$0.92	0.9%
Visa	V	$1.32	0.7%

Prosperity Stars

Now that we're well into the post–Great Recession recovery, our point of view shifts from recovery stars to those companies that should reap strong benefits from recovery. The list was rebuilt from the ground up and includes companies with a strong base in manufacturing (DuPont, Illinois Tool Works, W. W. Grainger, Johnson Controls), construction and infrastructure replacement (Fluor), new technologies, and plain old consumer optimism (Allergan, CarMax, Tiffany, Whirlpool, and Southwest).

▼ **Table 9: Prosperity Stars**

TOP 10 STOCKS FOR ECONOMIC PROSPERITY

Company	Symbol	Dividend	Yield%
Allergan	AGN	$0.20	0.2%
CarMax	KMX	—	—
DuPont	DD	$1.76	3.3%
Fluor Corporation	FLR	$0.64	1.0%
Illinois Tool Works	ITW	$1.52	2.3%
Johnson Controls	JCI	$0.76	2.1%
Southwest Airlines	LUV	$0.04	0.3%
Tiffany	TIF	$1.28	1.7%
W. W. Grainger	GWW	$3.35	1.5%
Whirlpool	WHR	$2.00	2.0%

Moat Stars

Finally, we get back to one of the basic tenets of value investing—the ability of a company to build a sustainable and unassailable competitive advantage. Value investing aficionados call such an advantage a "moat," for it represents a barrier to entry for competitors that will likely preserve that advantage for some time. The moat can come in the form of technology, the use of technology, a brand, enduring customer relationships, channel relationships, size or scale, or simply a really big head start into a business that makes it hard or even impossible for competitors to catch up. The appraisal of a moat is hardly an exact science; here we give our top 10 picks based on the size and strength (width?) of the moat.

This year we made a few adjustments, removing CarMax, which showed up on too many other lists, and Fair Isaac and McCormick because of signs of a little more competition (although both still have strong moats). We added Coca-Cola (the classic), Pall Corporation, and Monsanto, which seems again to be doing a good job defending turf lost when glyphosate patents expired.

▼ Table 10: Moat Stars

TOP 10 STOCKS FOR SUSTAINABLE COMPETITIVE ADVANTAGE

Company	Symbol	Dividend	Yield%
Apple	AAPL	$11.65	2.6%
Coca-Cola	KO	$1.12	2.6%
Iron Mountain	IRM	$1.20	2.8%
Monsanto	MON	$1.50	1.4%
Pall Corporation	PLL	$0.88	1.5%
Starbucks	SBUX	$0.84	1.4%
Sysco	SYY	$1.12	3.3%
Tiffany	TIF	$1.28	1.7%
Visa	V	$1.32	0.7%
W. W. Grainger	GWW	$3.35	1.5%

What Makes a *Best Stock* Best?

What is it that defines excellence—sustainable excellence—among companies? That's been a topic of considerable debate for years, and with all the study that's gone into it, it's amazing that nobody has hit upon a single formula for deciphering undeniable excellence in a company.

That's largely because it isn't as scientific as most of us would like or expect it to be. It defies mathematical formulation. Fundamentals such as profitability, productivity, and asset efficiency tell us how well a company has done and, by proxy, how well it is managed and how well it has done in the marketplace. Fundamentals are about what the company has already achieved and where it stands right now, and if a company's current fundamentals are a mess, stop right now—there isn't much point in going any further.

In most cases, what really separates the great from the good are the intangibles, the "soft" factors of market position, market acceptance, customer "love" of a company's products, its management, its aura. These features create competitive advantage, or "distinctive competence," as an economist would put it, that cannot be valued. Furthermore, and most importantly, they are more about what a company is set up to achieve in the future.

To paraphrase Buffett at his best: Give me $100 billion, and I could start a company; but I could never create another Coca-Cola.

Buffett means that Coca-Cola has already established a worldwide brand cachet; the distribution channels, customer knowledge, and product development expertise cannot be duplicated at any cost. They have an enduring grip on their markets. They can charge more for their products. They have a moat that insulates them from competition, or makes it much more expensive for competitors to participate. They're perceived by loyal customers as being top-line products worth paying more for.

A company with exceptional intangibles can control price and, in many cases, can control its costs.

LUV—A GREAT EXPERIENCE. BUT IS IT A GOOD INVESTMENT?

One way to learn a principle is to examine what happens when the principle does not apply. One industry where most of the fundamentals and almost all the intangibles work against it is the airline industry. Airlines cannot control price, because of competition, and because an airplane trip is an airplane trip. Aside from serving different snacks or offering better schedules, there is little an airline can do to differentiate their product, and almost nothing they can do to justify charging a higher price. Further, they have no control over costs such as fuel prices, union contracts, and airport landing fees. While some airlines offer good service, there is almost nothing they can do to distinguish themselves as excellent companies or excellent investments.

With these ills in mind, for 2 years we resisted the temptation to put Southwest, one of the most efficient, customer-focused, and best-managed businesses we know of, on our *100 Best* list. Great company, bad industry. But then, 2 years ago we decided to add them to the list anyway, as their business model and the continued floundering of their competitors should give them an edge that we feel investors may finally be willing to reward. We also thought they've been so good for so long that many of their customers will be willing to pay somewhat higher prices to stick with their offering. Indeed, there's recent evidence that their average revenue per ticket has risen substantially. They've also introduced some effective revenue enhancers, like priority check-in, a much more customer-friendly revenue booster than the annoying baggage fees charged by other carriers. These guys still get it, and we feel that their approach will put them farther ahead of the competition and allow them to overcome some of the industry's worst ills. Did it work out? Not initially, because fuel prices ruled in 2011 and early 2012. But the company finally took off in late 2012 and 2013, and it has become one of our best performers.

Strategic Fundamentals

Let's examine a list of strategic fundamentals that define, or keep score of, a company's success. This list can be used as a checklist, although it's hard to find a company that shows excellence in all of these areas.

Are Gross and Operating Profit Margins Growing?

We like profitable companies; who doesn't? But what really counts is the size of the margin and especially the growth. If a company has a gross margin (sales minus costs of goods sold) exceeding that of its competitors, that shows that it's doing something right, probably with its customers and/or with its costs. But competitive analysis is elusive; there is no dependable source of "industry" gross margins, and comparing competitors can be difficult because no two companies are exactly alike; it's easy to mix apples and oranges.

We like to see what direction gross margin is moving in—up or down. A growing gross margin also signals that the company is doing something right. That isn't perfect, either; as the economy moved from boom to bust, many excellent companies reported declines in gross and especially operating margins (sales minus cost of goods sold minus operating expenses) as they laid off workers and used less capacity. Still, in a steady-state environment, it makes sense to favor companies with growing margins. In a declining market, companies that can *protect* their margins will come out ahead.

Does a Company Produce More Capital Than It Consumes?

Make no mistake about it—we like cash. And pure and simple, we like it when a company produces more cash than it consumes.

At the end of the day, cash generation is the simplest measure of whether a company is being successful, especially over the long term. Sure, if a company buys an airplane or opens a factory or a bunch of stores in a given quarter, it will be cash-flow negative. But that should be a temporary thing; over the long haul, it should produce, not consume, cash. Companies that continually have to borrow or sell shares to raise enough cash to stay in business are on the wrong track.

So how do you determine this? You'll have to become familiar with the Statement of Cash Flows or equivalent in a company's financial reports. "Cash flow from operations" is usually positive and represents cash booked from sales less cost of goods sold, with adjustments for noncash items like depreciation and for increases or decreases in working capital. In simple terms, is the cash going into the cash register from the business?

"Cash used for investing purposes" or similar is a bit of a misnomer and represents net cash used to "invest" in the business—usually for capital expenditures, but also for short-term noncash investments like securities and a few other smaller items usually beyond scope. This figure is typically negative unless the company sells some part of its infrastructure. Over the long haul, cash generated from operations should well exceed cash used to invest in the business.

Companies in expansion mode may not show this surplus, and that's where "cash from financing activities" comes in. That's the cash generated from issuing debt or selling securities—or paying off debt or repurchasing shares, if things are going well—and dividends are included here as well. Again, a successful company will produce more cash—capital—from the business than it consumes, just as a successful household does the same, or else it goes into debt. Smart investors track this surplus over time.

Are Expenses under Control?

Again, just like your household, company expenses should be under control, and anything else, especially without explanation, is a yellow flag.

The best way to test this is to check whether the "Selling, General and Administrative" expenses (SG&A) are rising, and more to the point, rising faster than sales. If so, that's a yellow, not necessarily a red, flag, but if it continues, it suggests that something is out of control, and it will catch up with the company sooner or later. In the recent downturn, companies that were able to reduce their expenses to match revenue declines scored more points, too.

Is Noncash Working Capital under Control?

Working capital is a hard concept to grasp—even for small entrepreneurs who live with its ups and downs on a daily basis. Insufficient working capital is one of the biggest causes of death for small businesses, and working capital and especially changes in working capital can signal success or trouble.

Using a simplistic analogy, working capital is the circulatory lifeblood of the business. Money comes in and money goes out, and working capital is what circulates in the veins in between. In its purest sense, it is cash, receivables, and inventory, less short-term debts. It's what you own less what you owe aside from fixed assets like plant, stores, and equipment.

If receivables are increasing, that sounds like a good thing—more people owe you more money. But if receivables are rising and sales aren't, that suggests that people aren't paying their bills, or worse, the business has to finance more to achieve the same level of sales. Similarly, a rise in inventory without a rise in sales means that it costs the business more money—more working capital—to do the same amount of business. That costs twice, because unless the firm is lucky, more inventory means more obsolescence and potentially more deep-discount sales or more write-offs down the road.

So a sharp investor will check to see that major working capital items—receivables and inventory—aren't growing faster than sales; indeed, a company that generates more sales with a decrease in working capital is becoming more productive.

Is Debt in Line with Business Growth?

Like many other "fundamentals" items, you can tear your hair out looking at debt figures and trying to decide whether they're in line with asset levels, equity levels, and industry norms. A simpler test is to check and see whether long-term debt is increasing or decreasing, and in particular, whether it is increasing faster than business growth. Gold stars go to companies with little to no debt, and to companies able to grow without issuing mountains of long-term debt.

Is Earnings Growth Steady?

We enter the danger zone here, because the management of many companies have learned to "manage" earnings to provide a steady improvement, always "beating the street" by a penny or two. Stability is a good thing for all investors, and companies that can manage toward stability get extra points. It's worth checking for, but with the proverbial grain of salt.

Still, a company that is able to manage its sales, earnings, cash flow, and debt levels more consistently than competitors, and perhaps more consistently than what would be suggested by the ups and downs of the economy, is desirable—or at least more desirable than the alternatives.

Is Return on Equity Steady or Growing?

Return on equity (ROE) is another of those hard-to-grasp concepts, and it's another subjective measure when valuing assets and earnings. But at the end of the day, it's what all investors really seek: a return on their capital investments.

And like many other figures pulled from income statements and balance sheets, a ROE number, without any context, is hard to interpret. Does a 26.7 percent ROE mean, in itself, that a company is excellent? The figure sounds healthy, to be sure—it's a heck of a lot better than investing your money in a CD or T-bill. But because earnings and asset values are subjective, it may not represent true success. In fact, a company can increase ROE simply by borrowing money (yes!) and investing it into the business, even if it isn't invested as productively as other previous funds were invested. The math is complicated; we won't go into it here.

So the true test of ROE success is to check whether it is steady or increasing. Increasing—that makes sense. Why *steady*? Because if a company makes profits in a previous period and reinvests them in the business, that amount of money becomes part of equity (retained earnings). If the company reinvests productively, it will produce more returns, and ROE will at least keep up. If the company can't reinvest those earnings productively, ROE will drop—and perhaps it should be paying the earnings to you as dividends instead of investing them unproductively in the business. So if ROE is steady, the company still has good investments to make, and management is probably doing the right thing.

We should note that many investment analysts today prefer "Return on Invested Capital" (ROIC) as a metric over ROE. ROIC is return, or profit, divided by total equity *plus* debt. This gets you past the distortions that adding debt to the balance sheet might cause. Since the traditional balance sheet equation holds that "Assets = Liabilities + Capital," you can simply use total assets as the denominator—essentially the measure is "return on assets." Some analysts prefer to go farther by removing the cash balance from the asset denominator, to reflect the assets deployed and in use to generate returns and to get around the distortions of large reserve capital infusions often found at startup companies.

Does the Company Pay a Dividend?

Different people feel differently about dividends, and as shown earlier, we're placing a greater emphasis on dividend-paying stocks this year. After all, save for the eventual sale of the company to someone else, a dividend is the only true cash that an investor will realize from buying a stock in a corporation, other than by selling the stock. And, at least in theory, investors should receive some compensation for their investments once in a while.

Yet, many companies don't pay dividends or don't pay dividends that compete very effectively with fixed-income yields. Why do investors put up with this? Because, in theory anyway, a company in a good business should be able to reinvest profits more effectively than the investor can (or else why would the investor have bought the company in the first place?). And investors trust that reinvested profits will eventually bring the growth in company value that will be reflected in the share price, or eventual takeover or an eventual payment of a dividend or, better yet, growth in that dividend.

That's the theory, anyway. But there are still lots of companies that get away with paying no dividend at all. Can we tolerate this? Yes, if a company is really doing a great job with their retained profits, like Apple before they started paying dividends last year, or CarMax. But we favor companies that offer at least something to their investors in the short term, some return on their hard-earned and faithfully committed capital. If nothing else, it keeps management teams honest and shows that management understands that shareholder interests are up there somewhere on the list of priorities.

A dividend is a plus. Lack of a dividend isn't necessarily a deal breaker, but it suggests a closer look. A dividend reduction—and there were many in the past year—suggests poor financial and operational health, because the dividend is usually the last thing to go, but in some cases it reflects management prudence and conservatism. Best question to ask yourself: Would you have reduced the dividend if you were running the company? And down the road, does the company bring back the dividend as times get better? A no to either of these questions is troubling.

Finally, dividend payouts should be examined over time. We've seen, and included in our lists, a number of companies that have steadily increased dividends—many for each of the 10 previous years. We like this; it's just like getting an annual raise. And if you hold the stock long enough, the percentage return against your original investment can get quite large, even approaching 100 percent per year if the stock is held long enough and the dividend is raised persistently enough. Getting an ever-increasing dividend—and owning a stock that has most likely appreciated because the dividend has increased—is like having your cake and eating it, too—a true favorite among investors.

ARE VALUATION RATIOS IN LINE?

One of the most difficult tasks in investing is determining the true value—and per-share value—of a company. If this were easy, you'd just determine a value, compare it to the price, and if the price were lower than the value, push the buy button.

Professional investors try to determine what they call the "intrinsic value" of a company, which is usually the sum of all projected future cash flows of a company, discounted back to the present (remember, money received tomorrow is both less predictable and less valuable than money received now). They use complex math models, specifically, discounted cash flow (DCF) models, to project, then discount, earnings flows. But those models—especially for the individual investor—depend too much on the crystal ball accuracy of earnings forecasts, and the so-called discount rate is a highly theoretical construct beyond the scope of most individual investors. DCF models require a lot of estimates and number crunching, especially if multiple scenarios are employed, as they should be. They take more time than it's worth for the individual investor. If you're an institutional investor buying multimillion-share stakes, we would conclude otherwise.

Valuation ratios are a shorthand way to determine if a stock price is acceptable relative to value. By far and away the most popular of these ratios is the price-to-earnings (P/E) ratio, a measure of the stock price usually compared to TTM, or trailing twelve months' earnings, but also sometimes compared to future earnings.

The P/E ratio correlates well to your expected return on an investment you might make in the company. For instance, if the P/E is 10, the price is 10 times the past, or perhaps expected, annual earnings of the company. Take the reciprocal of that—1 divided by 10—and you get 0.10, or 10 percent. That's known as "earnings yield," the theoretical yield you'd get if all earnings were paid to you as dividends as an owner. Ten percent is pretty healthy compared to returns on other investments, so a P/E of 10 suggests success.

Of course, the earnings may not be consistent or sustainable, or there may be substantial risk from factors intrinsic to the company, or there may be exogenous risk factors, like the total meltdown of the economy. The more risk, the more instability, the lower the expected P/E should be because the earnings stream is less stable. If you think the earnings stream is solid and stable in the face of the risk, then the stock may be truly undervalued. Look for P/Es that (1) suggest strong earnings yield and (2) are favorable compared to competitors and the industry.

Apart from P/E, the price-to-sales ratio (P/S), price to cash flow (P/CF), and price to free cash flow (P/FCF) are often used as fundamentals yardsticks. Like P/E, these measures also have some ambiguities, and it's best to think about them in real-world, entrepreneurial terms. Would you pay three times annual sales for a business and sleep well at night? Probably not—unless its profit margins were exceptionally high. So if a P/S ratio is 3 or above, look out; opt for a business with a P/S of 1 or less if you can. Similarly, the price-to-cash-flow ratios can be thought of as true return going into your pocket for your investment; is it enough? Is it enough given the risk? And what about the difference between "cash flow" and "free cash flow"? The difference is mostly cash laid out for capital expenditures, so it's worth making this distinction, although the lumpiness of capital expenditures makes consistent application of this number elusive. Incidentally, we don't regard price-to-book value (P/B) ratios as that helpful, because the book value of a company can be very elusive and arbitrary unless most of a company's assets are in cash or other easy-to-value forms.

Companies with high P/E, P/S, P/B, and P/CF ratios aren't necessarily bad investments, but you need to have good reasons to look beyond these figures if they suggest truly inadequate business results.

Strategic Intangibles

When you look at any company, perhaps the bottom-line question follows the Buffett wisdom: If you had $100 billion in cool cash to spend (and we'll assume the genius intellect to spend it right), could you recreate that company?

If the answer is yes, it may still be a great company, but it may not be great enough to fend off competition and keep its customers forever. If the answer is no, the company truly has something unique to offer in the marketplace, difficult to duplicate at any cost. That distinctive competence, that sustainable competitive edge—whatever it is, a brand, a trade secret, a lock on distribution or supply channels—may be worth more than all the factories and high-rise office buildings and cash in the bank a company could ever have.

What we're talking about are the intangibles, the "soft" factors that make companies unique and that add up to more than the sum of their parts, the factors that ultimately drive future revenues. Intangibles not only define excellence, they define the future, while fundamentals mainly define the past. Seven key intangibles follow, although you'll think of more, and some industries may have some unique ones of their own, like intellectual property in the technology sector.

DOES THE COMPANY HAVE A MOAT?

A business moat performs much the same role as its medieval castle equivalent—it protects the business from competition. Whatever factors create the moat, ultimately those are the factors that prevent you, with your $100 billion, from taking their business. Moats are usually a combination of brand, product technology, design, marketing and distribution channels, and customer loyalty all working together to protect a company. A moat doesn't just protect the existence of a company, it helps it command higher prices and earn higher profits.

Whether a company has a narrow moat, a wide moat, or none at all is a subjective assessment for you to make. However, you can get some help at Morningstar (*www.morningstar.com*), whose stock ratings include an assessment of the moat.

Coca-Cola has a moat because of the sheer impossibility of surpassing its brand and brand recognition worldwide. CarMax has a moat because it is farther along in putting retail-style dealerships on the ground and applying management information technologies to its business than anyone else; it would take years for a competitor to catch up. Tiffany has a moat because of its immediately recognized brand and elegantly simple, stylish brand image and the enduring and timeless panache around that. The Moat Stars list presented earlier identifies the top 10 stocks with a solid and sustainable competitive advantage.

DOES THE COMPANY HAVE AN EXCELLENT BRAND?

It's hard to say enough about brand, especially in today's fast-moving, highly packaged, highly national and international marketplace. A strong brand means consistency and a promise to consumers, and consumers sold on a brand will prefer it over any other, almost regardless of price. People still buy Tide; Starbucks is still synonymous with high quality and ambience. Good brands command higher prices and foster loyalty, identity, and even customer "love."

Ask yourself if a company has a sought-after brand, a brand customers would pay extra to buy or align with, a brand that would be difficult to duplicate at any cost. Would customers rather fight than switch? Think about Starbucks, Coca-Cola, Tiffany, Smucker's, or Nike, or the brands within a house, like Frito-Lay (Pepsi), Tide (P&G), or Teflon (DuPont).

IS THE COMPANY A MARKET LEADER?

Market leadership usually—but not always—goes hand in hand with brand. The trick is to decide whether a company really leads in its industry. Often—but not always—that's a factor of size. The market leader usually has the highest market share, and the important point is that it calls the shots with regard to price, technology, marketing message, and so forth—other companies must play catch-up and often discount their prices to keep up. Apple is a market leader in digital music, Monsanto in systematized agriculture, Nike in sports apparel, and Starbucks in beverages—and so forth.

Excellent companies tend to be market leaders, and market leaders tend to be excellent companies. But this relationship doesn't always hold true—sometimes the nimble but smaller competitor is the excellent company and will likely assume market leadership eventually. Examples like CarMax, Perrigo, Valero, and Southwest Airlines can be found on our list.

DOES THE COMPANY HAVE CHANNEL EXCELLENCE?

"Channels" in business parlance means a chain of players to sell and distribute a company's products. It might be stores, it might be other industrial companies, it might be direct to the consumer. If a company is considered a top supplier in a particular channel, or a company has especially good relations with its channel, that's a plus.

Excellent companies develop solid channel relationships and become the preferred supplier in those channels. Companies such as Patterson, Deere, Fair Isaac, McCormick, Nike, Pepsi, Procter & Gamble, Sysco, and Whirlpool all have excellent relationships with the channels through which they sell their product.

DOES THE COMPANY HAVE SUPPLY-CHAIN EXCELLENCE?

Like distribution channels, excellent companies develop excellent and low-cost supply channels. They are seldom caught off guard by supply shortages and tend to get favorable and stable prices for whatever they buy. This is often not an easy assessment unless you know something about a particular industry. Nike and Target, or Procter & Gamble again, are examples of companies that have done a good job managing their supply chains.

DOES THE COMPANY HAVE EXCELLENT MANAGEMENT?

It's not hard to grasp what happens if a company *doesn't* have good management: Performance fails and few inside or outside the company respect the company. It's not easy for an investor to determine if a management team does a good job or acts in shareholder interests. Clues can include candor and honesty and the ability of company management to speak in accessible, easily understood terms about the company and company performance (it's worth listening to conference calls as a resource). A management team that admits errors and eschews other forms of arrogance and entitlement (i.e., luxury perks, office suites, aircraft) is probably tilting its interests toward shareholders, as is the management team that can cough up some return to shareholders once in a while in the form of a dividend.

This may be the most subjective and elusive assessment of all, as few investors work with these folks on a daily basis. Still, over time, you can garner a strong hunch about whether a management team is effective and on your side.

ARE THERE SIGNS OF INNOVATION EXCELLENCE?

This question seems pretty obvious, but it's not just about the products that a company sells. True, if the company is leading the industry in innovation, that's usually a good thing, for "first to market" definitely offers business advantages.

The less obvious part of this question is whether the company makes the best *use* of technology to make operations and customer interfaces as efficient and effective as possible. Southwest Airlines may have missed our list in the past because of the difficulty of achieving excellence in an industry where players can't control prices or costs. But they do make our list today, not only because of brand and management excellence, but also innovation excellence. Why? Simply because, after all of these years, amazingly, they still have the best, simplest, easiest-to-use flight booking and check-in in the industry. Sometimes these sorts of innovations mean a lot more than bringing new, fancy products and bells and whistles to the market. And one can also look to Apple, CarMax, FedEx, Itron, UPS, and Visa on our list for more obvious examples of companies that have deployed technology and innovative customer interfaces to achieve sustainable competitive advantage.

Choosing the *100 Best*

So with all of this in mind, just how was this year's *100 Best Stocks* list actually chosen?

The answer is more subtle than you might think. If we could give you a precise formula, you wouldn't need this book. You'd be able to do it yourself. In fact, every investor would be able to do it on his or her own. Our book would simply be the result of yet another stock screener. And every investor would invest in the same stocks. Is that a feasible or practical solution? Hardly. Everyone would scramble to buy the same 100 best stocks. The prices would be sky high, and the price of other stocks would melt to nothing.

SIGNS OF VALUE

Following are a few signs of value to look for in any company. This is not an exhaustive list by any means, but it's a good place to start:

- » Gaining market share
- » Can control price
- » Loyal customers
- » Growing margins
- » Producing, not consuming, capital (free cash flow)
- » Steady or increasing ROE
- » Management forthcoming, honest, understandable

SIGNS OF UNVALUE

. . . and signs of trouble, or "unvalue":

- » Declining margins
- » No brand or who-cares brand
- » Commodity producer, must compete on price
- » Losing market dominance or market share
- » Can't control costs
- » Must acquire other companies to grow
- » Management in hiding, off message, making excuses, difficult to understand, or in the news for all the wrong reasons

While we didn't apply a specific formula or screener to the universe of stocks, we did take a few measurable factors into account to narrow the list from thousands to a few hundred issues. Those factors came from several sources, but at this point we must tip our cap to Value Line and the research and database work they do as part of the Value Line Investment Survey. If you aren't familiar with Value Line, it's worth a look for any savvy individual investor, either online at *www.valueline.com* or, in many cases, at your local library. It is an excellent resource.

Here are 6 metrics we use as a starting point to select and sort stocks for further review:

- **S&P Rating** is a broad corporate credit rating reflecting the ability to cover indebtedness, in turn reflecting business levels, business trends, cash flow, and sustained performance. It's a bit like the credit score you might have used to determine your personal credit risk.

- Value Line Financial Strength Rating is used much like the S&P rating except that it goes further into overall balance sheet and cash flow strength. It should be noted that several companies with "B" ratings were selected; these are typically newer companies that will grow into A companies or that may have been hit harder by the recession than others.
- Value Line Earnings Predictability is what it sounds like, a calculated tendency of companies to deliver consistent and predictable earnings without surprises.
- Value Line Growth Persistence is again what it sounds like—the company's ability to consistently grow, even in weaker economic times.
- Value Line Price Stability reflects the stability and relative safety of a company. Again, we did not reject a company out of hand due to volatility; rather, if stability was low, we tried to make a case that the business, business model, and intangibles were worth the risk.
- Dividends and Yield. Companies that pay something are held in higher regard; however, again, it is not by any means an absolute criterion.

With these facts and figures in mind, the evaluation proceeded with a close eye on the "signs of value" and intangibles mentioned previously. Some consideration was also given to diversification; we did not want to overweight any sector or industry but strove to give you a healthy assortment of stocks to pick from across a variety of industries.

With these thoughts in mind, you can make more sense of the companies we picked. And of course, full disclosure and full disclaimer: We didn't do *all* the analysis. We couldn't have. It wouldn't have made any sense anyway, for things would have changed from the time we did it, and it might not match your preferences anyway. So it is of utmost importance for you to take our selections and analysis and make them yours—that is, do the due diligence to further qualify these picks as congruent with your investment needs.

Strategic Investing

Although this book is designed to help you pick the best stocks to buy, investing, by nature, goes well beyond simply buying stocks, just like owning an automobile goes far beyond buying a car. That said, we think a few words are in order.

We find that a lot of investors lose the forest in the trees, spending all of their energy trying to find individual stocks or funds without putting enough consideration into their overall investing framework. If they look at the big picture at all, they look at the formulaic covenants of asset alloca-tion, a favorite subject of the financial planning and advisory community, as though the difference between 50 percent equities and 60 percent equities makes all the different in the world. Sure, it might in the world of pension funds and other institutional investments, where a 10 percent adjustment could move millions into or out of a particular asset class and more or less toward safety, but what about a $100,000 portfolio? Does $10,000 more or less in stocks, bonds, or cash make that much difference?

Perhaps not. There's more to that story—doesn't it matter more which equities you invest in than just the fact that you're 60 percent in equities? So while asset allocation models make for nice pie charts, we prefer to approach big-picture portfolio constructs differently. Much of what follows—and a lot of other good investing "habits" as well—are covered in Peter's sister book *The 25 Habits of Highly Successful Investors* (Adams Media, 2012).

Start with a Portfolio in Mind

We're assuming you are not a professional investor. You have other things to do with your time, and time is of the essence. You cannot spend 40, 50, or 60 hours a week glued to a computer screen analyzing your investments.

To that assumption, we'll add another: that, as an individual inves-tor, you're looking to beat the market. Not by a ton—20 percent sustained returns simply aren't possible without taking outlandish risks. But perhaps if the market is up 4 percent in a year, you'd like to achieve, 5, 6, perhaps 7 percent without taking excessive risks. Or if the market is down 20 percent, perhaps you cut your losses at 5 or 10 percent. You're looking to do *some-what* better than the market.

Because of time constraints, and owing to your objective to do slightly better than average, we suggest taking a tiered approach to your portfolio. The tiers aren't based on the type of assets; they're based on the amount of activity and attention you want to pay to different parts of your portfolio. It's a strategic portfolio approach you would probably take if you were man-aging a small business—put most of your focus on the products and cus-tomers who might bring the greatest new return to your business; let the rest of your slow and steady customer base function as it has for the long term.

We suggest breaking up your portfolio into 3 tiers or segments. This can be done by setting up specific accounts, or less formally by simply applying the model as a thought process.

Active Portfolio Segmentation

OPPORTUNISTIC

ROTATIONAL

FOUNDATION

	CLASSIC	CONSERVATIVE	AGGRESSIVE
OPPORTUNISTIC	10-20%	5-10%	20-40%
ROTATIONAL	10-30%	5-10%	10-30%
FOUNDATION	50-80%	80-90%	30-70%

THE FOUNDATION PORTFOLIO

In this construct, each investor defines and manages a cornerstone foundation portfolio, which is long term in nature and requires relatively less active management. Frequently, the foundation portfolio consists of retirement accounts (the paradigmatic long-term investment) and may include your personal residence or other long-lived personal or family assets, such as trusts, collectibles, and so forth. The typical foundation portfolio is invested to achieve at least average market returns through index funds, quality mutual funds, and some income-producing assets like bonds held to maturity. A foundation portfolio may contain some long-term plays in commodities or real estate to defend against inflation, particularly in such commodities as energy, precious metals, and real estate trusts. The foundation portfolio is largely left alone, although as with all investments it is important to check it at least once in a while to make sure performance—and managers, if involved—are keeping up with expectations.

The Rotational Portfolio

You manage the rotational portfolio fairly actively to keep up with changes in business cycles and conditions. It is likely a set of stocks or funds that might be rotated or remixed occasionally to reflect business conditions or to get a little more offensive or defensive. More than the other portfolios, this portfolio follows the rotation of market preference among different kinds of businesses and business assets. The portfolio is managed to redeploy assets among market or business sectors, between aggressive and defensive business assets, from large- to small-cap companies, from companies with international exposure to those with little of the same, from companies in favor versus out of favor, from stocks to bonds to commodities, and so forth. Sector-specific exchange-traded funds are a favorite component of these portfolios, as are cyclical and commodity-based stocks like gold mining stocks.

Is this about market timing? Let's call it "intelligent" or "educated" market timing. Studies telling us that it is impossible to effectively time market moves have been around for years. It is impossible to catch highs and lows in particular investments, market sectors, or even the market as a whole. Nobody can find exact tops or bottoms. But by watching economic indicators and the pulse of businesses and the marketplace, long-term market performance can be boosted by well-rationalized and timely sector rotation. The key word is *timely*. The agile active investor has enough of a finger on the pulse to see the signs and invest accordingly.

While the idea isn't new, the advent of "low-friction" exchange-traded funds and other index portfolios makes it a lot more practical for the individual investors. What is a "low-friction" fund? They trade like a single stock—one order, one discounted commission. You don't have to liquidate or acquire a whole basket full of investments on your own to follow a sector. We should note that it's been possible to rotate assets in mutual fund families for years with a single phone call, but most funds in these families are less "pure" plays in their sector, and most families do not cover all sectors.

The Opportunistic Portfolio

The opportunistic portfolio is the most actively traded portion of an active investor's total portfolio. The opportunistic portfolio looks for stocks or other investments that seem to be notably under- or overvalued at a particular time. The active investor looks for shorter-term opportunities—perhaps a few days, perhaps a month, perhaps even a year—to wring out gains from undervalued situations.

The opportunistic portfolio also may be used to generate short-term income through covered option writing. Options are essentially a cash-based risk transfer mechanism whereby a possible but low-probability investment outcome is exchanged for a less profitable but more certain outcome. A fee or "premium" is paid in exchange for transferring the opportunity for more aggressive gain to someone else. You collect this fee. Effectively, you as the owner of a stock can convert a growth investment into an income investment, paying yourself a dividend for the ownership of the stock by selling an option. Is this risky? Actually, it is less risky than owning the stock without an option.

Curiously, the main objective of this short-term portfolio is to generate income, or cash. Most traditional investors look at the long-term, more conservative components of a portfolio to generate income through bonds, dividend-paying stocks, and so forth. In this framework, the short-term opportunistic portfolio actually does the heavy lifting in terms of generating cash income. An active investor might look to trade those stocks with varying degrees of frequency or to sell some options to generate cash. These "swing" trades usually run from a few days to a month or so, and may be day trades if things work out particularly well and move particularly fast. It should be emphasized again that day trades are not the active investor's goal or typical practice.

ARE RETIREMENT ACCOUNTS ALWAYS PART OF THE FOUNDATION?

The long-term objectives and nature of retirement accounts suggest normal inclusion as part of the foundation portfolio. In fact, retirement assets can be deployed as part of either the rotational or opportunistic portfolio. In fact, it might make a lot of sense. Why? Because returns generated are tax free, at least until withdrawn. Tax-free returns can compound much faster. Because of the importance of these assets, one should only commit a small portion to an actively managed opportunistic portfolio, but it can be a good way to juice the growth of this important asset base.

100 Best Stocks *and the Segmented Portfolio*

The next natural question is—"So how do I use the *100 Best Stocks* to construct my portfolio tiers?" The answer is really that selections from the *100 Best* list can be used in all tiers, depending on your time horizon and current price relative to value. If you see a stock on the *100 Best* list take a nosedive, and feel that nosedive is out of proportion to the real news and near-term prospects of the company, it may be a candidate for the opportunistic portfolio. If the stock makes sense as a relatively low-volatility, long-term holding (as many on our list do), it's a good candidate for the foundation portfolio. Likewise, if you feel that, say, health-care stocks are, as a group, likely to be in favor and are undervalued now, you can pick off the health-care stocks on the *100 Best* list as a rotational portfolio pick. Similarly, if you feel that large-cap dividend-paying stocks will do well, again you can use the *100 Best* list to feed into this hunch. Not surprisingly, we feel the *100 Best* stocks are of the highest quality and can be used with relatively less risk than most other stocks to achieve your objectives.

When to Buy? Consider When to Sell

If it's hard to figure out when to buy a stock, it's even harder to figure out when to sell. People get married to their investment decisions, feeling somehow that if it isn't right, maybe time will help and things will get better. Or they're just too arrogant to admit that they made a mistake. There are lots of reasons why people hold on to investments for too long a time. Here's the fundamental truth: Buying and selling should be much the same process. Let's look at it from the point of view of selling. When should you sell? Simply, when there's something else better to buy. Something else better for future returns, something else better for safety, something else better for timeliness or synchronization with overall business trends. That something else can be another stock, a futures contract, or a house. It can also be cash—sell that stock when . . . when what? When cash is a better investment. Or when you need the money, which is another way of saying that cash is a better investment.

Similarly, if you think of a buy decision as a best possible deployment of capital because there's no better way to invest your money, you'll also come out ahead. It really isn't that hard, especially if you've done your homework. And it's also made easier if you avoid rash overcommitments; that is, you avoid buying all at once in case you've made a mistake or in case better prices come later down the road.

ETFs: Different Route, Same Destination (Almost)

The *100 Best Stocks to Buy* series is about—well—the 100 best individual companies in which you can buy shares to build into your investment portfolio. The objective is to use these selections as a starting point to build a customized portfolio of your very own, a portfolio that earns decent, better-than-market, long-term returns from excellent companies while—because they're excellent companies—taking less risk than you would with most investments. And because you're doing it yourself, you save money on fees and expenses and come away with the pride of ownership of doing it yourself.

That said, not everyone has the time or inclination to do this this. Not everyone wants to sail through the treacherous channels of company financial information and the foggy mysteries of intangibles and marketplace performance to figure out which companies are really best to own and to keep the finger on the pulse to make sure they stay that way. You may want to own individual stocks. But just as buying a kit makes many aspects of building a new outdoor deck easier, so does buying a stock "kit": a product or package of stocks to do what you might otherwise have to struggle through on your own. If you could get such a kit product cheap enough and aligned to your needs, then why wouldn't you? It will save time, and you'll be firing up the barbecue and enjoying those outdoor parties with your friends a lot sooner. Or, perhaps at the risk of more tiring analogies, buying individual stocks is like ordering à la carte from a menu. You're not sure if what you're getting works together, so why not do a prix fixe to let the chef do some of the driving? Okay, enough . . .

Such is the impulse to find investment products—packages, prix fixe menus——that mimic the performance of the *100 Best* stocks. Honestly, we would love it if some fund company would come to us and "buy" our index to build a fund you could buy, but that hasn't happened yet. But in that spirit—and because we've written a lot about the merits of individual stock versus fund investing before—we'd like to offer this special section about using exchange-traded funds (ETFs) as a path to own portfolios crafted with many of the *100 Best Stocks* principles in mind.

The ETF Universe

We're talking about ETFs here, not traditional mutual funds. Although total traditional mutual fund assets still outweigh ETF-held assets by a factor of 8 to 1, traditional mutual funds are more expensive and haven't performed as well as ETFs—or the market benchmarks—over time. So we will limit this discussion to ETFs, but if you're working with a professional advisor or are limited to traditional funds through your 401(k) or some other investment platform, the discussion can apply to traditional funds, too.

ETFs are packaged single securities trading on stock exchanges (rather than directly through a mutual fund company), which create a basket of securities that track the composition of specially designed indexes. With most

ETFs (excluding "actively managed" ETFs) there are no fund managers making individual stock purchase or sale decisions. The fund follows the index.

These indexes started out as broad, bland, and obvious—the first ETF, the SPDR S&P 500 ETF Trust, has tracked the S&P 500 index since 1993. Since that inception, hundreds of new indexes have been created to track everything from broad baskets of stocks to the price of certain commodities in Australian dollars. Our job here is to identify the indexes—and the funds built around them—that mimic *100 Best Stocks* principles.

As of early 2013, there are some 1,391 exchange-traded products, of which 1,234 are ETFs and 157 are so-called "exchange-traded notes," or ETNs, which are actually fixed-income securities adjusted in value to track an index without actually owning the components of the index. The ETF space is growing by more than 100 funds every year and has amassed about $1.6 trillion in assets There are generalized and specialized ETFs covering stocks, bonds, fixed-income investments, commodities, real estate, currencies, and the so-called "leveraged and inverse" funds designed to achieve specialized investing objectives. Within each of those groups, the segments available could fill a chapter in and of themselves with divisions by market cap, style (growth versus value), industry, sector, strategy, country, and region—just to name a few.

ETF Advantages
There are numerous advantages of ETFs over traditional funds—reasons why they are "where the puck is going" in packaged investments:

- Easy to research. ETFs are relatively easy to understand and easy to screen using commonly found screening tools at online brokers.
- Transparency. It's easy to learn what individual stocks an ETF owns and what comprises the underlying index, both through the online portals and through the index providers' websites. (Want to know what's in the Focus Morningstar Health Care Index? Just put the index name into a search engine, and you'll get there.)
- Low fees, low cost. Fees typically range from 0.1 percent for the most generic index funds to 0.2–0.8 percent for more specialized funds—about half of the typical figures found in traditional mutual funds.
- Easy to buy and sell. It's like buying and selling an ordinary stock.
- Easy to match your objectives and style. New funds are showing up every day, and many match a quality, low-volatility, value-oriented style we're aligned with.

▼ *100 Best Stocks—ETF "Imitators"*

ETFS WITH STRONG *100 BEST* COMPOSITION AND STRATEGIES

ETF	Symbol	Sponsor	Total assets	Yield	Expense ratio (%)	1-yr perfor-mance	Inception date	$10K at inception	What attracted us:
S&P SPDR Dividend ETF	SDY	State Street	$11.7B	2.7%	0.38%	34.4%	11/1/05	$16,413	Diverse portfolio, "Dividend Aristocrats" index
First Trust Morningside Dividend Leaders	FDL	First Trust	$629.9M	3.4%	0.45%	27.1%	3/9/06	$14,145	Lots of *100 Best* stocks
iShares Dow Jones Select Dividend Index Fund	DVY	Blackrock	$12.4B	3.3%	0.40%	28.1%	11/3/03	$18,097	Growth plus income, lots of *100 Best* stocks
Powershares Buyback Achievers Portfolio	PKW	Invesco	$415.2M	1.0%	0.71%	36.5%	12/20/06	$14,709	Compelling strategy, strong long-term results
Market Vectors Wide Moat ETF	MOAT	Van Eck	$187.5M	0.5%	0.49%	32.8%	4/24/12	$11,624	Compelling strategy, new fund, low cost
Powershares S&P 500 Low Volatility Portfolio	SPLV	Invesco	$5.4B	2.6%	0.25%	27.4%	5/5/11	$13,470	Low-volatility focus, lots of *100 Best* stocks, low cost
iShares MSCI USA Minimum Volatility Index Fund	USMV	Blackrock	$3.7B	1.6%	0.15%	26.2%	10/18/11	$13,424	Low-volatility focus, lots of *100 Best* stocks, low cost
Powershares S&P High Quality Portfolio	SPHQ	Invesco	$228.7M	1.7%	0.70%	30.1%	12/6/05	$12,329	Growth and stability of dividends, lots of *100 Best* stocks

Dining with the 100 Best: *A Special ETF Menu*

Our *100 Best Stocks* list doesn't really follow any investment style. It isn't just growth or value. It isn't just large cap, it isn't just high yield, nor is it just tied to certain industries or sectors of the economy. It is a blend of excellent companies in the right businesses, doing well in those businesses, with a potential for strong, steady, and growing investor returns. There is no index or any other screenable classification to select those companies. If there were, there'd be little reason to publish this book.

So as we search for ETFs that run with the same tailwinds as our *100 Best* list, we start with the name of the fund and the index that the fund follows. "Dividend Achievers" or "Buyback Achievers" tells us we're looking on the right part of the menu. Then we dig in and look at the actual portfolio composition (again, most investing portals and brokerage sites let you do this—we use Fidelity (*www.fidelity.com*). If we see lots of *100 Best* stocks on the list, it confirms that we're on the right track.

Previously, you saw a list of 8 ETFs that we feel follow our *100 Best* style and principles that could be used to build or supplement parts of your portfolio.

Selecting ETFs is an art in itself and was covered in an earlier book we did in this series called *The 100 Best ETFs You Can Buy 2012*. Unfortunately that book didn't find a large enough market to be updated each year, but it is still useful in its original form. There are many other ETF resources, again at your online broker or through a specialized ETF portal called ETFdb (*www.etfdb.com*). This portal and its classification page (*www.etfdb.com/type*) can be helpful in finding individual ETFs that suit your taste.

We'll leave the ETF discussion here but will augment it further in future releases of the *100 Best Stocks* series, because ETFs are an increasingly important and viable complement to investing in individual stocks. The good news is that you can invest in ETFs and still follow the *100 Best* style.

Part II

THE 100 BEST STOCKS TO BUY

The 100 Best Stocks to Buy

Index of Stocks by Company Name (*New for 2014)

Company	Symbol	Category	Sector
—A—			
3M Company	MMM	Conservative Growth	Industrials
Abbott Laboratories	ABT	Growth and Income	Health Care
Aetna	AET	Conservative Growth	Health Care
Allergan	AGN	Aggressive Growth	Health Care
Amgen	AMGN	Conservative Growth	Health Care
Apple	AAPL	Aggressive Growth	Consumer Discretionary
Aqua America*	WTR	Growth and Income	Utilities
Archer Daniels Midland	ADM	Conservative Growth	Consumer Staples
AT&T	T	Growth and Income	Telecommunications Services
Automatic Data Processing	ADP	Conservative Growth	Information Technology
—B—			
Baxter	BAX	Aggressive Growth	Health Care
Becton, Dickinson	BDX	Conservative Growth	Health Care
Bemis*	BMS	Conservative Growth	Consumer Staples
—C—			
Campbell Soup	CPB	Conservative Growth	Consumer Staples
CarMax	KMX	Aggressive Growth	Retail
Chevron	CVX	Growth and Income	Energy
Church & Dwight	CHD	Aggressive Growth	Consumer Staples
Cincinnati Financial	CINF	Income	Financials
Clorox	CLX	Conservative Growth	Consumer Staples
Coca-Cola	KO	Conservative Growth	Consumer Staples
Colgate-Palmolive	CL	Conservative Growth	Consumer Staples
Comcast	CMCSA	Aggressive Growth	Telecommunications Services
ConocoPhillips	COP	Growth and Income	Energy
Corning*	GLW	Aggressive Growth	Information Technology
Costco Wholesale	COST	Aggressive Growth	Retail
CVS Caremark	CVS	Conservative Growth	Retail
—D—			
Deere	DE	Aggressive Growth	Industrials
Dominion Resources	D	Growth and Income	Utilities
Duke Energy	DUK	Income	Utilities
DuPont	DD	Growth and Income	Materials

Index of Stocks by Company Name (continued)

Index of Stocks by Company Name (continued)

—N—

NextEra Energy	NEE	Growth and Income	Utilities
Nike	NKE	Aggressive Growth	Consumer Discretionary
Norfolk Southern	NSC	Conservative Growth	Transportation

—O—

Otter Tail	OTTR	Growth and Income	Utilities/Industrial

—P—

Pall Corporation	PLL	Aggressive Growth	Industrials
Patterson	PDCO	Aggressive Growth	Health Care
Paychex	PAYX	Aggressive Growth	Information Technology
PepsiCo	PEP	Conservative Growth	Consumer Staples
Perrigo	PRGO	Aggressive Growth	Health Care
Praxair	PX	Conservative Growth	Materials
Procter & Gamble	PG	Conservative Growth	Consumer Staples

—Q—

Quest Diagnostics*	DGX	Aggressive Growth	Health Care

—R—

Ross Stores	ROST	Aggressive Growth	Retail

—S—

Schlumberger	SLB	Aggressive Growth	Energy
Seagate Technology	STX	Aggressive Growth	Information Technology
Sigma-Aldrich	SIAL	Aggressive Growth	Industrials
Southern Company	SO	Growth and Income	Utilities
Southwest Airlines	LUV	Aggressive Growth	Transportation
St. Jude Medical	STJ	Aggressive Growth	Health Care
Starbucks	SBUX	Aggressive Growth	Restaurants
State Street*	STT	Conservative Growth	Financials
Stryker	SYK	Aggressive Growth	Health Care
Suburban Propane	SPH	Income	Energy
Sysco	SYY	Conservative Growth	Consumer Staples

—T—

Target Corporation	TGT	Aggressive Growth	Retail
Tiffany	TIF	Aggressive Growth	Retail
Time Warner Inc.	TWX	Conservative Growth	Entertainment
Total S.A.	TOT	Growth and Income	Energy
Tractor Supply Company	TSCO	Aggressive Growth	Retail

Index of Stocks by Company Name (continued)

3M Company

❏ Ticker symbol: MMM (NYSE) ❏ S&P rating: AA– ❏ Value Line financial strength rating: A++
❏ Current yield: 2.5% ❏ Dividend raises, past 10 years: 10

Company Profile

The 3M Company is now a $30 billion diversified manufacturing technology company with leading positions in industrial, consumer and office, health care, safety, electronics, telecommunications, and other markets. The company has operations in more than 60 countries and serves customers in nearly 200 countries. Due to the breadth of their product line and the global reach of their distribution, the company has long been viewed as a bellwether for the overall health of the world economy. Over the past 5 years the company's stock has lagged the S&P into the recession and led the S&P during the recovery. 3M has had a history of sound management and is regularly among the leaders in everyone's "most admired" list of companies.

The company has been on an acquisition tear recently, capped off by its 3Q 2012 acquisition of the Avery Dennison office and consumer products business for $550 million. The well-known Avery labels are the flagship product of this group, but it markets a broad range of products for the office and education markets. 3M has made it clear that it plans to continue to buy into complementary markets and has set aside $2 billion in FY2013 for further acquisitions to supplement sales growth.

3M's operations are divided into 6 segments (approximate revenue percentages in parentheses):

- The Industrial and Transportation segment (34 percent) produces industrial tapes, abrasives, adhesives, and products for the separation of fluids and gases. They supply such markets as paper and packaging, food and beverage, electronics, and the automotive market.
- The Health Care segment (17 percent) serves markets that include medical clinics and hospitals, pharmaceuticals and dental and orthodontic practitioners. Products and services include medical and surgical supplies, skin health and infection prevention products, drug delivery systems, dental products, and antimicrobial solutions.
- The Safety, Security, and Protection Services segment (13 percent) serves a broad range of markets that increase the safety, security, and productivity of workers, facilities, and

systems. Major product offerings include safety and security products, energy control products, and roofing granules for asphalt shingles.

- The Consumer and Office segment (14 percent) serves markets that include retail, home improvement, building maintenance, and other markets. Products in this segment include office supply products such as the familiar tapes and Post-it notes, stationery products, construction and home improvement products, home-care products, protective material products, and consumer health-care products. This segment will grow considerably with the acquisition of the Avery Dennison office products line.

- The Display and Graphics segment (12 percent) serves markets that include electronic display, traffic safety, and commercial graphics. This segment includes optical film solutions for electronic displays, computer screen filters, reflective sheeting for transportation safety, and projection systems, including mobile display technology and visual systems products.

- The Electro and Communications segment (11 percent) serves the electrical, electronics, and communications industries, including electric utilities.

Products include electronic and interconnect solutions, telecommunications products, electrical products, and touch screens and touch monitors.

Financial Highlights, Fiscal Year 2012

The company reported revenue of $29.9 billion in fiscal 2012, basically flat year/year, but in line with estimates. Operating efficiency improvements accounted for a bump in earnings, but a dismal foreign exchange environment exacerbated the sales declines in some foreign markets. A softer-than-expected global consumer electronics market impacted sales in APAC, which grew a mere 0.1 percent.

Reasons to Buy

3M manufactures a broad line of products for end-user and industrial markets. The company makes many steady-selling products essential to manufacturing and day-to-day operations of other companies and organizations, and seemingly essential to most of us, e.g., Post-it Notes and Scotch tape. Currently priced at nearly $105 per share, the stock is trading close to its all-time high. Be not afraid, though, as 3M has a record of moderately outpacing the market (3M is a Dow 30 component) during bullish periods and has also held its value better than most during market downturns. The company grew its dividend another 8 percent last year, making for 11 consecutive years of growth. Their current yield of 2.5 percent is a nice bonus, even as some analysts point to price potential of $125 per share. Along those lines, we feel several large-cap value stocks are currently underpriced and will benefit from a move to quality when the current bull market tapers off. These shares are in the right place at the right time, with investors likely looking to tuck away some gains toward the end of 2013. These shares are up 17 percent over last year's price at this time when we recommended the stock on the strength of its international presence, its innovation, and its financials. These fundamentals have not changed, and we feel 3M still has room to grow, and significantly ahead of its Dow brethren. We also like the prospects for a rebound in the European markets in early 2014.

Reasons for Caution

With the European markets still in the doldrums, 3M will have to rely on its Americas and APAC markets to see them through 2013 and into the early part of 2014. EMEA sales were 23 percent of the company total, and the only region to show a year/year decline (down 3 percent). The company is forecasting an additional decline in western Europe through 2013 of as much as an additional 3 percent. The company's acquisition plans will not tax their cash reserves significantly, but between acquisitions and share repurchases the company has allocated $5 billion in cash, a pace they will not be able to sustain for more than a year or two.

SECTOR: **Industrials**
BETA COEFFICIENT: **0.80**
10-YEAR COMPOUND EARNINGS PER SHARE GROWTH: **10.0%**
10-YEAR COMPOUND DIVIDENDS PER SHARE GROWTH: **6.0%**

		2005	2006	2007	2008	2009	2010	2011	2012
Revenues (mil)		21,167	22,293	24,462	25,269	23,123	26,662	29,611	29,904
Net income (mil)		3,111	3,851	4,096	3,460	3,193	4,169	4,283	4,445
Earnings per share		3.98	5.06	5.60	4.89	4.52	5.75	5.96	6.33
Dividends per share		1.68	1.84	1.92	2.00	2.04	2.10	2.20	2.36
Cash flow per share		5.55	6.71	7.29	6.65	6.15	7.43	7.85	8.35
Price:	high	87.4	88.4	97.0	84.8	84.3	91.5	98.2	95.5
	low	69.7	67.0	72.9	50.0	40.9	68.0	68.6	82.0

3M Company
3M Center
St. Paul, MN 55144–1000
(651) 733-8206
Website: www.3m.com

Abbott Laboratories

◻ Ticker symbol: ABT (NYSE) ◻ S&P rating: AA ◻ Value Line financial strength rating: A++
◻ Current yield: 1.5% ◻ Dividend raises, past 10 years: 10

Company Profile

For many years "A Promise for Life" has been the slogan of Abbott Laboratories, founded in 1888 and one of the most diverse health-care manufacturers in the world. The company decided in 2012 that part of that promise would be better fulfilled by another entity, and in January 2013 spun off its pharmaceutical business into the newly created company AbbVie. Abbott Labs retained all other segments of its business and has no stake in AbbVie.

Abbott is now organized around its 4 largest business segments: Nutritional Products, Diagnostic Products, Medical Device Products, and its Established Products Division (essentially, its retained legacy pharmaceutical lines). The company's split is not unlike what's happening with some integrated oil companies, which are separating out R & D–intensive exploration and production components into separate companies.

Abbott continues to be a dominant player in the nutritional market, with a top share in the nutritional products market. The company's products are sold in more than 130 countries, with more than half its sales derived from international operations.

Currently, Abbott's leading brands include Freestyle (diabetes monitoring), Ensure (nutritional supplements for adults), and Similac (infant formula).

The company has widespread respect among the medical and financial community as one of the most solid and diversified health-related names, as well as one of the most innovative in the industry.

Financial Highlights, Fiscal Year 2012

The past year of Abbott Laboratories as a pharmaceutical supplier was another solid, steady performance. Some might go far as to say unspectacular, but the company has never been about the spectacular. For at least 15 years they've been about consistent performance, even through the worst of the 2007 recession and financial crisis. In 2012 Abbott's revenues, income, and operating and net margins all showed very healthy increases. The happy upshot of this (for our readers) was the performance of the stock, which hit a new high with 28 percent growth over the previous year. And, of further interest, the retained Diagnostics and Nutritional segments were the strongest drivers, while the pharmaceuticals business continued its trend of diminishing growth.

Reasons to Buy

Abbott is a very different company than it was just last year. Spinning off 40 percent of one's revenues will do that. But in fact (and this is what the company itself understood), Abbott was already 2 different companies operating as 1.

There is nothing on this planet like a modern pharmaceutical development operation. Yes, some of Abbott's remaining medical products undergo the same type of rigorous and mandated test regimes required of pharmaceuticals, and many have their success tied to governmental and institutional healthcare budgets, but to our knowledge, only airliners and pharmaceuticals have development cycles measured in decades. And you don't see Boeing in the baby-formula business.

Pharma is a risky, capital-intensive business. This doesn't mean it's a bad business, but when it's such a big part of a company that has other, less needy (but just as valuable) segments, the lesser stars tend to get short shrift. There's nothing inherently wrong with this approach, either, if you feel the lesser stars are put to best use as supporting players. But Abbott felt there was a great deal of untapped and underdeveloped value in its smaller lines (the remaining 60 percent of the company), and we agree. Early projections for the realigned company are for double-digit percentage growth in per-share earnings. The company is also confident that by redeploying resources on internal processes it can bump operating margin a full percentage point in 2013 alone.

Abbott's nutritional products are market leaders. Their baby formula is the dominant player worldwide, and the worldwide market is growing quickly (particularly in high-population developing markets). Other standout products include diabetes monitoring and treatment, an area that has shown strong volume growth recently.

Finally, we like Abbott's diagnostics and bio-assay business. Rapid diagnosis of common (and uncommon) diseases with a simple blood (or other fluid) assay is becoming a reality, and the advent of this technique will revise the practice of medicine everywhere. Abbott is well positioned here, with current products and the research base for further growth.

ABT has paid consecutive quarterly dividends since 1924 and has raised the dividend in each of the past 10 years. Obviously, the increases will stop in 2013, but the yield is still a respectable 1.5 percent.

Reasons for Caution

Major reorganizations and restructurings often bring some complexities and doubt; we'll continue to monitor this. The medical devices category (stents, etc.) has saturated in recent years, and both revenues and margins are declining. One must always watch politics and belt-tightening efforts in the health-care sector.

SECTOR: **Health Care**
BETA COEFFICIENT: **0.31 (prior company)**
10-YEAR COMPOUND EARNINGS PER SHARE GROWTH: **9.0% (prior company)**
10-YEAR COMPOUND DIVIDENDS PER SHARE GROWTH: **9.0% (prior company)**

	2005	2006	2007	2008	2009	2010	2011	2012
Revenues (mil)	22,337	22,476	25,914	29,528	30,764	35,167	39,000	39,874
Net income (mil)	3,908	3,841	4,429	4,734	5,745	6,500	7,290	8,119
Earnings per share	2.50	2.52	2.84	3.03	3.69	4.17	4.65	5.07
Dividends per share	1.10	1.18	1.30	1.44	1.60	1.76	1.88	2.01
Cash flow per share	3.42	3.51	4.05	4.32	5.00	5.90	6.60	6.90
Price: high	50.0	49.9	59.5	61.1	57.4	56.8	56.4	72.5
low	37.5	39.2	48.8	45.8	41.3	44.6	45.1	54.0

Abbott Laboratories
100 Abbott Park Road
Abbott Park, IL 60064–6400
(847) 937-6100
Website: www.abbott.com

CONSERVATIVE GROWTH

Aetna Inc.

❏ Ticker symbol: AET (NYSE) ❏ S&P rating: A+ ❏ Value Line financial strength rating: A ❏ Current yield: 1.5% ❏ Dividend raises, past 10 years: 2

Company Profile

Founded in 1853, Aetna is one of the nation's longest-lived insurers. Longevity, though a point of pride (and marketing value) among insurers, is not by itself a qualifying criterion for inclusion in our *100 Best Stocks* list. Today's Aetna, a product of a 1996 merger between Aetna Life and Casualty and U.S. Healthcare, is also one of the largest and most important diversified healthcare, insurance, and benefits companies in the United States.

The company's three distinct businesses are operated in 3 divisions. Health Care provides a full assortment of health benefit plans for corporate, small business, and individual customers, including PPO, HMO, point-of-service, vision care, dental, behavioral health, Medicare/Medicaid, and pharmacy benefits plans. The Group Insurance business provides group term life, disability, and accidental death and dismemberment insurance products primarily to the same sort of businesses that might sign up for its health plans. The Large Case Pensions business administers pension plans for certain existing customers.

The health-care business is by far the largest segment and the focal point of our selection of this company. The business insures some 35 million individuals. With impending health-care reforms, many of which are targeted at the insurance side of the industry, it would normally be hard to recommend such a company because of the uncertainty going forward and the general public dislike of health insurers. However, Aetna has proven itself to be a pacesetter among insurance providers, mainly through its support and innovations in the area of consumer-directed health care.

For example, with Aetna's consumer-directed HealthFund plans, subscribers become responsible for a portion of their own health-care costs and are given the tools to shop for health-care alternatives and maximize preventive care. Aetna originally led the way with some of the first health savings account–compatible products in 2001. Since then the company has led the industry in developing tools, such as the Aetna Navigator price transparency tool designed to help patients evaluate the cost and outcomes of procedures in different geographies.

The company also has championed patient- and doctor-accessible medical records and other techniques for making health-care delivery more efficient. Aetna is also a big believer in the use of analytics—using a "big data" approach to predict the types of medical conditions their covered clients are likely to encounter in the coming years based on correlations among contributing factors in their large data pool. Obviously, being able to tell a particular patient how to avoid a predicted condition is a big win for both parties. Predictability permits the company to assemble coverages appropriate to the patient's needs, saving money for both the company and the client.

Financial Highlights, Fiscal Year 2012

FY2012 results reflect the uncertainties in the overall health-care market. Revenues were up only slightly over FY2011, with earnings, after adjustments for one-time charges of nearly $1 billion, down just slightly due to several recent acquisitions. Improved "utilization"—that is, the reduction of the amount and cost of health care provided per subscriber—has taken hold over the past few years, probably a result of direct management, process improvements, and a general pattern of cost consciousness among both consumers and providers. That improved utilization reduces costs and drops straight to the bottom line, allowing Aetna to earn $5.15 a share, a 36 percent increase over FY2010 and the first time the company has exceeded $4.00 a share. Besides utilization, one factor was a drop of almost 10 percent of outstanding shares to 350 million through repurchases. Financially the company is clicking on all cylinders, and while share repurchases will continue, the company is cautious about the sustained rally, calling for FY2013 EPS of $5.00.

Reasons to Buy

As we said last year, Aetna is ahead of the pack in terms of both business and technology innovation. While the share price in 2012 was down and then back up an aspirin-inducing 30 percent, the company's fourth quarter 2012 was very strong in terms of revenue growth and expense ratio reduction, and the acquisition of Coventry Health Care and its prescription drug plan service should provide considerable returns in the coming year. The company's financials remain solid, with significant cash reserves. Last year saw another dividend increase (up 14 percent) and an additional $1.4 billion spent in share repurchase.

Reasons for Caution

Public and governmental scrutiny of health insurers has never been higher, and burgeoning health-care costs can be difficult for even a company of Aetna's capability and influence to manage. Cost increases have proven to be difficult to contain over the past decade in spite of many industry-led and government-mandated efforts. There are opportunities for an innovative player with a breakthrough model to enter this space, although the barriers to entry are daunting. Still, Aetna needs to remain a leader, staying ahead of trends as the new health-care environment evolves.

SECTOR: **Health Care**
BETA COEFFICIENT: **0.95**
10-YEAR COMPOUND EARNINGS PER SHARE GROWTH: **28.0%**
10-YEAR COMPOUND DIVIDENDS PER SHARE GROWTH: **5.5%**

	2005	2006	2007	2008	2009	2010	2011	2012
Revenues (mil)	22,492	25,146	27,600	30,951	34,765	34,246	33,700	36,596
Net income (mil)	1,344	1,602	1,842	1,922	1,236	1,555.5	1,850	1,658
Earnings per share	2.23	2.82	3.49	3.93	2.75	3.68	5.15	5.14
Dividends per share	0.02	0.04	0.04	0.04	0.04	0.04	0.45	0.70
Cash flow per share	2.73	3.63	4.36	5.07	3.83	5.20	6.25	6.43
Price: high	49.7	52.5	60.0	59.8	34.9	36.0	46.0	51.1
low	29.9	30.9	40.3	14.2	16.7	25.0	30.6	34.6

Aetna Inc.
151 Farmington Avenue
Hartford, CT 17405–0872
(860) 273-0123
Website: www.aetna.com

Allergan, Inc.

❑ Ticker symbol: AGN (NASDAQ) ❑ S&P rating: A+ ❑ Value Line financial strength rating: A+
❑ Current yield: 0.2% ❑ Dividend raises, past 10 years: 1

Company Profile

Allergan is a health-care products company making pharmaceutical, over-the-counter, and medical device items for the ophthalmic, neurological, dermatological, and urologic fields as well as for use in an assortment of cosmetic medical procedures such as breast aesthetics and obesity intervention, and other specialty medical markets. The company was founded in 1977 and originally marketed ophthalmic products for contact lens wearers and other products for eye inflammation and other disorders.

The company operates in 2 segments. The Specialty Pharmaceuticals segment markets the long-line ophthalmic products, including contact lens products, glaucoma therapy, artificial tears, and allergy- and infection-fighting products. Brand names include Restasis, Lumigan, Refresh, Alphagan, and Acuvail among others.

Specialty Pharmaceuticals also sells Botox for a variety of medical conditions and for cosmetic use. Botox is used not only for the familiar skin wrinkle therapies but also for neuromuscular disorders; recently it has been approved for use in treating chronic migraines, a new market with substantial potential. It has also been approved for an overactive bladder condition. In total, with these approvals, the "therapeutic" side of the Botox business (in contrast to the "cosmetic") is quite healthy; total Botox-related revenues are expected to grow at least 10 percent in FY2013 and perhaps more as these treatments become mainstream. Another migraine treatment has been acquired this year; see the following sections for details. The segment also offers a number of popular skin-care and acne medications for both acute care and aesthetic use, including acne care, psoriasis, and eyelash enhancement. Brand names include Aczone and Tazorac for acne and psoriasis, Vivite for aging skin care, and Latisse for eyelashes.

The Medical Devices Segment makes and markets breast implants for augmentation, revision, and reconstructive surgery. Obesity intervention products include the Lap-Band system and the Orbera Intragastic Balloon System (Allergan is seeking a buyer for this line). The segment also markets other skin and tissue regenerative products for aesthetic and recon-structive purposes for burn treat-ment and other traumas.

The approximate FY2012 business breakdown by revenue, almost unchanged from FY2011, is 47 percent eye care, 30 per-cent neuromuscular including Botox, 13 percent breast and facial implants, 3 percent obesity implants, 1 percent urological, and 5 percent other. Foreign sales continue to account for about 39 percent of the total.

Financial Highlights, Fiscal Year 2012

In March, Allergan completed its acquisition of MAP Pharmaceuti-cals, a development-stage company with one major product, Levadex, which is an inhaled therapy for the treatment of migraine headaches. Unfortunately, the approval process for Levadex has proven to be some-thing of a headache itself; no word on whether it's an approved treat-ment for this condition. The FDA has twice rejected the drug, most recently delaying its introduction by at least 8 months.

The company had a good FY2012, with revenues up approxi-mately 6.5 percent to $5.7 billion, but per-share earnings were up a full 13 percent to $3.84 per share. The fourth quarter of 2012 was par-ticularly strong, with net margins at a record high of 21.5 percent. The

company's projections for FY2013 are equally optimistic, in spite of their choosing to treat revenues from the obesity treatment product line as discontinued business. Per-share earnings are expected to rise 13 percent on increased sales of 7 percent.

Reasons to Buy

Allergan tends to be more econom-ically sensitive and cyclical than other pharmaceutical and medi-cal products companies because much of what they sell supports cosmetic, thus elective, and thus cash-paid (in contrast to insurance-paid) procedures. The share price over the past 20 years reflects this dynamic—rather than showing the slow, steady increases of a medical supplier like Johnson & Johnson, Allergan's share price moves with the broader economic trends and with a higher beta. Of course, this is a negative when the economy is soft, although the company sells enough regularly required prod-ucts such as eye-care products to not be hurt too much by bad times. We like the issue because it will do especially well in good times. New uses for Botox, such as the migraine treatments, over-active bladder symptoms, and oth-ers are also promising. We also like the prospects in overseas markets as treatments become available for a growing (and aging) middle class.

Reasons for Caution

In April 2013, the FDA again denied approval for Allergan's inhaled migraine treatment Levadex. The FDA's concern was not with the drug's efficacy or safety but with the packaging. Allergan believes the approval will be granted after further inspection of the packaging facility and, potentially, modification to the process.

Despite their thorough approval processes, pharmaceutical and medical device products come with an inherent risk of short- and long-term failure with painful financial and brand-image consequences. Cosmetic devices are particularly sensitive—witness what happened to Dow Corning with breast implants in the 1970s. And now, Allergan has recently begun to divest itself of its laparoscopic obesity treatments (the Lap-Band) due to concerns over complications and sketchy long-term effectiveness. Falling sales didn't help, either.

Last year we were somewhat cautious regarding Allergan's prospects, but we stayed with them and they managed to prove out. This year we're of the same mind, even though the company is well positioned with in-demand products and broader applications in good demographics. Allergan is currently trading at a 32 multiple and is a dividend payer in name only. This makes them unique in this book. They may not be the right stock for everyone, so we'll repeat the caution we offered last year: Pick your buying opportunities carefully.

SECTOR: **Health Care**
BETA COEFFICIENT: **0.90**
10-YEAR COMPOUND EARNINGS PER SHARE GROWTH: **15.0%**
10-YEAR COMPOUND DIVIDENDS PER SHARE GROWTH: **1.5%**

		2005	2006	2007	2008	2009	2010	2011	2012
Revenues (mil)		2,318	3,063	3,939	4,403	4,503	4,883	5,347	5,710
Net income (mil)		477	452	575	786	850	975	1,057	1,172
Earnings per share		1.78	1.51	1.86	2.57	2.78	3.16	3.41	3.84
Dividends per share		0.20	0.20	0.20	0.20	0.20	0.20	0.20	0.20
Cash flow per share		2.07	1.98	2.58	3.46	3.65	4.03	4.29	4.76
Price:	high	56.3	61.5	68.1	70.4	64.1	74.9	89.3	97.1
	low	34.5	46.3	52.5	29.0	35.4	56.3	68.0	81.3

Allergan, Inc.
2525 Dupont Drive
Irvine, CA 92612
(714) 246-4500
Website: www.allergan.com

CONSERVATIVE GROWTH

Amgen, Inc.

❑ Ticker symbol: AMGN (NASDAQ) ❑ S&P rating: A+ ❑ Value Line financial strength rating: A++
❑ Current yield: 2.0% ❑ Dividend raises, past 10 years: 2

Company Profile

Founded in 1980, Amgen is the world's largest and one of the first independent biotech medicines company. The company develops medicines and therapeutics based on advances in cellular and molecular biology, mainly for grievous or chronic illnesses such as cancer, kidney disease, rheumatoid arthritis, bone disease, inflammation, nephrology, and others.

In FY2012, the company generated most of its approximately $17 billion in revenues with just 9 major products (Aranesp, Enbrel, Epogen, Neulasia, Neupogen, Nplate, Prolia, Sinsipar, and Vectibix), which you probably haven't heard of unless you've been prescribed one or are in the medical profession. The explanations of these products are far too technical for most of us to comprehend. Witness the company literature describing its products: "Neulasta (pegfulgrastim), a pegylated protein based on the filgrastim molecule, and NEUPOGEN (filgrastim) a recombinant-methionyl human granulocyte colony-stimulating factor, (G-SCF), both [of which] stimulate the production of neutrophils (a type of white blood cell that helps the body fight infection)."

Okay, we're out of our depth here. Forget about not investing in a business you don't understand—how about a business you can't even pronounce? Ordinarily we'd be reluctant to recommend a company with only 9 major products—products we don't really understand—in such an R & D–intensive business and changing technology. But Amgen is an exception—maybe an exception for biotech in general—because it has turned these products into a cash machine. The company earned about $5 billion on that $17 billion in sales with $6 billion in cash flow and $24 billion in cash on the balance sheet—not bad for a limited product assortment.

While the company continues to invest almost 20 percent of revenues in R & D, it has also begun to return a little bit of capital to the investors. Quarterly dividends were initiated in FY2011 at $1.12 per share annually, increased to $1.44 in FY2012 and again to $1.88 for FY2013. Share buybacks have reduced share counts from 1.224 billion in 2005 to a present day 763 million.

Financial Highlights, Fiscal Year 2012

FY2012 revenues came in at just over $17.2 billion, 3 percent higher than FY2010 and matching the previous year's increase. Earnings came in at $5.20 per share, again just slightly ahead of FY2010. Both figures were affected by the new health-care reform legislation. Those numbers sound modest, but management now projects FY2012 revenues in the $16.1–$16.5 billion range, with earnings in the $5.90–$6.15 range, both healthy increases. These increases reflect a few modest acquisitions and development partnerships and greater acceptance of their major product offerings. They also reflect growth in developing markets. The company has several new products in late-stage development, mainly in oncological, inflammatory, and metabolic disease categories.

Reasons to Buy

Amgen is regarded as the dominant player in this biotech niche and has had success with R & D and approval processes thus far. The product pipeline is a big focus of attention for any drug company, particularly so for those companies with only a dozen or so active products. Amgen currently has 47 drugs in trials, with 14 of them in final Phase 3 trials. They've recently had very encouraging results from talimogene laherparepvec, the announcement of which spurred a small rally in the price of the stock.

Even with recent share price increases, the P/E is hovering in the 14 range, and with a net profit margin of 30 percent, the company generates huge volumes of cash. They have been active (and successful) in their acquisitions, having made 13 of them in the past 13 years. Will they continue to acquire smaller companies? As mentioned earlier, the company is placing more emphasis on current shareholder return through dividends and share buybacks. Not only does this juice up total returns, but it also reduces the temptation to make costly acquisitions.

The company recently announced a joint venture with a Chinese pharmaceutical company to manufacture (Amgen) and market (Zhejiang Beta Pharma) Vectibix for delivery to patients in China.

Reasons for Caution

With so much R & D and other expense going into a handful of products, any failure or FDA rejection can be very costly. The company is huge, but as with any biotech, fortunes can change quickly and in ways that may be difficult for lay investors to comprehend. With huge companies sometimes comes huge debt, and that's certainly the case with Amgen. They carry $27 billion in total debt and pay $1.1 billion per year in interest. To be fair, Pfizer and Merck also carry very significant debt loads, and for the same reason—carryover from acquisitions. The company, as mentioned, faces some impact from the new health-care reform legislation, and initiatives to reduce health-care costs could affect Amgen. And, we normally shy away from companies whose products we don't understand.

SECTOR: **Health Care**
BETA COEFFICIENT: **0.65**
10-YEAR COMPOUND EARNINGS PER SHARE GROWTH: **17.0%**
10-YEAR COMPOUND DIVIDENDS PER SHARE GROWTH: **NA**

	2005	2006	2007	2008	2009	2010	2011	2012
Revenues (mil)	12,420	14,268	14,771	15,093	14,642	15,053	15,500	17,265
Net income (mil)	3,710	4,181	3,761	4,196	4,931	4,941	4,680	4,987
Earnings per share	2.95	3.51	3.31	3.90	4.83	5.12	5.20	6.41
Dividends per share	—	—	—	—	—	—	1.12	1.44
Cash flow per share	3.72	4.41	4.57	5.03	6.01	6.39	6.60	7.95
Price: high	86.9	81.2	76.9	86.5	64.8	61.3	65.0	90.8
low	56.2	63.5	46.2	39.2	45.0	50.3	47.7	63.3

Amgen, Inc.
One Amgen Center Drive
Thousand Oaks, CA 91320
(805) 447-1000
Website: www.amgen.com

AGGRESSIVE GROWTH

Apple Inc.

❑ Ticker symbol: AAPL (NASDAQ) ❑ S&P rating: not rated ❑ Value Line financial strength rating: A++ ❑ Current yield: Nil ❑ Dividend raises, past 10 years: 1

Company Profile

Apple is one of the most closely watched companies in the world. They have gone from being a niche supplier of high-end gadgets to the bellwether of consumer technology and industrial design, and in many ways the health of the technology market altogether, as their product line spans consumer and professional. The company designs, manufactures, and markets personal computers, tablet computers, portable music players, cell phones, and related software, peripherals, downloadable content, and services. It sells these products through its own retail stores, online stores, and third-party and value-added resellers. The company also sells a variety of third-party compatible products such as printers, storage devices, and other accessories through its online and retail stores, and digital content through its iTunes store.

The company's products have become household names: the iPhone, iPod, iPad, and MacBook are just some of the company's hardware products. And while the software may be less well known, iTunes, QuickTime, OSX, and the emerging iCloud are important segments of the business, each with its own revenue stream.

Their product line, while comparatively narrow, is focused on areas where the user interface is highly valued. Apple has leveraged this focus on the user experience into a business that is far and away the most profitable in the industry.

Apple has become a case study in creating extraordinary value through innovation, innovative leadership, and marketing excellence. But while wildly successful, the company has come upon a test anticipated for some time: the passing of Steve Jobs in October 2011. Steve was clearly the driving and leading force in Apple's innovation, style, and success. It remains to be seen if the momentum can be maintained in the absence of this unique guiding light.

Financial Highlights, Fiscal Year 2012

Any other company on any other planet in the universe would be ecstatic to turn in the sort of numbers that Apple did in 2012. Sales up 44 percent. Earnings up 61 percent. Cash flow up 60 percent. Return on capital of 35 percent. These are mind-boggling numbers, and Apple has turned in this sort of performance for 14 straight quarters. But in the last half of calendar 2012, the bloom was off the rose. While the stock entered calendar 2012 at a price of $422 and rose as much as 300 points, by year end it was trading around $500 and has fallen further since. The main problem has been the declining profitability of the iPhone and flat volumes in the very popular iPad product. The company has plans to address those issues with follow-on products in the coming year, as well as a significant expansion of its business in China, where it enjoys very strong market share.

Apple recently announced a $100 million investment in domestic manufacturing, where the company will begin producing a new version of its Mac products later in 2013. Granted, this announcement was made just prior to Apple's appearance before a congressional committee to discuss their tax practices, but we applaud the move nonetheless.

Reasons to Buy

Apple's most well-known product, the iPhone, seems ubiquitous. The truth, however, is this: The iPhone has less than 20 percent market share. We think Apple slipped by not having lower-priced products ready when Android-based phones flooded the market, but the good news is that Apple still has 50

percent of the market's earnings with its lower volumes. The introduction of the iPhone 5S and some lower-priced models in the fall of 2013 should improve volumes at a possible hit to unit earnings.

Apple has taken some steps to address both their declining share price and the vocal critics of their massive cash hoard. For one, the company increased the dividend to $12.20 per share, or a current 2.8 percent yield. They also committed $60 billion to share repurchase over the next 10 quarters, meaning that share count (at current prices) would drop by 130 million shares, or 13.7 percent of the outstanding base. The company also said they would return $100 billion in total shareholder value in buybacks and dividends over the same period, which (if we're doing the math correctly) implies an average $4 billion/quarter in dividends, or about a 5.2 percent yield at the end of FY2015. Wow.

Wait a minute. Did we just spend a paragraph touting Apple as an income stock? Yep, we did. This is not a situation we foresaw last year, but we're probably in good company there. We did warn about the fuzzy product pipeline and the effects of a long run-up in the share price, and no doubt the recent decline in the share price can be partially put down to long-term shareholders taking a profit even if it meant taking less than $500/share. But the exit of the easy money has had the happy effect of pulling the share price down to an entry point unthinkable last year. The current P/E ratio relative to the market hasn't been this low since 1998, when the company was teetering on the edge of bankruptcy. Apple at $420 has never been "cheaper," it won't be cheaper for quite some time, and with the initiation of a strong dividend and the largest buyback program in the history of the world, we think it's an absolute steal.

Reasons for Caution

Phones, in our view, will never be as profitable on a per-unit basis for Apple as they have been for the past 3 years. Given the current user profile and user needs, revolutionary year-to-year advances in this product category are unlikely.

Frequently mentioned in the past few years is the potential for a "real" Apple TV, rather than the server/connectivity appliance currently sold under that name. While we would welcome something, anything, that would bring some elegance and rationality to what is without a doubt the most unfriendly and poorly thought-out collection of user interfaces in the consumer space (we like to gripe about our toys), we don't see an Apple-branded traditional television having a major impact on the market unless content-delivery methods are thoroughly sorted out.

SECTOR: **Consumer Discretionary**
BETA COEFFICIENT: **1.00**
10-YEAR COMPOUND EARNINGS PER SHARE GROWTH: **58.5%**
10-YEAR COMPOUND DIVIDENDS PER SHARE GROWTH: **NM**

	2005	2006	2007	2008	2009	2010	2011	2012
Revenues (mil)	13,931	19,315	24,006	32,479	36,537	65,225	108,249	156,508
Net income (mil)	1,254	1,989	3,496	4,834	5,704	14,013	25,922	41,733
Earnings per share	1.44	2.27	3.93	5.36	6.29	15.15	27.89	44.15
Dividends per share	—	—	—	—	—	—	—	2.65
Cash flow per share	1.72	2.59	4.37	5.97	7.12	16.42	29.85	47.92
Price: high	75.5	93.2	203.0	200.3	214.0	326.7	426.7	705.1
low	31.3	50.2	81.9	79.1	78.2	190.3	310.5	409.0

Apple Inc.
1 Infinite Loop
Cupertino, CA 95014
(408) 996-1010
Website: www.apple.com

Aqua America, Inc.

▫ Ticker symbol: WTR (NYSE) ▫ S&P rating: NA ▫ Value Line financial strength rating: B++▫ Current yield: 2.2% ▫ Dividend raises, past 10 years: 10

Company Profile

The strategic importance of water, and the efficiencies of operating water utilities across a wide geography, and their stability as investments have made water utilities a more desirable investment. Aqua America, Inc., a U.S.-based publicly traded water and wastewater utility, serving approximately 3 million customers in 10 states: Pennsylvania, Ohio, North Carolina, Illinois, Texas, New Jersey, Indiana, Florida, Virginia, and Georgia. Like many modern utilities, the company also owns a nonregulated subsidiary supplying industrial water and services with a new and special emphasis on the Pennsylvania, Texas, and Ohio shale industries. In mid-2012, the company and a partner deployed a new water pipeline specifically to serve Marcellus shale operators, eliminating some 4,000 water truck trips every two months.

The company has pursued growth aggressively through acquisitions, bringing in nearly 200 acquisitions and growth ventures in the past 10 years. Recently, the company announced acquisitions in Pennsylvania and Virginia and the divestiture of most of its portfolio in northern Florida. Normally we're not too thrilled with growth-by-acquisition strategies, but in this case it makes sense because a lot of local public jurisdictions and private operators see the logic in turning smaller plants over to a larger company, where economies of scale and management can take effect.

Financial Highlights, Fiscal Year 2012

Acquisitions and a few divestitures make true revenue and earnings trends hard to capture, but in FY2012 Aqua America grew revenues 6.5 percent, earnings 5.7 percent, and per-share earnings, hurt a bit by the issuance of 2 million new shares, only 5 percent. FY2013 projections are stronger, helped along by the unregulated sales of water into the shale industry; per-share earnings are projected to grow 24 percent on a 5.5 percent revenue increase.

Reasons to Buy

In the midst of a raging bull market, we make this choice in defense against the next pullback—we'd like to have a few choices that will likely be relatively immune from such an event. That, plus an interest in steadily growing cash returns, fuels our interest in Aqua America. Aqua America is a relatively small and simple business compared to a lot we look at. The company occupies a strategic position in a key utility area, especially as more water works become available as public sector operations are trimmed. The stock has an exceptionally low beta of 0.19, indicating stability, and persistently growing earnings and dividends. The payout percentage—dividends as a percent of net profits—has trended downward, and that, along with strong cash flow, suggests a pickup in the size of dividend increases. In fact, Value Line projects a 2014 dividend of 84 cents, which would be a 25 percent increase over the FY2012 level.

Reasons for Caution

Water distribution requires a lot of expensive infrastructure, and a lot of the current infrastructure is old—replacement costs could be high and a drag on earnings. If water stays "boring" in comparison to other, rising market sectors, we may be all wet; if the market does indeed pull back, and Aqua is able to make the best of its monopoly status in key markets, we may come out squeaky clean.

SECTOR: **Utilities**
BETA COEFFICIENT: **0.19**
10-YEAR COMPOUND EARNINGS PER SHARE GROWTH: **6.5%**
10-YEAR COMPOUND DIVIDENDS PER SHARE GROWTH: **7.5%**

		2005	2006	2007	2008	2009	2010	2011	2012
Revenues (mil)		496.8	533.5	602.5	627.0	670.5	728.1	712.0	757.8
Net income (mil)		91.2	92.0	95.0	97.9	104.4	124.0	144.8	153.1
Earnings per share		0.71	0.70	0.71	0.73	0.77	0.90	1.04	1.09
Dividends per share		0.40	0.44	0.45	0.51	0.55	0.58	0.63	.67
Cash flow per share		1.21	1.28	1.37	1.42	1.61	1.78	1.81	1.89
Price:	high	29.2	29.8	26.6	22.0	21.5	23.0	23.8	26.9
	low	17.5	20.1	18.9	12.2	15.45	15.5	19.3	21.1

Aqua America, Inc.
762 West Lancaster Ave.
Bryn Mawr, PA 19010
(610) 525-1400
Website: www.aquaamerica.com

Archer Daniels Midland Company

◻ Ticker symbol: ADM (NYSE) ◻ S&P rating: A ◻ Value Line financial strength rating: A+ ◻ Current yield: 2.2% ◻ Dividend raises, past 10 years: 10

Company Profile

ADM is one of the largest food processors in the world. It buys corn, wheat, cocoa, oilseeds, and other agricultural products, and processes them into food, food ingredients, animal feed and ingredients, and biofuels. It also resells grains on the open market. Rather than the finished consumer products most food processors are known for, ADM produces and distributes intermediate components for food product manufacture and is the largest publicly traded company in this business by far. Among the more important products are vegetable oils, protein meal and components, corn sweeteners, flour, biodiesel, ethanol, and other food and animal feed ingredients. Foreign sales make up about 48 percent of total revenue, and the recent acquisition of Australia's Grain-Corp will drive that higher.

The company is highly vertically integrated and owns and maintains facilities used throughout the production process. It sources raw materials from 60 countries on 6 continents, transports them to any of its 230 processing plants via its own extensive sea/rail/road network, and then transports the finished products to the customer.

The company operates in 3 business segments: Oilseeds Processing (39 percent of FY2012 sales), Corn Processing (14 percent), and Agricultural Services (47 percent). The Oilseeds Processing unit processes soybeans, cottonseed, sunflower, canola, peanuts, and flaxseed into vegetable oils. Crude vegetable oils are sold as is or are further refined into consumer products, while partially refined oils are sold for use in paints, chemicals, and other industrial products. The solids remaining from this processing are sold for a number of applications, including edible soy protein, animal feed, pharmaceuticals, chemical, and paper.

The Corn Processing segment milling operations (primarily in the United States) produce food products too numerous to list, but include syrup, starch, glucose, dextrose, and other sweeteners. Markets served include animal feeds and the vegetable oil market. Fermentation of the dextrose yields ethanol, amino acids, and other specialty food and feed products. The ethanol is processed for beverage stock or use as the base for ethanol-blended gasoline.

The Agricultural Services segment is primarily engaged in

buying, storing, cleaning, and transporting grains to/from ADM facilities and for export. It also resells raw materials into the animal feed and agricultural processing industries.

In early 2013, ADM announced the $3 billion acquisition of GrainCorp, Australia's largest grain distributor and processor, with which it already had an investment stake. The main strategy is to gain access to China and other Asian markets.

Financial Highlights, Fiscal Year 2012

After a strong FY2011, which saw increases in both prices and volumes and relatively cheap supply, the U.S. farm belt drought and softness in fuel demand and the ethanol industry gave us a glimpse at ADM's downside. Revenues grew a decent 10.4 percent to just over $89 billion, but the good news pretty much stops there. The drought lowered agricultural output and raised prices for corn, soybeans, and other fundamental inputs, leading to a 26 percent drop in year-over-year net income, and with a slight share count increase, a 28 percent drop in per-share earnings. FY2013 has started on a similar note, with first quarter per-share earnings down 33 percent, still affected by the drought (though initial indications call for a much better crop this year), soft ethanol, and challenges in the Brazilian ag sector, in which ADM has large investments. The

company is doing some rightsizing in the ethanol business and projects a moderate 10.6 percent improvement in per-share earnings on $90 billion in sales—these figures do not include GrainCorp. With strong cash flows, dividend increases are likely to continue, and we may see a resumption of share repurchases.

Reasons to Buy

Core businesses are strong and growing, and China, India, eastern Europe, and other emerging market growth will be particularly strong. Agriculture is still a key strategic business on a global basis, and increased demand for food and especially middle-class Western diets from emerging market customers bodes well. The company is and has been a strong player in the biofuels industry. While uncertainties continue in the ethanol and biofuels segment, the company's experience and scale in ethanol and biodiesel are strong positives, and the company should win as other smaller players exit the market.

There are 4 major suppliers that dominate the world market for commodity foodstuffs: Archer, Bunge, Cargill, and Dreyfus—the "ABCD" of world foods. Growth through selective acquisitions is an important factor to success in this business—if you miss an attractive opportunity, one of your competitors will not. ADM continues to make small acquisitions, most in the emerging markets of Asia, South America, and eastern Europe. Sales growth outside the United States has far outpaced domestic growth, and ADM's presence and extensive transportation capability give it a decided advantage over its smaller competitors, many of which are focused only in certain markets or certain industries. We like the solid track record for growth in dividends and overall shareholder value, which appears to be lagged somewhat by the growth in share price—but years like 2012 may show us why.

ADM's market and geographic breadth reduce its exposure to both climatic and political variables, and overall, we think solid plays in the food chain are a good place to be. The beta of 0.47 suggests the same.

Reasons for Caution

We saw how agricultural cycles and production can negatively impact this company, but we expect that the worst is over. Still, there's a cyclical component—caused more by nature than most—that's hard to ignore. ADM is heavily invested in the corn-ethanol-fuel processing chain. Ethanol has always existed at the very margins of the transportation fuels market, and continued softness in demand for gasoline will have a disproportionate effect on the profitability of ethanol. Federal policy toward ethanol subsidies and ethanol imports (primarily sugar-based ethanol from Brazil) both bear watching. Finally, the company does produce high fructose corn syrup; a pickup in nutritional health sentiment in the food and especially the beverage industry won't help.

SECTOR: **Consumer Staples**
BETA COEFFICIENT: **0.47**
10-YEAR COMPOUND EARNINGS PER SHARE GROWTH: **17.0%**
10-YEAR COMPOUND DIVIDENDS PER SHARE GROWTH: **12.5%**

	2005	2006	2007	2008	2009	2010	2011	2012
Revenue (mil)	35,944	36,596	44,018	69,816	69,207	61,692	80,676	89,038
Net income (mil)	744	1,312	1,561	1,834	1,970	1,959	2,036	1,496
Earnings per share	1.40	2.00	2.38	2.84	3.06	3.06	3.13	2.26
Dividends per share	0.32	0.37	0.43	0.49	0.54	0.58	0.62	0.69
Cash flow per share	2.44	3.00	3.51	3.97	4.21	4.49	4.54	3.56
Price: high	25.5	46.7	47.3	48.9	33.0	34.0	38.0	34.0
low	17.5	24.0	30.2	13.5	23.1	24.2	23.7	34.3

Archer Daniels Midland Company
4666 Faries Parkway, Box 1470
Decatur, IL 62525
(217) 424-5200
Website: www.adm.com

AT&T Inc.

❑ Ticker symbol: T (NYSE) ❑ S&P rating: A- ❑ Value Line financial strength rating: A+ ❑ Current yield: 4.9% ❑ Dividend raises, past 10 years: 9

Company Profile

Measured by revenue, AT&T continues to be the world's largest telecommunications holding company. Although known for years as the center of the wireline local and long-distance telecom service, it has evolved to be the largest provider of wireless, commercial broadband, and Wi-Fi services in the United States and has become a large player in consumer broadband services with its legacy ISPs and U-verse bundle product. At 56 percent of total revenues, the AT&T Wireless subsidiary has emerged as the largest business segment but has fallen slightly behind its biggest rival, Verizon, in term of the volume of user contracts. AT&T still has the resources to do most anything it wants to do in this space, though, and has plans to recover its lost ground.

Beyond these consumer and commercial products, the company's servers and trunk lines constitute a major part of the global Internet. Data and data services provided by this infrastructure now account for 23 percent of the sales mix.

Its traditional wireline subsidiaries account for another 20 percent of revenues and offer services in 13 states, and the wireless business provides voice coverage primarily for traveling U.S. customers and U.S. businesses in 220 countries. The company has long been focused on offering one-stop-shopping services—wireline, data, wireless, and other services with one price on one bill. These efforts have had varying success, but the U-verse product—an IP-based bundling of TV, data, and voice services turning the TV, the PC, and the cell phone into integrated display and transaction devices—is a particularly important development.

The company's strategy appears to center on the idea of migrating its customer base to smartphones, which brings a solid future revenue stream but carries a lot of upfront cost in the form of device subsidies and marketing/advertising expenses.

Financial Highlights, Fiscal Year 2012

AT&T saw a nice rebound in earnings fueled, somewhat ironically, by a downturn in the smartphone business. Fewer subsidized phones being sold meant fewer upfront outlays and less of a drag on the bottom line. Income returned to FY2010 levels following last year's dip. Earnings should continue to rise this year as the previous contract's revenue streams come on line. We can expect close to $2.60 per share for FY2013, about an 11 percent increase over FY2012.

Reasons to Buy

AT&T has been under pressure on several fronts in the broadband space with regard to their current offerings and their future plans for higher speeds and broader and more robust wireless coverage. The U-verse product works well in dense urban areas but cannot extend its reach much beyond inner suburbs. Late in 2012, AT&T announced a series of programs designed to address these issues and to leverage their wireline infrastructure, which has been underperforming in the past few years. The new Velocity IP project could grow the U-verse customer base by 33 percent by the end of 2015, potentially adding 8.5 million subscribers to a customer base that currently generates $170/month per subscriber. They will also double the number of fiber installations to multiunit buildings (to 1 million) and have started to replace older infrastructure with faster and more reliable equipment.

AT&T is also expanding its 4G LTE rollout by an additional 50 million provisioned units and expanding 4G coverage to 99 percent of its customer locations. The entire VIP (like that?) program will cost $14 billion but should provide AT&T better revenue opportunities, lower operating costs, and improved customer retention in areas where they are exposed.

AT&T has built a strong wireless base, especially going forward as millions use—and pay for—data access anywhere, anytime. We think a company that can charge $20 for 200mb of data is positioned well for the future, given the gobs of data used by nearly everyone and especially younger folks getting into the game. We see modest earnings growth bolstered in part by an aggressive buyback plan, with continued dividend increases on top of what is already one of the best dividend payouts for a quality company available today.

Reasons for Caution

Last year's failed T-Mobile bid and the loss of exclusivity on Apple's iPhone have put AT&T's wireless business in a bit of a pinch. Their ability to respond is not really in doubt, but the effectiveness of the response is not yet proven. And wireless will continue to be one of the most competitive businesses around—AT&T will have to continue to improve this service if they want to remain among the leaders. We continue to be concerned that the company is banking too much on smartphones, and perhaps too much on contracts, leaving behind a substantial market of "ordinary" wireless customers who prefer an unlocked phone with no contracts. This is a growing market that AT&T needs to address, evidenced by the company's loss of 69,000 contract users in the most recent quarter. This is a well-managed company with a solid earnings and dividend base, but even the best-managed companies can't change the laws of physics or gradual shifts in consumer preference.

SECTOR: **Telecommunications Services**
BETA COEFFICIENT: **0.70**
10-YEAR COMPOUND EARNINGS PER SHARE GROWTH: **3.9%**
10-YEAR COMPOUND DIVIDENDS PER SHARE GROWTH: **5.0%**

		2005	2006	2007	2008	2009	2010	2011	2012
Revenues (mil)		43,862	63,055	118,928	124,028	123,018	124,399	126,723	127,434
Net income (mil)		5,803	9,014	16,950	12,867	12,535	13,612	13,103	13,698
Earnings per share		1.72	2.34	2.76	2.16	2.12	2.29	2.20	2.33
Dividends per share		1.29	1.22	1.42	1.60	1.64	1.68	1.72	1.76
Cash flow per share		3.42	4.63	5.36	5.56	5.46	5.60	5.31	5.70
Price:	high	26.0	36.2	43.0	41.9	29.5	29.6	31.9	38.6
	low	21.8	24.2	32.7	20.9	21.4	23.8	27.2	29.0

AT&T Inc.
208 S. Akard Street
Dallas, TX 75202
(210) 821-4105
Website: www.att.com

CONSERVATIVE GROWTH

Automatic Data Processing, Inc.

❏ Ticker symbol: ADP (NYSE) ❏ S&P rating: AAA ❏ Value Line financial strength rating: A++
❏ Current yield: 2.9% ❏ Dividend raises, past 10 years: 10

Company Profile

"The Business behind Business" is the rather apt slogan employed by Automatic Data Processing, or ADP, as it is more widely known. ADP is the nation's largest provider of outsourced employer payroll, tax processing, employee benefits, and other automated and nonautomated human resources (HR) and other business services. Their business is not just a matter of stamping out paychecks, as some tend to think. These are services that are expensive and complicated to set up and maintain, and have nearly zero tolerance for failure. Small businesses and start ups in particular rely on companies like ADP to do these jobs well and keep them out of trouble with their employees, the IRS, and other regulatory agencies. Large companies outsource entire HR functions to ADP because HR and payroll is not where most companies want to apply their capital and resources—they want to be experts in their area of expertise. The reason ADP and their (few) competitors are well paid is because they're worth it.

The Employer Services unit accounts for about 70 percent of revenues and is engaged in payroll, tax, and other transaction processing for about 600,000 employers worldwide. These transactions include paychecks, direct deposit, FICA withholding tax payments, retirement and other benefits services, and reporting. About 80 percent of this business is in the United States, 13 percent in Europe, 5 percent in Canada, and 2 percent in Asia and Latin America.

The Professional Employer Organization Services unit provides a more complete, seamless HR back-end solution, branded as TotalSource, for about 5,600 clients, including personal HR consultation for employees and retirement plan administration. There are 47 TotalSource offices in 22 states. This unit accounts for about 18 percent of the business.

The remainder of ADP's business is primarily made up of the Dealer Services unit. Dealer Services provides a comprehensive and integrated dealership management solution (DMS), with bundled hardware and software designed to manage all dealership operations including sales management, inventory, HR, procurement, factory communications, warranty, accounting, and other functions. This DMS product is used by auto, truck, marine, motorcycle, and heavy equipment dealers, among others.

Financial Highlights, Fiscal Year 2012

ADP's products and services are directly tied to the level of employment, so FY2012 remained challenging even as FY2011 seemed promising. The protracted period of low employment growth and low interest rates were drags on both the top and bottom lines, respectively (ADP typically earns a "float" on cash held by the company while awaiting dispersal and redemption by employees). It wasn't all bad news, though, as revenues did grow 8 percent and per-share earnings grew 9 percent. The company also completed 7 acquisitions in 2012. Most of these were targeted at the health-care services markets, which are likely to get more complicated before they get simpler, making for a good opportunity to acquire long-term clients.

Reasons to Buy

While not an exceptional growth business, ADP over the past 3 years has shown very steady increases in core financials and (not surprisingly) share price. Others have moved into the market with innovative offerings designed to chip away at ADP's market share, but ADP has responded with new products of their own. ADP's new CEO has said that he will focus on faster product development and innovation to create value for the customer. Our feeling is that ADP is already the ideal cloud business model, one that can be packaged with features limited only by their ability to develop them and get them to market quickly. The customer base has never been more comfortable with the cloud, and we feel that soon ADP's established service model will be the norm for most businesses administrative functions. In the meantime, ADP will continue to be a safe, steady way to play the normal growth in the economy, with a bit of a short-term kicker in the form of the economic recovery. The company has a good brand in the business, and with the exception of Paychex (another *100 Best* stock), it has little substantial competition and should own, or co-own, this niche for a long time to come. Outsourcing trends should push more business their way, while acquisitions make the offering more complete and achieve international expansion.

The dividend is solid, and the company continues to raise it regularly and has been aggressive in buying back shares, reducing share count by 100 million to 490 million shares in the past 10 years. The company is almost debt free, with debt less than 1 percent of total capital.

Reasons for Caution

A relative newcomer to the payroll processing management market is Intuit, who have graduated from their core of smaller, resource-strained clients to score a number of larger and more lucrative accounts. They have a good base for growth, having made strong inroads with their tax and business accounting software installations.

SECTOR: **Information Technology**
BETA COEFFICIENT: **0.80**
10-YEAR COMPOUND EARNINGS PER SHARE GROWTH: **5.5%**
10-YEAR COMPOUND DIVIDENDS PER SHARE GROWTH: **14.0%**

	2005	2006	2007	2008	2009	2010	2011	2012
Revenues (mil)	8,499	8,881	7,800	8,776	8,867	8,927	9,879	10,665
Net income (mil)	1,055	1,072	1,021	1,162	1,208	1,207	1,254	1,389
Earnings per share	1.79	1.85	1.83	2.20	2.39	2.39	2.52	2.82
Dividends per share	0.61	0.68	0.83	1.04	1.24	1.34	1.42	1.55
Cash flow per share	2.34	2.42	2.30	2.74	2.85	2.92	3.07	3.40
Price: high	48.1	49.9	51.5	46.0	44.5	47.3	55.1	60.0
low	40.4	42.5	43.9	30.8	32.0	28.5	44.7	50.9

Automatic Data Processing, Inc.
1 ADP Boulevard
Roseland, NJ 07068
(973) 974-5000
Website: www.adp.com

AGGRESSIVE GROWTH

Baxter International Inc.

❏ Ticker symbol: BAX (NYSE) ❏ S&P rating: A+ ❏ Value Line financial strength rating: A++
❏ Current yield: 2.6% ❏ Dividend raises, past 10 years: 6

Company Profile

Baxter International develops, manufactures, and markets biopharmaceuticals, drug delivery systems, and medical equipment. Based in the United States, Baxter has operations in more than 100 countries and operates in 2 primary segments: Medical Delivery and Bioscience.

The Medical Products segment (56 percent of FY2012 revenues, same as last year) produces medication delivery equipment used to apply, inject, infuse, and otherwise deliver fluids and medications to the patient. The Medical Products segment also markets Baxter's industry-leading line of renal care products, including home-based kidney care products, primarily for the dialysis and end-stage kidney disease market. That segment was formerly broken out separately and makes up about 19 percent of Baxter's total revenue, but that's about to change.

The Bioscience segment (44 percent) produces pharmaceuticals mainly derived from blood plasma for treatment of hemophilia and other bleeding disorders, immune deficiencies, burns, and shock.

In December 2012, Baxter made an agreement to buy Swedish renal care equipment maker Gambro for about $4 billion. Based on projections, Gambro would add north of $1 billion in revenues to the mix, and increase the percentage of revenues coming from the dialysis market from 19 percent to something closer to 25 percent. This large acquisition, if approved, will require issuance of about $3 billion in new debt in addition to $1 billion in cash parked overseas committed to the deal and may hurt earnings a bit during 2013.

Also of note is a new Alzheimer's drug, called Gammagard, that should be released from Phase 3 trials into the market in mid-2013. Expectations are high. Finally, international sales make up about 58 percent of the total, with Europe accounting for about 32 percent, Asia Pacific 15 percent, and Latin America 12 percent.

Financial Highlights, Fiscal Year 2012

Baxter had a pretty good FY2012 but was a little off its FY2011 pace, in part because of currency headwinds, with a 2.1 percent increase in the top line and a 5.1 percent increase in per-share earnings. EPS was helped by a 24 million (4 percent) share buyback.

Additionally, the company hiked its healthy dividend 15 percent from FY2011, and has indicated another 23 percent raise this year. These raises, from 9 years of flat $0.58 per share dividends from 1998–2006 to a projected $1.80 per share in 2013 show a clear and favorable turnaround in the company's shareholder return policy. For FY2013, the company has guided for a 10 percent revenue increase, inclusive of Gambro, and a 2.6 percent per share net increase, reflective of another 5 million shares repurchased but also a hit of 10–15 cents per share in acquisition costs. EPS is projected at $4.65.

Reasons to Buy

Baxter is a solid play on medical supplies for recurring or chronic diseases and will do well as the population ages and as medication of these diseases expands into emerging markets. Baxter has been a strong player in its niches, particularly the Bioscience and renal products, and has enjoyed profit margins stronger than the industry average as a result. The Gambro acquisition only strengthens this position. The company has an ambitious and successful R & D program, with some 6.8 percent of sales being invested in R & D. In recent years the company has placed more emphasis on shareholder returns through buybacks and dividend increases.

Reasons for Caution

Health-care reform and related spending slowdowns may cut into demand for some of Baxter's products. International exposure can create growth but may also create a near-term drag from the strengthening of the dollar. If something bad happens in the Gammagard release, that could hurt, too. Finally, while we like the Gambro acquisition, it does inject an element of risk.

SECTOR: **Health Care**
BETA COEFFICIENT: **0.53**
10-YEAR COMPOUND EARNINGS PER SHARE GROWTH: **10.0%**
10-YEAR COMPOUND DIVIDENDS PER SHARE GROWTH: **7.0%**

		2005	2006	2007	2008	2009	2010	2011	2012
Revenues (mil)		9,849	10,378	11,263	12,348	12,562	13,056	13,893	14,100
Net income (mil)		958	1,464	1,826	2,155	2,330	2,368	2,471	2,516
Earnings per share		1.52	2.23	2.79	3.38	3.80	3.98	4.31	4.53
Dividends per share		0.58	0.58	0.72	0.91	1.07	1.18	1.27	1.46
Cash flow per share		2.46	3.13	3.80	4.52	5.02	5.25	5.50	5.90
Price:	high	41.1	48.5	61.1	71.5	61.0	61.9	62.5	68.9
	low	33.1	35.1	46.1	47.4	45.5	40.3	47.6	49.0

Baxter International Inc.
1 Baxter Parkway
Deerfield, IL 60015
Website: www.baxter.com

CONSERVATIVE GROWTH

Becton, Dickinson and Company

◻ Ticker symbol: BDX (NYSE) ◻ S&P rating: A+ ◻ Value Line financial strength rating: A++
◻ Current yield: 2.2% ◻ Dividend raises, past 10 years: 10

Company Profile

Becton, Dickinson is a global medical technology company focused on improving drug delivery, enhancing the diagnosis of infectious diseases and cancers, and advancing medical lab work and drug discovery. The company develops, manufactures, and sells medical supplies, devices, laboratory instruments, antibodies, reagents, and diagnostic products through its 3 segments: BD Medical, BD Diagnostics, and BD Biosciences. These products are sold to health-care institutions, life science researchers, clinical laboratories, the pharmaceutical industry, and the general public. International sales account for about 56 percent of the total. BD is a familiar brand both for observant patients in clinics, medical offices, and hospitals and for the nursing and medical community.

The company operates in 3 worldwide business segments: Medical (53 percent of FY2012 sales), Biosciences (14 percent), and Diagnostics (33 percent).

The BD Medical segment produces a variety of drug delivery devices and supplies, including hypodermic needles and syringes, infusion therapy devices, intravenous catheters, insulin injection systems, regional anesthesia needles, and prefillable drug-delivery systems for pharmaceutical companies.

BD Diagnostics offers system solutions for collecting, identifying, and transporting blood and other specimens, as well as instrumentation for analyzing these specimens. Testing systems include those for sexually transmitted diseases, microorganism identification and drug susceptibility, and certain types of cancer screening. The business also provides customer training and business management services.

BD Biosciences provides research tools and reagents to accelerate the pace of biomedical discovery. Clinicians and researchers use BD Biosciences' tools to study genes, proteins, and cells to understand disease, improve technologies for diagnosis and disease management, and facilitate the discovery and development of new therapeutics.

Financial Highlights, Fiscal Year 2012

FY2012 was a year of met expectations for BDX, but not much

more. The Medical and Diagnostics businesses outperformed, but the Biosciences segment fell short due to weakness in research spending across several of their markets. Overall, revenues were off 1 percent, with earnings off 12 percent due to unfavorable currency translations and the added costs associated with several acquisitions.

The first 2 quarters of FY2013 have been very positive for BDX. Financials have significantly exceeded expectations, with revenues up 4 percent and per-share earnings up a healthy 18 percent. Credit the widespread and extended flu season in early calendar 2013 (we're not kidding—you say "ah-choo" and BDX hears "cha-ching"). The Q2 earnings would have been even better but for a new tax on medical devices, the effect of which amounted to about $.05/share on earnings.

Reasons to Buy

Becton, Dickinson continues to be as recession-proof as any stock on our list, while also offering decent growth potential, especially in earnings, cash flow, and dividends. The company has achieved double-digit growth in earnings, cash flow, dividends, and book value for the past 10 years, and revenue growth has only slightly missed that mark. Operating margins are consistently strong in the high 20 percent range.

The company launched 10 new products in 2012 and benefitted from the prior year's acquisitions, which added 1 percent to their growth. Emerging markets were an area of particular strength, with sales in China up nearly 25 percent. Emerging markets now account for 23 percent of total sales. The company put its strong cash flow to good use in 2012, acquiring 3 smaller business lines to supplement its Biosciences offerings.

The company is well branded and well established in all of its markets, and it offers a solid way to play the long-term "health" of the health-care industry. BDX used $1.9 billion in support of its share price in 2012 via share repurchase and dividends (the company has a 40-year run of annual dividend increases).

Reasons for Caution

For better or worse, health care in the United States appears to be an issue on which many political careers will be based over the next few decades. We'd like to think that some stability is just around the corner, but perhaps there is simply too much money at stake. Whatever the reason, health care seems destined to be a political football for years to come. The recent tax placed on some medical devices will raise money, and in so doing may increase the likelihood of additional taxes down the road. We understand that joint replacement hardware is now coming under scrutiny, which we can no doubt blame on the attractive demographics. U.S.-based companies in the health-care industry have done very well in the past few decades, and the thinking in Washington seems to be that now may be the time for them to kick in.

SECTOR: **Health Care**
BETA COEFFICIENT: **0.65**
10-YEAR COMPOUND EARNINGS PER SHARE GROWTH: **12.5%**
10-YEAR COMPOUND DIVIDENDS PER SHARE GROWTH: **15.5%**

	2005	2006	2007	2008	2009	2010	2011	2012
Revenues (mil)	5,415	5,835	6,560	7,156	7,160	7,372	7,828	7,708
Net income (mil)	692	841	978	1,128	1,220	1,185	1,272	1,123
Earnings per share	2.66	3.28	3.84	4.46	4.95	4.94	5.61	5.36
Dividends per share	0.72	0.86	0.98	1.14	1.32	1.48	1.64	1.80
Cash flow per share	4.60	5.08	5.82	6.60	7.13	7.25	8.27	8.30
Price: high	61.2	74.2	85.9	93.2	80.0	80.6	89.4	80.6
low	49.7	58.1	69.3	58.1	60.4	66.5	72.5	71.6

Becton, Dickinson and Company
1 Becton Drive
Franklin Lakes, NJ 07417–1880
(201) 847-5453
Website: www.bd.com

CONSERVATIVE GROWTH

Bemis Company, Inc.

❏ Ticker symbol: BMS (NYSE) ❏ S&P rating: A ❏ Value Line financial strength rating: A ❏ Current yield: 2.7% ❏ Dividend raises, past 10 years: 10

Company Profile

Freshness, *Convenience*, and *Sterility* are the three buzzwords that adorn the top of the company's home page, and go a long way to explain their value add in the food chain. Bemis makes all kinds of packaging, mainly for the food and pharmaceutical industries. Flexible Packaging includes bags, wraps, and containers, many with a pressure-sensitive or zipper closure, and all labeled for the client's products, roll out of 78 facilities to the end of packing lines in 12 countries. The Pressure Sensitive product group makes a line of pressure-sensitive materials, clearly for use in their own packaging, but also for the printing, graphic design, and technology markets. Those custom-designed graphics on the sides of large vans and other vehicles start out as a Bemis pressure-sensitive film. About 30 percent of sales are international.

Financial Highlights, Fiscal Year 2012

FY2012 was a mixed year for Bemis, with a 3.4 percent drop in revenues from FY2011, which was a banner year for the company. Earnings were also slightly down from the 2010–2011 level, but a moderately aggressive share buyback program resulted in an 8 percent gain in earnings per share for FY2012. Continued share buybacks and some restructuring programs to rightsize the operational base and product mix are expected to turn around what had been gradually decaying margins—and a decrease in plastic resin prices will also help—to drive an 11 percent gain in per-share earnings in FY2013 on modestly increased sales. Share buybacks are projected in the 1.5 percent range each year, and dividend increases have run at a very steady 4 percent.

Reasons to Buy

This is not an exciting company, but they do provide critical packaging technologies to the industries they serve. New and innovative food packaging designs are becoming more desired as convenience and quality outweigh cost as a priority; the new packaged salads are a good example of packaging for a product not packaged before; new zip-close containers for lunchmeats, cheeses, etc. show how the package is moving up the value-add scale. The company has a significant beach-head in growing Latin American markets, China, and Australia, and is investing in new technologies and applications such as package design enhancements for microwaving and easy-open packages for elderly customers (we especially applaud this one!), and new technologies and delivery systems for the health-care and pharmaceutical industries. Cash flow and cash returns to shareholders are steady and increasing. The inherent low volatility is suggested by the low beta of 0.69; the fact that the stock has done little in the past 10 years makes us think there's some share price growth somewhere in this package.

Reasons for Caution

To a degree, Bemis lies in the "crack the whip" zone of both the food industry and energy prices. When food prices rise, consumers get more sensitive to price and may hesitate to pay for convenience packaging. And when energy prices go up, that does bad things to plastic resin prices, and this company makes almost everything it sells out of plastic. Aside from those two downsides, it's really a pretty safe and steady—if not exciting—business.

SECTOR: **Consumer Staples**
BETA COEFFICIENT: **0.69**
10-YEAR COMPOUND EARNINGS PER SHARE GROWTH: **3.5%**
10-YEAR COMPOUND DIVIDENDS PER SHARE GROWTH: **7.0%**

	2005	2006	2007	2008	2009	2010	2011	2012
Revenues (mil)	3,474	3,639	3,649	3,779	3,515	4,835	5,323	5,139
Net income (mil)	162.5	195.6	181.6	166.2	147.2	203.3	184.1	173.8
Earnings per share	1.51	1.83	1.74	1.65	1.38	1.83	1.99	2.15
Dividends per share	0.72	0.76	0.84	0.88	0.90	0.92	0.96	1.00
Cash flow per share	2.99	3.32	3.38	3.29	2.81	3.84	3.87	3.66
Price: high	32.5	35.0	36.5	29.7	31.4	34.3	34.4	33.9
low	23.2	27.8	25.5	20.8	16.8	25.5	2.2	29.5

Bemis Company, Inc.
One Neenah Center, 4th Floor
Neenah, WI 54957
(920) 727-4100
Website: www.bemis.com

Campbell Soup Company

◻ Ticker symbol: CPB (NYSE) ◻ S&P rating: A- ◻ Value Line financial strength rating: B++
◻ Current yield: 2.5% ◻ Dividend raises, past 10 years: 9

Company Profile

Campbell Soup Company is the world's largest, as they like to say, "maker of convenience foods." To most of the free world, that still translates to soup and the ubiquitous pop-culture-iconic Campbell's Soup can. But there is a lot more to this story.

While there are 20 such brands under the Campbell roof, the original Campbell's Soup is still far and away the most important. The company owns 60 percent of the prepared soup market. Their 3 top soups are 3 of the top 10 grocery products sold in the United States every week. Approximately 80 percent of U.S. households purchase the soup, and the average inventory on hand is 6 cans. Few brands have enjoyed such penetration and loyalty.

The company has 5 reporting segments. To highlight the company's own vision of breadth beyond soup, the former U.S. Soup division (including U.S. Sauces), is in the Simple Meals division, reflecting a stronger targeting and message around the concept of convenience. Other divisions include U.S. Beverages, Global Baking and Snacking, International Simple Meals and Beverages, and North America Foodservice. Within each segment reside the many familiar brands that constitute the business: Swanson, Prego, Pace, V8, Pepperidge Farm, Arnott's, Wolfgang Puck, and, of course, Campbell's.

Campbell's products are distributed to 120 countries worldwide and are sold through its own sales force and through distributors. U.S.-based operations account for 70 percent of revenue in FY2012, down 10 percent from FY2011. Products are manufactured in 20 principal facilities within the United States and in 14 facilities outside the country, primarily in Australia, Europe, and Asia/Pacific. The vast majority of these facilities are company owned.

Campbell's product strategy continues to center on 3 large, global categories—simple meals, baked snacks, and healthy beverages—which they feel are well aligned with broad consumer trends. The company's growth strategy has evolved toward greater innovation in product marketing and brand recognition and new packaging designed to broaden use in today's fast-paced economy, as well as a healthy dose of internationalization. New store displays and branding advertise soups in 4 easily recognized categories: Classic Favorites, Healthy & Delicious, Taste Sensations, and Healthy Kids. The company has stepped up R & D through its new Pepperidge Farm Innovation Center, where all baked goods R & D takes place. We feel that all of these activities will move the brand forward while maintaining core values and the core customer base. "Nourishing Peoples' Lives Every Day" should play well in the international space, a frontier the company is just beginning to capitalize on.

Financial Highlights, Fiscal Year 2012

Campbell continued its run of low growth in sales for another year, but the feeling here is this is about to end. For FY2012, though, revenues were nearly identical to FY2011, while earnings dropped off a bit due to some restructuring charges and additional promotions undertaken by the company to build brand strength. Per-share earnings were off 4 percent, offsetting a steeper earnings decline with a small share buyback.

The big news in 2012 was Campbell's $1.55 billion cash purchase of Bolthouse Farms from a private equity firm. Bolthouse, based in Bakersfield, is best known for its line of natural carrot snacks and vegetable and fruit juices. Campbell feels this brand will give

the company better exposure to millennials, a market not well addressed by Campbell's traditional brands. They also see increased demand for wholesome, natural snacks and juices increasing among the Hispanic and boomer demographics.

The company also announced the closing of 2 of its less-used facilities, with charges to be taken in FY2013.

Reasons to Buy

Brand strength is a key reason to stock a few shares of Campbell in your investment pantry. Campbell owns the number 1 or number 2 position in each of the product categories in which it participates. It dominates the $4 billion U.S. soup market.

Beyond that, we see FY2011 and FY2012 as investment years. We like the new focus on innovation and think this company could kick-start growth with a few product category and packaging winners, not to mention the still largely untapped international opportunity. Campbell isn't trying to capture the remaining 40 percent of the soup market that it doesn't own; it's trying to grow the overall size of the market and letting their 60 percent share do the talking. The company is releasing dozens of new soup products with creative flavors and packaging concepts in the coming year. They're also entering new markets with veggie snacks and fruit juices, and a larger offering of vegetable juices. These are all strong growth markets with excellent demographics. Their retail partners are excited about the changes, and this is reflected in the analysts' estimates of a 10 percent growth in sales for FY2013. It may also help to explain the recent 20 percent run-up in the share price.

Reasons for Caution

Even with the recent emphasis on innovation, the company's brands and core customer base are aging, and adoption of new products may prove slow, especially among the younger set. As others, like Coca-Cola, have found out over the years, there are risks inherent with tinkering with a long-established brand such as Campbell's. We would hope that Campbell succeeds with its new ventures without pulling the rug out from under the old ones. We still like Cream of Mushroom on a rainy day, even if we have no idea what it's made of.

SECTOR: **Consumer Staples**
BETA COEFFICIENT: **0.50**
10-YEAR COMPOUND EARNINGS PER SHARE GROWTH: **5.0%**
10-YEAR COMPOUND DIVIDENDS PER SHARE GROWTH: **3.5%**

		2005	2006	2007	2008	2009	2010	2011	2012
Revenues (mil)		7,548	7,343	7,867	7,998	7,586	7,676	7,715	8,480
Net income (mil)		707	681	771	798	771	842	846	783
Earnings per share		1.71	1.66	1.95	2.09	2.15	2.45	2.54	2.44
Dividends per share		0.69	0.74	0.82	0.88	1.00	1.05	1.15	1.16
Cash flow per share		2.42	2.41	2.78	3.07	2.87	3.25	3.48	3.35
Price:	high	31.6	40.0	42.7	40.8	35.8	37.6	35.7	37.2
	low	27.3	28.9	34.2	27.3	24.8	24.6	29.7	31.2

Campbell Soup Company
1 Campbell Place
Camden, NJ 08103–1799
(856) 342-6428
Website: www.campbellsoup.com

AGGRESSIVE GROWTH

CarMax, Inc.

❑ Ticker symbol: KMX (NYSE) ❑ S&P rating: not rated ❑ Value Line financial strength rating: B+
❑ Current yield: Nil ❑ Dividend raises, past 10 years: NA

Company Profile

"The Way Car Buying Should Be." That's the slogan used by this clean-cut chain of used vehicle stores and superstores and its new big-box, retail-like model for selling cars. CarMax buys, reconditions, and sells cars and light trucks at 120 retail centers in 60 metropolitan markets, mainly in the Southeast, Midwest, and California, but gradually moving to a more nationwide footprint. The company specializes in selling cars that are under 6 years old with less than 60,000 miles and in excellent condition; the cars are sold at a competitive price for their condition in a no-haggle environment. The price is the price; the emphasis is on the condition of the vehicles and on a helpful and friendly sales and transaction process. Sales representatives are compensated for cars they sell, but not in such a way that drives them to push the wrong car on a customer. The company sold some 447,728 used vehicles in FY2013, up 9.7 percent from 408,080 in FY2012 and 13 percent beyond the 396,181 sold in FY2011. They are gaining footholds in new markets such as Denver and the D.C. area, and most reports suggest they are gaining market share

in the markets they serve with a high degree of customer satisfaction. Further, the health of the economy and consumer spending have swung car buying into a higher gear—but with newfound consumer prudence. Many of these purchases are heading to the 1- to 6-year-old used car sector of the business, where prices are 40–60 percent lower than comparable new cars. In addition to "retail" used car sales, CarMax is a big player in auto wholesaling, having moved about 325,000 units mostly taken in trade; the company is the world's largest used car buyer. The company also earns income through its financing unit, known as CarMax Auto Finance, or CAF.

CarMax also has service operations and sells extended warranties and other products related to car ownership. The company has state-of-the-art web-based tools as well as other aids designed to make the car selection, buying, and ownership experience easier, including an iPhone/iPad app that generated a 5 percent increase in traffic to Car-Max's websites. As CarMax puts it, customers request four things when they buy a car:

1. Don't play games
2. Don't waste my time
3. Provide security
4. Make car buying fun

The company's offering is aimed at reducing these concerns and providing the right experience. The offering continues to be unique in the industry, and competitors would have a long way to go to catch up.

During FY2013 the company opened 10 new stores, including Denver and Jacksonville, FL, and a small format store in Harrisonburg, VA, as a model for future expansion. In FY2014 (which ends in February 2014), the company plans to open 13 new stores in 8 new markets, including the St. Louis and Philadelphia areas. The company plans to open 10–15 new stores in each of the next two fiscal years.

Financial Highlights, Fiscal Year 2013

FY2013 saw a further continuation of the post-recession recovery begun in FY2011. Sales rose a healthy 8 percent to $10.8 billion, reflecting increased store counts, unit volumes, and a slightly improved per-vehicle gross profit of $2,141. Total sales volumes increased about 12 percent, while same-store volumes increased about 6 percent. The company also reported increases in financing and extended warranty

volumes. Total and per-share earnings did not quite track sales because of expenses related to opening new stores, but gross used vehicle profits increased 12 percent, wholesale profits 11 percent, and auto financing profits 15 percent. The company announced a $500 million share repurchase plan in early 2013, the first of its kind and a sign of increased returns to shareholders.

Reasons to Buy

Quite simply, CarMax continues to be a buy if you believe the traditional dealer model is broken and if you believe people will continue to see value in late-model used vehicles.

Additionally, CarMax brings the latest in business intelligence and analytic models to the car-marketing process, in procurement, merchandising, pricing, and selling the vehicles. Do green Jeep Cherokees sell well in Southern California? Then let's find some, put them on the lot there, and set a market-based price. KMX is well ahead of the industry in making analysis-based supply and selling decisions and has quite successfully deployed analytic tools to adjust prices and inventories quickly to market conditions, a competency that bodes well for the future.

CarMax is clearly taking market share from traditional used car dealers. The company estimates that it has only 6 percent of the current market for 0- to 10-year-old used vehicles. Further, there are close to 70,000 new and used car dealerships in the United States; that number will shrink over the next few years while CarMax builds brand strength and reputation in this important market and gains operational strength and experience to support it. The company is positioned well both for organic growth through market share and for geographic growth; there is still plenty of fertile ground for new growth especially in the Northeast and Northwest and smaller metro areas. Additionally, earnings growth will be aided by increased market dominance, which should help both pricing and per-vehicle cost, and used car supply should loosen as more units purchased new in the post-recession recovery show up on the used market.

Reasons for Caution

CarMax will always be somewhat vulnerable to economic cycles, the availability of credit, and the availability of quality used vehicles to resell. As this company is still in the growth phase, and new dealerships involve putting lots of new cars on the ground, working capital needs are extensive, and cash returns to shareholders have not met our norms; however, the new share repurchase program takes a step toward changing that.

SECTOR: **Retail**
BETA COEFFICIENT: **1.45**
10-YEAR COMPOUND EARNINGS PER SHARE GROWTH: **12.9%**
10-YEAR COMPOUND DIVIDENDS PER SHARE GROWTH: **NA**

	2006	2007	2008	2009	2010	2011	2012	2013
Revenues (mil)	6,560	7,466	8,200	6,974	7,400	8,975	10,004	10,800
Net income (mil)	148.1	198.6	182.0	59.2	281.7	380.9	413.8	425.0
Earnings per share	0.70	0.92	0.83	0.27	1.26	1.67	1.79	1.85
Dividends per share	—	—	—	—	—	—	—	—
Cash flow per share	0.83	1.08	1.05	0.52	1.52	1.95	2.19	2.25
Price: high	17.4	27.6	29.4	23.0	24.8	30.0	37.0	38.2
low	12.3	13.8	18.6	5.8	6.9	18.6	22.8	24.8

CarMax, Inc.
12800 Tuckahoe Creek Parkway
Richmond, VA 23238
(804) 747-0422
Website: www.carmax.com

Chevron Corporation

❑ Ticker symbol: CVX (NYSE) ❑ S&P rating: AA ❑ Value Line financial strength rating: A++
❑ Current yield: 3.1% ❑ Dividend raises, past 10 years: 10

Company Profile

Chevron is the world's fourth-largest publicly traded, integrated energy company based on oil-equivalent reserves and production. It is engaged in every aspect of the oil and gas industry, including exploration and production, refining, marketing and transportation, chemicals manufacturing and sales, and power generation.

Active in more than 180 countries, Chevron (formerly Chevron-Texaco via the 2001 merger) has reserves of 7.2 billion barrels of oil and 25.9 trillion cubic feet of gas, with a daily production capacity of 2.6 million barrels of oil-equivalent and 4 billion cubic feet of gas per day. In addition, it has global refining capacity of more than 2 million barrels per day (bpd) and operates more than 22,000 retail outlets (including 4,093 of their own) around the world. The company also has interests in 30 power projects now operating or being developed. The upstream capacity is concentrated in North America, Africa, Asia, and the Caspian Sea area, with less exposure to the Middle East than some competitors. The company is more concentrated in oil (less in

gas) than some of its competitors, although the company has invested in new shale gas developments. The emphasis on oil has been a strength recently as oil prices have climbed, while gas prices have fallen to levels not seen in 50 years.

Its downstream (refining/retailing) businesses include 4 refining and marketing units operating in North America, Europe, West Africa, Latin America, Asia, the Middle East, and southern Africa. Downstream also has 5 global businesses: aviation, lubricants, trading, shipping, and fuel and marine marketing.

The company's global refining network comprises 23 wholly owned and joint-venture facilities that process more than 2 million barrels of oil per day. Gasoline and diesel fuel are sold through more than 22,000 retail outlets under 3 well-known consumer brands: Chevron in North America; Texaco in Latin America, Europe, and West Africa; and Caltex in Asia, the Middle East, and southern Africa.

Chevron is the number 1 jet fuel marketer in the United States and third worldwide, marketing 550,000 barrels per day in 80 countries. The company's fuel and marine marketing business is a leading global supplier and marketer of fuels, lubricants, and coolants to the marine and power markets, with about 500,000 barrels of sales per day.

Financial Highlights, Fiscal Year 2012

Chevron's recovery from the recession was not as smooth as other producers. The company had some coughs and stumbles and a rough idle that lasted through late FY2010. Starting in FY2011, though, the company has been firing on all cylinders. FY2012 offered a small setback in revenues as crude prices softened somewhat, even though refinery output made up a large part of the difference on higher gasoline prices. Natural gas prices are still weak, even as the company prepares several major projects in exploration and development of natural gas fields. In all, sales and earnings were just off of FY2011's record marks, but not by much.

Chevron once again raised its dividend, by a healthy 14 percent.

Reasons to Buy

Relatively modest increases in recent global demand for petroleum has afforded Chevron the opportunity to retool some of its production and refining capacity without impacting deliveries. As demand increases over the next few years, preferential use of these more efficient facilities should produce higher yields at lower costs. Chevron achieved a reserve replacement rate of over 110 percent in FY2012 and has the ability to produce far in excess of its anticipated demand through 2013.

Chevron's gas production fields and liquefaction and port facilities under construction in Western Australia will not come on line for a few years, but they will be an important income generator for many years. Japan has to import all of its fuel and has extensive port facilities for the handling of LNG (liquid natural gas). As of now, over 80 percent of Chevron's LNG from Wheatstone is covered under long-term agreements to Asian customers, including Japanese electric utilities.

The company is most exposed to some of the best sectors and geographies in the business and has established a good brand and track record for discovery, production, and downstream operations. The company has cut back its refining base a bit, but will likely remain in the refining business for the long term, to their benefit. The company has a solid record of earnings, cash generation, and cash distribution, and shareholders should be rewarded in the long term.

Reasons for Caution

The most immediate risks to Chevron's share price, as we see it, are these: One, industrial producer prices in China have been falling for nearly a year, which is sending signals of a weakening economy and is bad news for commodity suppliers who will be pressured by factories. Two, the United States is actually making headway in its goal of becoming a net energy exporter, which would not be a problem for Chevron except for…Three, the combined effect of the first two risks will be to make the dollar stronger and lower the dollar price of Chevron's products on the world market. Will this scenario play out? It's too early to tell. Most commodity suppliers are scrambling to get China all of the materials it needs at whatever price they're willing to pay (almost). In that light, we don't see China's economy slowing down as a result of supply-side problems, and demand for their products should revive as the Euro recovers.

SECTOR: **Energy**
BETA COEFFICIENT: **0.95**
10-YEAR COMPOUND EARNINGS PER SHARE GROWTH: **15.0%**
10-YEAR COMPOUND DIVIDENDS PER SHARE GROWTH: **8.5%**

	2005	**2006**	**2007**	**2008**	**2009**	**2010**	**2011**	**2012**
Revenues (bil)	198.2	210.1	220.9	273	172.6	204.9	253.7	241.9
Net income (bil)	14.1	17.1	18.7	23.9	10.5	19.0	26.9	26.2
Earnings per share	6.54	7.80	8.77	11.67	5.24	8.48	13.44	13.32
Dividends per share	1.75	2.01	2.32	2.53	2.66	2.84	3.09	3.51
Cash flow per share	8.96	10.09	12.11	16.69	10.95	15.99	19.98	20.05
Price: high	66.0	76.2	95.5	104.6	79.8	92.4	111.0	118.5
low	49.8	53.8	65.0	55.5	56.1	66.8	102.1	95.7

Chevron Corporation
6001 Bollinger Canyon Road
San Ramon, CA 94583–2324
(925) 842-5690
Website: www.chevron.com

AGGRESSIVE GROWTH

Church & Dwight Company, Inc.

❑ Ticker symbol: CHD (NYSE) ❑ S&P rating: BBB ❑ Value Line financial strength rating: A+
❑ Current yield: 1.8% ❑ Dividend raises, past 10 years: 7

Company Profile

Church & Dwight is the world's largest producer of sodium bicarbonate, which turns out to be an incredibly versatile compound. Safe to ingest (and actually good for you, in many cases), it can also tear the rust off of steel and deodorize a litter box. Useful applications for sodium bicarbonate, much to the delight of CHD shareholders, appear to be endless. Being able to produce this material at the lowest cost is a big part of CHD's success, but it's not the entire story. The bigger story is about how this company built a brand and a series of products based on sodium bicarbonate, known to most of us as baking soda. These well-known products are marketed under the Arm & Hammer brand, a brand deployed across several product categories. The company has sold this iconic product continually since its founding in 1846—the product's longevity owing to its versatility. The full list is too long to print here, but sodium bicarbonate is used in the chemical industry, in baking, cleaning, agriculture (as both a soil and feedstock amendment), medicine, and the paper industry. It's an abrasive, a deodorizer, a leavening agent, a water purifier, an antacid, a dialysate (treatment for kidney failure), a blowing agent for plastics . . . the list goes on.

Church & Dwight is a fairly quiet, low-profile company that has gradually learned the ropes of contemporary consumer staple marketing. Sodium bicarbonate is not the company's only product, but it is at the core of most of its businesses. Most of the bicarbonate-based products are sold under the well-known and iconic Arm & Hammer brand, a brand that the company has learned to leverage into a number of product categories beyond ordinary cleaners, including toothpaste, deodorant, carpet and room deodorizers, cat litter, detergents, and others. It is an excellent brand extension story. About 40 percent of the company's U.S. consumer products are sold under the brand name Arm & Hammer and derivative trademarks, such as Arm & Hammer Dental Care Toothpaste and Arm & Hammer Super Scoop Clumping Cat Litter. Fueled largely by acquisitions since 2001, the brand portfolio now extends well past Arm & Hammer. Other major brands include Trojan, OxiClean, Spinbrush, First Response, Nair, Orajel, and XTRA.

In 2003, the company acquired the former Unilever oral care business in the United States and Canada, comprising the Mentadent, Pepsodent, and Aim toothpaste brands, and exclusive licensing rights to Close-Up toothpaste. Late in 2005, the company expanded its oral-care business with the acquisition of the Spinbrush battery-operated toothbrush business from Procter & Gamble. In August 2006, the company expanded its household brand portfolio with the acquisition of the net assets of Orange Glo International.

The company claims the Arm & Hammer brand appears in more grocery aisles than any other brand, and that the brand appears in over 90 percent of American homes. Most of the company's brands, Arm & Hammer and XTRA in particular, are marketed as "value" selections at attractive price points. In today's more frugal environment, this goes a long way toward explaining the company's recent success.

Financial Highlights, Fiscal Year 2012

Church & Dwight turned in another solid year of top- and bottom-line increases in FY2012, with particular strength in the fourth quarter. In the final quarter, earnings were up 30 percent year/year, and revenues grew 11 percent versus just 3 percent in the previous quarter. Driving the growth in sales was a 17 percent increase in the Consumer Domestic unit. The company expects to generate over $1.2 billion in free cash flow over the next 3 years, so we may see even more activity in acquisitions. In 2012 the company acquired Avid Health, the leader in gummy-form vitamins and supplements, for $650 million in cash. The deal should bring with it about $60 million in earnings in FY2013.

Reasons to Buy

Ten years ago, Church & Dwight had one iconic consumer brand, and its net sales were just over $1 billion. They now have more than 80 brands and nearly $3 billion in annual sales. The growth in their base of core brands has accelerated over the past 5 years, and the company is actively seeking further acquisitions. So far, they've done an excellent job of integrating the acquired brands into the core business as well as leveraging their core brand into new products. This is a solid defensive stock that's been behaving like a growth stock. They're in a very competitive industry and are a top player in most of their markets, and yet still produce growth and income increases—a 40 percent dividend increase in 2012 to go along with 30 percent rise in the average share price.

Another way to look at it: The $8.5 billion market cap makes this company a good value—one to own if, say, we had $8.5 billion to invest—and that may get some of its larger rivals thinking about owning it, too.

Reasons for Caution

While core brand expansion has been very successful, and while recent acquisitions have been successful, we tend to be cautious about companies that tend to overly rely on acquisitions as a growth strategy. It's easy to make a mistake, even though the company has had an excellent track record so far. The company is also exposed to raw material and commodity price increases, but seems to have been able to pass them on so far.

SECTOR: **Consumer Staples**
BETA COEFFICIENT: **0.60**
10-YEAR COMPOUND EARNINGS PER SHARE GROWTH: **17.0%**
10-YEAR COMPOUND DIVIDENDS PER SHARE GROWTH: **16.0%**

	2005	2006	2007	2008	2009	2010	2011	2012
Revenues (mil)	1,737	1,946	2,221	2,422	2,521	2,589	2,715	2,922
Net income (mil)	123	143	169	201	249	286	315	350
Earnings per share	0.92	1.04	1.23	1.43	1.74	1.98	2.20	2.45
Dividends per share	0.12	0.13	0.13	0.17	0.23	0.31	0.68	0.92
Cash flow per share	1.32	1.49	1.70	1.94	2.37	2.51	2.75	2.92
Price: high	19.8	21.8	28.6	32.5	31.2	35.5	46.3	59.3
low	16.1	16.3	21.2	23.8	22.7	29.5	33.8	44.2

Church & Dwight Company, Inc.
469 North Harrison Street
Princeton, NJ 08543
(609) 683-5900
Website: www.churchdwight.com

INCOME

Cincinnati Financial Corporation

❏ Ticker symbol: CINF (NASDAQ) ❏ S&P rating: BBB ❏ Value Line financial strength rating: B++
❏ Current yield: 3.3% ❏ Dividend increases, past 10 years: 10

Company Profile

It's always nice when a stock picked almost exclusively for income turns into a solid growth performer, too. Cincinnati Financial provided a 37 percent increase in share price during the course of our 2013 measurement period for a 41.5 percent total performance—not bad for a "boring" insurance company, no?

Cincinnati Financial Corporation (CFC), founded in 1968, is engaged primarily in property casualty insurance marketed through independent insurance agents in 37 states. The company, one of the 25 largest property and casualty insurers in the nation, operates in 4 segments: Commercial Lines Property Casualty Insurance, Personal Lines Property Casualty Insurance, Life Insurance, and Investments. Commercial Lines account for about 71 percent of premium revenues, Personal Lines about 29 percent; all insurance products are sold through independent agencies.

Cincinnati Financial fully or partially owns a series of subsidiary companies that actually provide and manage the insurance products marketed by the company and its agents. Its standard market property casualty insurance group includes two subsidiaries: the Cincinnati Casualty Company and the Cincinnati Indemnity Company. This group writes a range of business, homeowner, and auto policies.

The 2 noninsurance subsidiaries of Cincinnati Financial are CSU Producer Resources, which offers insurance brokerage services to CFC's independent agencies so their clients can access CFC's excess and surplus lines insurance products, and CFC Investment Company, which offers commercial leasing and financing services to CFC's agents, their clients, and other customers. Like all property and casualty insurers, CFC earns income from underwriting (premiums collected less casualty payouts) and from investing the vast pool of cash generated through premiums stored up until a loss occurs.

Financial Highlights, Fiscal Year 2012

In FY2012, despite Hurricane Sandy, which did not affect the company as much as some had feared, CFC turned in a breakout year. In recent years the company had offset a soft underwriting business hampered by natural catastrophes and a poor economic climate with modest gains from its investment business. FY2012 gave us the stronger pricing environment, improved business conditions for commercial customers, a relative lack (despite Sandy) of loss-producing catastrophes, and a better investing environment to boot. In FY2012, the underwriting loss came in at -$0.51, which was better than FY2011's -$3.28. Meanwhile, investment gains, hurt somewhat by continued low interest rates, remained virtually flat at $3.26 per share (compared to $3.24), but the current bull market bodes well for next year at least, while underwriting income continues to improve. All told, a continued recovery in underwriting and an increase in interest rates could produce some impressive earnings results; in the meantime, the company has relatively low debt for this industry and should be able to keep paying a healthy dividend for the foreseeable future.

Reasons to Buy
CFC enjoys both a loyal customer base and a loyal agency base. Measured by premium volume, the company is ranked as the number 1 or number 2 carrier among 75 percent of the agencies that have represented them for the past 5 years. The company has invested in new pricing and modeling analytics to sharpen its approach to pricing and customer relationships. CFC is on firm financial footing with a dividend covered by investment income and cash flow and a relatively low 12 percent long-term debt as a percentage of total capital. Despite the recent financial storm, dividend payouts have increased slowly and steadily each year. From here forward, the company is uniquely positioned to benefit from interest rate increases, which will help investment income, and underwriting income is likely to improve as well. We would hope that would turn into a more rapidly rising dividend payout, although the conservative approach would be to hold back on large dividend increases until underwriting income turns positive.

Reasons for Caution
Interest rates on the industry's traditional investment instruments may continue to be weak for some time. Competition is stiff, and a large natural catastrophe could hurt. But the biggest concern is that the stock may have gotten ahead of itself, with a current yield dropping from 4.5 percent to 3.3 percent just based on recent share price growth. Although this is a great stock to own, new investors should look for good entry points. Even if you're afraid of rising interest rates, this is a pretty solid pick and still one of the best plays in the insurance sector.

SECTOR: Financials
BETA COEFFICIENT: 0.78
10-YEAR COMPOUND EARNINGS PER SHARE GROWTH: 2.0%
10-YEAR COMPOUND DIVIDENDS PER SHARE GROWTH: 8.5%

		2005	2006	2007	2008	2009	2010	2011	2012
Total assets (mil)		16,003	17,222	16,637	13,369	14,440	15,095	15,668	16,548
Net income (mil)		386	496	610	344	215	273	121	392
Earnings per share		3.17	2.82	3.54	2.10	1.32	1.68	0.74	2.40
Dividends per share		1.21	1.34	1.42	1.53	1.57	1.59	1.60	1.62
Underwriting inc. per share		1.32	1.04	1.83	(0.94)	(2.19)	(1.80)	(3.28)	(0.51)
Price:	high	45.9	49.2	48.4	40.2	29.7	32.3	34.3	41.0
	low	38.4	41.2	36.0	13.7	17.8	25.3	23.7	30.1

Cincinnati Financial Corporation
6200 S. Gilmore Road
Fairfield, OH 45014
(513) 870-2000
Website: www.cinfin.com

The Clorox Company

❑ Ticker symbol: CLX (NYSE) ❑ S&P rating: BBB+ ❑ Value Line financial strength rating: B++
❑ Current yield: 3.0% ❑ Dividend raises, past 10 years: 10

Company Profile

A leading manufacturer and marketer of consumer cleaning and other household products, Clorox markets some of consumers' most trusted and recognized brand names, including its namesake bleach and cleaning products, Green Works natural cleaners; Fresh Step and Scoop Away cat litter; Kingsford charcoal; Hidden Valley, KC Masterpiece, and Soy Vey dressings and sauces; Brita water-filtration systems; Glad bags, wraps, and containers; and Burt's Bees natural personal care products. By sales, the more mundane liquid bleach products, trash bags, and charcoal dominate sales, contributing 14, 13, and 11 percent of sales, respectively. In the U.S., Clorox owns the number 1 or number 2 market share position with 90 percent of its products.

The company is divided into 4 segments, with the percent of FY2012 sales and net profits in parentheses:

■ Cleaning Products (31 percent of sales, 36 percent of net profits) includes laundry, home care, and professional cleaning products. Home-care products include disinfecting sprays and wipes, toilet bowl cleaners, carpet cleaners, drain openers, floor mopping systems, toilet and bath cleaning tools, and premoistened towelettes. Professional products are for institutional, janitorial, and foodservice markets, and include bleaches, disinfectants, food-storage bags, and bathroom cleaners.

■ Lifestyle (16 percent, 25 percent) offers food products, including salad dressings, seasonings, sauces, and marinades; personal-care lines (Burt's Bees); and water filtration products under the Brita brand.

■ Household Products (31 percent, 28 percent) offers charcoal under the Kingsford and Match Light brands, as well as cat litter, plastic bags, wraps, and containers under some of the brands mentioned above.

■ International (22 percent, 11 percent) is set up as a separate entity to market and distribute an assortment of U.S.-made and locally made brands.

To give an idea how far Clorox has come as a consumer company, it was founded in 1913 as the Electro-Alkaline Company. It has been known as the Clorox Company since 1957, although it was owned by archrival Procter & Gamble from 1957 until 1969 when the FTC forced divestiture to promote competition.

Financial Highlights, Fiscal Year 2012

FY2012 turned out to be a fairly strong rebound year after the company took a $258 million impairment charge in FY2011 related to its Bert's Bees acquisition, which wiped out about half its earnings for that year. Revenues posted a 4.5 percent gain in FY2012 but still ended up a bit shy of 2009 and 2010 figures—currency translation is one factor. Earnings followed a similar path, strong compared to the impaired FY2011 but not quite what the company saw in 2009 and 2010, in a large part due to increased commodity costs that took about 20 percent out of the bottom line figure. Per-share earnings, helped along by significant buybacks in 2011 and 2012, advanced to $4.10, the second highest in its history. Going forward, the company projects a 3–5 percent overall top-line growth rate and plans to most aggressively grow its Professional segment at a 10–15 percent rate to tap into health-care and

other disinfecting markets. Per-share earnings are projected to climb 6 percent as input costs moderate.

Reasons to Buy

Even in a slowing consumer market, Clorox, due to its strong brand position and market share, has proven itself able to increase prices in the past. As a personal preference, we especially like the Green Works products, which, unlike many "green" products, seem to actually work and to have become a standard on store shelves.

That said, many consumers have switched away from name-brand products; just how many remains to be seen. Clorox has proven itself to be a strong, well-managed, and shareholder-oriented defensive player. Dividend raises have been strong and persistent, and the company has reduced share count almost 40 percent since 2004. The stock has tended to trade in a very tight range even with negative news; with a beta of 0.40 it is a safety and stability play.

Reasons for Caution

We've seen the lessons of high commodity prices and of dipping too far into the acquisition pool, as was the case in the Burt's Bees acquisition. We remain concerned that the company could be tempted again into poor acquisitions to spur growth, as it's pretty challenging to grow demand and market share for bleach, trash bags, and charcoal. Finally, the stock has posted some fairly aggressive new highs with a P/E over 20, a bit rich for this kind of company— choose entry points carefully.

SECTOR: **Consumer Staples**
BETA COEFFICIENT: **0.40**
10-YEAR COMPOUND EARNINGS PER SHARE GROWTH: **8.0%**
10-YEAR COMPOUND DIVIDENDS PER SHARE GROWTH: **10.5%**

	2005	2006	2007	2008	2009	2010	2011	2012
Revenues (mil)	4,388	4,644	4,847	5,273	5,450	5,534	5,231	5,468
Net income (mil)	517	443	496	461	537	603	258	543
Earnings per share	2.88	2.89	3.23	3.24	3.81	4.24	2.07	4.10
Dividends per share	1.10	1.14	1.31	1.66	1.88	2.05	2.25	2.44
Cash flow per share	4.66	4.17	4.55	4.82	5.22	5.68	3.51	5.56
Price: high	66.0	66.0	69.4	65.3	65.2	69.0	75.4	76.7
low	52.5	56.2	56.2	47.5	59.0	59.0	60.6	66.4

The Clorox Company
1221 Broadway
Oakland, CA 94612
(510) 271-2270
Website: www.clorox.com

CONSERVATIVE GROWTH

The Coca-Cola Company

❏ Ticker symbol: KO (NYSE) ❏ S&P rating: A+ ❏ Value Line financial strength rating: A++
❏ Current yield: 2.7% ❏ Dividend raises, past 10 years: 10

Company Profile

The Coca-Cola Company is the world's largest beverage company. For more than 100 years, the company has mainly produced concentrates and syrups, which it then sells to independent bottlers worldwide. These bottlers add water (still or carbonated, depending on the product), sugar, and other (often local) ingredients, then bottle and distribute the products to restaurants, retailers, and other distributors. The company owns the brand and is responsible for consumer brand marketing initiatives, while the distributors handle all downstream merchandising. The company operates in more than 200 countries and markets nearly 500 brands of concentrate. These concentrates are used to produce more than 3,000 different branded products, including Coca-Cola.

In 2010, the company took a big step toward full integration of its supply chain with the purchase of the North American operations of Coca-Cola Enterprises (CCE), the largest of its network of bottlers, in order to streamline distribution and marketing, give greater control of pricing, and cut about $350 million in redundant costs. At the same time, Coke sold distribution in Norway, Sweden, and a future in Germany back to CCE, reaffirming the third-party bottler model in international, or at least European, markets. The company continues on a path to acquire some of its smaller bottling franchises.

The company continues to strive to expand its beverage offerings beyond the traditional carbonated soda drinks. Major brands besides Coke include Minute Maid juices, Dasani and Evian bottled waters, Powerade and Full Throttle sports beverages, Nestea iced teas, and major brands such as Ayataka Green Tea and I Lohas water in Japan and others similarly local to their markets.

The total numbers are staggering: 500 brands, 16 of which have reached $1 billion in sales, 27.7 billion cases worldwide, which equates to 620 billion servings per year, 1.8 billion beverages consumed per day, and 21,080 servings per second, all processed through more than 300 bottlers serving 200 countries, and all handled through the world's largest beverage distribution system. In terms of unit case volume, 79 percent of all sales are overseas—29 percent in Latin America, 18 percent in Eurasia/Africa, 18 percent in the Pacific, and 14 percent in Europe. In revenue terms, the company counts about 59 percent as overseas sales.

Financial Highlights, Fiscal Year 2012

For FY2012, worldwide total volumes grew 4 percent. While North American sales grew only 2 percent and Europe dropped 1 percent, the rest of the international business carried the year. Total revenues were up 3 percent, while total earnings increased 1 percent. Without currency effects, both numbers would have been 2–3 percent higher. Per-share earnings increased 2.6 percent on the heels of a 57 million share buyback, about 1.3 percent of outstanding shares, a pattern that is likely to accelerate. For FY2013, the company expects about a 2 percent growth in sales but some improvement in margins as the bottler consolidations take hold, and it is projecting a 5.5 percent increase in total earnings. These returns are finding their way to shareholders—Coke increased its dividend 10 percent in early 2013 and authorized a 500 million share buyback program.

Reasons to Buy

"I like to bet on sure things," Warren Buffett said, on why he'll never sell a share of Coke stock. That pretty much sums it up, and the reasons to buy Coke continue to be solid. The company has category leadership, especially globally, in soft drinks, juices and juice drinks, and ready-to-drink coffees and teas. They're number 2 globally in sports drinks, and number 3 in packaged water and energy drinks. In Coca-Cola, Diet Coke, Sprite, and Fanta, they own 4 of the top 5 brands of soft drink in the world.

The Coca-Cola name is probably the most recognized brand in the world and is almost beyond valuation. Indeed, Mr. Buffett once uttered the classic line about brand strength and intangibles in reference to Coke: "If you gave me $100 billion and said take away the soft drink leadership of Coca-Cola in the world, I'd give it back to you and say it can't be done."

Coke has traditionally been a steady hedge stock and offers a solid dividend with a steady and recently accelerating track record of dividend growth. The company boasts—quite rightly—about having raised dividends in each of the past 50 years. It is also as close to a pure play on international business as you'll find in a U.S. company. Finally, the low beta of 0.51 confirms its low-volatility credentials.

Reasons for Caution

Sales in established markets—the U.S. and Europe—are still flat or only slightly improving, probably caused in part by interest in health and reducing obesity. The company is largely past the bottling franchise acquisitions, but it is still a very complex business to manage. The bottling business is lower margin, which plainly shows up in the results, with net profit margins dipping from the low 20s to 19 percent recently—still not a bad number all in all and forecasted to improve as more synergies are realized.

As Coke consumers ourselves, we continue to be concerned at the erosion of Coke products in favor of Pepsi in many restaurants and fast-food chains. We realize that PepsiCo owns a number of fast-food chains and has a captive market there, but we wonder how and why Coke is losing this important distribution and brand recognition channel, especially as far more people seem to specify Coke than Pepsi when ordering their cola. It makes us wonder whether there are larger elephants in their sales and marketing room. It also serves as an example of what you, as an astute individual investor, can yourself observe about your companies in the course of daily life.

SECTOR: Consumer Staples
BETA COEFFICIENT: 0.51
10-YEAR COMPOUND EARNINGS PER SHARE GROWTH: 9.0%
10-YEAR COMPOUND DIVIDENDS PER SHARE GROWTH: 10.0%

	2005	2006	2007	2008	2009	2010	2011	2012
Revenues (mil)	23,104	24,088	28,857	31,944	30,990	35,123	46,554	48,017
Net income (mil)	5,014	5,568	5,981	7,050	6,824	8,144	8,932	9,019
Earnings per share	1.09	1.19	1.29	1.51	1.47	1.75	1.92	1.97
Dividends per share	0.56	0.62	0.68	0.76	0.82	0.88	0.94	1.02
Cash flow per share	1.29	1.40	1.54	1.79	1.75	2.09	2.41	2.46
Price: high	22.6	24.7	32.2	32.8	29.7	32.9	35.9	40.7
low	20.2	16.7	22.8	20.1	18.7	24.7	30.6	33.3

The Coca-Cola Company
One Coca-Cola Plaza
Atlanta, GA 30313
(404) 676-2121
Website: www.coca-cola.com

Colgate-Palmolive Company

❑ Ticker symbol: CL (NYSE) ❑ S&P rating: AA- ❑ Value Line financial strength rating: A++
❑ Current yield: 2.4% ❑ Dividend raises, past 10 years: 10

Company Profile

Colgate-Palmolive is the second-largest global producer of detergents, toiletries, and other household products. The company manages its business in 2 straightforward segments: Oral, Personal, and Home Care; and Pet Nutrition. The Oral, Personal, and Home Care division produces and markets a number of familiar brands and products: Ajax, Palmolive, Irish Spring, Softsoap, Mennen, and SpeedStick, as well as the familiar Colgate brand of oral care products. These brands are strong: Colgate owns 44 percent of the worldwide oral care market and 22 percent each of the personal care and home care markets. Hill's pet food brand represents 13 percent of Colgate's total sales.

Colgate is also strong in the global consumer products market, with a presence in more than 200 countries and territories. About 82 percent of its business is international, and about 50 percent of that business is in emerging markets.

Financial Highlights, Fiscal Year 2012

FY2012 left most investors with a smile on their face. Revenues were up 2 percent on increased unit volume of 3.5 percent, while earnings were up 2 percent as well. Profitability would certainly have been better without currency headwinds (the downside of such high levels of international sales). Growth in the Asia/Africa region was very encouraging, with a revenue increase of 7 percent over last year and representing 20 percent of global sales.

The company remains committed to its Hill's brand of pet foods, which has disappointed of late. The company has put in place several programs to restore sales. And in FY2012, the company announced yet another increase in the dividend of 7 percent.

Reasons to Buy

Colgate's brands are market leaders. They have a 45 percent share of the global toothpaste market and 33 percent of the manual toothbrush market. They're number 1 or 2 with many of their other brands, including Ajax and Softsoap, and have many other well-established brands. Strong brands lead to pricing power. The company's "first to market" global strategy has given them a formidable foothold in emerging markets like China and India.

Colgate is a conservatively run company that prefers slower organic growth over quick (but expensive) acquisitions. They rarely have a downside surprise—they tend to meet or beat their estimates. They plow money back into the company and achieve profitability through operational excellence, rather than paying for gross margins at any price. This is a solid defensive play with a good dividend, real earnings growth, and real earnings predictability.

Looking at the bigger picture, Colgate is probably a safer, steadier alternative in the consumer staples marketplace than Procter & Gamble (another *100 Best* stock), as it is less prone to reach for new, rapidly changing markets, such as cosmetics, and less apt to try to grow through acquisitions. This company is about slow, steady returns with little risk and little market volatility in bad times. The company touts not just 10 but 50 consecutive years of dividend increases. We also like the company's orientation toward international and especially emerging markets, although currency adjustments create another source of volatility.

Reasons for Caution

At its current price of $112/share, CL is trading at 23 times forward earnings, which is a bit steep for what is normally considered a defensive play. Colgate participates in an increasingly competitive market, requiring more frequent new product rollouts and related marketing expenses just to keep up. Also, the Colgate business will not stimulate aggressive investors.

SECTOR: **Consumer Staples**
BETA COEFFICIENT: **0.60**
10-YEAR COMPOUND EARNINGS PER SHARE GROWTH: **9.5%**
10-YEAR COMPOUND DIVIDENDS PER SHARE GROWTH: **12.5%**

	2005	2006	2007	2008	2009	2010	2011	2012
Revenues (mil)	11,397	12,238	13,790	15,330	15,327	15,564	16,734	17,085
Net income (mil)	1,351	1,353	1,737	1,957	2,291	2,203	2,431	2,472
Earnings per share	2.43	2.46	3.20	3.66	4.37	4.31	4.94	5.15
Dividends per share	1.11	1.28	1.44	1.56	1.72	2.03	2.27	2.44
Cash flow per share	3.42	3.71	4.21	4.54	5.29	5.14	5.94	6.19
Price: high	57.2	67.1	81.3	82.0	87.4	86.1	94.9	111.0
low	48.2	53.4	63.8	54.4	54.5	73.1	74.9	87.2

Colgate-Palmolive Company
300 Park Avenue
New York, NY 10022–7499
(212) 310-2291
Website: www.colgate.com

AGGRESSIVE GROWTH

Comcast Corporation

❑ Ticker symbol: CMCSA (NASDAQ) ❑ S&P rating: BBB+ ❑ Value Line financial strength rating: B+ ❑ Current yield: 2.2% ❑ Dividend raises, past 10 years: 4

Company Profile

Comcast is one of the nation's leading providers of communications services and information and entertainment content passed through those services. The core business is Comcast Cable, the familiar cable TV network that has evolved into a conduit for delivering bundled high-speed Internet services, phone services, and on-demand content. This business serves some 23 million subscribers in 39 states.

The company has been evolving its information and entertainment business over the years through its ownership of regional sports networks and national channels such as the Golf Channel, E! (an entertainment channel), Fandango (a moviegoer's website), and others. The company took a major leap forward as a content provider with the early 2011 closing of the acquisition of 51 percent of NBCUniversal, almost instantly turning the company into not only a connectivity powerhouse but a media powerhouse as well through its ownership of Universal Pictures among other assets. In March 2012, Comcast completed the purchase by acquiring the remaining 49 percent of NBCUniversal from General Electric, the previous parent corporation.

Comcast is now regarded as the largest integrated content development and distribution business in the United States.

The company has been building its Xfinity Internet portal brand to compete with satellite operators and such offerings as AT&T U-verse and Verizon FiOS. Comcast also announced a new Internet 2go wireless Internet service through a 4G network. In short, Comcast has evolved from being a lackluster cable TV service to a full-scale communications utility with some of the highest performance products on the market, using the Xfinity platform to draw customers in for the rest of its service bundle. The company now has nearly as many Internet service customers (19 million) as it does cable subscribers (23 million), with more than 10 million phone service connections thrown in for good measure. The company is now also rolling out its on-demand Streampix platform to compete with Netflix video on demand for customers not on the Xfinity platform.

The vast majority of Comcast customers are residential, although the company also offers a business class service to meet the needs of small and midsized organizations. The company also owns the Philadelphia 76ers and Flyers and a series of Universal theme parks through the NBCUniversal subsidiary.

Financial Highlights, Fiscal Year 2012

The NBCUniversal partnership continued to boost profits at Comcast. NBCUniversal generated just over two-thirds of Comcast's operating income in FY2012 on about one-third of the company's total revenue. The highlight reel included $1.4 billion in revenue from the London Olympics and the 2012 Super Bowl, and total operating income of $4.1 billion. In the Cable Communications segment, revenues from residential video (representing just over half of the segment's $40 billion) grew only 2.5 percent while their high-speed Internet revenue grew more than 9 percent. A standout was their Business Services line, which grew another 34 percent in FY2012 and has nearly doubled over the last 2 years.

A couple of large one-time transactions generated cash for the company in FY2012. First was the sale of some wireless spectrum licenses from SpectrumCo (a joint venture) to Verizon Wireless, from which Comcast netted $2.3 billion and a bundle of cross-selling agreements with Verizon. Second was a redemption by A&E Television Networks of NBCUniversal's equity interest in A&E for $3 billion in cash.

Reasons to Buy

The idea of including Comcast in last year's guide took some getting used to. We like to include companies that we admire, and, like a lot of people, we rank cable providers right up there with used car dealers. We saw a lot to like with their numbers and added them on that basis. This year we had no qualms. Comcast is doing very well with their business and is well positioned for growth, with a number of growing markets and a solid infrastructure base with which to service them. Comcast is one of those companies that has spent years building its product and infrastructure and is now finally figuring out how to utilize it more profitably while at the same time offering a better value proposition to customers. Although there are some risks in entering the oft-fickle media business, we generally like Comcast's efforts to make the most of its network. What really intrigues us at this point is the on-demand services for both video and TV. While Netflix and others are bringing such services to market, because of bandwidth and other considerations, they probably make the most sense to deliver through the extremely high bandwidth of a cable system. Comcast owns the largest such system and is putting it to good use— and starting to question whether the competitors should be able to use its network. While such thinking can annoy customers and bring out the antitrust regulators, it should serve to build business, and the Xfinity offering makes this much more consumer friendly. In short, Comcast is doing a lot of the right things both in the marketplace and financially. And the results of those successes are being paid back to shareholders in a big way.

Reasons for Caution

The net neutrality debate is ongoing. We feel that the truce of zero-price rules has worked well and is the best deal for the end user. It allows users to deal directly with content providers, which is a healthier market model than one driven by hidden and passed-on costs (see the health-care industry for a doomsday scenario

of this dynamic). If the company becomes too aggressive in the media content market, and particularly if it restricts others from using its "last mile" of cable, that could bring some grief in the court of public opinion, not to mention regulation. The company faces extreme competition in most of its markets, although it may have at least a temporary bandwidth advantage at present.

For all the improvements the company has made, the share price hasn't been that exciting—of course, therein may lie the opportunity.

Finally, lest you think we've gone all soft on our feelings about certain cable company business practices, consider that the company's top two executives make over $50 million combined and have a controlling interest in the voting Class B shares.

SECTOR: **Telecommunications Services**
BETA COEFFICIENT: **0.95**
10-YEAR COMPOUND EARNINGS PER SHARE GROWTH: **28.3 percent**
5-YEAR COMPOUND DIVIDENDS PER SHARE GROWTH: **18.2%**

		2005	2006	2007	2008	2009	2010	2011	2012
Revenues (mil)		22,255	24,966	30,895	34,256	35,756	37,937	55,842	62,570
Net income (mil)		1,098	2,235	2,287	2,701	3,638	3,535	4,377	6,023
Earnings per share		0.33	0.47	0.74	0.91	1.26	1.29	1.58	2.29
Dividends per share		—	—	—	0.25	0.27	0.38	0.45	0.60
Cash flow per share		1.84	1.48	2.82	3.10	3.57	3.89	4.44	5.26
Price:	high	22.8	28.7	29.6	22.5	17.3	21.2	27.2	38.2
	low	17.0	16.2	17.3	12.1	10.3	14.3	19.2	24.3

Comcast Corporation
One Comcast Center
Philadelphia, PA 19103
(215) 665-1700
Website: www.comcast.com

GROWTH AND INCOME

ConocoPhillips

❏ Ticker symbol: COP (NYSE) ❏ S&P rating: A ❏ Value Line financial strength rating: A++
❏ Current yield: 4.4% ❏ Dividend raises, past 10 years: 9

Company Profile

Take two big companies in the energy production and distribution business. They're both huge. One, a refiner and marketer with thousands of gas stations, tanker trucks, terminals, and tank farms, sells about $180 billion a year with an average operating margin of 9.3 percent and a net margin of about 2.5 percent. The other business does about $62 billion a year with 44 percent operating margins and 12 percent net margins. Which one would you rather own shares in? The larger, lower-margin refining and marketing business? Or the smaller, high-margin exploration and production business?

As it turns out, ConocoPhillips investors were able to make that choice in 2012. The company spun off its massive refining and distribution business into another publicly traded company running under the familiar Phillips 66 name. And which choice would have suited you better as an investor? Perhaps the new Phillips 66 (symbol PSX) would have during 2012, as a major improvement in refining margins caused in part by shifting to more local supplies of crude oil, came forward; PSX did quite well (as did other refiners), perhaps better than expected. Our Valero Energy pick adds a focused downstream refining/retail business to the mix; we chose to retain ConocoPhillips to stay closer to the exploration and production segment, which we still feel will do well in the long run, while refining is more cyclical. With the removal of Marathon Oil, ConocoPhillips is now the only pure E&P play on our list, and we applaud them for taking this bold step.

The remaining COP is still headquartered in Houston, TX, and operates in more than 33 countries (was 40) with about 17,000 employees (was 30,000) and $62 billion in annual revenues (was about $245 billion), a notable shift in the numbers at the bottom of this review. The company that's leftover generated about three-quarters of the profit on one-quarter of the revenue, with different capital budgeting and working capital needs, management expertise, and other requirements; hence COP's decision to pursue this path. (Marathon did it the year before and others are likely to do it.)

"Exclusively E&P" is the company's new motto. The new exploration and production core primarily explores for, produces, transports, and markets crude oil, natural gas, and natural gas liquids on a worldwide basis. The company's E&P operations are geographically diverse, producing in the United States, including a large presence in Alaska's Prudhoe Bay, Norway, the United Kingdom, western Canada, Australia, offshore Timor-Leste in the Timor Sea, Indonesia, China, Vietnam, Libya, Nigeria, Algeria, and Russia.

Beyond the split, the company has been working hard to right-size itself, selling certain other far-flung properties—some in Russia, for instance. The company has also invested heavily in U.S.-based assets and production in the new Bakken, Eagle Ford, and Permian shale fields, and now 29 percent of total production and 23 percent of reserves are based in the Lower 48, with another 14 percent of production and 20 percent of base in Alaska.

Financial Highlights, Fiscal Year 2012

Due to the split, the financials are a bit hard to follow in their regular form; a first glance of the numbers would suggest a mild disaster, but of course that's not the case. FY2012 revenues came in at just over $62 billion, and yes, that is down even on an apples-to-apples basis mainly because of distressed natural gas prices. Operating margins and profits were also slightly lower due to lower prices and somewhat reduced fixed costs absorption; beyond that it is simply too difficult to compare profit performance in such a year. The company is investing heavily in E&P, with a $16 billion capital budget (for which there is plenty of capital from recent sales), and as such, the company is targeting a 3–5 percent production growth going forward. Next year's "compares" will once again be difficult, as some good-sized asset sales came midyear. Revenues are projected at "only" $54 billion, but margins are expected to rise considerably. The aggressive share repurchase program has stalled for the moment, but we expect that to pick up again, too, and notably the new company kept the same dividend as before despite the split.

Reasons to Buy

There is a lot to like here. ConocoPhillips made a bold move to focus on what it does best, both operationally and geographically. The remaining business is less vulnerable to refining and pricing cycles. Beyond the split, the company has divested itself of about $12 billion in assets, moves that would on the surface cause some panic but in this case seem destined to improve focus, make a strong competitive run at the bigger integrated oil companies, and produce more profits. With a strong U.S. base, COP is less exposed to political risks, and it stands to benefit for any rise in oil and especially gas prices. Cash flow is strong, and, for a company with its growth potential, the dividend is attractive.

Reasons for Caution

The split may bring some hiccups, but we think it will continue to be a smooth transition, as it was for Marathon. It may take a year or two for everything to settle down so that investors can really track and understand ongoing performance. Like most energy companies, the ambiguities of exploration and geopolitics add a bit more uncertainty to the risk profile.

SECTOR: **Energy**
BETA COEFFICIENT: **1.21**
10-YEAR COMPOUND EARNINGS PER SHARE GROWTH: **9.0%**
10-YEAR COMPOUND DIVIDENDS PER SHARE GROWTH: **12.5%**

	2005	2006	2007	2008	2009	2010	2011	2012
Revenues (bil)	179.4	183.7	187.4	240.8	149.3	189.4	244.8	62.0
Net income (bil)	13.64	15.55	11.89	15.86	5.35	9.80	12.2	7.50
Earnings per share	9.55	9.66	9.14	10.66	3.59	5.92	8.76	5.95
Dividends per share	1.18	1.44	1.64	1.88	1.91	2.16	2.64	2.64
Cash flow per share	10.27	14.19	14.86	16.80	9.85	12.50	15.65	11.25
Price: high	71.5	74.9	90.8	96.0	57.4	68.6	77.4	78.3
low	41.4	54.9	61.6	41.3	34.1	48.5	68.0	50.6

ConocoPhillips
600 North Dairy Ashford
Houston, TX 77079–1175
(212) 207-1996
Website: www.conocophillips.com

AGGRESSIVE GROWTH

NEW FOR 2014

Corning Incorporated

◻ Ticker symbol: GLW (NYSE) ◻ S&P rating: NA ◻ Value Line financial strength rating: B+
◻ Current yield: 2.8% ◻ Dividend raises, past 10 years: 5

Company Profile

When you think of Corning, you think of glass. All kinds of glass—drinking glasses, glass tableware, and that sort of thing. And if you were around in the '60s, you may remember that well-known white cookware with the little blue flowers on the side.

But things change, and so has Corning. Today's Corning is a premier technology company, more precisely, a technology materials company. If you use a smartphone, a tablet, a laptop PC, or a flat-panel television, chances are pretty good that the glass on the screen comes from Corning. And a good amount of the data you see on that screen may have come through glass-based fiber optic materials supplied by—guess who—Corning.

In fact, Corning operates in 5 segments, all centered on the glass business. Display Technologies (36 percent of FY2012 sales) makes a lot of those screens, actually referred to as "glass substrates for liquid crystal displays." Telecommunications (27 percent) makes fiber optic cable and an assortment of connectivity and other products related to fiber for telecommunications companies,

LAN, and data center applications. Specialty Materials (17 percent) provides a wide assortment of high-tech, glass-based materials, including those specialty glass screens for smartphones, tablets, etc., which they have cleverly branded as Corning Gorilla Glass for its endurance characteristics. Also out of this division comes a new bendable display substrate known as Willow Glass and a host of glass and ceramic products and formulations used in the semiconductor industry, precision instruments, and even astronomy and ophthalmology. The Environmental Technologies segment (12 percent) makes ceramic substrates and filters for emission control systems, mostly for gasoline and diesel engines. The Life Sciences segment (8 percent) makes laboratory glass and plastic wares, and it just completed the acquisition of a similar business from Becton, Dickinson.

The company competes with a number of suppliers, mostly Japanese, on a variety of fronts, but also has a 50–50 joint venture with Samsung in the display business (Samsung Corning) and a joint venture with Dow Chemical in silicon products and technologies that produces seals, lubricants, etc. from silicon materials.

Financial Highlights, Fiscal Year 2012

FY2012 was a mixed year for Corning, with 2 strong currents moving in opposite directions. The business was hurt by the big drop in the value of the yen to the dollar precipitated by Japanese central bank policy. Businesses that have a lot of Japanese competitors, such as Corning, suddenly found themselves facing much stronger price competition, especially in the display business. That "hurt" was offset to a degree by a strong performance in the Gorilla Glass business, which has reached $1 billion in sales and is likely to keep going with new anti-glare materials and—who knows—even flexible screens. But the "help" didn't offset the "hurt" completely. Operating margins dropped substantially from 35 to 30 percent, and with less volume to absorb costs, net profit dropped almost 39 percent to $1.7 billion. This is a profitable company—even that level of profits drove a 21.6 percent net profit margin even after a 6 percent higher tax rate for the year. The "hurt" was mainly on profits because of pricing; gross revenues managed a 1.5 percent gain. For FY2013 the company is projecting a 3.6 percent revenue increase but another slight decrease

on the bottom line and in margins; recovery is expected by FY2014.

Reasons to Buy

We like companies that stand to benefit no matter how a market plays out. Our CarMax pick benefits whether Ford or Toyota or Hyundai win; CarMax sells used cars no matter what. At least for glass displays, Corning is in the same position—whether Samsung or Apple comes out on top of the smartphone contest, Corning wins. Whether tablets or PCs lead the personal computing market, Corning wins. The explosion in smart devices and the new technologies Corning is likely to bring to that space create some excitement down the road.

And the core businesses aren't too shabby, either. The company endured a huge boom-bust cycle with the first buildout of the Internet during the dot-com bubble, and suffered the consequences. But having a piece of the world's largest fiber optic supplier and technology leader isn't such a bad thing, either. Across the board, Corning is investing a lot (in fact, 9.3 percent of revenues in R & D) to differentiate their products through innovation.

Finally, this company is profitable, with plenty of cash flow, and is starting to return cash to shareholders both in the form of dividends and in share buybacks; the dividend yield is quite decent for this type of company, and is growing.

Reasons for Caution

While its product portfolio is broader than it was 15 years ago, supplying well beyond the telecom industry, the company is still subject to business and inventory cycles. Glass, without the right amount of innovation, is a commodity business, and the recent strengthening of Japanese competition through the lower yen presents a big new challenge. If you think Japanese policymakers will drive the currency lower to spur local business and consumption, Corning may not be the place to be.

SECTOR: **Information Technology**
BETA COEFFICIENT: **1.45**
10-YEAR COMPOUND EARNINGS PER SHARE GROWTH: **3.5%**
10-YEAR COMPOUND DIVIDENDS PER SHARE GROWTH: **NM**

	2005	2006	2007	2008	2009	2010	2011	2012
Revenues (mil)	5,579	5,174	5,860	5,948	5,395	6,632	7,890	8,012
Net income (mil)	1,299	1,785	2,267	2,424	2,114	3,275	2,620	1,728
Earnings per share	0.85	1.12	1.41	1.53	1.35	2.07	1.76	1.15
Dividends per share	—	—	0.10	0.20	0.20	0.20	0.23	0.32
Cash flow per share	1.17	1.51	1.83	2.01	1.86	2.64	2.49	1.85
Price: high	22.0	29.6	27.3	28.1	19.5	21.1	23.4	14.6
low	10.6	17.5	18.1	7.4	9.0	15.5	11.5	10.6

Corning Incorporated
One Riverfront Plaza
Corning, NY 14831
(607) 974-9000
Website: www.corning.com

Costco Wholesale Corporation

❏ Ticker symbol: COST (NASDAQ) ❏ S&P rating: A+ ❏ Value Line financial strength rating: A+
❏ Current yield: 1.2% ❏ Dividend raises, past 10 years: 9

Company Profile

Costco Wholesale Corporation operates a multinational chain of membership warehouses, mainly under the Costco Wholesale name, that carry brand-name merchandise at substantially lower prices than are typically found at conventional wholesale or retail sources. The warehouse sales model was designed to help small to medium-sized businesses reduce costs in purchasing for resale and for everyday business use, but as most know, the individual consumer has been their big growth driver. The company capitalizes on size and operational efficiencies, like "cross-docking" shipments directly from manufacturers to stores, to deliver attractive pricing to its customers. The company does not do delivery, nor does it run billing or accounts receivable for sales accounts—sales are "where is" for cash or cash equivalents. Costco is the largest membership warehouse club chain in the world based on sales volume, the fifth-largest general retailer in the United States, and the seventh-largest general retailer in the world.

Costco carries a broad line of product categories, including groceries, appliances, television and media, automotive supplies, toys, hardware, sporting goods, jewelry, cameras, books, housewares, apparel, health and beauty aids, tobacco, furniture, office supplies, and office equipment. The company also operates self-service gasoline stations at a number of its U.S. and Canadian locations. Approximately 52 percent of sales come from food, beverages, alcohol, sundries, and snacks. Another 17 percent come from hardlines—electronics, appliances, hardware, automotive, office supplies, and health and beauty aids—and 10 percent from softlines—primarily clothing, housewares, media, jewelry, and domestics—and the rest, including gasoline, pharmacy, optical, and other services, form a catch-all "other" category. The emergence of Costco as a grocer of choice cannot be missed.

Additionally, Costco Wholesale Industries, a division of the company, operates manufacturing businesses, including special food packaging, optical laboratories, meat processing, and jewelry distribution.

Costco is open only to members of its tiered membership plan.

As of mid-2013 Costco has 627 locations: 449 in the United States and Puerto Rico, 85 in Canada, 33 in Mexico, 24 in the U.K., 33 in Asia, and 3 in Australia. The company plans to open an additional 14 warehouse clubs through the end of FY 2013.

Financial Highlights, Fiscal Year 2012

Costco came out of the recession like it never happened and has not looked back. FY2011 was an excellent year, and FY2012 continued the roll, with sales up nearly 12 percent and earnings up 17 percent. Per-share earnings hit a record high of $3.89, which helps to explain how a no-frills retailer with razor-thin margins can be trading at 23 times forward earnings. Membership fees increased 11 percent, and membership retention reached 90 percent in North America and over 86 percent worldwide (if you're new to Costco, understand that membership fees account for nearly all of the company's profit). This high retention is particularly notable in that the company raised its membership charges last year by an average of 8 percent. Comps for the year were 7 percent, down from 2011's heady 10 percent but in line with historical averages.

Reasons to Buy

You have to admire a retailer that can get paid in cash and buy merchandise on credit. Costco claims that, for a significant percentage of their inventory, the product is sold long before they have to pay for it. The company's margins may be narrow, but it may be the easiest 1.5 percent ever made at retail.

Costco is in an attractive best-of-both-worlds niche: They are a price leader consistent with the attitudes of today's more frugal consumer, yet they enjoy a reputation for being more upscale than their competition. We also continue to like the international expansion and think the formula will play well overseas. Any U.S. resident who has hosted a visitor from abroad knows that Costco is a favored destination during the visit. We expect international expansion will be one of the company's primary growth drivers over the next 10 years. The company has a strong brand in a highly competitive sector, is gaining market share, and has a strong management track record. Although the 1.2 percent yield isn't that much of an attraction, the company has raised it each year since initiating it in 2004. The company increased its stock repurchase authorization to $4 billion during FY2011 but has not, as yet, seen fit to spend any of it.

Reasons for Caution

One concern is the dependence on low-margin food and sundry lines. With the ramp-up of Walmart and

Target groceries and stiff competition elsewhere, Costco may not always be the food source of choice. That said, food does get customers into the store, and gets them into the store more than once a week.

While we admire the performance of the business, we're not sure it completely supports some of the share price projections we see from some analysts. A forward P/E of around 23 is a 40 percent premium to its peer retailers as a group, though we have no problems with this if the company's growth plans come to fruition.

SECTOR: **Retail**
BETA COEFFICIENT: **0.75**
10-YEAR COMPOUND EARNINGS PER SHARE GROWTH: **9.5%**
10-YEAR COMPOUND DIVIDENDS PER SHARE GROWTH: **22.7%**

		2005	**2006**	**2007**	**2008**	**2009**	**2010**	**2011**	**2012**
Revenues (mil)		52,935	60,151	64,400	72,483	71,422	77,946	88,915	99,137
Net income (mil)		989	1,103	1,083	1,283	1,086	1,307	1,462	1,741
Earnings per share		2.03	2.30	2.37	2.89	2.57	2.93	3.30	3.97
Dividends per share		0.45	0.49	0.55	0.61	0.68	0.77	0.89	1.03
Cash flow per share		3.12	3.50	4.05	4.48	4.25	4.85	5.34	6.13
Price:	high	51.2	57.9	72.7	75.2	61.3	73.2	88.7	106.0
	low	39.5	46.0	51.5	43.9	38.2	53.4	69.5	78.8

Costco Wholesale Corporation
999 Lake Drive
Issaquah, WA 98027
(425) 313-8203
Website: www.costco.com

CONSERVATIVE GROWTH

CVS Caremark Corporation

❑ Ticker symbol: CVS (NYSE) ❑ S&P rating: BBB+ ❑ Value Line financial strength rating: A
❑ Current yield: 1.5% ❑ Dividend raises, past 10 years: 10

Company Profile

Stanley and Sid Goldstein were distributing health and beauty products in the early 1960s when they decided to branch out into retailing, opening their first Consumer Value Store in Lowell, MA, in 1963. The CVS chain had grown to 40 outlets by 1969, the year they sold the business to Melville Shoes. Melville underwent a restructuring in the mid-1990s, spinning off CVS and other retail units.

Stan and Sid should be proud. CVS is now the largest pharmacy health-care provider in the United States. Its flagship domestic drugstore chain operates 7,400 retail and specialty pharmacy stores in 42 states, Puerto Rico, and the District of Columbia. The company holds the leading market share in 32 of the 100 largest U.S. drugstore markets, more than any other retail drugstore chain. Over time, it has expanded through acquiring other players in the category—Osco, Sav-On, Eckerd, and Longs Drugs. CVS's purchase of Longs Drugs in 2008 vaulted the company into the lead position in the U.S. drug retail market, ahead of Walgreens.

Stores are situated primarily in strip shopping centers or free-standing locations, with a typical store ranging in size from 8,000 to 12,000 square feet. Most new units being built are based on either a 10,000-square-foot or 12,000-square-foot prototype building that typically includes a drive-thru pharmacy. The company says that about half of its stores were opened or remodeled over the past 5 years.

The Caremark acquisition in 2007 transformed CVS from strictly a retailer into the nation's leading manager of pharmacy benefits, the middlemen between pharmaceutical companies and individuals with drug benefit coverage. The Caremark acquisition forms the core of the company's Pharmacy Benefits Management (PBM) operations, which have some 65,000 pharmacy outlets including hospitals and clinics as well as the previously mentioned retail stores. The company dispenses some 775 million prescriptions a year, and the Pharmacy Services segment now makes up about 65 percent of sales.

The company's MinuteClinic concept is especially interesting in today's climate of managing health-care costs. CVS now has 657 clinics in 25 states offering basic health services like flu shots and such in a convenient retail environment. All but 12 of these clinics are located in CVS stores, naturally serving to drive traffic into the stores and vice versa. The company also operates mail order and online pharmacies for regular and chronically ill patients.

Financial Highlights, Fiscal Year 2012

Many of our stocks for this issue had good results FY2012, but probably none better than CVS. The company grew revenues 15 percent (representing $16 billion) and per-share earnings 23 percent to $3.44 (midrange estimates were for $3.23 per share). The integration issues arising from recent acquisitions appear to be in the rear-view mirror, and the company has done a good job retaining customers absorbed during the disagreement between Walgreens and Express Scripts.

Although the dividend isn't large, the company seems dedicated to raising it regularly and has been fairly aggressive in share repurchases since making its big acquisitions in the mid-2000s.

Reasons to Buy

Nearly 1 of every 4 prescriptions in the U.S. is filled by CVS. These prescriptions are dispensed to a population that is disproportionately older, more financially secure, and insured. That goes beyond the typical positives seen for this industry: the graying of the population, the rather effortless spending on health care that still goes on. The company continues to feel that its leadership in Sunbelt states will capitalize on this megatrend. The recent federal health-care overhaul left Medicare Part D basically untouched, which encourages caregivers to use generic drugs whenever possible, and generics, while cheaper overall, generate higher margins for the pharmacy. Over the next 5 years, more than $50 billion in branded drugs will lose patent protection, creating further opportunities for generics and driving pharmacy margins even higher. And between 2013 and 2014, another 3 million people will become eligible for Medicare Part D, raising the total to nearly 35 million.

Finally, the company has served up another 5-way: 10 years of double-digit compounded sales, earnings, cash flow, dividend, and book value growth over the period. That said, the dividend yield remains modest, but it is pegged for a 40 percent bump in 2013.

Reasons for Caution

The PBM business continues to be challenging from both a sales and profitability standpoint. Compounding this risk is the fact that CVS's fortunes are more closely tied to health care than are its competitors, Walgreens and Walmart, which have larger general retail operations. Finally, the company has some fairly serious debt service associated with its many buyouts and share repurchases.

SECTOR: **Retail**
BETA COEFFICIENT: **0.85**
10-YEAR COMPOUND EARNINGS PER SHARE GROWTH: **12.5%**
10-YEAR COMPOUND DIVIDENDS PER SHARE GROWTH: **13.0%**

	2005	2006	2007	2008	2009	2010	2011	2012
Revenue (mil)	37,006	43,814	76,330	87,472	98,729	98,413	107,273	123,133
Net income (mil)	1,172	1,343	2,637	3,589	3,803	3,700	3,766	4,401
Earnings per share	1.45	1.60	1.92	2.44	2.63	2.67	2.80	3.44
Dividends per share	0.14	0.16	0.24	0.26	0.30	0.35	0.50	0.65
Cash flow per share	2.15	2.50	2.59	3.37	3.73	3.75	4.10	5.00
Price: high	31.6	36.1	42.6	44.3	38.3	37.8	39.5	49.8
low	22.0	26.1	30.5	23.2	23.7	26.8	31.3	41.0

CVS Caremark Corporation
One CVS Drive
Woonsocket, RI 02895
(914) 722-4704
Website: www.cvs.com

Deere & Company

▢ Ticker symbol: DE (NYSE) ▢ S&P rating: A ▢ Value Line financial strength rating: A++ ▢ Current yield: 2.2% ▢ Dividend raises, past 10 years: 10

Company Profile

Founded in 1837, Deere & Company grew from a one-man blacksmith shop into a worldwide corporation that today does business in more than 160 countries and employs more than 40,000 people around the globe. Deere has a diverse base of operations reporting into 3 segments: Agriculture and Turf, Construction and Forestry, and Financial Services.

Deere has been the world's premier producer of agricultural equipment for nearly 50 years. The Agriculture and Turf segment produces and distributes tractors, loaders, combines, harvesters, seeding, mowers, hay baling, tilling, crop care and application, snow removal, and other equipment. If it's used on a farm and requires an engine, Deere likely offers it. With the Construction and Forestry segment, Deere is also the world's leading manufacturer of forestry equipment and a major manufacturer of heavy construction equipment (Caterpillar being the market leader in this segment). They're also the world leader in premium turf-care equipment and utility vehicles in both the commercial and consumer markets.

As the company reports it, revenue for the Agriculture and Turf segment is about 81 percent of the $33.5 billion in FY2012 revenue; the Construction and Forestry segment makes up the remainder. The Financial Services segment rolls its revenue into the other segments and only segment profits are reported.

The Financial Services segment includes John Deere Credit, which is one of the largest equipment finance companies in the United States, with more than 1.8 million accounts, a managed asset portfolio of nearly $16 billion, and a contribution of $460 million in profits, or about 15 percent of the total. It provides retail, wholesale, and lease financing for agricultural, construction, and forestry equipment; commercial and consumer equipment, including lawn and ground care; and revolving credit for agricultural inputs and services. These services are available in all of Deere's largest markets, including Argentina, Australia, Brazil, Canada, France, and Germany. Overall, international sales account for about 41 percent of the total.

Financial Highlights, Fiscal Year 2012

Despite hard times in the U.S. farm sector in 2012, Deere had a very good fiscal year. Revenues plowed ahead almost 14 percent, helped along most by a strong international sector, while earnings advanced about 9.5 percent. Per-share earnings, aided along by a 4.7 percent share buyback, rose 15 percent to a record $7.64, a level approaching almost twice that seen before the Great Recession, and the 10-year compounded earnings growth of 25 percent is one of the highest you'll see for a company this size. The dividend was hiked 18 percent in FY2012, and another raise in early FY2013 pencils out to another 14 percent increase.

For 2013 the fields may not be quite so fertile, as farm machinery demand particularly from emerging overseas markets is starting to moderate; the company expects only a 5 percent year-over-year growth in the dominant Agriculture and Turf segment. They do project, however, a decent year for the Construction and Forestry segment, driven largely by the home-building recovery. The company projects a 10 percent EPS growth on a 7.5 percent growth in revenues.

Reasons to Buy

"Nothing runs like a Deere" is the company's apt slogan, and as far as industrial companies go, Deere has achieved almost unparalleled excellence over the years. They have an outstanding brand (and one of the most popular logos for hats, jackets, and so on, worn by people who have barely seen a farm field!) and reputation in the agriculture industry, and we see the ag industry as strong and strategic far into the future as global living standards improve and emerging markets develop. Farm incomes continue to rise worldwide. The company is making good progress in developing markets, particularly in Brazil and India. The business cycle is also turning positive for the smaller Construction and Forestry segment.

Beyond its products, Deere has established an almost unassailable brand leadership with its services and customer-centered innovations. Deere, more than others, puts its people in the field (literally) to figure out what agriculture professionals really need, and they work with their customers closely to sell their products through a solid dealer network.

The company is now opening factories in places where before they only had sales offices. Deere factories in Brazil, China, India, and Russia will be producing engines, construction equipment, farm machinery, and tractors. These facilities will come online in 2013 and 2014, supplementing the output from the combine factory in India that went live in 2012. New finance operations, critical to the company's sales, were opened last year in Russia, Chile, Thailand, and India.

Finally, cash flow is very strong, and the company has a solid track record of keeping its shareholders in mind. Eight of the 10 years have produced record revenues and earnings. In the same period the share base has dropped 20 percent and dividends have increased 312 percent.

Reasons for Caution

The company is, and always will be, vulnerable to cycles in the farm sector and more recently, international demand. Recent softness in commodity prices may foretell another down cycle on the farm; it's too early to tell—but farmers, who buy this stuff, can get cautious pretty quickly. The company's beta of 1.58 reflects this long-term volatility and cyclicality. Recent public-sector belt tightening both at the federal and state level may hurt the farming business, as will any protracted rise in energy prices. These are mostly short-term risks in a company with an enormous brand and long-term track record.

SECTOR: **Industrials**

BETA COEFFICIENT: **1.58**

10-YEAR COMPOUND EARNINGS PER SHARE GROWTH: **22.0%**

10-YEAR COMPOUND DIVIDENDS PER SHARE GROWTH: **13.0%**

	2005	2006	2007	2008	2009	2010	2011	2012
Revenues (mil)	19,401	19,884	21,489	25,804	20,756	23,573	29,466	33,501
Net income (mil)	1,447	1,453	1,822	2,053	1,198	1,865	2,799	3,065
Earnings per share	2.94	3.08	4.01	4.70	2.82	4.35	6.63	7.64
Dividends per share	0.61	0.78	0.91	1.06	1.12	1.16	1.52	1.79
Cash flow per share	3.85	4.09	5.12	6.01	4.05	5.72	8.34	9.56
Price: high	37.4	50.7	93.7	94.9	56.9	84.9	99.8	89.7
low	28.5	33.5	45.1	28.5	24.5	46.3	59.9	69.5

Deere & Company
One John Deere Place
Moline, IL 61265
(309) 765-8000
Website: www.deere.com

Dominion Resources, Inc.

◻ Ticker symbol: D (NYSE) ◻ S&P rating: A- ◻ Value Line financial strength rating: B++ ◻ Current yield: 3.7% ◻ Dividend raises, past 10 years: 10

Company Profile

Dominion Resources is one of our family of 4 Eastern Seaboard utility holding companies, all having in common growing markets, a growing commercial base, favorable regulatory environments, and more alternative energy in the mix than most—see Duke Energy, NextEra Energy, and Southern Company, also on our *100 Best* list.

Dominion continues to be among the nation's largest producers and distributors of energy, although it has accelerated a program to downsize its wholesale power business and has recently closed or sold some of its merchant power operations, to focus more on the regulated electric and gas transmission industries. Before the effects of 5 recent plant divestitures, the company had 28,000 megawatts of regulated and nonregulated power generation and 6,300 miles of electric transmission lines. In the gas business, the company owns 11,000 miles of natural gas pipelines as well as the nation's largest underground natural gas storage system. The company currently serves retail energy customers in 12 states, mainly in VA, NC, PA, OH, and CT. The company is investing in new facilities in its core service area and a major gas export terminal on the Chesapeake Bay.

In its strategic transformation, Dominion has migrated from a mix of about 46 percent regulated and 54 percent nonregulated energy businesses in 2006 to almost 90–100 percent regulated versus unregulated today. The strategy is to be best in class in more stable, regulated industries, to avoid the ups and downs of unregulated wholesale businesses, and to focus on areas of solid economic growth. The markets have responded, giving Dominion a 10 percent price-to-earnings premium compared to peers, compared to a 12 percent discount back in October 2012.

Financial Highlights, Fiscal Year 2012

Consolidated results for FY2012 appear lackluster, due to divestitures and a relatively mild 2012 weather pattern. Revenues dipped some 9.1 percent, but perhaps confirming the company's overall reinvention strategy, earnings and earnings per share stayed almost exactly the same, and as a reward to shareholders the company posted a 7 percent dividend increase and indicated similar increases forthcoming. For FY2013, the company is guiding earnings in the $3.20–$3.50

range, the midpoint of which would be 22 percent ahead of FY2012.

Reasons to Buy

Dominion's core businesses are healthy. The consolidation to regulated industries seems to be working, and the strong presence in the gas distribution and storage business is a good play in the new shale fracking era and gives it a growth component. The company is well positioned in the Pennsylvania and New York shale regions, and with the new (over)supply it's better to be in the distribution and storage business than in exploration and production. Fuel costs for the electric business, at 47 percent of revenues, are lower than most. The size of dividend increases has been growing as the company is able to pay out more

of its earned cash in a more stable regulated environment.

Reasons for Caution

The company has a larger nuclear exposure than most at 28 percent of generating capacity; that can be good in times of rapidly increasing fossil fuel prices but bad when unforeseeable events occur and/or when natural gas is the bargain fuel of the day. The company has been making an aggressive transformation in an industry not known for big change; we suppose this could add a risk factor, but so far, so good. Finally, recent share prices have taken the company to the low end of our acceptable yield range for this type of company. The more growth-oriented gas distribution businesses will probably help in the longer term but make the shares more expensive now.

SECTOR: Utilities
BETA COEFFICIENT: 0.43
10-YEAR COMPOUND EARNINGS PER SHARE GROWTH: 7.0%
10-YEAR COMPOUND DIVIDENDS PER SHARE GROWTH: 3.5%

	2005	2006	2007	2008	2009	2010	2011	2012
Revenues (mil)	17,971	16,482	15,674	16,290	15,131	15,197	14,379	13,093
Net income (mil)	1,033	1,704	1,414	1,781	1,585	1,724	1,603	1,605
Earnings per share	1.50	2.40	2.13	3.04	2.64	2.89	2.76	2.75
Dividends per share	1.34	1.38	1.46	1.58	1.75	1.83	1.97	2.11
Cash flow per share	3.71	4.91	5.08	5.07	4.82	5.10	5.05	5.25
Price: high	43.5	42.2	49.4	48.5	39.8	45.1	53.6	55.6
low	33.3	34.4	39.8	31.3	27.1	36.1	42.1	48.9

Dominion Resources, Inc.
P.O. Box 26532
Richmond, VA 23261–6532
(804) 819-2156
Website: www.dom.com

INCOME

Duke Energy

❏ Ticker symbol: DUK (NYSE) ❏ S&P rating: A- ❏ Value Line financial strength rating: A ❏ Current yield: 4.1% ❏ Dividend raises, past 6 years: 6

Company Profile

Those of you familiar with this North Carolina–based utility holding company, but who haven't looked at it in a while, might be in for a surprise or two. First is the $75 (recent) share price, compared to years trading in the $15–20 range. Explanation: The company decided to do a reverse split in mid-2012. Second, and at the same time, the company acquired Progress Energy, greatly expanding its foothold in the Southeast and Florida. If you haven't looked at it for, say, ten years, the company was reformed in 2007 also after spinning off most of its midstream gas business into a new company, Spectra Energy, which is why our data table goes back only to that point in time.

So, you may rightly ask, what is Duke today, and should you invest in it? Duke Energy Corporation is still a utility provider and operator working primarily in the Southeast and Midwest but with operations outside those areas, including some international operations. The company has 3 operating segments: U.S. Franchised Electric and Gas, Commercial Power, and International Energy.

The U.S. Franchised Electric and Gas segment generates, transmits, distributes, and sells electricity as a regulated utility in most of North Carolina, northern and western South Carolina, southwestern Ohio, Indiana, and northern Kentucky, including the Greater Cincinnati area. It also transports and sells natural gas to 500,000 customers in southwestern Ohio and northern Kentucky. With the Progress acquisition, the company spread into the north half of Florida as well as increased the size of other markets, especially in western North Carolina. This segment supplies electric service to approximately 7.2 million residential, commercial, and industrial customers (up from 4 million prior to the acquisition) with approximately 289,900 miles of distribution lines and a 32,200-mile transmission system. The company is relatively heavily invested in nuclear power, with some 33 percent of its power provided this way (53 percent coal, 13 percent other).

The Commercial Power segment's main business is to generate power to sell into the unregulated wholesale market, with about 6,800 megawatts of generating capacity located mainly in the Midwest. The Duke Energy Generating Services subsidiary within this segment develops and operates renewable energy projects, including some newly acquired solar arrays in North Carolina and Arizona. One subsidiary within this segment also offers onsite energy solutions and utility services for large customers, including municipalities and large factory complexes.

The International Energy segment operates and manages power-generation facilities and sells and markets electric power, natural gas, and other energy products outside the United States, mainly in Latin America.

In total, the company is one of the largest, if not the largest, public utility in the United States.

Financial Highlights, Fiscal Year 2012

Revenues, earnings, and share count took a step function higher with the Progress acquisition; it's not an easy task to comment on the apples-to-apples progress (pardon the pun) of the original business, particularly with a measure of acquisition costs thrown in. We'll start with the share count, which increased some 58 percent to 705 million shares. Working backward, earnings per share dropped slightly from $4.14 to $3.71,

reflecting acquisition costs and a six-cent charge related to a plant closure. Outside of those issues, the core earning power per share looks unchanged and is expected to rise substantially to $4.35 per share in FY2013. Revenues rose 35 percent with the acquisition and a slight dampening effect from mild weather, and will rise another 29 percent next year as Progress is integrated into the whole for a full year. All through this period the dividend has been increased about 2 percent each year.

Reasons to Buy

Duke has always been a well-managed utility operating in solid markets with a growing customer base, and that base has now been extended. The North Carolina customer base is diverse and especially attractive as more companies and individuals move there to enjoy lower costs of living and costs of doing business. The new northern Florida base is also a strong and prosperous region.

We actually like its nuclear exposure, as we do think nuclear power will return to the electricity generating stage in a bigger way. Duke will have the advantage of experience and existing infrastructure and is gaining experience with other renewables as well, perhaps paving the way to a less fossil-fuel-driven future.

Reasons for Caution

For many, nuclear power is a reason for caution, and we certainly would want to diversify utility holdings to avoid overexposure to utilities with nuclear facilities. Like most utilities, Duke depends on regulatory rate relief to grow revenues, and so the regulatory environment is critical—but it has a favorable history. Like most utilities and other fixed-income surrogates, the share price has been driven up as investors search for yield—which becomes a problem if interest rates finally start to rise.

SECTOR: **Utilities**
BETA COEFFICIENT: **0.32**
10-YEAR COMPOUND EARNINGS PER SHARE GROWTH: **NA**
10-YEAR COMPOUND DIVIDENDS PER SHARE GROWTH: **NA**

		2005	2006	2007	2008	2009	2010	2011	2012
Revenues (mil)		—	10,607	12,720	13,207	12,731	14,272	14,529	19,624
Net income (mil)		—	1,080	1,522	1,279	1,461	1,771	1,848	2,148
Earnings per share		—	2.76	3.60	3.03	3.39	4.02	4.14	3.71
Dividends per share		—	—	2.58	2.70	2.82	2.91	2.97	3.03
Cash flow per share		—	7.86	8.11	7.34	7.58	8.49	8.68	6.80
Price:	high	—	—	63.9	61.9	53.8	55.8	66.4	71.1
	low	—	—	50.7	40.5	35.2	46.4	50.6	59.6

Duke Energy Corporation
550 South Tryon St.
Charlotte, NC 28202–1803
(704) 382-3853
Website: www.duke-energy.com

GROWTH AND INCOME

E. I. du Pont de Nemours and Company (DuPont)

◻ Ticker symbol: DD (NYSE) ◻ S&P rating: A ◻ Value Line financial strength rating: A++ ◻ Current yield: 3.3% ◻ Dividend raises, past 10 years: 5

Company Profile

Although the company is known to many as a chemical company, today's DuPont is reawakening as a world leader in science and technology with important end product ingredients in a range of disciplines. The company has always been a technology leader with such well-known inventions as Nylon, Rayon, Teflon, and Kevlar, but until recently has been taken in more as a commodity producer than an innovator. We see signs of change in that reputation, toward its own "market-driven science" business vision.

The company continues to evolve with the 2012 divestiture of the Performance Coatings Division, which it had indicated its intention to auction off earlier in the year. That auction netted $4 billion after tax, which was the company's target, and the business accounted for some 19 percent of total revenues in FY2011. That move leaves 7 operating divisions.

■ The Agriculture (30 percent of FY2012 revenues) segment delivers a portfolio of products and services specifically targeted to achieve gains in crop yields and productivity, including Pioneer brand seed products and well-established brands of insecticides, fungicides, and herbicides. Pioneer develops, produces, and markets corn hybrid and soybean varieties and sells wheat, rice, sunflower, canola, and other seeds under the Pioneer and other brand names.

■ Electronic and Communications (8 percent) makes high-tech materials for the semiconductor industry. E&C supplies differentiated materials and systems for photovoltaics (solar), consumer electronics, displays, and advanced printing.

■ Nutrition and Health (10 percent) consists of the recently acquired Danisco's specialty food ingredients business and Solae, a majority-owned venture with Bunge Limited, which is engaged in developing soy-based technologies. The segment is a provider of solutions for specialty food ingredients, health, and safety. Products include cultures, emulsifiers, gums, natural sweeteners, and soy-based food.

- Industrial Biosciences (3 percent) develops and manufactures a wide range of enzymes, the biocatalysts that enable chemical reactions, on a large scale. The segment's enzymes add value and functionality to products and processes, such as animal nutrition, detergents, food manufacturing, and ethanol production.

These first 4 businesses add on to the traditional core businesses:

- Performance Chemicals (21 percent) delivers a range of industrial and specialty chemical products such as fluorochemicals (refrigerants, Teflon) and titanium-based pigments to industrial customers, including plastics and coatings, textiles, mining, pulp and paper, water treatment, and health-care manufacturers.
- Performance Materials (19 percent) supplies high-performance polymers, films, plastics, and substrates to a variety of industries from automotive to aerospace and consumer durable goods manufacturers.
- Safety and Protection (11 percent) makes protective fibers and clothing, including bulletproof apparel; disinfectants; and protective building surfaces—Tyvek house wrap is one of the bigger brands here.

The company has operations in 90 countries worldwide, and about 61 percent of consolidated net sales are made to customers outside the United States.

DuPont has one of the largest R & D budgets of any company in the world and operates more than 75 R & D centers worldwide. DuPont's core research is concentrated at its Wilmington, Delaware, facilities. DuPont's modern research is focused on renewable bio-based materials, biofuels, energy-efficient technologies, safety products, and alternative energy technologies.

Financial Highlights, Fiscal Year 2012

Not surprisingly in light of the Performance Coatings divestiture, which happened midyear 2012, revenues were down some 8.3 percent, but up about 3 percent on an apples-to-apples basis. Unit volumes did better, as currency exchange took another 2 percent from the top line. Agriculture was strong, with increasing volumes and pricing, and a nice 14 percent gain from FY2011. Weaker areas included Electronics and Communications, with its exposure to PV (solar panels), and Performance Chemicals, due to a decline in titanium dioxide (white pigment) and fluoropolymer. Net profits and per-share earnings declined about 15 percent, again related to the divestiture. Going forward, operating and net margins are expected to improve, and some of the inventory destocking that had been occurring should end; the company projects a 14 percent earnings increase on a 5 percent revenue gain and a 1.5 percent share buyback.

Reasons to Buy

DuPont continues to succeed in reinventing itself as an innovation leader and to capitalize on innovation and product leadership in established categories. Not that this company doesn't have experience with innovation—quite the opposite, in fact—but the problem seems to be in getting recognized for its innovation. The product pipeline continues to be full, individual product margins remain strong, and the company's biggest moneymakers still dominate their markets.

The company visualizes itself as a "fast growing science company" set to capitalize on "global megatrends"—population growth, alternative energy production, and so forth. The improvement of worldwide food production is at the center of its new growth initiatives. The company has brand leadership in many categories, and is committed to shareholder returns with a solid dividend track record and a resumption of share buybacks.

Reasons for Caution

The company still needs to overcome the stigma of a commodity producer. For better or worse, DuPont made some bets in the alternative energy industry, supplying materials for solar applications and biofuels, which haven't done as well as expected. We believe the company will adjust properly to the corrections in these markets and is well positioned in its others.

SECTOR: **Materials**
BETA COEFFICIENT: **1.53**
10-YEAR COMPOUND EARNINGS PER SHARE GROWTH: **0.5%**
10-YEAR COMPOUND DIVIDENDS PER SHARE GROWTH: **1.5%**

		2005	2006	2007	2008	2009	2010	2011	2012
Revenues (mil)		26,639	27,421	29,378	30,529	26,109	31,505	37,961	34,812
Net income (mil)		2,300	2,684	3,034	2,477	1,853	3,032	3,698	3,137
Earnings per share		2.32	2.88	3.28	2.73	2.04	3.28	3.93	3.33
Dividends per share		1.46	1.48	1.52	1.64	1.64	1.64	1.64	1.70
Cash flow per share		3.97	4.40	4.89	4.33	3.70	4.80	5.67	5.19
Price:	high	54.9	49.7	53.9	52.5	35.6	50.2	57.0	57.5
	low	37.6	38.5	42.3	21.3	16.0	31.9	37.1	4.7

E. I. du Pont de Nemours and Company
1007 Market Street
Wilmington, DE 19898
(800) 441-7515
Website: www.dupont.com

CONSERVATIVE GROWTH

Eastman Chemical Company

❑ Ticker symbol: EMN (NYSE) ❑ S&P rating: BBB ❑ Value Line financial strength rating: A
❑ Current yield: 1.8% ❑ Dividend raises, past 10 years: 3

Company Profile

For every company that stays at the party too long, there's another that knows when it has had enough. Rather than stay and drink the last of whatever's left, it drives home safely and wakes up the next morning clear headed and ready to work. Actually, we wouldn't know too much about that last part, but we imagine it must happen that way somewhere. In any case, Eastman is an example of a company that got out in time. They owned a domestic market that was dying (photographic film chemistry) and managed to exit with a few tears but no long-term ill effects. The same (unfortunately) cannot be said for their former parent company, Kodak, which stayed behind to do keg-stands and ended up sleeping in the bathtub. As of early 2012, Kodak is operating under Chapter 11 bankruptcy protection,

Eastman is one of those "better living through chemistry" companies with a history of solving problems and providing standard, high-tech, and high-precision materials to industries ranging from food and beverage to toys to medical equipment to computers and electronics.

The company is organized into 4 product groups, all of which have something more or less to do with petrochemicals:

- Performance Chemicals and Intermediates (PCI, 36 percent of sales) produces "acetyl and olefin streams" that eventually become strategic ingredients for agricultural chemicals, fibers, food and beverage ingredients, laundry-care products, pharmaceuticals, and medical devices and other specialty applications.
- Coatings, Adhesives, Specialty Polymers, and Inks (CASPI, 27 percent of sales) produces resins and other components designed to improve the appearance and performance of paints, coatings, inks, adhesives, and similar products.
- Fibers (27 percent) produces materials and finished fibers for everything from cigarette filters to clothing and home furnishings.
- Specialty Plastics (18 percent) produces specialty materials and films for, among other things, liquid crystal displays (LCDs).

Obviously there could be considerably more detail in these descriptions, but it would probably only be meaningful to those with a strong chemistry or materials background. The upshot: Eastman makes a lot of strategically important materials that support a lot of manufacturing processes for common and fairly high-volume items, such as beer bottles. Additionally, these materials are used in considerable amounts in overseas manufacturing. Eastman has adapted by setting up plants in 10 countries and driving foreign sales to 52 percent of the total.

Financial Highlights, Fiscal Year 2012

Eastman has clearly worked through the worst of the effects of the Great Recession. The company turned in an excellent FY2012 with fairly broad-based increases in revenues and income. Per-share earnings, even after issuing 17 million additional shares as part of the Solutia deal, are up to record levels and are nearly 3 times their 2009 levels. Operating margins continue to improve (up 15 percent last year) as a result of internal investment in improved processes, with further increases expected in FY2013. The company has obviously worked to improve its core financials, to the point that the Solutia debt looks to be easily managed via Eastman's greatly expanded cash flow.

Reasons to Buy

Although Eastman lies on the edge of the "buy businesses you understand" test, it's obvious from the numbers and especially the improving margins that the company really does produce things vitally important to manufacturing mainstream and advanced products. Successful product development has always been a key strength for Eastman, but the company has grown margins very steadily over the past few years through careful investments in business restructuring, cost-cutting measures, and additions to its output capacity. Eastman is well positioned for continued organic growth with excellent cash flow, solid projected earnings growth, and good liquidity. We like their international expansion in the face of stiffening competition from Asia. FY2013 looks very promising with realistic expectations for sales increases in the 17–19 percent range and an earnings bump of perhaps 25 percent.

Reasons for Caution

Eastman's fortunes will follow those of the larger manufacturing sector in general and, to a lesser extent, the feedstock (petroleum) market more specifically. Petro pricing is stable at the moment and is expected to remain so in the near term, but there is always risk of turmoil here, both political and speculative. The company is still carrying a heavy debt load from the acquisition of Solutia in 2011, and their continued prudence in paying that down and a focus on organic growth will be needed going forward. We do not expect to see significant increases in the dividend or share repurchases until the bulk of this debt is dealt with.

SECTOR: **Materials**
BETA COEFFICIENT: **1.30**
10-YEAR COMPOUND EARNINGS PER SHARE GROWTH: **15.5%**
10-YEAR COMPOUND DIVIDENDS PER SHARE GROWTH: **1.0%**

	2005	**2006**	**2007**	**2008**	**2009**	**2010**	**2011**	**2012**
Revenues (mil)	7,059	7,450	6,830	6,720	5,047	5,842	7,178	8,102
Net income (mil)	485	416	423	342	265	514	653	802
Earnings per share	2.97	2.50	2.53	2.25	1.82	3.48	4.56	5.38
Dividends per share	0.88	0.88	0.88	0.88	0.88	0.90	0.99	1.08
Cash flow per share	4.94	4.33	4.71	4.20	3.72	5.62	6.76	7.55
Price: high	30.9	30.6	39.2	39.1	31.0	42.3	55.4	68.2
low	22.0	23.7	28.8	12.9	8.9	25.9	32.4	39.2

Eastman Chemical Company
200 South Wilcox Drive
Kingsport, TN 37662
(423) 229-2000
Website: www.eastman.com

AGGRESSIVE GROWTH

Fair Isaac Corporation

❑ Ticker symbol: FICO (NYSE) ❑ S&P rating: not rated ❑ Value Line financial strength rating: B++
❑ Current yield: 0.2% ❑ Dividend raises, past 10 years: 2

Company Profile

Fair Isaac Corporation provides decision support analytics, software, and solutions to help businesses improve and automate decision making and risk management. The most well-known and best example of these solutions is the FICO score—an analytic single-figure estimate of a consumer's creditworthiness used in the credit industry and for other purposes such as employment and insurance.

FICO provides its analytic solutions and services to a variety of financial and other service organizations, including banks, credit-reporting agencies, credit card–processing agencies, insurers, telecommunications providers, retailers, marketers, and health-care organizations. It operates in 3 segments: Applications, Scores, and Tools. The Applications segment provides decision and risk management tools, market targeting products, and fraud detection tools and associated professional services. The Scores segment includes the business-to-business scoring solutions; myFICO solutions, delivering FICO scores for consumers; and associated professional services. The Tools segment provides software products and consulting services to help organizations build their own analytic tools.

Financial Highlights, Fiscal Year 2012

FICO is well past the Great Recession crunch, which saw a sharp slackening of demand as financial services firms reduced spending and as credit and loan activity diminished altogether. The demand for traditional credit-scoring products has resumed, though not at previous levels, and revenues haven't reached the record $826.4 million achieved in 2006. What has emerged as a stronger growth driver is the analytics provided by the Applications segment, primarily in fraud prevention and in marketing analytics, predicting consumer behavior and so forth. This segment now accounts for about two-thirds of the business (and fraud solutions are 25 percent of that). While the revenues at the Scoring division advanced only 4 percent last year, the Applications division was ahead 11 percent.

For FY2012 in total, revenues advanced just a bit over 9 percent, compared to a diminished 1.9

percent in FY2011 over FY2010. As a company that provides software and information, most of its cost structure is relatively fixed in the form of staff—cost of goods sold is almost insignificant—so, as such, is driven by volumes. Thus, earnings rose 29 percent, and aided by a persistent 2.5 percent share buyback per-share earnings actually rose some 42.5 percent. For FY2013, the company projects another strong performance, with revenues in the $760–770 million range (up 13 percent) and per-share earnings, hurt somewhat by acquisition costs for a few small takeovers, up about 10 percent.

Reasons to Buy

"Big data" and related analytics are hot right now as more companies learn how to use them more efficiently and effectively to manage different parts of their business. There are a number of companies, large and small, in the analytics business, but few have the brand reputation, product packaging, and leadership enjoyed by FICO. The company is the gold standard for this type of product and is more turnkey and easy for customers who don't have advanced mathematicians and software engineering staffs to buy. As a consequence, and with the brand recognition of the FICO score, the company has attained a pretty large moat on its brand and is a good example of how packaging and market definition can be as important as the product.

We also think a stabilizing financial industry with new rules, fewer workers, and a greater recognition for risk and risk management will bode well for the FICO product suite. Financial and other decision-making FICO products offer a good combination of streamlining and sophistication. Long term, we can easily see their modeling approaches being further extended to analyze customer behavior and provide decision support for insurability, employability, acceptance into schools, and even customer behaviors in stores or online, other areas well beyond a consumer's ability to repay extended credit. International demand for FICO's products continues to grow, too, notably in China, where fraud protection is a big business.

Going forward, the base scoring business should continue to recover, and the Applications business should be a healthy growth engine. At less than $1 billion in revenues and with only 2,155 employees, this company has room to grow and offers a nice alternative to the much larger businesses on our *100 Best* list.

The dividend remains inconsequential, but it doesn't take a genius to figure out the company's policy of providing shareholder returns in the form of cash. Share counts have dropped from almost 70 million in 2004 to just under 35 million at present—this drop in fact has amplified the earnings per-share performance considerably but also represents real return to remaining shareholders.

Reasons for Caution

Most of the changes afoot in the credit card and financial services industry bode well for FICO, but we wonder if credit-scoring demand will ever be what it was in 2004–07. There is more competition in the scoring arena from the 3 major credit bureaus (who now act as both a channel and a competitor, always a delicate situation) and from a product called VantageScore being marketed by the bureaus, which looks a lot like a FICO score but isn't. The company's business is still heavily tied to transaction volumes and financing, although less so moving forward as analytics and big data take center stage. Software companies always run a certain amount of technology risk; this should also be considered. There is some public concern that scoring models oversimplify lending and insurability decisions and should not be used or relied on so heavily. Finally, as we've seen, the company is vulnerable to economic downturns.

SECTOR: **Business Services**
BETA COEFFICIENT: **1.49**
10-YEAR COMPOUND EARNINGS PER SHARE GROWTH: **8.5%**
10-YEAR COMPOUND DIVIDENDS PER SHARE GROWTH: **10.5%**

	2005	2006	2007	2008	2009	2010	2011	2012
Revenues (mil)	798.7	825.4	822.2	744.8	630.7	605.6	619.7	676.4
Net income (mil)	134.5	103.5	104.7	81.2	65.1	64.5	71.6	92.0
Earnings per share	1.86	1.50	1.82	1.64	1.34	1.42	1.79	2.55
Dividends per share	0.08	0.08	0.08	0.08	0.08	0.08	0.08	0.08
Cash flow per share	2.91	2.57	3.03	2.49	2.15	2.36	2.58	3.20
Price: high	48.5	47.8	41.8	32.2	24.5	27.0	38.5	47.9
low	32.3	32.5	32.1	10.4	9.8	19.5	20.0	34.6

Fair Isaac Corporation
901 Marquette Avenue, Suite 3200
Minneapolis, MN 55402–3232
Phone: (612) 758-5200
Website: www.fairisaac.com

AGGRESSIVE GROWTH

FedEx Corporation

◻ Ticker symbol: FDX (NYSE) ◻ S&P rating: BBB ◻ Value Line financial strength rating: A ◻ Current yield: 0.6% ◻ Dividend raises, past 10 years: 9

Company Profile

FedEx Corporation is the world's leading provider of guaranteed express delivery services and a major player in the overall small shipment and small package logistics market. The corporation is organized as a holding company, with 4 individual businesses that compete collectively and operate independently under the FedEx brand. The familiar FedEx Express operation offers overnight and deferred air service to 57,000 drop-off locations, operating 688 aircraft and approximately 50,000 ground vehicles to support this business. The company also offers freight services for less time-sensitive items. The company has ventured into specialized logistics services with its comprehensive FedEx Services, which also includes the former Kinko's copy and office centers, now operating under the FedEx/Kinko's brand.

The company's operations include:

- The world's largest express transportation company (FedEx Express)
- North America's second-largest ground carrier for small-package business shipments (FedEx Ground)
- The largest U.S. regional less-than-truckload freight company (FedEx Freight)
- A "24/7" option for urgent shipments, providing nonstop, door-to-door delivery in the contiguous United States, Canada, and Europe (FedEx Custom Critical)
- The largest-volume customs filer in the United States, providing freight forwarding, advisory services, and trade technology (FedEx Trade Networks)

In total, the company operates an enormous logistics network of 688 aircraft, 180,000 ground vehicles, over 700 World Service Centers, over 1,800 FedEx Office locations, nearly 7,000 authorized Ship Centers, and more than 43,000 Drop Boxes. The company has about 280,000 employees. In FY2012, the Express segment accounted for 62 percent of revenues, Ground 22 percent, Freight 12 percent, and Services 4 percent.

Financial Highlights, Fiscal Year 2012

Following up on its strong rebound year in FY2011, FedEx kept the momentum going in FY2012 with solid growth in the top and bottom lines; particularly the bottom line, where earnings grew 40 percent to just over $2 billion. With these results, the company was able to grow capital expenditures (ground fleet improvement, largely) and strengthen their cash position. Growth in cash flow was particularly strong and looks to improve further through FY2014. Operating as they do on fairly thin margins, cash flow is both a key indicator and driver of overall health for a fast-turnover company like FedEx. When cash flow is on the rise here, further earnings increases are likely to follow.

As the economy continues to emerge from the recession and commerce and manufacturing resume toward full scale, FedEx's top line reaped the benefits in FY2012. Revenues advanced 9 percent to $42.7 billion. Not surprisingly, e-commerce is creating considerable single-shipment volume, and the new economy-minded SmartPost offering, which uses the U.S. Postal Service for end customer delivery, has gained a lot of traction. FedEx Ground had a particularly strong showing this year. Including the FedEx SmartPost business, the company's ground parcel market share grew to nearly 30 percent.

The big multiplier here is the fact that their revenue per ground freight parcel actually grew 7 percent, even as they were growing market share.

Reasons to Buy

The company delivered a very large pot of income in FY2012. After the rise in capital expenditures and retained cash, however, shareholders found themselves last in line for the soup and got no dumplings; a small increase in the dividend and a flat share price through the year was all that was left. Both of these were tied to the relatively high expectations for the share price entering the year. After another year of proven returns and a reasonable 16 P/E multiple, though, we feel the share price will benefit in the long term from the reduced expectations of FY2013.

The company recently renewed a lucrative $10.5 billion contract with the U.S. Postal Service. A 7-year deal, the contract calls for FedEx to supplement the Postal Service's package and overnight delivery services. As long as the USPS can pay their bills (a safe bet), this is good business for FedEx.

FedEx has a strong brand and offers a diverse set of services, really a complete logistics solution, for a large group of customers. The continued resurgence in the economy and growth in online shopping and delivery will certainly help volumes and pricing, and the continuing shift to e-commerce gives a boost to this recovery. The resumption of strong U.S. exports not only helps volume but also helps fill up planes traveling from the United States. The logistics business is always ripe for innovation, and FedEx has long been an innovator in the transportation and small-package shipment business, not only with new services, but also with new tools to help customers track shipments and manage their supply chains in real time; we expect this to continue.

Reasons for Caution

The momentum created in FY2011 and FY2012 has not carried forward into FY2013 as well as had been hoped, but the reasons are understood. A moderation in the Asian air-freight market has led to overcapacity and considerable pressure on margins. Second, a voluntary severance program will record higher costs than had been anticipated. The result of these two factors will likely be a miss against FY2013 estimates. The good news is this will also likely mean a pull-back in the share price and a buying opportunity for careful investors.

The company is always vulnerable to fuel prices, particularly if cost increases come faster than they can be recovered in rates and fuel surcharges—as is often the case. Finally, while cash flows are strong, this company must occasionally purchase or lease aircraft, and this and other capital expenditures can put a big dent in cash flows.

SECTOR: **Transportation**
BETA COEFFICIENT: **1.00**
10-YEAR COMPOUND EARNINGS PER SHARE GROWTH: **8.0%**
10-YEAR COMPOUND DIVIDENDS PER SHARE GROWTH: **11.0%**

	2005	2006	2007	2008	2009	2010	2011	2012
Revenues (mil)	29,363	32,294	35,214	37,953	35,497	34,734	39,204	42,680
Net income (mil)	1,449	1,885	2,073	1,821	1,173	1,184	1,452	2,032
Earnings per share	4.82	5.98	6.67	5.83	3.76	3.76	4.90	6.41
Dividends per share	0.29	0.33	0.37	0.40	0.44	0.44	0.48	0.52
Cash flow per share	9.74	11.13	12.39	12.13	10.09	10.01	11.13	13.08
Price: high	105.8	120.0	121.4	99.5	92.6	97.8	98.7	97.2
low	76.8	96.5	89.5	53.9	34.0	69.8	64.1	82.8

FedEx Corporation
942 South Shady Grove Road
Memphis, TN 38120
(901) 818-7200
Website: www.fedex.com

Fluor Corporation

◻ Ticker symbol: FLR (NYSE) ◻ S&P rating: A- ◻ Value Line financial strength rating: A++
◻ Current yield: 1.0% ◻ Dividend raises, past 10 years: 3

Company Profile

Fluor is one of the world's largest publicly owned engineering, procurement, construction, maintenance, and project management companies. They provide a diverse portfolio of large-scale infrastructure development expertise and services, primarily for 5 industry segments:

- Oil and Gas (35 percent of revenue, 43 percent of gross profit in 2012) where they serve all facets of the traditional energy industry, including upstream, downstream, and petrochemical markets, including oilfields, refineries, and pipelines.
- Industrial and Infrastructure (44 percent of revenue, 16 percent of profits) is their most diverse organization, which includes transportation, mining, life sciences, telecom, manufacturing, and commercial and institutional projects. This segment also covers the emerging alternative energy projects, including major windmill farm developments.
- Government (12 percent of revenue, 20 percent of profits) addresses the U.S. Departments of Energy, Defense, and Homeland Security.
- Global Services (6 percent of revenue, 23 percent of profits) provides operations and maintenance, supply chain, equipment services, and contract staffing.
- Power (3 percent of revenue, 2 percent of profits) designs, builds, commissions, and retrofits electric generation facilities using coal, natural gas, and nuclear fuels.

Financial Highlights, Fiscal Year 2012

Fluor had a good FY2012. New bookings of $27 billion brought the year-end backlog to $38.2 billion, down slightly from FY2011 year-end. Revenues for the year were a record $27.6 billion, up 18 percent over FY2011's already strong tally. Per-share earnings were up 27 percent to $4.30 (does not include one-time charges, see the following table). All in all, it's a very good report, and one that positions them well for their new initiative, which is a greater level of vertical integration.

With its solid capital structure, the company sees an opportunity to secure a larger portion of future contracts by making strategic acquisitions and/or forming joint ventures. The idea is to procure or partner with modular construction and fabrication specialists who can deliver on prebuilt (as opposed to build-on-site) engineered components. Building fabrication facilities at a work site at time of need and then rebuilding them elsewhere has become more expensive than building in a low-cost fixed facility and then shipping the product to the site.

Reasons to Buy

The good news for Fluor in FY2012 was the significant level of new awards. The better news for the year was the breadth of the new awards. The company operates in 5 distinct segments of the economy, which serves to spread the risk when any one segment happens to be in a down cycle, which is not uncommon. What is uncommon is when all 5 sectors are growing and awarding new contracts at the same time, and that's where Fluor is now. Fluor also happens to be in a good cash position and so can bid, and bid aggressively, on this new work.

For investors tolerant of some economic risk, Fluor's shares represent a solid way to play an economic recovery, as well as the continued need to replace old infrastructure.

General large-scale construction should regain health across all industries, including oil and gas, as the construction cycle becomes more favorable. In our view, the company has two growth kickers not to be ignored: their presence in the alternative energy industry, and their presence in the utility infrastructure industry. Both will see waves of new investment to capitalize on new energy technologies; in addition, there are thousands of miles of old water pipes, electric lines, and other infrastructure that is due, or overdue, for replacement. These 2 megatrends will boost Fluor's business for quite some time to come. Top-line revenue projections call for healthy growth of 10 percent plus for the next 2 years, and the company's conservative financial management will likely reap the best results from this increased activity.

Reasons for Caution

Fluor recently lost a $400 million arbitration hearing in the U.K. when the board ruled that Fluor was not entitled to recover the costs of reinspection and rework on the Greater Gabbard wind farm. Fluor was general contractor on the project and would normally be entitled to recover these costs, which were incurred when the customer claimed that a series of structural components used in the project were faulty. Most observers were surprised by the ruling, given Fluor's excellent reputation and its willingness to take on high-risk programs. We mention this because a Fluor project in our backyard, the eastern span of the San Francisco Bay Bridge, is now at schedule risk due to the discovery of a large number of faulty structural components, specifically broken bolts in the seismic-protection structures. Depending on how this plays out, Fluor may find itself in a similar situation here.

The Industrial group could be a bit of a wild card as mining contracts, particularly in China, are in a down cycle with no clear end in sight. The group's Infrastructure segment is keeping busy, however, offsetting much of the uncertainty.

SECTOR: **Industrials**
BETA COEFFICIENT: **1.35**
10-YEAR COMPOUND EARNINGS PER SHARE GROWTH: **14.5%**
10-YEAR COMPOUND DIVIDENDS PER SHARE GROWTH: **4.5%**

	2005	2006	2007	2008	2009	2010	2011	2012
Revenues (mil)	13,161	14,079	16,691	22,326	21,990	20,849	23,381	27,577
Net income (mil)	227	264	410	673	685	358	594	722
Earnings per share	1.31	1.48	2.25	3.67	3.75	1.98	3.40	4.30
Dividends per share	0.32	0.32	0.40	0.50	0.50	0.50	0.50	0.77
Cash flow per share	1.90	2.21	3.14	4.61	4.85	3.11	4.71	5.76
Price: high	39.6	51.9	86.1	101.4	50.5	67.3	75.8	64.7
low	25.1	36.8	37.6	28.6	41.7	41.2	44.2	45.0

Fluor Corporation
6700 Las Colinas Blvd
Irving, TX 75039
Tel: (469) 398-7000
Website: www.fluor.com

FMC Corporation

◻ Ticker symbol: FMC (NYSE) ◻ S&P rating: A- ◻ Value Line financial strength rating: A ◻ Current yield: 1.0% ◻ Dividend raises, past 10 years: 6

Company Profile

FMC Corporation is a diversified chemical company serving global agricultural, industrial, and consumer markets. Founded in 1883 as the Bean Spray Pump Company, FMC (they were also Farm Machinery Company at one point in their history) continues to serve the agricultural market in 1 of its 3 newly aligned operating segments: Agricultural Solutions, FMC Health and Nutrition, and FMC Minerals. The company is 1 of the world's largest producers of strategic materials, including phosphorous, hydrogen peroxide, and various lithium compounds.

FMC Agricultural Solutions (43 percent of revenues) provides crop protection and pest control products for worldwide markets. The business offers a solid portfolio of insecticides and herbicides and is considered an industry leader for its innovative packaging.

The new FMC Health and Nutrition segment includes most of the older Specialty Chemicals organization, minus the lithium compounds and the Peroxygens business, which is being considered for divestiture. Health and Nutrition, which represents 20 percent of the business, is the world's leading producer of alginate, carrageenan, and microcrystalline cellulose, which are key thickening, texturing, stabilizing, and fat substitute ingredients used in the food industry.

The new FMC Minerals segment combines all of the company's lithium-based businesses and Alkali Chemicals business under one reporting segment. FMC Lithium is one of the world's leading producers of lithium-based products and recognized as the technology leader in specialty organolithium chemicals and related technologies. Among other things, the lithium compounds produced at FMC are key ingredients in many emerging battery technologies. FMC Alkali Chemicals (31 percent of FY2012 revenues) is the world's largest producer of natural soda ash and is the market leader in North America. Downstream products include sodium bicarbonate, sodium cyanide, sodium sesquicarbonate, and caustic soda. You may not have heard of many of these products, which typically are used to manufacture things like glass, paper, detergents, tires, and electronic components, among other things—and ship by the rail tank car load—but they are vital ingredients to a number of key industries worldwide.

Speaking of which, about 63 percent of the company's overall business comes from overseas.

Financial Highlights, Fiscal Year 2012

FMC closed out a strong FY2012 performance with a good fourth quarter and solid year-over-year revenue and earnings increases. The Agricultural Solutions segment is on a roll, and we expect continued growth through FY2013. The businesses that will make up the new FMC Health and Nutrition and the FMC Minerals segments did not enjoy the same growth in FY2012 as they had in FY2011, but the reorganization should improve operating leverage within the businesses. In this light, the company has issued revised improved guidance for the full year, with expectations for an EPS midpoint of $4.00.

Reasons to Buy

The company is very optimistic about its prospects moving forward. The recent and ongoing infrastructure changes, coupled with an improved economic outlook in general, have led management to forecast sales of $5.5 billion and $1.2 billion in gross margin by the close of FY2015. These are some significant gains and would indicate (with historical average ratios) a share price in the $88–$92 range.

FMC is well positioned in several areas of relative strategic importance in the chemical industry, in particular the agriculture, biopolymer, and lithium compounds businesses. The strength of the economic rebound, combined with these leadership positions in specialty markets, bodes well for the company. Pricing strength, improving margins, and strong international sales (65 percent of sales in 2012) all add to a promising picture.

As an example of FMC's strategic portfolio, the company is the leading supplier of lithium-based compounds used in the lithium-ion battery industry. Lithium batteries are used extensively in technology products such as laptops, music players, tablets, and automobiles like the Tesla Model S, the Chevrolet Volt, and the Nissan Leaf. All of the early hybrid cars and many of those still in production use nickel metal hydride (NiMH) battery chemistry, but lithium batteries deliver higher power density at a much lower weight. They can also be recharged more quickly. Lithium chemistry batteries for motorcycle and boating use are already quite popular for their low weight and indefinite shelf life.

FMC is a key player in a broad consortium of U.S.-based companies working to establish a dominant domestic lithium battery industry. Lithium battery technology is viewed by many as a key to the future of the automotive industry, and some have said that the country that makes the batteries will make the cars.

The (reasonably certain) divestiture of the Peroxygens unit will free up capital that will be used "to expand share repurchases and fund growth activities," according to the CEO.

Reasons for Caution

While the company occupies a leadership position in several important chemical and ingredient markets, FMC can't get away completely from its role as a commodity producer, particularly in such compounds like soda ash. As such, competition and business cycles will always play a role in growth and stability. Additionally, while the company did start paying dividends in 2006, the cash return rate could really be better. Additionally, recent share prices seem to already include a lot of the good news; waiting for good entry points would be advisable.

SECTOR: **Materials**
BETA COEFFICIENT: **1.25**
10-YEAR COMPOUND EARNINGS PER SHARE GROWTH: **11.0%**
10-YEAR COMPOUND DIVIDENDS PER SHARE GROWTH: **NM**

		2005	2006	2007	2008	2009	2010	2011	2012
Revenues (mil)		2,150	2,347	2,633	3,115	2,826	3,116	3,378	3,748
Net income (mil)		1,721.9	216.4	132.4	351	305	353	429	483
Earnings per share		2.20	2.74	3.40	4.63	4.15	4.83	5.98	3.48
Dividends per share		—	0.18	0.21	0.24	0.25	0.25	0.30	0.35
Cash flow per share		2.00	2.27	2.62	3.27	2.97	3.41	3.98	4.51
Price:	high	16.0	19.5	29.5	40.1	31.6	41.0	46.5	59.4
	low	10.8	12.5	17.8	14.2	17.5	25.4	31.9	42.9

FMC Corporation
1735 Market Street
Philadelphia, PA 19103
(215) 299-6000
Website: www.fmc.com

GROWTH AND INCOME

General Mills, Inc.

❑ Ticker symbol: GIS (NYSE) ❑ S&P rating: BBB+ ❑ Value Line financial strength rating: A+
❑ Current yield: 3.1% ❑ Dividend raises, past 10 years: 8

Company Profile

General Mills is the second-largest domestic producer of ready-to-eat breakfast cereals and the sixth-largest food company in the world. Their sales are broken out into 3 major segments: U.S. Retail (63 percent of revenues), International (25 percent), and Bakery and Foodstuffs (12 percent).

Major cereal brands include Cheerios, Wheaties, Lucky Charms, Total, and Chex. Other consumer packaged food products include baking mixes (Betty Crocker and Bisquick); packaged meals; Progresso soups; Green Giant vegetables; Hamburger Helper; snacks (Pop Secret microwave popcorn, Bugles snacks, etc.; Pillsbury dough products; organic foods; and other products, including Nature Valley, Yoplait, Go-Gurt, and Colombo yogurt.

In the International sector, General Mills sells recognized brands such as Häagen-Dazs ice cream, Old El Paso Mexican foods, and Green Giant vegetables. The company is in a 50–50 joint venture with Nestlé in international food distributor Cereal Partners Worldwide. Those international businesses have sales and marketing organizations in 33 countries.

Financial Highlights, Fiscal Year 2012

For momentum-oriented investors, FY2012 was another dull one. The company actually reported a 2 percent decline in cereal revenues and a 4 percent decline in its Yoplait franchise. For cereals, the sense is that it might be generic competition and a continued move into healthier products; for Yoplait the emergence of competing Greek yogurt products is the bugaboo. However, the international segment was strong and commodity input prices finally moderated. All together, revenues moved up 12 percent, but this was largely due to the full-year integration of Yoplait; net earnings and EPS rose about 3.3 percent. Estimates call for a slightly stronger performance in FY2013, with a 6 percent organic revenue growth and a similar growth in earnings and EPS with a moderate share buyback possibly in the cards.

Reasons to Buy

General Mills continues to enjoy solid brand strength and a strong position in a very competitive cereal and packaged food market. Recent trends have pointed to brand leveraging (e.g., Chocolate Cheerios, Wheaties Fuel), and the results have been encouraging. There's evidence that the recession forced more people to eat at home, and those folks are starting to return to more premium brands found on store shelves. Finally, additional international expansion may bring some opportunity.

Earnings, operating margins, and cash flows have all followed a slow but cash-rich track upward. The company bolted Yoplait on without issuing any additional shares and only a small amount of debt. The long-term policy aimed at share repurchases has brought the share count down from 758 million in 2004 to 640 million recently, although there was a brief pause in 2012 as the Yoplait acquisition was digested. Dividend raises have

ranged from 9 to 17 percent in the past 3 years; the most recent raise was 15 percent. Finally, General Mills continues to be a notably safe and stable stock with a beta of 0.18.

Reasons for Caution

The company is strongly affected by commodity prices and cycles. The stock recently woke up after years of very conservative but slightly upward movement, probably based on investors chasing the high yield. Dividends have gone up appreciably, and the stock price has risen in lockstep, but if investors see a flattening of dividends or an increase in interest rates, this stock could suffer—new investors should look for bargain entry points.

SECTOR: **Consumer Staples**
BETA COEFFICIENT: **0.18**
10-YEAR COMPOUND EARNINGS PER SHARE GROWTH: **8.5%**
10-YEAR COMPOUND DIVIDENDS PER SHARE GROWTH: **7.0%**

		2005	2006	2007	2008	2009	2010	2011	2012
Revenues (mil)		11,244	11,640	12,442	13,652	14,691	14,796	14,880	16,658
Net income (mil)		1,100	1,090	1,144	1,288	1,367	1,571	1,652	1,707
Earnings per share		1.37	1.45	1.59	1.78	1.99	2.30	2.48	2.56
Dividends per share		0.62	0.67	0.72	0.79	0.86	0.96	1.12	1.22
Cash flow per share		2.09	2.13	2.30	2.50	2.78	3.09	3.29	3.47
Price:	high	26.9	29.6	30.8	36.0	36.0	39.0	40.8	41.9
	low	22.3	23.5	27.1	25.5	23.2	33.1	34.5	36.6

General Mills, Inc.
One General Mills Blvd.
Minneapolis, MN 55426
(763) 764-7600
Website: www.generalmills.com

Harman International Industries

◻ Ticker symbol: HAR (NYSE) ◻ S&P rating: BB- ◻ Value Line financial strength rating: B+
◻ Current yield: 1.4% ◻ Dividend raises, past 10 years: 1

Company Profile

Harman International is one of the world's leading producers of audio and infotainment solutions for an increasingly mobile society. That sounds like marketing copy, but it's a true depiction of this company.

Harman, probably more than any other supplier in the world, has made a partner out of their former customer, the automobile manufacturer. How? By selling a branded product in the car. Where there used to be only one logo, one brand, in the interior of an automobile, now there are two—the manufacturer's and brands offered by Harman. It's not unusual to find Infinity, JBL, Mark Levinson, and several other Harman brands front and center on the dashboard of over half of the popular car lines today.

Indeed, Harman is really an automotive company, with 74 percent of FY2012 sales coming from this business, while consumer audio is 11 percent and professional audio is 10 percent. The company claims (as of July 2012) to have "a cumulative estimated $16.1 billion of future awarded Infotainment and Lifestyle automotive business," which they are quick to make clear

does not imply committed business or booked orders. But $16.1 billion is a big number, and big numbers count for a lot in the rock-n-roll business.

Financial Highlights, Fiscal Year 2012

Harman turned it to past 11 in '12 with a healthy improvement in sales (up 18 percent) and earnings (up 41 percent). In a strong cash position, the company retired nearly all of its long-term debt and increased its dividend for the first time in many years, from $.05 to $.30. The company's transformation into an automotive supplier should provide it with some relief from the rapidly changing whims of its traditional consumer audio customer base. The company is also focusing on emerging markets, with country managers and staff now in place in Brazil, Russia, India, and China. Sales for these regions in FY2012 grew 31 percent to $529 million, and the company expects continued significant growth there.

Still, there are a lot of brands hanging around, and a fair amount of duplication in the company's structure. As a consequence, the company announced recently the closing of a manufacturing plant in the U.K. and the layoff of some 500 employees (approximately 4 percent of the base). The company also announced the restructuring of its product lines into a more coherent form, with just 3 main lines, better aligned with its new mission as primarily an automotive supplier.

Reasons to Buy

Auto manufacturers had known for some time that they were leaving a lot of money on the table for the aftermarket electronics industry but couldn't figure out how to sell those customers a high-end Delco or Ford radio. Harman stepped in with some of the most respected brands in traditional home electronics and turned their problem into a big win for both parties. Now Harman owns a substantial piece of the automotive design-in market, where they partner with the auto companies to provide infotainment systems—those integrated systems that all work together to provide sound, video, wireless communications, navigation, Internet access, and climate control on demand and in all parts of the vehicle. As Harman evolves, the integration of digital automotive electronics with personal digital devices (e.g., the iPod) offers a huge opportunity. The company is also leveraging this idea to "smart" hotel room adaptations,

where you can plug in your device to get your music and tap into your chosen personal information. Major automotive manufacturers such as Tata, BMW, Geely (China–Volvo), Volkswagen, and others have been signing large long-term contracts with Harman to provide these systems. And once you have a brand associated with a car, manufacturers are reluctant to design you out.

Automobile purchases appear to be on the rebound, with light vehicle purchases in the U.S. likely to increase by 20 percent over the next 2 years. This is great news for all auto suppliers, and none more than Harman, as they can benefit in the U.S. while the Euro market tries to gather steam.

Reasons for Caution

Harman buys a lot of brands. Some of these brands turn into money, but some don't. The company recently announced a minor restructuring, the timing of which (at the beginning of an economic upcycle) seems curious to these eyes, but then we're not in the rock-n-roll business. Harman is vulnerable to economic cycles and particularly those in the auto industry, and downturns in discretionary consumer audio purchases will amplify auto industry woes. Audio and infotainment tastes can be fickle, so the company will have to quickly embrace the latest trends.

SECTOR: Consumer Discretionary
BETA COEFFICIENT: 1.50
10-YEAR COMPOUND EARNINGS PER SHARE GROWTH: 7.5%
10-YEAR COMPOUND DIVIDENDS PER SHARE GROWTH: 9.0%

	2005	2006	2007	2008	2009	2010	2011	2012
Revenues (mil)	3,030	3,248	3,551	4,112	2,891	3,364	3,772	4,364
Net income (mil)	233	268	25	146	(56)	60	149	211.2
Earnings per share	3.31	3.94	4.14	2.35	(1.01)	0.85	2.08	2.83
Dividends per share	0.05	0.05	0.05	0.05	0.05	0.05	0.05	0.30
Cash flow per share	5.27	6.02	6.17	5.10	1.32	2.70	3.89	4.96
Price: high	130.5	115.9	125.1	73.8	40.3	53.4	52.5	52.8
low	68.5	74.6	69.5	9.9	9.2	28.1	25.5	34.1

Harman International Industries
400 Atlantic St.
Stamford, CT 06901
(202) 393-1101
Website: www.harman.com

GROWTH AND INCOME

Health Care REIT, Inc.

❑ Ticker symbol: HCN (NYSE) ❑ S&P rating: BBB ❑ Value Line financial strength rating: B++
❑ Current yield: 4.0% ❑ Dividend raises, past 10 years: 10

Company Profile

Health Care REIT, as the name clearly conveys, is a real estate investment trust investing primarily in senior living and medical care properties primarily in the U.S. It is our first venture into the REIT space and is intended as a steady growth plus income investment and to provide some exposure to real estate in our *100 Best Stocks* portfolio.

The trust operates in 3 primary business segments. The first and largest is referred to as the Seniors Housing "triple net" segment and is involved primarily in owning senior housing properties and leasing them to qualified operators in return for a steady income stream. This segment currently owns 576 properties, almost all in the U.S., concentrated in high-cost urban areas mostly on the coasts, and contributes $719 million, or about 40 percent of revenues. The second and fastest-growing segment is the Seniors Housing Operating segment, which operates some of the facilities owned by the REIT and others owned by third parties. It operates 154 properties in 27 states and contributes about 39 percent to revenues. The third major segment is Medical

Facilities, which operates office space set up for medical purposes, inpatient and outpatient medical centers, and life science laboratories in 36 states, contributing about 22 percent of revenues. The REIT owns and/or operates some 1,025 properties in all and within the portfolio, operates assisted living, skilled nursing, independent living, and the medical centers just mentioned.

The Health Care REIT employs a conscious and stated strategy of being in markets with high barriers to entry and with a more upscale, affluent retiree base. Markets such as Boston, New Jersey, Seattle, and major coastal California cities are territories for the Health Care REIT. The median revenue per occupied room for this REIT is $6,668 per month, compared to a national median of $3,962. In the markets that HCR operates in, the average single-family home cost runs 60 percent higher than the national average, and household incomes are 40 percent higher. Eighty percent of facilities are in the 31 most affluent U.S. metropolitan areas. The facilities are newer, more attractive, and desirable, as a trip through their website at *www.hcreit.com* will show.

The company made a big expansion move in 2012 with the acquisition of the real estate portfolio of Sunrise Senior Living, with its 125 properties mainly in California and the West. The company now also operates senior centers in Canada and the United Kingdom.

REITs, obviously, play on the real estate market, and in this case, in the high-value-add segment of health care. So by investing in such a REIT, you are investing in real estate and in the health-care industry, and with the property mix owned by the Health Care REIT, you're investing in the aging population. In this case in particular, you're investing in the willingness of the more affluent segments of the elderly population to spend for a pleasant retirement. REITs are typically good income producers, as they are required by law to pay a substantial portion of their cash flow to investors. The accounting rules are different, and REIT investors should focus on Funds From Operations (FFO), which is analogous to operating income; net income figures have depreciation expenses deducted, which can vary in timing and not always be realistic. Funds From Operations (FFO) support the dividends paid to investors.

Financial Highlights, Fiscal Year 2012

The acquisition of Sunrise Senior Living added to an already healthy portfolio. Net operating income (NOI)—another pure measure of REIT activity—rose 4 percent on a same-store basis, including an 8.6 percent rise in income from the operating segment. The Sunrise acquisition drove an increase in private pay to 82 percent from approximately 71 percent in FY2011. Funds From Operations (FFO) rose about 3.2 percent over FY2011, while the dividend was raised 4.2 percent. Guidance for FY2013 calls for an FFO of $3.80 per share, an 8 percent increase, as real estate markets solidify and recent acquisitions take root.

Reasons to Buy

Health Care REIT is a solid way to play the steady growth of the health-care industry and the aging demographic. REITs are a relatively risk free, income-oriented way to play the steady growth of this intersection of trends. Rents—and rent growth—are better than average, and its income payout is stable and growing. With its concentration on private-pay services, Health Care REIT will avoid some of the exposure to Medicare utilization management initiatives and related cutbacks that many others in the sector are exposed to.

Reasons for Caution

Because of their differences from ordinary corporations, it may be difficult to understand this investment, particularly the financial performance of REITs, especially a complex REIT like this one, which has both traditional property investments and operating company investments. One could also question, going forward, whether retirees will be as well heeled as they are today, with deterioration in retirement savings and increased costs. Finally, recent prices have reflected the continuing rebound in real estate in general, driving prices of this REIT along with many others to new highs, near those achieved in 2006; caveat emptor.

SECTOR: **Health Care**
BETA COEFFICIENT: **0.83**
10-YEAR COMPOUND FFO PER SHARE GROWTH: **3.0%**
10-YEAR COMPOUND DIVIDENDS PER SHARE GROWTH: **2.5%**

	2005	2006	2007	2008	2009	2010	2011	2012
Revenues (mil)	3,474	3,639	3,649	3,779	3,515	4,835	5,323	5,139
Net income (mil)	162.5	195.6	181.6	166.2	147.2	203.3	184.1	173.8
Funds from operations per share	3.03	2.97	3.12	3.38	3.13	3.08	3.41	3.52
Earnings per share	1.06	1.32	1.26	1.35	1.22	0.49	0.60	0.98
Dividends per share	2.46	2.54	2.62	2.70	2.72	2.74	2.84	2.96
Price: high	39.2	43.0	48.6	54.0	46.7	52.1	55.2	62.8
low	31.2	32.8	35.1	30.1	25.9	38.4	41.0	52.4

Health Care REIT, Inc.
4500 Dorr Street
Toledo, OH 43615
(419) 247-2800
Website: www.hcreit.com

Honeywell International Inc.

❑ Ticker symbol: HON (NYSE) ❑ S&P rating: A ❑ Value Line financial strength rating: A++
❑ Current yield: 2.2% ❑ Dividend raises, past 10 years: 7

Company Profile

Honeywell is a diversified international technology and manufacturing company operating in 4 business segments, engaged in the development, manufacturing, and marketing of aerospace products and services (31 percent of sales); control technologies for buildings, homes, and industry (40 percent); automotive products (15 percent); and specialty materials (14 percent).

The Aerospace segment primarily makes cockpit controls, power generation equipment, and wheels and brakes for commercial and military aircraft and for airports and ground operations. It also makes jet engines for regional and business jet manufacturers. Products include avionics, auxiliary power units (APUs), aircraft lighting, and landing systems. Honeywell's Automation and Control Solutions segment is best known as a maker of home and office climate-control equipment. It also makes home automation systems; thermostats; sensing and combustion controls for heating, A/C, and other environmental controls; lighting controls; security systems and sensing products; and fire alarms. This segment produces most of the components of what is known in the trade and advertising lingo as a "smart building." The company estimates that its products are at work in some 150 million homes and 10 million commercial buildings worldwide.

The Specialty Materials operation makes a wide assortment of specialty chemicals and fibers, which are sold primarily to the food, pharmaceutical, petroleum refining, and electronic packaging industries. Petroleum refining catalysts and carbon fiber materials are among the more important and fastest-growing products in this segment.

The Transportation System segment consists of a portfolio of parts and supplies for the automotive industry. With the sale of its retail consumer automotive brands, this group is now focused on OEM components such as sensors and braking systems. The consumer brand divestiture accounted for about $1 billion of the $37 billion business. U.S. exports represent about 14 percent of sales in 2012, while foreign manufactured products and services represent 41 percent of total sales.

Financial Highlights, Fiscal Year 2012

FY2012 brought Honeywell a fairly modest 3 percent increase in revenues but a very immodest 11 percent (adjusted) increase in earnings. Improvements in operations led to an adjusted increase in gross margin of 1.4 percent, which is something worth looking for as an investor. Operating efficiencies, once gained, tend to stick around for a year or more. The company is looking for further gains in operating margin in FY2013 of up to 0.5 percent. The global economy was fairly lackluster in 2012, but Honeywell made the most of its positions in the air transport, construction, and energy markets, where it holds strong positions with in-demand products.

Reasons to Buy

Demand for the company's aircraft equipment is driven primarily by expansion in the global jetliner fleet, particularly jets with 100 or more seats. However, in 2012, business and general aviation original equipment sales increased by 34 percent, while regional and transport original equipment sales grew at "only" 11 percent. Aircraft hardware sales always lead to aircraft spares contracts and aircraft service contracts, so a few years of large sales volumes (such as we've seen from Honeywell in 2011 and 2012) will lead to a significant chain of future revenue.

Honeywell has outlined its key growth vectors as international ("globalization"), safety and security, energy efficiency, and energy generation. We like this rather diverse but timely set of focal points. In particular, Honeywell is positioned well with regard to the growing awareness of the value of energy efficiency. Over the next few years we see a lot of movement toward green practices in building design and use, and no one has a stronger portfolio of lighting and temperature control systems than Honeywell. Over half of the company's portfolio, across all 4 segments, is in the area of energy efficiency. The company also has a valuable distribution network and existing customer base in all of its businesses. The company has a solid balance sheet and participates almost exclusively in high-margin businesses, particularly with the divestiture of the consumer auto business. The company's major initiatives for 2013 include several cost-cutting and efficiency programs, which are the sort of programs that will yield benefits for 2014.

Reasons for Caution

Honeywell did just over $4 billion in business to the U.S. government in FY2012. This number will probably decline as a result of the sequestration policy, but there are no other factors which would negatively impact existing or future programs. Many of the industries Honeywell sells to—in particular, the aerospace industry—are and probably will always be low-growth businesses. Finally, the company continues to depend on acquisitions for a portion of its growth, and in FY2012 that amounted to over half of its 3 percent growth in revenue. The company is well funded for this strategy, but results from acquisitions are often unpredictable.

SECTOR: **Industrials**
BETA COEFFICIENT: **1.15**
10-YEAR COMPOUND EARNINGS PER SHARE GROWTH: **2.5%**
10-YEAR COMPOUND DIVIDENDS PER SHARE GROWTH: **5.5%**

	2005	2006	2007	2008	2009	2010	2011	2012
Revenues (mil)	27,653	31,367	34,589	36,556	30,908	33,370	36,500	37,665
Net income (mil)	1,736	2,078	2,444	2,792	2,153	2,342	2,998	3,552
Earnings per share	1.92	2.52	3.16	3.75	2.85	3.00	3.79	4.48
Dividends per share	0.83	0.91	1.00	1.10	1.21	1.21	1.37	1.53
Cash flow per share	2.93	3.59	4.39	5.03	4.07	4.27	5.11	5.72
Price: high	39.5	45.8	62.3	63.0	41.6	53.7	62.3	64.5
low	32.7	35.2	43.1	23.2	23.1	36.7	41.2	52.2

Honeywell International Inc.
101 Columbia Road
P.O. Box 2245
Morristown, NJ 07962–2245
(973) 455-2222
Website: www.honeywell.com

CONSERVATIVE GROWTH

Illinois Tool Works Inc.

❑ Ticker symbol: ITW (NYSE) ❑ S&P rating: A+ ❑ Value Line financial strength rating: A++
❑ Current yield: 2.4% ❑ Dividend raises, past 10 years: 10

Company Profile

Illinois Tool Works is a longstanding multinational conglomerate involved in the manufacture of a diversified range of industrial products, mainly components, fasteners, and other "ingredients" for manufacturers. Customers include the automotive, machinery, construction, food and beverage, and general industrial markets. The company currently operates some 800 decentralized and modestly sized business units in 58 countries, employing approximately 65,000. Some of the products are branded and familiar, like Wolf and Hobart kitchen equipment and Paslode air power tools; most are obscure and only known to others in their industries. Overseas sales account for about 59 percent of the total.

The company announced the divestiture of a majority interest in its Decorative Surfaces (countertops, etc.) business but continues to be organized into 8 major segments, each contributing fairly equally to revenue:

■ Industrial Packaging (14 percent of revenues) includes steel, plastic, and paper products used for bundling, shipping, and protecting goods in transit. Primary brands include Acme, Signode, Pabco, and Strapex. Major end markets served are primary metals, general industrial, construction, and food/beverage.

■ Specialty Products (14 percent) is a hodgepodge of businesses that includes Diagraph (industrial marking and coding systems), Fastex (engineered components for the appliance industry) and ZipPak reclosable plastic packaging.

■ Test & Measurement and Electronics (13 percent) supplies equipment and software for testing and measuring of materials, solder and other materials for PC board manufacturing and microelectronics assembly. Brands include Brooks Instrument, Bushler, Chemtronics, Instron, Magnaflux, and Speedline Technologies.

■ Automotive OEM (13 percent) includes transportation-related components, fasteners, and polymers, as well as truck remanufacturing and related parts and service for the automotive manufacturer market. Important brands include Deltar Interior Components, which makes things like interior door handles.

- Polymers and Fluids (13 percent) businesses produce adhesives, sealants, lubrication and cutting fluids, and hygiene products for an assortment of markets. Their brands include Futura, Krafft, Devcon, Rocol and Permatex and such brands as Raiu-X and Wynn's for the automotive aftermarket.

- Food Equipment (11 percent) produces commercial food equipment and related service, including professional kitchen ovens, refrigeration, mixers, and exhaust and ventilation systems. Major brands include Hobart, Traulsen, Vulcan, and Wolf.

- Construction Products (11 percent) concentrates on tools, fasteners, and other products for construction applications. Their major end markets are residential, commercial, and renovation construction. Brands include Ramset, Paslode, Buildex, and Proline.

- The Welding segment (11 percent of revenues) produces equipment and consumables associated with specialty power conversion, metallurgy, and electronics. Their primary products include arc-welding equipment and consumables, solder materials, equipment and services for electronics assembly, and airport ground support equipment. Primary brands include AXA Power, Hobart, and Weldcraft.

Financial Highlights, Fiscal Year 2012

ITW continues to enjoy its comeback from the Great Recession, and a greater health due to favorable trends in the auto industry and in U.S. manufacturing overall. FY2012 revenues grew about 9 percent, and per-share earnings turned in a similar performance. The company bought back some 7 percent of its outstanding shares and raised the dividend 6 percent, an investor-friendly use of the company's rather substantial cash flows. Since 2003, the company has reduced share count 24 percent even as the acquisition train rolls on.

The Decorative Surfaces divestiture and currency headwinds will moderate revenues for FY2013 to a projected 2 percent drop (2–4 percent higher without the divestiture). Earnings per share are projected to advance another 5 percent driven by slightly higher margins and continued share repurchases.

Reasons to Buy

Buying shares of ITW is like buying a mutual fund of medium-sized manufacturing businesses you've probably never heard of but would definitely like to own. The company is well diversified and serves many markets. The company has solid models for making acquisitions, and seems to do better than most conglomerates historically in choosing candidates and then managing them once they're in the fold. The company seems to do an equally good job of turning opportunity into cash flow and using that cash flow to enhance shareholder returns, as exemplified by the steady record of dividend increases each year since 1994. Finally, the balance sheet is strong, with long-term debt only 14 percent of total capital and net profit margins exceeding 10 percent, both healthy for the type of business(es) ITW is engaged in.

Reasons for Caution

ITW is by nature tied to some of the more volatile elements of the business cycle, so it may not be the best pick for investors living in fear of the next downturn. Conglomerates are notoriously difficult to manage (it's hard enough to manage one business, let alone 800); any sign of cracks in this structure should be taken seriously. While acquisitions are part of the growth strategy, the company, thus far, keeps them small and does not depend on acquiring other big names, but the disruptions of a big acquisition (which is unlikely) could pose problems.

SECTOR: **Industrials**
BETA COEFFICIENT: **1.16**
10-YEAR COMPOUND EARNINGS PER SHARE GROWTH: **7.0%**
10-YEAR COMPOUND DIVIDENDS PER SHARE GROWTH: **13.5%**

	2005	2006	2007	2008	2009	2010	2011	2012
Revenues (mil)	12,922	14,055	16,169	15,869	13,876	15,870	17,787	17,924
Net income (mil)	1,494	1,717	1,826	1,583	969	1,527	1,852	1,921
Earnings per share	2.60	3.01	3.36	3.05	1.93	3.03	3.74	4.06
Dividends per share	0.61	0.71	0.91	1.15	1.24	1.27	1.38	1.46
Cash flow per share	3.34	3.87	4.44	4.56	3.27	4.17	5.06	5.55
Price: high	47.3	53.5	60.0	55.6	51.2	52.7	59.3	63.3
low	39.3	41.5	45.6	28.5	25.6	40.3	39.1	47.4

Illinois Tool Works Inc.
3600 West Lake Avenue
Glenview, IL 60026
(847) 724-7500
Website: www.itwinc.com

CONSERVATIVE GROWTH

International Business Machines

❏ Ticker symbol: IBM (NYSE) ❏ S&P rating: AA ❏ Value Line financial strength rating: A++
❏ Current yield: 1.7% ❏ Dividend raises, past 10 years: 10

Company Profile

Big Blue is the world's leading provider of computer hardware and services. Really—we should say services and hardware. Get the drift? IBM makes a broad range of computers, mainframes, and network servers. But the company has morphed over the years into a software and services company; it is number 2 behind Microsoft in the software business. IBM is also an innovation and new product development leader, for years leading the world in the number of U.S. patents issued.

IBM is divided into 4 principal business units. The largest, at 38 percent of revenues, the Global Technology Services unit, is really an IT service, offering cloud computing, analytics, and other applications outsourcing. The Global Business Services unit (18 percent) is also a service unit but now provides its service on customer sites through consulting, application design, systems integration, and similar services. The Software unit (24 percent) supplies primarily "middleware" products that make everything in an IT environment work together. The Systems and Technology group, which is the unit that most closely harkens back to the "Big Iron" days, is now just 17 percent of the business. Finally, the Financing unit (2 percent) helps the company market it all.

It's not hard to see how the company has evolved from the old "Big Blue" maker of mainframes. They still produce high-margin commercial servers and enterprise-level installations, but in recent years, as a deliberate, and frankly, envied strategy, they have exited the lower-margin hardware businesses, such as consumer PCs, laptops, and hard drives.

Financial Highlights, Fiscal Year 2012

Big Blue has had an interesting revenue story for the past 8 years. Revenues go up, revenues go down, revenues stay flat—it doesn't seem to matter, as the earnings just keep rising year after year. FY2012 was a good example: Revenues dropped 2 percent, but operating margin rose 160 basis points and earnings climbed 5 percent. Per-share earnings rose a full 10 percent as the company bought back another 5 percent of its shares.

This is all a function of IBM's continuing strategy of shedding its marginally profitable business and expanding its business in growth areas, either organically or through acquisition.

Reasons to Buy

Once viewed as a teetering giant of the computer industry with a massive intellectual property portfolio but an uncertain product strategy, IBM has, over the past decade, successfully reinvented itself as a powerhouse in the Software and Services sector. Further, IBM seems positioned "where the puck is going" in the IT world, a fact not lost on HP and other competitors trying to emulate the business model. Not long ago, many companies felt they had to have in-house information technology departments to service their IT needs. Now, most have found that it's far more efficient to contract those services out to someone who can provide data warehousing, website development and maintenance, regional/national/global IT infrastructure, etc., without requiring a commitment in fixed assets. This is where IBM has leveraged their expertise, and as this trend continues and as businesses increase their reliance on these services, IBM benefits. As the common architecture becomes more cloud-like, we also feel IBM will benefit.

In an unusual move for the tech sector, IBM takes a long-term view of their business. They're working from a business strategy they put in place back in FY2000 and are still measuring their progress against goals that were set 13 years ago. Their goals for 2015 include $20 in per-share earnings, generating half of their profit from software, and delivering $70 billion in shareholder returns. Nobody does this, except IBM.

They began getting out of low-margin tech businesses long before it was the cool thing to do—in fact, they pretty much invented the idea. With that end in mind, they are in negotiations to sell their low-end server business to Lenovo, following their PC divestiture years ago. Since this move began in 2000, their pretax margins have increased from 10 percent to 22 percent, and their free cash flow has gone from $6.2 billion to $18.2 billion per year. Since 2000, more than 50 percent of this $237 billion in cash has gone to share repurchases and another 12 percent has gone to dividends.

They continue to innovate and are in a great position to acquire whatever technology they choose not to develop internally. They have world-class semiconductor design and production facilities and license their design, manufacturing, and packaging services and products.

While all IT companies are vulnerable to economic cycles, IBM services income is largely based on long-term contracts, which are not as subject to the vagaries of the world economy as would be sales of hardware alone.

Reasons for Caution

IBM has carved out a very large chunk of the outsourced IT business. Innovation in this area can be rapid and disruptive, and margins can shrink precipitously as a result. IBM will have to stay ahead of the curve with innovative and compelling products and defensive product strategies in order to maintain revenue growth.

Competition in the services area is heating up, with Hewlett-Packard's purchase of EDS and Oracle's acquisition of Sun Microsystems. These two moves have created competitors with strong synergies and a compelling sales pitch to new and existing customers.

Finally, IBM has a larger exposure to governments and government contracts than many of its competitors. While this can be stabilizing in hard times, this time we feel that a massive and widespread public sector belt tightening could hurt the company.

SECTOR: **Information Technology**
BETA COEFFICIENT: **0.85**
10-YEAR COMPOUND EARNINGS PER SHARE GROWTH: **12.0%**
10-YEAR COMPOUND DIVIDENDS PER SHARE GROWTH: **18.0%**

	2005	2006	2007	2008	2009	2010	2011	2012
Revenues (bil)	91.1	91.4	98.8	103.6	95.8	99.9	106.9	104.5
Net income (bil)	8.5	9.4	10.4	12.3	13.4	14.8	15.9	16.6
Earnings per share	5.22	6.01	7.18	8.93	10.01	11.52	13.06	14.37
Dividends per share	0.78	1.10	1.50	1.90	2.15	2.50	2.90	3.30
Cash flow per share	8.71	9.56	11.28	13.28	14.11	16.01	17.77	19.04
Price: high	99.1	97.4	121.5	130.9	132.3	147.5	194.9	211.8
low	71.8	72.7	88.8	69.5	81.8	116.0	146.6	177.3

International Business Machines Corporation
New Orchard Road
Armonk, NY 10504
(800) 426-4968
Website: www.ibm.com

CONSERVATIVE GROWTH

International Paper Company

◻ Ticker symbol: IP (NYSE) ◻ S&P rating: BBB ◻ Value Line financial strength rating: B+ ◻ Current yield: 2.5% ◻ Dividend raises, past 10 years: 4

Company Profile

International Paper Company (International Paper), incorporated in 1941, is a global paper and packaging company complemented by a North American merchant distribution system with primary markets and manufacturing operations in North America, Europe, Latin America, Russia, Asia, and North Africa.

The company acquired rival Temple-Inland in mid-2012, expanding its packaging material capacity and customer base. By the end of 2012, the company operated 28 pulp, paper, and packaging mills (up from 20 in 2011), 187 converting and packaging plants (up from 142), 18 recycling plants (same), and 3 bag facilities (also the same), all in the United States. Production facilities in Europe, Asia, Latin America, and South America include 11 pulp, paper, and packaging mills, 65 converting and packaging plants, and 2 recycling plants.

The company operates in 3 segments (with FY2012 sales in parenthesis): Industrial Packaging (69 percent), Printing Papers (20 percent), and Consumer Packaging (12 percent), with distribution and forestry divisions supporting the 3 product segments. The Temple acquisition shifted the product mix approximately 8 percent towards Industrial Packaging from Printing Papers.

The Industrial Packaging segment produces containerboard, including linerboard, whitetop, recycled linerboard, and saturating craft. About 80 percent of the company's production (70 percent before Temple) is converted into corrugated boxes and other packaging. The company also recycles a million tons of corrugated, mixed, and white paper through 21 recycling plants.

The Printing Papers segment produces uncoated printing and writing papers, including papers for use in copiers, desktop and laser printers, and digital imaging. Market pulp is used in the manufacture of printing, writing, and specialty papers; towel and tissue products; and filtration products. Pulp is also converted into nonpaper products such as diapers and sanitary napkins.

The Consumer Packaging segment produces somewhat finer materials including bleached sulfate board for making packaging for food, cosmetics, pharmaceuticals, etc.

In early 2013 the company reached an agreement to sell the Temple-Inland Building Products division for $750 million, or about 20 percent of the original Temple purchase price.

Financial Highlights, Fiscal Year 2012

The company has recovered nicely from a very sharp 2008–09 dip related to the recession. During that time the dividend was cut by two-thirds and the share price dropped almost 90 percent, quite a wild ride for investors. While the company did have to borrow to fund some operations, it never reported a loss even during this down cycle. In FY2011, earnings recovered to $1.29 billion on sales of $26 billion, both levels that far exceeded annual sales and earnings in the peak prerecession year of 2007. Then Temple came along, and though it promises about $300 million in cost-savings synergies, acquisition costs and a softer margin environment brought earnings down again. FY2012 sales rose about 7 percent, consistent with the Temple acquisition. However, earnings and per-share earnings dropped substantially. The good news: Realized synergies should drive earnings up about 15 percent in FY2013 and 10 percent more in FY2014. The recession spawned a number of cost-savings moves, which could lead to a stronger upside if paper prices strengthen, but market conditions may continue to be a headwind. The dividend was raised 10 percent in FY2012 to an all-time high, indicating management's confidence in the long-term prospects for the business and orientation towards shareholders. The strong cash flows certainly support that move, although we'd like to see the company resume its share buyback program, too.

Reasons to Buy

We still like to include a few turnaround situations, because patient investors can be amply rewarded by well-executed turnarounds. Indeed, the company has recovered well from its black eye received in the Great Recession. Brands, supply chains, customers, channels, and general operational and market experience are already in place; the company just needs to prune the dead branches and make it all work. The company completed much of this "tree work" successfully and just added the Temple-Inland "tree" to its forest. Now that that acquisition is·complete, the company is likely to return to improving margins through marketing and operational improvements; that's probably a good place to be going forward. Continued international expansion probably makes sense, and the company has recently made some small plays in Brazil and Turkey. We think the company is well managed, is a solid player in a fairly steady industry, and is oriented toward returning cash to shareholders.

Reasons for Caution

Based on its price ($4.3 billion), core commodity business, and recent results, the Temple-Inland acquisition may have been expensive, but it bodes well for market share and ultimately pricing power down the road. For the most part,

IP is in a commodity business with a high reliance on corrugated boards and raw packaging materials, and the company will have to overcome that stigma—by adding value to its products and international presence. We are also concerned that enhanced Internet experiences and tablet devices may be reducing the amount of computer-generated printing, but that only affects a segment accounting for 20 percent of the business. Cost-reduction initiatives may prove unable to keep up with soft market conditions.

SECTOR: **Materials**
BETA COEFFICIENT: **2.21**
10-YEAR COMPOUND EARNINGS PER SHARE GROWTH: **5.0%**
10-YEAR COMPOUND DIVIDENDS PER SHARE GROWTH: **-1.0%**

	2005	2006	2007	2008	2009	2010	2011	2012
Revenues (mil)	24,097	21,995	21,890	24,829	23,366	25,179	26,034	27,833
Net income (mil)	513	635	963	829	378	644	1,292	749
Earnings per share	1.06	2.18	2.70	1.96	0.88	1.48	2.96	1.70
Dividends per share	1.00	1.00	1.00	1.00	0.33	0.40	0.98	1.09
Cash flow per share	3.85	3.63	4.15	5.02	4.27	4.78	6.00	5.08
Price: high	42.6	38.0	41.6	33.8	27.8	29.3	33.0	39.9
low	27.0	30.7	31.0	10.2	3.9	19.3	21.5	27.3

International Paper Company
6400 Poplar Avenue
Memphis, TN 38197
(901) 419-4957
Website: www.internationalpaper.com

Iron Mountain Incorporated

❏ Ticker symbol: IRM (NYSE) ❏ S&P rating: BB- ❏ Value Line financial strength rating: B ❏ Current yield: 3.1% ❏ Dividend raises, past 10 years: 3

Company Profile

The name implies security and invulnerability, and as such, Iron Mountain is the world's leading provider of secure record, document, and information-management services. Businesses that require off-site, secure storage, and/or archiving of data contract with IRM.

In general, IRM provides 3 major types of service: records management, data protection and recovery, and information destruction. All 3 services include both physical and electronic media.

Revenues accrue to the company mainly through 2 streams—storage and services. Storage revenues consist of recurring per-unit charges related to the storage of material or data. The storage periods are typically many years, and the revenues from this service account for just over half of IRM's total revenue over the past 5 years. Service revenue comes from charges for any number of services, including those related to the core storage service and others such as temporary access, courier operations, secure destruction, data recovery, media conversion, and the like.

In 2012 the company added a third source of revenue—rental space for third-party data centers, both as standalone systems and as co-locations for current storage customers. The same traits that make for good storage (cool, dark spaces with controlled ventilation and a high level of physical security) also make an excellent environment for servers.

Although its roots are in document management, the company offers digital archiving and services, which are analogous to the services done for paper, except that they are done for e-mail, e-statements, images, and other electronic documents. It also includes web-based archiving of computer, server, and website data, as well as storage of backup or disaster-recovery digital media. The company sold a portion of this business to HP's Autonomy in early 2011 but continues to offer these services through partnerships. IRM also offers tailored industry-specific services for industries such as health care. The company also offers value-add services in organizing, indexing, and facilitating search through documents and records.

IRM's client base is deep and diverse. They have over 90,000 clients, including 94 percent of the *Fortune* 1,000 and over 90 percent of the FTSE 100. They have over 1,000 facilities in 165 markets worldwide, and they are 6 times the size of their nearest competitor. The company has strengthened its competitive position by acquiring some 44 smaller competitors in local markets since 1998.

Financial Highlights, Fiscal Year 2012

The company's financial picture is in flux at the moment, so year/year comparisons may not be entirely meaningful. As part of its conversion to a new capital structure, the company is undergoing a number of one-time charges, the exclusion of which will make comps difficult. Nonetheless, we can say that Iron Mountain's business level has remained basically flat over the period of 2008 through 2012. Earnings in FY2012 (absent the aforementioned one-time charges) were up only slightly on operating margin. The company has raised its dividend to $0.98 and repurchased some 7 percent of its outstanding shares.

Reasons to Buy

When President Eisenhower signed into law the Cigar Excise Tax Extension of 1960 (a more sweeping protection from cheap Cuban imports coming just a few years later), included was an amendment that gave small investors the ability to directly participate in large portfolios of income-producing real estate. Prior to that, investing in hotels and the like was a game strictly for large institutions. The legislation enabled the creation of the REIT (real estate investment trust), an organizing structure for companies that derive at least 75 percent of their income from real estate, typically in the form of rents.

Iron Mountain has initiated the process of restructuring itself as an REIT. If they gain IRS approval, the company will begin operating as an REIT on January 1, 2014. They then have a year to disgorge all of their accumulated earnings and profits (about $1.5 billion) to shareholders in the form of dividends. Sounds like an opportunity for the investor, but there are some real risks to consider.

REITs have some interesting features. For one, an REIT has to distribute 90 percent of its earnings to its shareholders in the form of dividends. In return, the REIT is not taxed on any of those earnings. Thus the company can cut its tax bill dramatically—in rough numbers, IRM would have saved about $120 million on its FY2012 tax bill. The REIT structure also allows the company to repatriate cash held in foreign accounts without paying U.S. taxes on it. For many companies, this is the reason to convert, and for investors, a potential windfall.

For most of us, the dividend increases will be very welcome. We can expect significant expansion of the dividend after the restructuring, and we believe the share price will also increase well above its recent price of $39/share. Since the recession, REITs have beaten the growth in the S&P 500 by over 220 percent. This optimism is reflected in the current price, as the current P/E ratio is over 35. Get in early, we think.

Reasons for Caution

The biggest risks for the IRM investor involve the conversion to an REIT. First, the IRS may not approve the application. Second, after approval, IRM will have to spend a fair amount of money on this conversion process, some $400 million over the course of a few years. Finally, Congress may in the future make some material changes to the REIT laws that could have the effect of invalidating all of the advantages that IRM envisioned as part of the REIT conversion.

Another complication is the issue of debt. An REIT cannot deduct the interest it pays on debt financing, so Iron Mountain will be busy retiring debt and issuing new equity in the form of shares. Issuing shares will dilute the base, so the company will issue these shares gradually, even as it buys back shares (at market) to stabilize the price. This process will also put a strain on capital and will take several years.

SECTOR: **Information Technology**
BETA COEFFICIENT: **0.95**
5-YEAR COMPOUND EARNINGS PER SHARE GROWTH: **14.5%**
10-YEAR COMPOUND DIVIDENDS PER SHARE GROWTH: **NM**

		2005	2006	2007	2008	2009	2010	2011	2012
Revenues (mil)		2,078	2,350	2,730	3,055	3,014	3,127	3,027	3,005
Net income (mil)		114	129	153	152	195	230	255	215
Earnings per share		0.57	0.64	0.76	0.78	0.96	1.15	1.25	1.25
Dividends per share		—	—	—	—	—	0.34	0.86	0.98
Cash flow per share		1.52	1.69	2.01	2.19	2.55	2.75	3.25	2.95
Price:	high	27.6	27.5	35.7	34.1	29.4	26.2	32.9	35.5
	low	16.3	20.8	23.0	15.3	15.5	18.3	22.3	24.9

Iron Mountain Incorporated
745 Atlantic Avenue
Boston, MA 02111
Website: www.ironmountain.com

AGGRESSIVE GROWTH

Itron, Inc.

❏ Ticker symbol: ITRI (NASDAQ) ❏ S&P rating: BB ❏ Value Line financial strength rating: B+
❏ Current yield: Nil ❏ Dividend raises, past 10 years: NA

Company Profile

Itron is the world's largest provider of standard and intelligent metering systems for residential and commercial gas, electric, and water usage. Intelligent meters, in addition to tracking raw usage over a period of time, can also measure at the point of use operating parameters such as pressure, temperature, voltage, phase, etc. This information can be extremely valuable to the supplying utility but has in the past been difficult and expensive to obtain.

Itron supplies a range of products from basic meters that are read manually to meters that act as network devices and transmit their data in real time to the managing utility and/or to the consuming customer. Products and systems are produced and sold in 3 groupings:

- Standard metering—basic meters that measure electricity, gas, or water flow by electrical or mechanical means, with displays but no built-in remote reading or transmission capability.
- Advanced metering—these units, depending on the country and the communications technologies available—transmit usage data remotely through telephone, cellular, radio frequency (RF), Ethernet, or power line carrier paths. Among other value-adds, these meters transmit usage data for billing, thereby eliminating the need for on-site meter reading—a big savings for utility companies.
- Smart metering—smart meters collect and store interval data and other detailed info, receive commands, and interface with other devices through assorted communication paths to thermostats, smart appliances, and home network and other advanced control systems.

Itron also sells a range of software platforms for utilities and building managers for the management of the installed base and the analysis and optimization of usage, and it is active in developing so-called "smart grid" solutions for utilities and utility networks. The company also markets advanced metering initiative (AMI) contracts to utilities, where it installs devices and monitors and optimizes power usage for a utility.

The company was founded in 1977 and in 2004 acquired the electric meter operations of Schlumberger, which at the time was the largest global supplier of this equipment. At present, electric meters represent about 47 percent of the business, gas meters about 29 percent, and water meters the remaining 24 percent. The company has about 8,000 customers in 130 countries, and about 52 percent of the business comes from overseas. The company recently acquired SmartSynch, a provider of metering and communications systems using cellular technology.

Financial Highlights, Fiscal Year 2012

As expected when we added this company to the list last year, revenues and earnings slumped a bit in FY2012 because of the completion of 5 major advanced metering initiative, or AMI, contracts. Aside from these contract completions, which sliced about $150 million in revenues from 5 key customers, revenues advanced about 6 percent. These developments, combined with some cost-saving restructuring, some uncertainty about the renewal of R & D tax credits, and R & D efforts for the next generation of products have slowed the company down in the first part

of 2013 but probably represent a cyclical low. FY2013 revenues are projected in the $2.0–$2.1 billion range and earnings between $3.00 and $3.25—essentially a flat year. But 2014 looks better: Contracts with major U.S. customers and a possible contract with Tokyo Electric for 27 million smart meters all suggest better results for the year.

Reasons to Buy

Can you picture a day when you might manage your energy consumption, device by device, in your home using your smartphone? Even if you're away from home? And the day when utilities can monitor usage in real time to shift supply of a resource like electricity that virtually cannot be stored? Where solar energy generated from one locale on a sunny day is moved to another with clouds and rain?

If you believe that the need for managed energy efficiency will only grow in the future, Itron is a good place to be. As utilities modernize, reduce costs, and replace infrastructure, Itron products and networks will be in the sweet spot. Internationally, utilities are adding infrastructure, as well as replacing it, and Itron is positioned well for that, too. Worldwide, only about 12 percent of 2.5 billion meters are "smart" or "advanced."

Conceptually, these ideas make for a fine story, but as with so many similar companies they retain the question, "Yeah, but does this company make money?" In Itron's case, even though it is in a flat spot currently, the answer in general is yes, with decent earnings and especially cash flows even now, and we think this company will do better as time goes on and more utility infrastructure is replaced. This technology, and its cost savings, is proven. Over time, this company, like the utility industry it supports, has been relatively stable for a technology stock, and at recent prices, the stock continues to look like a good growth holding to sock away for the future. At the same time, while there is no dividend for the moment, the company has been repurchasing shares and has authorized a 2 million share repurchase—which would represent about 5 percent of the float.

Reasons for Caution

Companies that sell good ideas don't always grow, particularly if the size of their markets is limited or they are particularly conservative about spending money; that might describe the utility industry, which has been spending money on a lot of other things lately, including new gas-fired plants. Energy credits and subsidies are always subject to change. Finally, we cited as one of our reasons for caution last year a "jargony" and confusing website that didn't add much to our (or a customer's) understanding of the company and its products. Happily (and now more of a reason to buy than a reason for caution), the company has upgraded its website with new "solutions" and "products & services" pages among others—much better!

SECTOR: **Information Technology**
BETA COEFFICIENT: **1.66**
10-YEAR COMPOUND EARNINGS PER SHARE GROWTH: **14.0%**
10-YEAR COMPOUND DIVIDENDS PER SHARE GROWTH: **NA**

		2005	2006	2007	2008	2009	2010	2011	2012
Revenues (mil)		553	644	1,464	1,909	1,687	2,259	2,434	2,178
Net income (mil)		20.3	56.4	87.3	117.6	44.3	133.9	156.3	130.5
Earnings per share		1.84	2.16	2.78	3.36	1.15	3.27	3.85	3.25
Dividends per share		—	—	—	—	—	—	—	—
Cash flow per share		2.34	2.79	4.24	4.96	2.53	4.85	5.56	4.85
Price:	high	53.9	73.7	112.9	109.3	69.5	81.9	64.4	50.3
	low	21.5	39.4	51.2	34.3	40.1	52.0	26.9	33.3

Itron, Inc.
2111 North Moller Rd.
Liberty Lake, WA 99019
(509) 924-9900
Website: www.itron.com

The J. M. Smucker Company

❑ Ticker symbol: SJM (NYSE) ❑ S&P rating: NA ❑ Value Line financial strength rating: A+
❑ Current yield: 2.2% ❑ Dividend raises, past 10 years: 10

Company Profile

"With a name like Smucker's, it has to be good!" This ad jingle says it all about this eastern Ohio–based firm, a leading manufacturer of jams, jellies, and other processed foods for years. Thanks in large part to divestitures from the Procter & Gamble food division and other companies, it has grown itself into a premier player in the packaged food industry.

Smucker manufactures and markets products under its own name, as well as under a number of other household names such as Crisco, Folgers, Laura Scudder's, Hungry Jack, Eagle, Pillsbury, Jif (why not sell the peanut butter if they sell the jelly?) and, naturally, Goober (a combination of peanut butter and jelly in a single jar). The company also produces and distributes Dunkin' Donuts and Folgers coffee and produces an assortment of cooking oils, toppings, juices, and baking ingredients. The company has revitalized such brands as Folgers and Jif through improved marketing, channel relationships, and better focus on the success of these brands. Overall, the company aims to sell the number one brand in the various markets it serves. Operations are centered in the United States, Canada, and Europe, with about 10 percent of sales coming from overseas.

Even as a nearly $6 billion a year enterprise, the company still retains the feel of a family business, with brothers Tim and Richard Smucker sharing the CEO responsibilities as chairman and president respectively.

Financial Highlights, Fiscal Year 2012

Smucker reversed last year's drop in earnings with strong growth in their beverage lines. Revenues and earnings were both up 9 percent, due in part to reduced input costs (following 2 straight years of increases). The company's K-Cup products in their own brands continue to slug it out in a very competitive, but still very profitable, single-serving market. Earnings here will need to be watched. The company continues to make significant increases in the dividend and reinvest in its own shares, much to the delight of your authors.

The company extended the geography and brand base in 2012 with a couple of strategic acquisitions. In January it acquired a majority of the Sara Lee North American foodservice coffee and beverage business, and in March it acquired a 25 percent equity interest in a manufacturer and marketer of oats products headquartered in China. The company has been buying back some shares since a twofold increase related to the P&G acquisitions in 2008—between 2 and 5 percent of shares outstanding since then—so earnings per share increased about 3 percent during FY2011. Cash flows remained strong, over $7 per share, supporting the dividend, buybacks, and the share price.

Reasons to Buy

This is a very well-managed company with an excellent reputation in its markets. In recent years, it has a proven track record in buying and revitalizing key brands, the most prominent being former Procter & Gamble food brands and International Multifoods brands. We expect this trend to continue. The company's aggressive moves into coffee and other beverages were well timed and have provided a boost to the bottom line. They have ramped up marketing efforts significantly in support of 90 new products introduced in FY2012, offering very aggressive promotions at the consumer level.

Cash flow is very strong in this vertically integrated producer. Cash flow per share has more than doubled in the past 5 years and should double again in the next 4. This is a promising scenario for a company that has shown a taste and talent for acquisitions as of late. The base for steady growth is well established over the long term. Steady and safe: Smucker is the peanut butter and jelly sandwich of the investing landscape.

Reasons for Caution

The prepared food business is very sensitive in the short term to commodity and energy costs. As the company relies more and more on coffee products for earnings growth, it will find itself exposed to instability in the cost of raw materials and transportation. Yes, these are costs that also affect all of their competitors, but Smucker is in competition with a number of low-margin brands and has customers (such as Walmart) who have enormous buying power. Smucker will need to rely on brand strength and breadth should the economy slow again.

Also, the company currently trades at nearly 19 times forward earnings, which is high in this industry. The stock has been bought up in the past couple of quarters, but we feel it has room to move. Still, a buyer might benefit by waiting until the shares are back in the double digits before moving in.

SECTOR: **Consumer Staples**
BETA COEFFICIENT: **0.70**
10-YEAR COMPOUND EARNINGS PER SHARE GROWTH: **13.5%**
10-YEAR COMPOUND DIVIDENDS PER SHARE GROWTH: **10.5%**

	2005	**2006**	**2007**	**2008**	**2009**	**2010**	**2011**	**2012E**
Revenues (mil)	2,155	2,148	2,525	3,758	4,605	4,826	5,526	5,900E
Net income (mil)	155.1	164.6	178.9	321.4	520.3	566.5	535.6	570E
Earnings per share	2.65	2.89	3.15	3.77	4.15	4.79	4.73	5.25E
Dividends per share	1.08	1.14	1.22	1.31	1.40	1.68	1.88	2.04
Cash flow per share	3.97	3.94	4.42	3.73	5.60	7.06	6.75	7.60E
Price: high	51.7	50.0	64.3	56.7	62.7	66.3	80.3	89.4
low	43.6	37.2	46.6	37.2	34.1	53.3	61.2	70.5

The J. M. Smucker Company
One Strawberry Lane
Orrville, OH 44667
(330) 682-3000
Website: www.smuckers.com

GROWTH AND INCOME

Johnson & Johnson

❑ Ticker symbol: JNJ (NYSE) ❑ S&P rating: AAA ❑ Value Line financial strength rating: A++
❑ Current yield: 3.2 percent ❑ Dividend raises, past 10 years: 10

Company Profile

With FY2012 sales of $67 billion, Johnson & Johnson is the largest and most comprehensive health-care company in the world. JNJ offers a broad line of consumer products and over-the-counter drugs, as well as various other medical devices and diagnostic equipment.

The company has 3 reporting segments: Consumer Health Care ($14.4 billion in FY2012 sales), Medical Devices and Diagnostics ($27 billion), and Pharmaceuticals ($25 billion). In those segments, Johnson & Johnson has more than 275 operating companies in 60 countries, selling some 50,000 products in more than 175 countries. Among Johnson & Johnson's premier assets are its well-entrenched brand names, which are widely known in the United States as well as abroad. And as a marketer, JNJ's reputation for quality has enabled it to build strong ties to commercial health-care providers.

The company has a stake in a wide variety of health segments: anti-infectives, biotechnology, cardiology and circulatory diseases, diagnostics, gastrointestinals, minimally invasive therapies, nutraceuticals, orthopedics, pain management, skin care, vision care, women's health, and wound care.

The company's vast portfolio of well-known trade names includes Band-Aid adhesive bandages; Tylenol; Stayfree, Carefree, and Sure & Natural feminine hygiene products; Mylanta; Pepcid AC; Motrin; Sudafed; Zyrtec; Neosporin; Neutrogena; Johnson's baby powder, shampoo, and oil; Listerine; and Reach toothbrushes.

The company is typically fairly active with acquisitions, acquiring small niche players to strengthen its overall product offering. In 2012, J&J completed its acquisition of trauma devices maker Synthes for $21.3 billion by merging it with the company's existing DuPuy operation.

Financial Highlights, Fiscal Year 2012

Johnson & Johnson has a dominant and stable franchise in a secure and lucrative industry. We like the model of steady, recurring income from solid consumer brands such as Tylenol combined with more aggressive and lucrative ventures into pharmaceuticals and surgical products. In 2012 the company generated 25 percent of sales from products introduced in the past 5 years.

The company's revenue and earnings performance continues to be a bit softer than most investors would like, and 2012 was no exception to the longer-term trend. Revenues grew 8.5 percent, earnings just slightly under that at 8.0 percent. The company faced a number of hurdles in 2012 with a strong dollar, continued effects of the McNeil products (Tylenol and others) being produced under a consent decree following a recall, and a decision to exit certain stent markets. Still, the fourth quarter showed broad-based gains that brought the year to a close slightly ahead of most estimates, and these gains have grown larger still in early FY2013.

Reasons to Buy

A term we don't hear much anymore in the investment arena is *blue chip*. A name taken from the highest-value poker chip on the table, it was used to describe a stock into which you could put your money without fear. A blue-chip stock was where you put money that you would normally put in a bank, if banks would only pay dividends and occasionally offer you more than a toaster as an incentive to stick around. Johnson & Johnson has been a blue chip for as long as there have been blue chips. In 2012 and into early 2013, the company has added a new wrinkle to the appeal—share price increases of nearly 30 percent. Our recommendation last year highlighted their growth in international markets and continued high yield, but acknowledged their "modest growth prospects." We still think JNJ is fundamentally a conservatively run company whose growth prospects are on the lower end of this book's scale, but clearly the company, even trading at a 14 multiple, has great appeal in the investment community. And even if it's more often unexciting for the growth and momentum investor, JNJ's business model reminds us of the blue chips—steady earnings and cash flow combined with a healthy dividend and share repurchases, leading to very gratifying total shareholder returns. Dividends, by the way, have not only been raised 10 consecutive years, but the increases are substantial, 5–10 percent or more each year with another 15 percent expected over the next two years (are your wage increases this large?). We feel that JNJ is rock solid with modest growth prospects and little long-term downside.

Reasons for Caution

The U.S. government is considering fines against JNJ for problems with their sales practices. The fines may reach $2 billion, but the real concern is that language in the government's findings may leave the door open for private lawsuits. With $20 billion cash on hand, the sharks will circle. Final documents were issued in the summer of 2013—the wise investor will want to keep an eye on this.

SECTOR: **Health Care**
BETA COEFFICIENT: **0.65**
10-YEAR COMPOUND EARNINGS PER SHARE GROWTH: **11.0%**
10-YEAR COMPOUND DIVIDENDS PER SHARE GROWTH: **13.0%**

		2005	2006	2007	2008	2009	2010	2011	2012
Revenues (mil)		50,514	53,324	61,095	63,747	61,897	61,587	65,030	67,224
Net income (mil)		10,411	11,053	10,576	12,949	12,906	13,279	13,867	14,345
Earnings per share		3.35	3.73	4.15	4.57	4.63	4.76	5.00	5.10
Dividends per share		1.28	1.46	1.62	1.80	1.93	2.11	2.25	2.40
Cash flow per share		4.25	4.60	5.23	5.70	5.69	5.90	6.25	6.45
Price:	high	70.0	69.4	68.8	72.8	65.9	66.2	66.3	72.7
	low	59.8	56.6	59.7	52.1	61.9	56.9	64.3	61.7

Johnson & Johnson
One Johnson & Johnson Plaza
New Brunswick, NJ 08933
(800) 950-5089
Website: www.jnj.com

Johnson Controls Inc.

❑ Ticker symbol: JCI (NYSE) ❑ S&P rating: BBB+ ❑ Value Line financial strength rating: A
❑ Current yield: 2.2% ❑ Dividend raises, past 10 years: 9

Company Profile

Johnson Controls is a fairly low-profile U.S. manufacturer with 3 principal businesses that just now happen to all be in favor for the first time in years. JCI is a large manufacturer of automotive parts and subassemblies, heating ventilation and air conditioning (HVAC) and other energy controls, and an assortment of battery technologies and products. Their products are found in more than 12 million homes, 1 million commercial buildings, and are installed in more than 30 million new vehicles every year. Their business operates in 3 segments: Automotive Experience, Building Efficiency, and Power Solutions.

Their automotive business (51 percent of FY2012 revenues, 46 percent of profits) is one of the world's largest automotive suppliers, providing seating and overhead systems, door systems, floor consoles, instrument panels, cockpits, and integrated electronics. Customers include virtually every major automaker in the world, including newer start ups and plants in China. The business produces automotive interior systems for original equipment manufacturers (OEMs) and operates in 29 countries worldwide. Additionally, the business has partially owned affiliates in Asia, Europe, North America, and South America. In March 2012, the company said that it had retained outside consultants to explore the option of selling off its automotive interior electronics business, primarily responsible for displays and phone link products.

Building Efficiency (35 percent of revenues, 35 percent of profits) is a global leader in delivering integrated control systems, mechanical equipment, services, and solutions designed to improve the comfort, safety, and energy efficiency of nonresidential buildings and residential properties with operations in more than 125 countries. Revenues come from facilities management, technical services, and the replacement and upgrade of controls/HVAC mechanical equipment in the existing buildings and "smart buildings" market.

The Power Solutions business (14 percent of revenues, 33 percent of profits) produces lead-acid automotive batteries, serving both automotive original equipment manufacturers and the general vehicle battery aftermarket. They also offer absorbent glass mat (AGM), nickel metal hydride, and lithium-ion battery technologies to power hybrid vehicles.

Financial Highlights, Fiscal Year 2012

Last year we said that Johnson Controls was in the right place at the right time with all 3 of its businesses. While we still believe that was true, Europe in 2012 turned out to be the wrong place all of the time, and JCI (and all other automotive suppliers) got no love from across the pond. After a terrific 2011 performance driven by the recovery in the U.S. auto industry, we all had high hopes that Europe would turn around as well, but some of the EU countries decided they'd rather walk than drive.

JCI's revenue grew a mere 2.5 percent, while earnings ticked up 4.5 percent. Not terrible, but definitely not what we were expecting when we gave JCI a strong recommendation last year. If there's a bright side, it's that a good portion of JCI's 4.5 percent came from improvements in operating efficiency, which will help down the road. Other good news came from the company's Power Solutions operations, which is experiencing higher than expected growth in volume while also maintaining its position as the company's most profitable segment (on a percentage basis).

Reasons to Buy

JCI was one of the great recovery stories coming out of the Great Recession, with revenues increasing 40 percent in 2 years and share price quadrupling in just over 3 quarters. This rapid growth was driven largely by renewed confidence in the health of the U.S. automobile industry. That confidence has borne out, but the European market and manufacturing base are still lagging. JCI's FY2012 was essentially flat and the first 3 quarters of FY2013 are likely the same, but prospects for a turnaround in the European market in calendar 2014 are encouraging.

Domestic automobile purchases are on the rebound, and in a big way. Light vehicle purchases in the U.S. have increased by 1.5 million units per year since late 2009. The most recent sustained average (prior to the financial crisis) was during 2003–2007 where sales averaged 17 million units per year. We're now close to 15 million/year, still 2 million under what looks like the new steady run rate. Considering that the average age of cars on the road is still increasing and auto financing has never been easier, it could be hard to argue against 18 million units/year by the end of 2014. Add in growth in emerging markets, and you might be sitting pretty on a Johnson seat.

The company recently added 30 percent capacity to its automated facility in China to keep up with local demand for air-conditioning units. They are also building a second automotive battery factory in (where else?) China.

Finally, growth in share value from auto parts suppliers have outpaced the S&P by over 200 percent over the first two quarters of FY2013, and JCI's FY2013 EPS projections have been revised upward to $2.60–$2.70, ahead of last year's performance.

Reasons for Caution

If we haven't emphasized enough what a haunted house the European auto market is, then we aren't doing our job. Remember that entire countries have been saved from the brink of collapse, but not by much. Many Europeans, assuming they can afford gas, are not going to be replacing their cars as often as they used to. Is this a permanent condition? Not likely, and the truth is that many of the countries most affected were not big car markets to begin with. Nonetheless, the current European Union economic landscape may be with us for a while longer than we expect.

SECTOR: **Industrials**
BETA COEFFICIENT: **1.30**
10-YEAR COMPOUND EARNINGS PER SHARE GROWTH: **7.5%**
10-YEAR COMPOUND DIVIDENDS PER SHARE GROWTH: **12.0%**

	2005	2006	2007	2008	2009	2010	2011	2012
Revenues (mil)	27,883	32,235	34,624	38,062	28,497	34,305	40,833	41,995
Net income (mil)	909	1,028	1,252	1,400	281	1,365	1,665	1,749
Earnings per share	1.50	1.75	2.09	2.33	0.47	2.00	2.42	2.54
Dividends per share	0.33	0.37	0.44	0.52	0.52	0.52	0.68	0.74
Cash flow per share	2.60	2.95	3.34	3.63	1.48	3.00	3.45	3.70
Price: high	25.1	30.0	44.5	36.5	28.3	40.2	42.9	35.9
low	17.5	22.1	28.1	13.6	8.4	25.6	24.3	23.4

Johnson Controls Inc.
P. O. Box 591
Milwaukee, WI 53201–0591
(414) 524-2375
Website: www.johnsoncontrols.com

GROWTH AND INCOME

Kellogg Company

❏ Ticker symbol: K (NYSE) ❏ S&P rating: BBB+ ❏ Value Line financial strength rating: A ❏ Current yield: 2.5% ❏ Dividend raises, past 10 years: 9

Company Profile

Founded in 1906, Kellogg is the world's leading producer of breakfast cereal and convenience foods, including cookies, crackers, toaster pastries, cereal bars, frozen waffles, meat alternatives, and pie crusts. The company's brands include Kellogg's, Keebler, Pop-Tarts, Eggo, Cheez-It, Nutri-Grain, Rice Krispies, Murray, Austin, Morningstar Farms, Famous Amos, Kashi, and, as of June 2012, Pringles. The company sells most of these brands in overseas markets.

The company operates in 2 segments: Kellogg North America (NA) and Kellogg International, with International generating about 37 percent of revenue. NA operations are further divided into Cereals, Snacks, and Frozen/Specialty categories. The company produces more than 1,500 different products, manufactured in 19 countries and marketed in more than 180 countries around the world. The company operates manufacturing facilities in 16 countries in addition to the United States.

Financial Highlights, Fiscal Year 2012

Ongoing financials for FY2012 were somewhat mixed—although sales were better than expected (up nearly 8 percent), income was flat due to continued cost inflation in raw materials, mainly due to weather conditions and spiky transportation costs. The company took this opportunity to make investments in the brands and in internal process improvements, with results expected in 2014.

Reasons to Buy

Kellogg owns just over a third of the U.S. market for ready-to-eat cereals, which makes them the most recognized brand and market leader in the most mature food category in the world. They continue to respond to customer demand for new and interesting products, many with a health bent, with various new versions of Mueslix, Granola, Special K, and other brands.

In 2012 the company completed only its second major purchase in the past 20 years (the other being Keebler in 2001). The acquisition of the Pringles brand from Procter & Gamble vaulted the company into a new realm of the snack food business, tripling its international snack revenues. The product is available in over 80 flavors, including regional favorites. The popularity of the product is expected to open up new distribution channels for other Kellogg products, particularly in Europe and Asia.

We like Kellogg's growth in international markets. Special K is growing at double-digit rates internationally and at triple-digit rates in India.

The last 9 very positive months aside, the company has a compelling history of slow but steady growth. It's very unusual to see the share price move as quickly as it has recently, but we're not complaining. And it's worth noting that there hasn't been anything like a bubble in Kellogg's share price in their history.

Reasons for Caution

Many of the major food producers in the U.S., including Kellogg, General Mills, and Hershey, have seen large percentage gains in their share price from January through May 2013—the big K is up 18 percent over this period. Most explanations revolve around a softening in the cost of raw materials and the strong dividend positions of all 3 companies. This is all great news if you took our recommendation on Kellogg last year, but if you're buying now, you'll want to look the prices over carefully and make sure you're getting a fair entry point. Kellogg's share price is at an all-time high as we go to press, driving the yield down to 2.5 percent.

And, there's no guarantee that we won't see a recurrence in the disastrous drought conditions that drove corn and other commodity prices higher in 2011 and 2012.

SECTOR: **Consumer Staples**
BETA COEFFICIENT: **0.55**
10-YEAR COMPOUND EARNINGS PER SHARE GROWTH: **8.0%**
10-YEAR COMPOUND DIVIDENDS PER SHARE GROWTH: **5.0%**

		2005	2006	2007	2008	2009	2010	2011	2012
Revenues (mil)		10,177	10,907	11,776	12,822	12,575	12,397	13,175	14,197
Net income (mil)		980	1,004	1,103	1,148	1,212	1,247	1,225	1,297
Earnings per share		2.26	2.51	2.76	2.99	3.17	3.30	3.35	3.37
Dividends per share		1.06	1.14	1.24	1.30	1.43	1.56	1.67	1.74
Cash flow per share		3.39	3.41	3.78	3.99	4.35	4.48	4.55	4.83
Price:	high	47.0	51.0	56.9	58.5	54.1	56.0	57.7	57.2
	low	42.4	42.4	48.7	35.6	35.6	47.3	48.1	46.3

Kellogg Company
One Kellogg Square
P. O. Box 3599
Battle Creek, MI 49016–3599
(269) 961-6636
Website: www.kelloggcompany.com

GROWTH AND INCOME

Kimberly-Clark

◻ Ticker symbol: KMB (NYSE) ◻ S&P rating: A ◻ Value Line financial strength rating: A++
◻ Current yield: 3.4% ◻ Dividend raises, past 10 years: 10

Company Profile

Kimberly-Clark develops, manufactures, and markets a full line of personal care products, mostly based on paper and paper technologies. Well known for their ubiquitous Kleenex brand tissues, KMB also is a strong player in bath tissue, diapers, feminine products, incontinence products, industrial and health-care-related paper products, and others.

The company operates in 4 segments: Personal Care, Consumer Tissue, K-C Professional & Other, and Health Care. The Personal Care segment provides disposable diapers, training and youth pants, and swim pants; baby wipes; and feminine and incontinence care products, and related products. Brand names include Huggies, Pull-Ups, Little Swimmers, Good-Nites, Kotex, Lightdays, Depend, and Poise. The Consumer Tissue segment offers facial and bathroom tissue, paper towels, napkins, and related products for household use under the Kleenex, Scott, Cottonelle, Viva, Andrex, Scottex, Hakle, and Page brands. The K-C Professional & Other segment provides paper products for the away-from-home, that is, commercial/institutional marketplace under Kimberly-Clark, Kleenex, Scott, WypAll, Kimtech, KleenGuard, Kimcare, and Jackson brand names. The Health Care segment offers disposable health-care products, such as surgical drapes and gowns, infection control products, face masks, exam gloves, respiratory products, pain management products, and other disposable medical products.

The company was founded in 1872 and is headquartered today in Dallas, TX, with a historical, technology, and manufacturing base in the Fox River Valley in Wisconsin.

Financial Highlights, Fiscal Year 2012

FY2012 would bring only tears of joy, no tears of fear or trepidation to be mopped up by Kimberly-Clark investor Kleenexes. Sales and operating performance have always had a steady and rock-solid character, but during the year, a combination of operational improvements and share buybacks delivered a 24 percent growth in per-share earnings for the year on sales growth of a modest 1.6 percent and a net profit growth of 21 percent. The savings are reflective of $250 million in reduced costs from its Project FORCE—Focus on Reducing Costs Everywhere—program. These savings in overhead and other factors offset higher input and raw material costs through the year. The company continues to streamline for FY2013, calling for a continuation of moderate sales growth rates. Sales are expected to grow in the 0–3 percent range, but organic sales growth, which takes out the effects of the European diaper discontinuance, currency, and other factors, is expected to grow in a healthy 3–5 percent range. Similarly, and helped along by share buybacks and a moderation of input cost increases, per-share earnings are expected to grow in the 5–8 percent range. The company just budgeted $1.3 billion for share buybacks and increased the dividend 9.5 percent to $2.92 annually, a strong showing for shareholders and shareholder interests. KMB has reduced its share count from 501 million in 2003 to about 390 million at the end of 2012.

Reasons to Buy

Kimberly-Clark has shown itself to be a steady and solid business in all kinds of economic climates. The relatively high yield and strong track record of raising dividends and buying back shares is a definite plus. Operating margins have regained the 20 percent level, a level not seen

since 2006. Strong cash flow has financed strategic business investments, including international expansion in emerging markets, product innovations, and strategic marketing. The company continues to be rock solid, with a microscopic beta of 0.32 and with shareholder interests a consistent priority.

The company has stellar brands and should do well expanding them into overseas markets, a relatively untapped frontier compared to some of its peers. Also, compared to some peers, especially Procter & Gamble, the company is less inclined to go for "glamour" markets such as cosmetics, choosing instead to add to margins through operating efficiencies and scale. Safety-oriented investors may find this approach preferable. In addition, Value Line gives the company an A++ for financial strength and a top rating for safety, the latter of which it has maintained since 1990.

Reasons for Caution

While the paper products business is steady, it isn't easy to see where substantial additional growth would come from. The company, rightly so, is targeting international expansion, but competition and currency fluctuation make the results far from certain. The cost of pulp and paper raw materials will always be volatile. Companies like KMB have sometimes come to rely on acquisitions for growth; KMB has, so far, largely resisted this temptation but that could change. Finally, investors and the markets have recognized KMB's consistent excellence and have bid up the price to record levels recently. Expectations, once quite modest, are now sky-high for this issue. Investors should shop carefully for entry points while seeking long-term safety and growth in cash returns.

SECTOR: **Consumer Staples**
BETA COEFFICIENT: **0.32**
10-YEAR COMPOUND EARNINGS PER SHARE GROWTH: **3.0%**
10-YEAR COMPOUND DIVIDENDS PER SHARE GROWTH: **9.0%**

	2005	2006	2007	2008	2009	2010	2011	2012
Revenues (mil)	15,903	16,747	18,266	19,415	19,115	19,746	20,846	21,063
Net income (mil)	1,803.7	1,844.5	1,861.6	1,698.0	1,884.0	1,843	1,591	1,750
Earnings per share	3.78	3.90	4.25	4.14	4.52	4.45	3.99	4.42
Dividends per share	1.80	1.96	2.08	2.27	2.38	2.58	2.76	2.92
Cash flow per share	5.74	6.10	6.34	5.98	6.40	6.53	6.78	6.70
Price: high	68.3	68.6	72.8	69.7	67.0	67.2	74.1	88.3
low	55.6	56.6	63.8	50.3	43.1	58.3	61.0	70.5

Kimberly-Clark Corporation
P.O. Box 619100
Dallas, TX 75261
(972) 281-1200
Website: www.kimberly-clark.com

CONSERVATIVE GROWTH

The Kroger Company

❑ Ticker symbol: KR (NYSE) ❑ S&P rating: BBB ❑ Value Line financial strength rating: B++
❑ Current yield: 1.8% ❑ Dividend raises, past 10 years: 7

Company Profile

Kroger is the nation's largest retail grocery store operator, with about 2,424 supermarkets, 791 convenience stores, and 348 specialty jewelry stores operated around the country. Supermarket operations account for about 94 percent of total revenue and are located in 31 states with a concentration in the Midwest (where it was founded) and in the South and West, where it grew mostly by acquisition. The company is dominant in the markets it serves, with a number 1 or 2 market share position in 36 of its 44 major markets.

Kroger operates through a series of store brands many of you will be familiar with but probably did not associate with the Kroger name, including King Soopers, Fred Meyer, Smiths, Fry's, Ralph's, Dillons, Smith's, Baker's, and an assortment of others. The typical Kroger supermarket is full service and well appointed with higher-margin specialty departments like health foods, seafood, floral, and other perishables. The Fred Meyer stores carry a large assortment of general merchandise in addition to groceries, turning them into modern-era

big-box department stores; the company has 128 stores in all that meet this format, mostly in the West. There are also 146 "warehouse" stores under the Food4Less brand and 78 "marketplace" stores with expanded offerings similar to Fred Meyer to complement the supermarkets. About 1,169 "supermarket fuel centers" and 1,949 pharmacies round out the supermarket picture. Finally, the company has a considerable presence in manufacturing its own store-branded food items, with 37 such plants located around the country.

Financial Highlights, Fiscal Year 2012

Helped along somewhat by the calendar, which added an extra week for FY2012 ending in February 2013, Kroger turned in a 7 percent growth in revenues (about 2 percent of that related to the calendar) and a more substantial 19.2 percent growth in total earnings. The increased earnings combined with a 9 percent reduction in share count led to a 31 percent increase in earnings per share. Despite the competition from the likes of Walmart, the company has been able to drive a same-store sales increase for 9 straight years and is showing that it can hold the line in margins better than some. Operating expenses (SG&A) as a percent of revenue have declined for 8 straight years. For FY2013 the company projects per-share earnings in the $2.71–$2.79 range, off of FY2012's torrid growth rate but still respectable and as of now assuming 0 to a modest share repurchase, but current cash flow suggests that both dividends and share repurchases could well increase during the year.

Reasons to Buy

Kroger has done a good job in a tough market. Major discount retailers like Walmart and Target have stepped into the grocery business with a fairly significant price advantage, yet so far Kroger has been able to fend them off by focusing on product breadth, the shopping experience, and strategic price reductions. This success has been little recognized by the market until recently, where the shares, which traded flat for years despite solid earnings, cash

flow, and dividend growth, have started to rise. Our kudos, too, for reducing the share count some 30 percent since 2005. In addition, we like the Fred Meyer quality grocery-plus-department-store format, a more pleasant and balanced shopping experience than either Walmart or Target and a format that Kroger could do well to roll out nationwide. The company also has a good toehold on the low-price warehouse food business with Food4Less. All told, this is a well-managed company that continues to dominate its niches.

Reasons for Caution

You can't think "full-service grocer" without raising the fear of competition from discounters, and the recent recession trained a lot of shoppers to look for the lowest possible prices, even if they had to go to 2 or 3 stores to complete a week's shopping. If the conventional grocery store format is condemned to the dustbin of retail history, Kroger could be vulnerable, but we feel it has enough clout and experience in new formats to adapt.

SECTOR: **Retail**
BETA COEFFICIENT: **0.38**
10-YEAR COMPOUND EARNINGS PER SHARE GROWTH: **3.5%**
10-YEAR COMPOUND DIVIDENDS PER SHARE GROWTH: **NM**

	2005	2006	2007	2008	2009	2010	2011	2012
Revenues (bil)	6,055	6,611	7,023	7,600	7,673	8,219	9,037	9,675
Net income (mil)	958	1,115	1,181	1,249	1,122	1,118	1,192	1,423
Earnings per share	1.31	1.54	1.69	1.90	1.73	1.74	2.00	2.63
Dividends per share	—	0.26	0.30	0.36	0.37	0.40	0.44	0.53
Cash flow per share	3.07	3.39	3.83	4.15	4.12	4.38	5.05	5.98
Price: high	20.9	24.5	31.9	31.0	26.9	24.1	25.8	27.1
low	15.1	18.0	22.9	22.3	19.4	19.1	21.1	21.0

The Kroger Company
1014 Vine Street
Cincinnati, OH 45202
(513) 762-4000
Website: www.kroger.com

AGGRESSIVE GROWTH

Macy's, Inc.

❏ Ticker symbol: M (NYSE) ❏ S&P rating: BBB- ❏ Value Line financial strength rating: B+
❏ Current yield: 2.0% ❏ Dividend raises, past 10 years: 5

Company Profile

Macy's is now by far the largest operator of department stores in the U.S. The company operates under 2 brand names, Macy's and Bloomingdale's, and operates about 850 stores in 45 states, Puerto Rico, and Guam. Macy's has been assembled over the years from a large assortment of famed department store predecessors including Marshall Field, May, and a portfolio of names once under ownership of Federated Department Stores, including Lazarus, Weinstocks, Dillard, Abraham & Straus, I. Magnin, and others. The company, in current form, was assembled after Federated emerged from bankruptcy in 1992.

In addition to department stores, Macy's operates its own credit card operations and an internal merchandising group that, among other things, develops and markets a number of familiar proprietary brands such as Charter Club, Club Room, Hotel Collection, Tommy Hilfiger, Ellen Tracy, and now, the Martha Stewart Collection. Private label brands now account for 19 percent of sales. The company also operates 90 specialty stores including outlets and furniture stores. The online presence, macys.com, continues to grow and is strategically more integrated with the sales process. It's easy to shop online, then see the product, pick it up, and importantly, pay the online price at the store. The sales mix is approximately 62 percent women's clothing, shoes, and accessories; 23 percent men's and children's; and 15 percent home and miscellaneous.

Financial Highlights, Fiscal Year 2012

Macy's continues to ride a combination of economic recovery and a series of internal operational improvements to find a successful new growth trajectory in a business that many had given up on. Same-store sales improved 3.3 percent, which is somewhat diminished from last year's 5.3 percent but on a stronger "comp" base. Almost all of this growth is accounted for by online sales, which advanced over 40 percent during the year, for the second year in a row, almost double the increases experienced in previous years. Total sales advanced about 4.7 percent to $27.7 billion, finally exceeding the boom years prior to the recession. Operational improvements in procurement and supply chain, combined with improved and more locally customized merchandising and improved profitability from its proprietary credit card, grew net profit margins back to 5.0 percent after reaching 4.7 percent in FY2012, and a continued nice recovery from the recessionary levels of 2–3 percent. It makes sense now to compare Macy's results to stronger years, and indeed for the past 10 years the 5.0 percent net profit margin level was only achieved once, in 2005. Most of the increase has come from operating costs, not gross margin improvements, suggesting that retail price competition (and discounting) are still substantial. The company continues to invest in itself, buying back almost $1 billion in stock in the first 9 months of FY2012 and authorizing $1.5 billion for future buybacks. The company retired almost 20 million shares in FY2012, bringing its total from 547 million shares in 2005 to about 395 million at the end of 2012. Not too surprisingly, especially in light of these factors, Macy's grew per-share earnings some 16.3 percent on the previously mentioned single-digit sales growth figures. Earnings growth should continue into FY2013, with EPS for the year recently guided up another 18 percent to $3.91–$3.95 per share.

Reasons to Buy

Justifiably perhaps, most investors would perceive Macy's and the department store business to be yesterday's news, as big-box retailers and the Internet have taken over. True, those players have snatched important parts of the retail business, but the department store idea has made a comeback with more affluent, brand-conscious, and experience-conscious shoppers. The stores have been upgraded, merchandise assortments made more exciting, and service has improved. Merchandise assortments have been localized and are now more exciting and edgier and more aimed at the younger set. Department stores aren't just for grandma any longer. The company has managed its image and product well and has turned the new interest and a more scientific approach to management into solid bottom-line results.

The integration of online and physical stores into an integrated experience is one of the best such efforts we've seen. Additionally, the company has achieved savings by merging back-end inventories between stores and online channels—online orders can be filled with excess merchandise from stores, for example. Recent stumbles and lackluster market performance by competitors, notably J. C. Penney, have also helped. Cash flow is almost double reported per-share earnings, and, through dividend increases and share buybacks, Macy's continues to lure investors through its front doors.

Reasons for Caution

The economy, of course, is always a risk, and any return to higher levels of unemployment, foreclosures, taxes, or any other factors that would make customers feel less flush will hurt. The high beta of 1.68 bears out the economic sensitivity of this issue. Macy's still relies heavily on promotional discounts and special sale events, which have probably become habitual shopping practice among many customers; we suspect that relatively few customers actually pay full price for most of what they buy. Additionally, free shipping promotions on Macys.com may compromise operating margins. While Macy's is increasing its appeal to the younger set, the Internet is still a big contender here, although the growth in Macys.com is encouraging.

SECTOR: **Retail**
BETA COEFFICIENT: **1.68**
10-YEAR COMPOUND EARNINGS PER SHARE GROWTH: **3.5%**
10-YEAR COMPOUND DIVIDENDS PER SHARE GROWTH: **15.0%**

	2005	**2006**	**2007**	**2008**	**2009**	**2010**	**2011**	**2012**
Revenues (mil)	22,390	26,970	26,313	24,892	23,489	25,003	26,405	27,686
Net income (mil)	1,111	1,147	970	543	595	867	1,238	1,410
Earnings per share	2.56	2.16	2.18	1.29	1.41	2.03	2.88	3.45
Dividends per share	0.51	0.52	0.53	0.20	0.20	0.20	0.35	0.80
Cash flow per share	3.76	4.85	5.42	4.33	4.29	4.77	5.61	6.34
Price: high	39.0	45.0	46.7	28.5	20.6	26.3	33.3	42.2
low	27.1	32.4	24.7	5.1	6.3	15.3	21.7	32.3

Macy's, Inc.
7 West Seventh St.
Cincinnati, OH 45202
(513) 579-7000
Website: www.macys.com

CONSERVATIVE GROWTH

McCormick & Company, Inc.

❑ Ticker symbol: MKC (NYSE) ❑ S&P rating: A- ❑ Value Line financial strength rating: A ❑ Current yield: 2.0% ❑ Dividend raises, past 10 years: 10

Company Profile

McCormick manufactures, markets, and distributes spices, herbs, seasonings, flavors, and flavor enhancers to consumers and to the global food industry. They are the largest such supplier in the world. Customers range from retail outlets and food manufacturers to foodservice businesses.

McCormick's U.S. Consumer business (about 59 percent of sales and 79 percent of operating profits), its oldest and largest, manufactures consumer spices, herbs, extracts, proprietary seasoning blends, sauces, and marinades. Spices are sold under an assortment of recognizable brand names: McCormick, Lawry's, Zatarain's, Thai Kitchen, Simply Asia, Clubhouse, Billy Bee, Produce Partners, Golden Dipt, Old Bay, and Mojave. Industrial customers include foodservice, food-processing businesses, and retail outlets. The Industrial segment was responsible for 41 percent of sales and 21 percent of operating profits.

Many of the spices and herbs purchased by the company, such as black pepper, vanilla beans, cinnamon, and herbs and seeds, must be imported from countries such as India, Indonesia, Malaysia, Brazil, and the Malagasy Republic. Other ingredients such as paprika, dehydrated vegetables, onion, garlic, and food ingredients other than spices and herbs originate in the United States.

The company was founded in 1889 and has approximately 7,500 full-time employees in facilities located around the world. Major sales, distribution, and production facilities are located in North America and Europe. Additional facilities are based in Mexico, Central America, Australia, China, Singapore, Thailand, and South Africa. International sales account for about 40 percent of the total. The company has recently deployed more informative print and web content with recipes and other information to spur cooking with spices. The company does a lot of innovation in the area of flavors and flavor trends, and we also like a new packaging initiative—called Recipe Inspirations—to sell prepackaged spices set to cook a particular meal; this launch has been successful.

Financial Highlights, Fiscal Year 2012

The spice and ingredient business is a fairly slow, steady business at most times, but, aided by a growing number of people eating at home to control expenses in response to the recession, a habit that continues as we emerge from it, McCormick had an excellent FY2012, and the stock continued to reach new highs. Revenues increased almost 10 percent, driven by a combination of increased base demand, new products and packages, and strong brand loyalty. For the most part, McCormick was able to pass on price increases mostly commensurate with ingredient cost increases it experienced, leading to a rise in total earnings and earnings per share of about 11 percent, an improvement from last year's 6 percent. For 2013 the company expects these growth rates in earnings to moderate a bit to the 6–8 percent range on a sales growth rate of 6 percent. International sales are expected to be a primary growth driver.

Reasons to Buy

As a strong pure play in the seasonings business, McCormick is the largest branded producer of seasonings in North America, and they're the largest private-label producer of seasonings as well, giving them a substantial level of price protection. McCormick is not just a producer, however—they also create new seasoning products. In fact, every year since 2005, between 13 percent and 18 percent of their industrial business sales have come from new products launched in the preceding 3 years. Keeping up with changing tastes requires McCormick to produce that new, hot flavor and to come up with new and interesting flavors and blends of existing seasonings. The company has also tapped existing niches, for example, reporting a 40 percent increase in flavorings sold into the Hispanic market since 2006. The company continues to acquire in the Asian market, with an agreement in mid-2012 to acquire Wuhan Asia-Pacific Condiments, Ltd.

On the consumer side, as amateur cooks ourselves we continue to feel that people would use more spices if they only knew how to use them. The website and its recipe offerings and the prepackaged Recipe Inspirations meal kits will get the less-experienced cooks using spices more effectively in their own cooking. Doesn't that prepackaged Country Herb Chicken & Dumplings, which deploys 6 prepackaged McCormick spices, sound good? In our view, these initiatives, combined with continuing growth in the health-conscious segment by learning to replace fat flavoring with spice flavoring, will add to a solid business base for the company.

McCormick's sales have increased every year for the past 50 years, and the company has paid a dividend every year since 1925. In 2012, they raised the dividend for the twenty-seventh consecutive year. The profitability, stability, and defensive nature of the company and its business continue to present an attractive combination for investors.

Reasons for Caution

Downsides include the rising cost of ingredients and the sourcing of many of these ingredients in geopolitically unstable regions. Top-line growth is likely to remain moderate except by acquisition. While earnings and share-price growth have been steady, they don't add a lot of "spice" to an aggressive portfolio. That said, we don't see people's tastes in taste diminishing anytime soon.

SECTOR: **Consumer Staples**
BETA COEFFICIENT: **0.41**
10-YEAR COMPOUND EARNINGS PER SHARE GROWTH: **10.0%**
10-YEAR COMPOUND DIVIDENDS PER SHARE GROWTH: **11.0%**

	2005	**2006**	**2007**	**2008**	**2009**	**2010**	**2011**	**2012**
Revenues (mil)	2,592	2,716	2,916	3,177	3,192	3,339	3,650	4,014
Net income (mil)	215	202	230	282	311	356.3	380	408
Earnings per share	1.56	1.72	1.92	2.14	2.35	2.65	2.80	3.04
Dividends per share	0.64	0.72	0.80	0.88	0.96	1.04	1.12	1.24
Cash flow per share	2.24	2.45	2.64	2.83	3.08	3.39	3.55	3.85
Price: high	39.1	39.8	39.7	42.1	36.8	47.8	51.3	66.4
low	29.0	30.1	33.9	28.2	28.1	35.4	43.4	49.9

McCormick & Company, Inc.
18 Loveton Circle
P. O. Box 6000
Sparks, MD 21152–6000
(410) 771-7244
Website: www.mccormick.com

AGGRESSIVE GROWTH

McDonald's Corporation

❏ Ticker symbol: MCD (NYSE) ❏ S&P rating: A ❏ Value Line financial strength rating: A++
❏ Current yield: 3.2% ❏ Dividend raises, past 10 years: 10

Company Profile

McDonald's Corporation operates and franchises the ubiquitous golden arches McDonald's restaurants. At 2012 year-end, there were approximately 34,010 restaurants in 118 countries, up from 33,510 at the end of 2011. Some 81 percent of these restaurants are operated by franchisees; the remainder by the company. Franchisees pay for and own the equipment, signs, and interior of the businesses and are required to reinvest in them from time to time. The company owns the land and building or secures leases for both company-operated and franchised restaurant sites.

Revenues to the company come in the form of sales from company-owned stores and rents, fees, royalties, and other revenue streams from the franchisees. The company continues to sell off company stores to increase the dominance of the franchising business, which benefits cash flow and reduces operational costs and exposure to commodities prices.

McDonald's continues to dominate the fast-food hamburger restaurant market segment with a market share approaching 50 percent, while the nearest competitors, Burger King and Wendy's, have market shares in the low to mid-teens. In the overall fast-food segment, McDonald's is still the single biggest player with a 19 percent market share by revenue, followed by Doctor's Associates, Inc. (Subway) with a 10 percent share. The company is facing some stiffer competition from Five Guys Burgers and Fries and some more local names like In-N-Out Burger and Burgerville, but these companies have not taken significant share as of yet.

An iconic brand worldwide, the company generates about 68 percent of its revenue and 57 percent of profits outside the United States.

Financial Highlights, Fiscal Year 2012

FY2012 was a mixed deal for McDonald's, with international and especially European headwinds offsetting some success with promotions in the U.S. involving value menus and the Monopoly games. For the year, sales rose approximately 2.1 percent to a record $27.57 billion, while earnings were down just a fraction to $5.46 billion.

Share buybacks reduced share count about 2 percent, thus earnings per share increased about 2 percent anyway. Increased food costs also reduced operating and net margins slightly. For FY2013 the company will continue to expand the franchise model, experiment with new menu innovations, remodel restaurants, and reduce share counts, but it will still encounter the headwinds of competition, post-recessionary malaise, high food costs, and the end of the payroll tax holiday. These many moving parts are expected to lead to a slightly more healthy revenue gain approaching 5 percent, with per-share earnings advancing about 8 percent to $5.80.

Reasons to Buy

In the early part of the decade, McDonald's had been adding mainly company-owned stores in an effort to boost revenues. They aren't as profitable as franchises, and there were signs that people were becoming tired of the menu and more concerned about health. In 2003, McDonald's initiated a new strategy that called for increasing sales at its existing stores by expanding menu options, expanding store hours, and renovating stores. The customer base adapted well to all of these initiatives. The company also began franchising a higher percentage of its stores, driving revenue with reduced capital expense. The

strategy has paid off with operating margins in particular. Those margins have grown from the mid-20s to the mid-30s, with most of that increase coming in the 2008–2010 time frame, a tough period for most restaurants. At the same time, share buybacks have reduced share counts from 1.26 billion in 2005 down to about 1.0 billion. These factors have produced substantial shareholder returns, much of which is actually getting returned to shareholders, as the dividend has climbed from 24 cents per share to $2.87 per share in the 10-year period. As a result, the share price is now 8 times its 2003 low and is a steady and safe stock with a beta of 0.38. McDonald's continues to be an iconic name in overseas markets, and continues to offer "quality, service, convenience, and value" to restaurant-goers worldwide.

Reasons for Caution

It seems like fast-food restaurants go through a cycle—menus get boring, they get taken to task over health and obesity issues, the stores get stale. Then they refurbish the menu, refurbish the stores, and add healthy items with a dose of PR to alleviate the negatives, and everything is all right for a few years. McDonald's may be ready for another one of those rebalancing and enhancing periods. We are a bit concerned about the new "fresh ingredient" competition from the likes of In-N-Out, but the McDonald's model still has a lot of loyalty with a lot of people and seems to come through these periods with flying colors, as it did after 2003. Finally, like all in the food business, McDonald's is vulnerable to ingredient price swings. As a result, the next leg of growth is harder to foresee, but that said, current performance and shareholder returns remain strong.

SECTOR: Restaurants
BETA COEFFICIENT: 0.38
10-YEAR COMPOUND EARNINGS PER SHARE GROWTH: 12.5%
10-YEAR COMPOUND DIVIDENDS PER SHARE GROWTH: 26.0%

	2005	2006	2007	2008	2009	2010	2011	2012
Revenues (mil)	20,460	21,586	22,787	23,522	22,745	24,075	27,008	27,567
Net income (mil)	2,509	2,873	3,522	4,201	4,451	4,970	5,503	5,465
Earnings per share	1.97	2.30	2.91	3.67	4.11	4.60	5.27	5.36
Dividends per share	0.67	1.00	1.50	1.63	2.05	2.26	2.53	2.87
Cash flow per share	2.98	3.43	4.06	4.85	5.20	5.95	6.75	6.95
Price: high	35.7	44.7	63.7	67.0	64.8	80.9	101.0	102.2
low	27.4	31.7	42.3	45.8	50.4	61.1	72.1	83.3

McDonald's Corporation
One McDonald's Plaza
Oak Brook, IL 60523
(630) 623-3000
Website: www.mcdonalds.com

CONSERVATIVE GROWTH

McKesson Corporation

❑ Ticker symbol: MCK (NYSE) ❑ S&P rating: A– ❑ Value Line financial strength rating: A++
❑ Current yield: 0.75% ❑ Dividend raises, past 10 years: 4

Company Profile

McKesson Corporation is America's oldest and largest health-care services company and engages in 2 distinct businesses to support the health-care industry. Pharmaceutical and medical-surgical supply distribution is the first and by far the largest business: The company is the largest such distributor in North America. The company delivers to approximately 40,000 pharmaceutical outlets as well as hospitals and clinics throughout North America from 28 domestic and 17 Canadian distribution facilities.

Second, and not to be ignored, is a technology solutions business that provides clinical systems, analytics, clinical decision support, medical necessity and utilization management tools, electronic medical records, supply-chain management, and connectivity solutions to hospitals, pharmacies, and an assortment of health-care providers. While the distribution business, at $119 billion for FY2012, continues to provide 97 percent of the company's revenue, the information technology business is no less important and is a $3.3 billion business all by itself. McKesson's software and hardware IT solutions are installed in some 70 percent of the nation's hospitals with more than 200 beds, and 52 percent of hospitals overall.

The company offers products and services covering most aspects of pharmacy and drug distribution, including not only physical distribution and supply-chain services but also a line of proprietary generics and automated dispensing systems, record-keeping systems, and outsourcing services used in retail and hospital pharmacy operations.

In late 2010, the company completed a $2.16 billion acquisition of U.S. Oncology, a distributor of products targeted to the cancer-care industry. With that acquisition, McKesson became the leading supplier of materials, technology, and operational platforms to the oncological community, and that acquisition has performed well. In early 2012, the company acquired the Katz Group Canada, a major distributor supplying more than 1,000 Canadian pharmacies. The company finalized the acquisition of medical supplies distributor PSS World Medical during FY2013.

Financial Highlights, Fiscal Year 2012

The McKesson business is about as close to recession-proof as one can become, but the flip side of that is relatively small gains when things start to recover. Revenues grew a modest 1 percent, almost all of it in the Distribution business. Improving margins, however, drove a moderate 12.7 percent increase in net earnings, and combined with share buybacks, earnings per share advanced a healthy 22.6 percent. The company has retired 25 percent of the 304 million outstanding shares it had on the books in 2005. Cash flow continues to be strong, and the board has authorized another $500 million for buybacks. Per-share earnings guidance for FY2013, however, indicates slower growth to the $7.10–$7.30 per share range.

Reasons to Buy

The distribution business has proven to be rock solid and will likely continue that way. Demographics and the addition of millions to the insured health-care rolls will keep demand moving in the right direction. McKesson dominates its niches and is a go-to provider of much of what hospitals and clinics need to operate. Additionally, hospitals and other care providers are starting to get the memo that it is time to improve utilization and operational efficiency, and McKesson's technology solutions are hard to ignore, although many might do so at first glance, as they are only 3 percent of the business. As most distributors do, McKesson operates on very thin margins; the expansion of technology services and generic equivalent drugs should eventually become a growth driver as efficiency measures continue to catch on. The company has a strong track record of stability and is well managed; the stock has many of the characteristics of a true long-term equity holding.

Reasons for Caution

Some, and perhaps much, of the optimism previously mentioned has already been priced into the stock. The relatively deliberate growth pace in its two primary businesses suggests the temptation of acquisitions; the company has done okay here thus far but there is always some danger. Additionally, and as mentioned, the company does operate on thin margins and as such has a low tolerance for mistakes or major changes in the health-care space that could be brought on by legislation or regulation. While we applaud the aggressive buyback strategy, we'd like to see a bit more return to shareholders in the form of cash dividends; that said, the company has tripled the indicated dividend since 2007.

SECTOR: **Health Care**
BETA COEFFICIENT: **0.79**
10-YEAR COMPOUND EARNINGS PER SHARE GROWTH: **16.0%**
10-YEAR COMPOUND DIVIDENDS PER SHARE GROWTH: **10.5%**

	2005	**2006**	**2007**	**2008**	**2009**	**2010**	**2011**	**2012**
Revenues (mil)	88,050	92,977	101,703	106,632	108,702	112,084	121,010	122,455
Net income (mil)	737	881	1,021	1,194	1,251	1,316	1,463	1,516
Earnings per share	2.34	2.89	3.43	4.28	4.58	5.00	6.05	6.33
Dividends per share	0.24	0.24	0.24	0.48	0.48	0.72	0.76	0.80
Cash flow per share	3.30	3.99	5.03	6.03	6.37	7.18	8.40	9.30
Price: high	52.9	55.1	68.4	68.4	65.0	71.5	87.3	100.0
low	30.1	44.5	50.5	28.3	33.1	57.2	66.6	74.9

McKesson Corporation
One Post Street
San Francisco, CA 94104
(415) 983-8300
Website: www.mckesson.com

AGGRESSIVE GROWTH

Medtronic, Inc.

❏ Ticker symbol: MDT (NYSE) ❏ S&P rating: A+ ❏ Value Line financial strength rating: A++
❏ Current yield: 2.3% ❏ Dividend raises, past 10 years: 10

Company Profile

Medtronic is the world's largest manufacturer of implantable medical devices and is a leading medical technology company, providing lifelong solutions to "alleviate pain, restore health, and extend life," primarily for people with chronic diseases. The 6 business segments are (with contribution to FY2012 revenues in parenthesis):

- Cardiac Rhythm Disease Management (31 percent) develops products that restore and regulate a patient's heart rhythm as well as improve the heart's pumping function. This segment markets implantable pacemakers, defibrillators, Internet and non-Internet–based monitoring and diagnostic devices, cardiac resynchronization devices, and minimally invasive catheter ablation equipment.
- Cardiovascular (21.5 percent) develops products and therapies that treat a wide range of vascular diseases and conditions. These products include coronary, peripheral, and neuro-vascular stents; stent graft systems for diseases and conditions throughout the aorta; angioplasty technologies; and distal protection systems. The segment also develops products that are used in both arrested and beating heart bypass surgery and markets the industry's broadest line of heart valve products for replacement and repair.
- Medtronic Spinal and Biologics (20 percent) develops and manufactures products that treat a variety of disorders of the cranium and spine, including traumatically induced conditions, deformities, herniated discs and other disc diseases, osteoporosis, and tumors. The Biologics business is the global leader in biologics regeneration and pain therapies across a variety of musculoskeletal applications including spine, orthopedic trauma, and dental.
- Neuromodulation (11 percent) employs many technologies used in heart electrical stimulation to treat diseases of the central nervous system. It offers therapies for movement disorders; chronic pain;

urological and gastroentero-
logical disorders, including
incontinence, benign prostatic
hyperplasia (BPH), enlarged
prostate, and gastroesophageal
reflux disease (GERD); and
psychological diseases.

- Diabetes (9 percent) offers
  advanced diabetes management solutions, including
  insulin pump therapy, glucose
  monitoring systems, and treatment management software.
- Surgical Technologies (8
  percent) develops products for
  ear, nose, and throat–related
  diseases and certain neurological disorders; among them are
  precision image-guided surgical systems.

Financial Highlights, Fiscal Year 2012

Increased competition and higher
utilization (translation: cost containment and deferral of elective surgeries) continued to moderate top-line
growth to a modest 2.1 percent
increase over FY2011. The trends
affected all segments equally. Helped
in part by a share count decrease of
about 3.7 percent, earnings per share
rose 7.2 percent to $3.70.

Dividends increased another
7 percent and have increased in
orderly fashion over the past 10
years. For FY2013, the company
expects improved international
sales but an offset from currency

exchange and the new 2.3 percent
medical device tax.

Reasons to Buy

The name Medtronic is synonymous
with medical technology. That said,
its solid financials and steady growth
make it far different from a typical
tech stock. The company gets 45 percent of its sales overseas, and international expansion continues to be
part of the story, especially in emerging markets, as MDT-supported
medical procedures become mainstream. The R & D footprint, with
9,000 employed scientists and 9.2
percent of revenues spent on R &
D, also bode well for the future, and
there are a number of important new
products in the pipeline.

The company is a pioneer technology leader and a successful innovator in many surgical and implant
technologies, including the restora-
tion of normal brain function and
chemistry to millions of patients
with central nervous system disorders. The company's DBS (Deep
Brain Stimulation) systems treat
disorders by modulating the nervous system with electrical stimulation, chemicals, and biological
agents delivered in precise amounts
to specific sites in the brain and
spinal cord. This system has been
used successfully to treat the most
severe symptoms of conditions such
as Parkinson's disease, and this and
other new products, especially in

the neuromodulation segment, should enhance prospects.

Medtronic has enjoyed steady growth and has achieved the quintuple-play—double-digit compounded ten-year growth in revenues, earnings, cash flow, dividends, and book value. The dividend, relatively generous for a tech company of this sort, has tripled in 8 years. The stock price has run a predictable cycle each year, with steady growth and reasonable entry points observed each year.

Reasons for Caution

Medtronic may be entering the mature lifecycle phase in many of its product lines, meaning future growth opportunities may be harder to come by. The trend toward improved utilization in the United States is probably here to stay, but deferred procedures will be made up at some point. Earnings growth, while steady, is not very exciting and is hardly accelerating, and it remains to be seen how the new medical device tax will affect long-term earnings. This is a slow, steady performer, and we continue to hope that the company doesn't get too aggressive with acquisitions and instead focuses on making the most of its internally generated new products and international growth opportunities.

SECTOR: **Health Care**
BETA COEFFICIENT: **0.91**
10-YEAR COMPOUND EARNINGS PER SHARE GROWTH: **12.0%**
10-YEAR COMPOUND DIVIDENDS PER SHARE GROWTH: **17.0%**

	2005	2006	2007	2008	2009	2010	2011	2012
Revenues (mil)	11,292	12,299	13,515	14,599	15,817	15,933	16,184	16,500
Net income (mil)	2,687	2,798	2,984	3,282	3,576	3,647	3,447	3,790
Earnings per share	1.86	2.21	2.41	2.61	2.92	3.22	3.46	3.70
Dividends per share	0.36	0.41	0.47	0.63	0.82	0.90	0.97	1.04
Cash flow per share	2.80	2.96	3.22	3.45	3.96	4.16	4.13	4.60
Price: high	58.9	59.9	58.0	57.0	44.9	46.7	43.3	44.6
low	48.7	42.4	44.9	28.3	24.1	30.8	30.2	35.7

Medtronic, Inc.
710 Medtronic Parkway N. E.
Minneapolis, MN 55432–5604
(763) 505-2692
Website: www.medtronic.com

Molex Incorporated

❑ Ticker symbol: MOLX (NASDAQ) ❑ S&P rating: NA ❑ Value Line financial strength rating: A
❑ Current yield: 3.2% ❑ Dividend raises, past 10 years: 7

Company Profile

Molex is one of the largest suppliers to the worldwide electrical and electronics manufacturing industries. They provide both industry-standard and custom parts for a balanced mix of automotive, aerospace, consumer, commercial, medical, and industrial applications. Their catalog includes more than 100,000 electromechanical components, including connectors, cabling, backplanes, sockets, and switches, among others, designed in all sizes, shapes, and levels of integrity for all environments. Molex's products are sold both direct and via one of the largest distribution networks in the industry. Typical direct customers include large ODMs (original design manufacturers) such as Foxconn, Flextronics, and SCI, as well as OEMs such as carmakers who build their own product. They also provide custom design and contract manufacturing services. The company has over 33,000 employees and operates nearly 40 manufacturing locations in 16 countries. Sixty percent of sales are to Asia (where most electronics manufacturing occurs) with 26 percent to the Americas and 14 percent to Europe.

For FY2012 the customer breakdown was 26 percent information technology, 23 percent telecom, 18 percent consumer electronics, 17 percent automotive, 13 percent industrial, and 3 percent other. The $45 billion worldwide market for the type of interconnects that represent the bulk of Molex's revenue is well fragmented, with the top 10 suppliers accounting for just over half of the overall market; Molex is number two with an approximately 8 percent share.

Financial Highlights, Fiscal Year 2012

FY2010 and FY2011 were rebound years: FY2012, unfortunately, not so much. Unfavorable foreign currency translations and new product startup costs hurt sales, margins, net earnings, and cash flows, leading to a largely flat to slightly down year on all accounts. Despite that, the company increased its dividend 17 percent to 82 cents a share and is expected to increase it again to 88 cents in FY2013. For FY2013 the company expects new products to come on line, and its FY2012 acquisition of Affinity Medical Technologies should bolster its presence in the medical segment. All told, revenues are projected to rise about 8 percent from this lackluster base year, while earnings may lag that figure a bit as new products and acquisitions come on line.

Reasons to Buy

Interconnects are the Rodney Dangerfield of high-tech: no respect, no respect at all. And while it's true that the materials and manufacturing processes for the bulk of this industry's products have been, historically, pretty low-tech, there is a subset of Molex's catalog that makes possible many of the current leading-edge designs. As devices (such as smartphones and tablets) get smaller and provide more functionality, the internal connections also have to get smaller and provide higher-speed operation. These interconnect modules, typically custom-designed for each application, are where the high margins live. They require sophisticated design and fabrication techniques, and this is where Molex excels.

The company's vision for the future is to be able to design anywhere, manufacture anywhere, and sell anywhere. Having design, manufacturing, and admin resources close to the customer is a big advantage in a rapid-turn environment, but it's also very difficult to do in the traditionally low-margin interconnect business. The company has

had a lot of success in recent years creating this capacity while keeping overhead costs moderate and margins high.

The company is also making the most of new product development and has achieved pricing power in many of its segments. Longer term, we like the idea that run-of-the-mill machines like cars and appliances are being made smarter and smarter—that bodes well for needing the kinds of high-performance interconnects that Molex provides. The economic recovery also bodes well, and with a doubling of the cash account to $700 million in two years ($4 per share) we expect smart acquisitions and improving cash returns to investors, something Molex has already shown a willingness to offer.

Reasons for Caution

Molex competes in a fragmented market with a large number of capable players, all looking at many of the same customers for the next big win. These high-margin design wins are a big part of market leadership, and these wins are highly sought after. Compounding the sales challenges are the issues with raw materials—gold and copper are a significant component of Molex's costs, and it appears that predicting prices on those two commodities will continue to be a challenge, as it has been for several years now. Finally, while we like the idea of Molex connectors in washing machines, other more mainstream technologies such as PCs are going through some upheaval, which may temper demand in some key product areas as the market adapts to new technologies.

SECTOR: **Industrials**
BETA COEFFICIENT: **1.61**
10-YEAR COMPOUND EARNINGS PER SHARE GROWTH: **5.0%**
10-YEAR COMPOUND DIVIDENDS PER SHARE GROWTH: **22.0%**

	2005	**2006**	**2007**	**2008**	**2009**	**2010**	**2011**	**2012**
Revenues (mil)	2,549	2,861	3,266	3,328	2,582	3,007	3,587	3,489
Net income (mil)	196	264	263	254	52.4	192	308	289
Earnings per share	1.03	1.38	1.42	1.40	0.30	1.10	1.76	1.63
Dividends per share	0.15	0.20	0.30	0.45	0.61	0.61	0.70	0.82
Cash flow per share	2.27	2.60	2.72	2.85	1.76	2.47	3.14	2.98
Price: high	30.0	40.1	32.3	30.6	22.4	23.7	28.5	28.5
low	23.8	25.6	23.5	10.3	9.7	17.5	18.5	21.9

Molex Incorporated
2222 Wellington Court
Lisle, IL 60532
(630) 969-4550
Website: www.molex.com

AGGRESSIVE GROWTH

Monsanto Company

❑ Ticker symbol: MON (NYSE) ❑ S&P Rating: A+ ❑ Value Line financial strength rating: A
❑ Current yield: 1.5% ❑ Dividend raises, past 10 years: 8

Company Profile

Monsanto was once a major chemical company with a broad pedigree ranging from saccharine to sulfuric acid to Agent Orange and DDT. Monsanto was absorbed into Pharmacia Upjohn in 2000, which kept its pharmaceutical products and spun off the agricultural products business into a "new" Monsanto in 2002. Today's Monsanto provides a set of technology-based agricultural products for use in farming in the United States and overseas. The company views its business as providing better-quality foods and animal feedstocks while reducing the costs of farming.

The company has 2 primary business segments: Seeds and Genomics, and Agricultural Productivity. The Seeds and Genomics segment (72 percent of FY2012 revenues) produces seeds for a host of crops, most importantly corn and soybeans, but also canola, cotton, and a variety of vegetable and fruit seeds. Most of the seed products are bioengineered to provide greater yields and to be more resistant to insects and weeds. Familiar to many consumers, especially those who travel in the Midwest, is the DeKalb seed brand.

The Agricultural Productivity segment (28 percent) offers glyphosate-based herbicides, known as Roundup to most of us, for agricultural, industrial, and residential lawn and garden applications. Beyond this market-leading product, the division also offers other selective herbicides for control of pre-emergent annual grass and small seeded broadleaf weeds in corn and other crops. Monsanto owns many of the major brands in both the seed and herbicide markets. The company also partners with other agricultural and chemical companies such as Cargill, BASF, and Biotechnology Inc. to develop other high-tech agricultural and food-processing solutions.

In recent years, the company underwent some upheaval as patents on its flagship Roundup herbicide system expired, almost immediately followed by reports that certain weeds were developing immunity to it anyhow, and cheaper foreign competitors were starting to invade its garden. Beyond that, they alienated some of their farmer base with pricing and marketing practices for their seed and herbicide systems. These reports and a sag in earnings brought the stock price from the 70s to the mid 40s in mid-2010. Since then, the company has taken steps to modernize its herbicide offerings and become less dependent on them, to develop the core seed businesses further, and to focus on developing markets like Latin America and China, making them less dependent on the "one-trick" Roundup pony. We continue to applaud these moves.

The two big stories, aside from the transition beyond dependence on Roundup, are international growth and legal patent protection on their seed and herbicide systems. Both look to be plusses at this time.

Financial Highlights, Fiscal Year 2012

After a weak and somewhat unsettling year in FY2010, Monsanto started its comeback to previous levels in FY2011 but the comeback started first on the top line, while profits lagged as the Roundup franchise lost some of its luster. In FY2012, the comeback really started to grow and bear fruit, led by the Seeds and Genomics segment and international expansion, particularly in Latin America. The drought, which increases demand for genetically modified seed stocks, and higher commodity prices have both created a strong "macro" environment for Monsanto products. FY2012 revenues sprouted ahead some 14.3 percent, while margin improvements drove net profits up

almost 23 percent. Initial FY2013 results are very promising, and the company is projecting solid results, with earnings per share up some 25 percent to $4.80 on a top-line growth of about 12.5 percent.

Reasons to Buy

Monsanto will provide business schools with an excellent case study in becoming too dependent on one product and watching that product decline—and responding by retrenching back to its core strengths for a resurgence. The company continues to lead in technology applied to agricultural use and continues to advance in biotech applications in its Seeds and Genomics segment while advancing its products in the Agricultural Productivity segment with glyphosate-related products as well. All of this is working in the backdrop of global agriculture, a healthy and important sector in which to own worldwide leadership. It appears that revenues, margins earnings, cash flow, and dividends are all moving in the right direction at an accelerating pace.

Reasons for Caution

While the growth statistics appear strong, technology-based cyclical companies like Monsanto can hit a wall pretty quickly. Monsanto is positioned well to take advantage of agricultural upcycles, such as we're in now, but if crop prices and planted acreage fall, the company may suffer in the short term. In recent years, however, these downcycles have proved short-lived. Somewhat to our surprise, the recent drought actually helped the company.

Not everyone—including its customer base of farmers—is happy with Monsanto. Many have been outspoken for years about the power and practices of the company, and some of that angst has turned into possible legal headwinds. One farmer in Indiana has brought a case that will test the power of Monsanto—and many others in far-distant sectors of the tech space—to handle the sale of its products the way software companies sell licenses. The farmer claims that he can plant soybean

seed from plants originally generated from Monsanto seed—with its genetic makeup—without paying Monsanto. Monsanto claims it sells the seed like a software license—it and anything else produced or copied from it are its intellectual property. In May, the Supreme Court unanimously ruled in favor of Monsanto.

Bottom line—Monsanto has some challenges in the customer relations area, in addition to these legal challenges. We'd also like to see a little more cash returned to investors as dividends or share buybacks, but we can also see that the company is investing its profits in its own business successfully.

SECTOR: **Industrials**
BETA COEFFICIENT: **0.92**
10-YEAR COMPOUND EARNINGS PER SHARE GROWTH: **22.0%**
10-YEAR COMPOUND DIVIDENDS PER SHARE GROWTH: **22.5%**

	2005	2006	2007	2008	2009	2010	2011	2012
Revenues (mil)	6,294	7,344	8,563	11,365	11,724	10,502	11,822	13,516
Net income (mil)	565.7	722.1	1,027	1,895	2,448	1,327	1,615	2,045
Earnings per share	1.05	1.31	1.98	3.39	4.41	2.41	2.93	3.70
Dividends per share	0.34	0.34	0.55	0.83	1.01	1.08	1.14	1.20
Cash flow per share	2.06	2.28	2.85	4.50	5.49	3.57	4.07	5.00
Price: high	39.9	53.5	116.3	145.8	93.4	87.1	78.7	94.8
low	25.0	37.9	49.1	63.5	66.6	44.6	58.9	69.7

Monsanto Company
800 North Lindbergh Boulevard
St Louis, MO 63167
(314) 694-1000
Website: www.monsanto.com

Mosaic Company

❑ Ticker symbol: MOS (NYSE) ❑ S&P rating: BBB ❑ Value Line financial strength rating: A
❑ Current yield: 1.7% ❑ Dividend raises, past 10 years: 2

Company Profile

We generally shy away from commodities producers. Why? Because it's hard to establish a brand or a competitive advantage. Typically the business becomes a race to the bottom, where the low-cost producer wins. But if you're the low-cost producer, you probably aren't making much money—and you probably won't stay the low-cost producer for long.

We prefer companies that have other routes to establishing—and maintaining—a competitive advantage. But there are commodities, and then there are strategic commodities. What do we mean by that? Well, some commodities are more important—and in more constrained supply—than others. And if a company can invest itself wholly in these commodities, and establish a dominant market share and position in doing so, it will establish a competitive advantage.

That's where the Mosaic Company comes in. Mosaic, formed in 2004 through a merger of Cargill's fertilizer operations with IMC Global, is the dominant world producer in the so-called "P+K" market—that's phosphorus and

potassium, for those of you who shied away from high school chemistry. And in case you're not clear on why P and K are important, they are vital fertilizer ingredients and hence essential to most of the world's agriculture production. Plants require more potassium than any other nutrient besides nitrogen, and it is important to root system development and many processes that form plant starch and proteins. Potassium is mined and sold in its oxide form known more popularly as potash. Phosphorus is a vital component of photosynthesis for plant metabolism and growth.

Mosaic is the largest combined P+K producer in the world. About two-thirds of the business is phosphorus and a third potash. Both minerals are produced commercially in a limited number of places in the world. Mosaic has interests in the important locations in North and South America, notably Florida phosphorus mines and potash mines in Saskatchewan, Michigan, New Mexico, and Peru. Through a network of processing and packaging plants in several countries, the company sells its product in approximately 40 countries. As a percentage of FY2012 sales, the United States accounted for 40 percent, Brazil 22 percent, India 15.4 percent, China 3.4 percent, and the remaining 19 percent made up of most of the rest of the agricultural free world.

Financial Highlights, Fiscal Year 2012

Not surprisingly, Mosaic's fortunes are driven by what is happening in the agriculture world, and the news from down on the farm, despite the 2012 drought in the U.S., has been pretty good lately. Several factors, including increasing overseas demand for basic foodstuffs, has driven crop prices up, and when that happens, more crops are planted and farmers are willing to spend more to grow them. That's pretty simple economics, and the world recovery from recession is helping that along

That said, Mosaic is subject to inventory cycles in planting and storage by downstream farmers and distributors, and when the agricultural economy sours, Mosaic and other companies in this business can see some sharp downturns. Total revenues plummeted some 35 percent from FY2009 to FY2010, only to recover most of that in FY2011 and top it by another 11 percent in FY2012, achieving a record $11.1 billion in top-line sales. Not too

surprisingly, margins and earnings follow the revenue swings. Per-share earnings rebounded smartly along with the revenues to a record $4.42 in FY2012. In part to soften the inventory cycle, the company has entered some long-term agreements at relatively lower prices, particularly in China and India. That, combined with another minor glut in the supply chain, is expected to reduce potash prices some 10 percent and hurt margins. In turn, that will spur moderate earnings growth to a modest 3 percent during FY2013. The company expects the international sector to grow faster than the U.S., which diversifies the demand base but also hurts pricing and margins. The company, which bought back 5 percent of its shares in FY2011, switched shareholder return "horses," doubling its dividend twice during FY2012 to an indicated $1.00 per share per year.

Reasons to Buy

Particularly for those interested in investing in commodities, we think this is some of the most fertile ground on which to stand. Demand for food will only increase over time, and Mosaic is the largest and 1 of only 5 major free world producers of P+K. The combination of prime mining sites, size, and operational efficiency in its processing and distribution operations should lead to at least maintaining, if not expanding, market share. While some of the recent expansion trends, including long-term Chinese contracts, hurt short-term profitability somewhat, we applaud the efforts to expand and simultaneously stabilize the business. And we enthusiastically applaud the dividend hikes and the dedication to returning cash to shareholders in general, whatever form that may take.

Reasons for Caution

Commodity markets and commodity producers are inherently volatile, and any reduction in planting or backup in inventory, not to mention overall global economic weakness or short-term droughts as experienced in the U.S., can drive prices down in a heartbeat. Particularly in the mining business, adjusting to these cycles can be difficult; it's a hard ship to turn. As we said, we applaud the company's efforts to be less impacted by these cycles.

SECTOR: **Materials**
BETA COEFFICIENT: **1.39**
10-YEAR COMPOUND EARNINGS PER SHARE GROWTH: **NM**
10-YEAR COMPOUND DIVIDENDS PER SHARE GROWTH: **NM**

	2005	2006	2007	2008	2009	2010	2011	2012
Revenues (mil)	4,397	5,304	5,774	9,812	10,298	6,759	9,937	11,108
Net income (mil)	167.6	82.6	342.5	1,962.2	1,909.7	862.8	1,942.2	1,930
Earnings per share	0.47	0.18	0.80	4.38	4.28	1.93	4.34	4.42
Dividends per share	—	—	—	—	0.20	0.20	0.20	1.00
Cash flow per share	0.99	1.15	1.67	5.20	5.11	2.94	5.35	5.73
Price: high	18.0	23.5	97.6	103.3	62.5	76.9	59.5	62.0
low	12.4	13.3	19.5	21.9	31.2	37.7	44.9	44.4

Mosaic Company
3033 Campus Drive
Plymouth, MN 55441
(800) 918-8270
Website: www.mosaicco.com

GROWTH AND INCOME

NextEra Energy, Inc.

❑ Ticker symbol: NEE (NYSE) ❑ S&P rating: A- ❑ Value Line financial strength rating: A ❑ Current yield: 3.6% ❑ Dividend raises, past 10 years: 10

Company Profile

NextEra is a full-service utility, power-generating unit, and utility services provider built around the utility stalwart Florida Power & Light, which formally changed its name to NextEra in 2010. NextEra not only represents an evolution in name but also a hint to how the company does business and expects to do business in the future as a leader in clean and large-scale alternative energy sourcing for the power market.

Headquartered in Juno Beach, FL, FPL Group's principal operating subsidiaries are NextEra Energy Resources, LLC, and the original Florida Power & Light Company, one of the largest rate-regulated electric utilities in the country. FP&L serves 4.6 million customer accounts in eastern and southern Florida. Through its subsidiaries, NextEra collectively operates the third-largest U.S. nuclear power generation fleet and has a significant presence in solar and wind generation markets.

As a nonregulated subsidiary, NextEra Energy Resources, LLC (or NEER), is a wholesale energy provider and a leader in producing electricity from clean and renewable fuels and, unlike many other alternative-energy driven businesses, is a viable standalone business entity. It has 4,700 employees at 115 facilities in 24 states and has solar and wind farms, nuclear energy facilities, and gas infrastructure operations not just in Florida but in 22 states and Canada. NEER's energy-producing portfolio includes 8,569 megawatts of wind generation facilities in 17 states and Canada, which is estimated to comprise 18 percent of the entire wind power generating capacity in the U.S.; 2,721 mW of nuclear generation in four facilities, 2,700 mW of traditional natural gas–fired generation, 1,168 mW in hydro and oil facilities, and 940 mW of solar projects. NEER recently purchased 2 solar energy farms, totaling 40mW, from industry leader First Solar Inc. All told, not only do the alternative energy platforms reduce fuel costs, but the total energy mix produces levels of sulfur dioxide (the cause of acid rain) some 90 percent below the average for the U.S. electric industry, a nitrous oxide emission rate 80 percent below the industry and a carbon dioxide (CO_2) emission rate

51 percent below industry averages. The subsidiary accounts for nearly a third of NextEra's total revenue—and nearly half of its profits—a healthy return for an alternative energy–based operation. Recently the NEER subsidiary has redirected its business toward longer-term contracts, which can hurt short-term profitability but help stabilize future revenues and earnings.

The company has a few small but promising nonregulated subsidiaries, offering design and consulting services for other alternative and conventional utility providers. Its FPL FiberNet subsidiary specializes in high-bandwidth data transmission from telecommunications locations to cell phone towers, mainly in Florida, Texas, and other areas in the South. Finally, the company was named number one overall among electric and gas utilities on *Fortune*'s 2012–13 World's Most Admired Companies list for a seventh straight year.

Financial Highlights, Fiscal Year 2012

Revenues in FY2012 dropped to $14.256 billion largely reflecting the sale of 4 gas-fired generating plants in late 2011. Total and per-share earnings dropped a corresponding amount. The company expects modest growth to return in FY2013 with earnings in the $4.70–$5.00 range, and has also offered an FY2014 target range of $5.05–$5.65, as post-recession energy usage recovers and as the regulatory environment continues to be generally favorable for rates.

Reasons to Buy

For those who believe that alternative energy is the future for large-scale power generation, NextEra is the best play available. The Recovery Act of 2009 contains a number of tax incentives for the deployment and use of renewable and nuclear sources, and NextEra is well positioned to take advantage. The company continues to grow alternative energy capacity on all fronts, particularly wind and solar, and continues to make money on these efforts. All of this adds to the solid and traditional FP&L regulated utility base; this company has the steady feel of a traditional utility with a bit more interest in the form of alternative energy plays and leading-edge power utility technology. Cash flow is very strong and supports both the dividend and continued investments in alternative energy production.

Reasons for Caution

The company's FPL subsidiary is still a regulated utility and may not always receive the most accommodating treatment. Additionally, alternative energy tax credits may not be around forever. The dividend yield, while still healthy for a company with future growth prospects in an up-and-coming industry, is still a little low by current utility standards—reflecting

in part the fact that investors have already put a lot of energy into this stock, and the price accounts for its prospects. Buyers should continue to look for good entry points.

SECTOR: **Utilities**
BETA COEFFICIENT: **0.50**
10-YEAR COMPOUND EARNINGS PER SHARE GROWTH: **7.5%**
10-YEAR COMPOUND DIVIDENDS PER SHARE GROWTH: **6.5%**

	2005	2006	2007	2008	2009	2010	2011	2012
Revenues (mil)	11,846	15,710	15,263	16,410	15,646	15,317	15,341	14,256
Net income (mil)	885	1,261	1,312	1,639	1,615	1,957	2,021	1,911
Earnings per share	2.32	3.23	3.27	4.07	3.97	4.74	4.82	4.56
Dividends per share	1.42	1.50	1.64	1.78	1.89	2.00	2.20	2.40
Cash flow per share	6.18	6.77	6.85	8.03	8.75	9.60	9.29	8.70
Price: high	48.1	55.6	72.8	73.8	60.6	56.3	61.2	72.2
low	35.9	37.8	53.7	33.8	41.5	45.3	49.0	58.6

NextEra Energy, Inc.
700 Universe Boulevard
Juno Beach, FL 33408
(561) 694-4697
Website: www.nexteraenergy.com

AGGRESSIVE GROWTH

Nike, Inc.

❑ Ticker symbol: NKE (NYSE) ❑ S&P rating: A+ ❑ Value Line financial strength rating: A++
❑ Current yield: 1.5% ❑ Dividend raises, past 10 years: 10

Company Profile

Nike's principal business activity is the design, development, and worldwide marketing of footwear, apparel, equipment, and accessory products. Nike is the largest seller of athletic footwear and athletic apparel in the world, but a big part of the story is how they are extending beyond traditional footwear and apparel. Their products are sold through retail accounts, Nike-owned retail outlets, its website, and a mix of independent distributors and licensees in more than 190 countries around the world.

Nike does no manufacturing—virtually all of their footwear and apparel items are manufactured by independent contractors outside the United States, while equipment products are produced both in the United States and abroad.

Nike's shoes are designed primarily for athletic use, although a large percentage of these products are worn for casual or leisure purposes. Their shoes are designed for men, women, and children for running, training, basketball, and soccer use, although they also carry brands for casual wear.

Nike sells apparel and accessories for most of the sports addressed by their shoe lines, as well as athletic bags and accessory items. Nike apparel and accessories are designed to complement their athletic footwear products, feature the same trademarks, and are sold through the same marketing and distribution channels. All Nike-branded products are marketed with the familiar "swoosh" logo, one of the most recognized and successful branding images in history.

Nike has a number of wholly owned subsidiaries, or "affiliate brands," including Converse, Hurley, Jordan Brand, and Nike Golf, which variously design, distribute, and license dress, athletic, and casual footwear, sports apparel, and accessories. The company sold its Cole-Haan and Umbro subsidiaries in 2012. In FY2012, these subsidiary brands accounted for just under 15 percent of total revenues.

Of the total $21 billion in 2012 Nike brand revenues (excluding subsidiaries) approximately 42 percent comes from North America, 21 percent from Western Europe, 12 percent from China, 6 percent from central and eastern Europe,

4.3 percent from Japan, and 16 percent from other emerging markets. Growth for the emerging markets was 25 percent year over year, for China 23 percent, and for North America 17 percent. It's not hard to see the strength of the Nike brand abroad.

Financial Highlights, Fiscal Year 2012

Nike's sales gained speed in FY2012, up some 15.7 percent over FY2011, which was up 9.7 percent from an unusually soft FY2010. During 2012 the company split its stock 2 for 1 and bought back some 36 million shares, about 4 percent of its float, and raised its annual dividend 17 percent to 70 cents annually—all solid results considering that it was a period of higher input costs and slightly lower gross margins. On a constant currency basis, the company expects high single to low double-digit growth rates for FY2013 with earnings per share expected to grow in the 12 percent range. Demand for its products continues to be strong in all regions, and input costs may ease during the year. The company is quite sensitive to foreign exchange, and a strong dollar can diminish results.

Reasons to Buy

Why buy Nike? In a word, brand. The Nike brand and its corresponding swoosh continue to be one of the most recognized—and sought after—brands in the world. It is a lesson in simplicity and image congruence with the product behind it. Nike doesn't sit still with it; rather, the company is learning to leverage it into more products outside the traditional athletic wear circuit—golf clubs, golf balls, even a new line of GPS watches and apps to find, say, a new route for your run and to track your performance right on your phone. The company continues to invest in innovation in all of its segments, including new fabrics, colors, uniform materials, and digital linkages to make active lifestyles more productive and fun. Further, Nike doesn't just limit the brand appeal to athletes: Slogans like "Just Do It" and "If you have a body, you're an athlete" emphasize the appeal and lifestyle across all segments of the population. We think this is drop-dead smart.

Of course, solid brand and brand reputation lead to category leadership and, hence, higher profitability, and Nike has finished far ahead of the pack in this area, too. The brand and moat created by the brand seem to have nowhere to go but forward, and improved manufacturing efficiencies, strong channel relationships, and international exposure, particularly in China, all keep the company moving faster in the right direction. Despite its size, the company continues to deliver double-digit earnings, cash flow, and dividend growth. We continue to like the combination of protected profitability through brand excellence, combined with a clean conservative balance sheet, providing a good combination of safety and growth potential—and we like the fact that they are returning more of the proceeds to shareholders.

Reasons for Caution

Two things could put hurdles in Nike's path. The first is higher commodity input prices. Second, the company is continually in the news—and the rumor mill—for unfair labor practices and child labor violations in some of its foreign manufacturing plants. The company doesn't actually own or operate these plants, but the rumors can stick nonetheless. A particularly egregious violation could tarnish the brand, but there have been none to date.

SECTOR: **Consumer Discretionary**
BETA COEFFICIENT: **0.85**
10-YEAR COMPOUND EARNINGS PER SHARE GROWTH: **14.5%**
10-YEAR COMPOUND DIVIDENDS PER SHARE GROWTH: **17.0%**

	2005	2006	2007	2008	2009	2010	2011	2012
Revenues (mil)	13,740	14,955	16,326	18,627	19,176	19,014	20,862	24,128
Net income (mil)	945	1,392	1,458	1,734	1,727	1,907	2,133	2,223
Earnings per share	1.12	1.32	1.43	1.72	1.76	1.93	2.20	2.37
Dividends per share	0.24	0.30	0.36	0.44	0.49	0.53	0.60	0.70
Cash flow per share	1.32	1.60	1.72	2.07	2.12	2.23	2.60	2.83
Price: high	22.5	25.3	34.0	35.3	33.3	46.2	49.1	57.4
low	18.8	18.9	23.7	21.3	16.1	30.4	54.7	42.6

Nike, Inc.
One Bowerman Drive
Beaverton, OR 97005
(503) 671-6453
Website: www.nikeinc.com

CONSERVATIVE GROWTH

Norfolk Southern Corporation

❑ Ticker symbol: NSC (NYSE) ❑ S&P rating: BBB+ ❑ Value Line financial strength rating: B+
❑ Current yield: 2.0 ❑ Dividend raises, past 10 years: 10

Company Profile

Norfolk Southern Corp. was formed in 1982 as a holding company when the Norfolk & Western Railway merged with the Southern Railway. Including lines received in the split takeover (with CSX) of Conrail, the current railroad operates 21,000 route-miles of track in 22 eastern and southern states. They serve every major port on the East Coast of the United States and have the most extensive intermodal network in the east.

Company business in FY2012 was about 26 percent coal, coke, and iron ore; 20 percent intermodal; 13 percent agricultural and consumer products; 12 percent metals and construction; and 29 percent other. Within those categories, the railroad transports the usual mix of raw materials, intermediate products such as parts, and manufactured goods.

In the late 1990s, the company split the acquisition of northeastern rail heavyweight Conrail with rival CSX corporation, so it has considerable operations in the Northeast and Midwest in addition to its traditional southern base. The heaviest traffic corridors are New York–Chicago; Chicago–Atlanta; Appalachian coalfields to the port of Norfolk, VA, and Sandusky, OH; and Cleveland–Kansas City. The company has a diverse base of large Midwestern factories and large and smaller southern factories and basic materials producers in the coal and lumber industry, giving a well-diversified traffic base.

The company has been an innovator in the intermodal business, that is, combining trucking and rail services—with its Triple Crown services, centered on the Roadrailer, a train of coupled-together highway vans on special wheelsets. At the terminal, a cab simply backs up to the van and drives it off.

The company provides a number of logistics services and has substantial traffic to and from ports and overseas destinations. The company has an active program to attract lineside customers to build freight volumes.

Financial Highlights, Fiscal Year 2012

Norfolk Southern was chugging along nicely as the economy improved in FY2010 and FY2011, with record revenues and sales gains near 10 percent. Then, a funny thing happened to natural gas prices. The new availability of cheap gas, European and Chinese softness, and new regulations all blended together to derail coal-hauling revenues. As a portion of the company's revenues, coal dropped from 31 percent in FY2011 to 26 percent in FY2012. Soft coal shipments dropped revenues about 1.2 percent and net earnings a bit more, about 5.6 percent. Even so, a substantial 5 percent share buyback resulted in the modest 2 percent earnings per share increase after a 27 percent increase the previous year. Lower coal volumes hurt the excellent operating ratio (ratio of variable operating costs to total costs) to 71.7, still an excellent figure and good enough for the number two position behind *100 Best* stock Union Pacific.

Reasons to Buy

NSC and its competitors have all been hurt by the coal slowdown, but there are some silver linings, both short and long term. For the short term, increased exploration and production of crude oil in places like North Dakota have changed around oil supply chains in the U.S., and since there are no pipelines to serve the need, trainloads of oil are moving from this and a few other booming regions to eastern refineries. The boom has also brought new business moving other commodities used in the new fracking extraction process. Longer term, a widening of the Panama Canal, scheduled to go into use in 2014, will expand Asian trade into southern and eastern ports (a lot of which now comes into the West Coast). Norfolk Southern continues to do an excellent job sizing its physical plant and managing costs, as evidenced by the operating ratio mentioned earlier. NSC has proven over the past 30 years that it can compete effectively for long-haul truck business with its intermodal offerings and has some of the most competitive service and terminal structures in the business. It has gained market share from trucks. Additionally, NSC serves some of the more dynamic and up-and-coming manufacturing markets in the United States, namely, Asian and other foreign-owned manufacturing facilities found particularly in the Southeast. The company has created a Heartland Corridor time freight and double-stack container routing between Chicago and the East Coast, reducing distance by 250 miles and, more importantly, transit times from 4 to 3 days. Additionally, the company is about to complete similar improvements on its Crescent Corridor between Louisiana and New Jersey. Such innovations will further assert the company's leadership. Additionally, we like the strength and diversity coming from serving the domestic and especially the foreign-owned auto industry—the company serves plants for (in alphabetical order) BMW, Chrysler, Ford, General Motors, Honda, Isuzu, Mazda, Mercedes-Benz, Mitsubishi, Nissan, Subaru, Suzuki, and Toyota.

Finally, cash flow continues to be strong, dividend raises are consistent, and the company authorized repurchase of another 50 million shares, about a sixth of the current float.

Reasons for Caution

While the coal slowdown seems to be under control and accounted for in the stock price, it is still a very important commodity; a further downturn would hurt. Additionally, higher fuel prices can hurt, but this is usually offset somewhat by increased use of rail transport as customers are looking to save on fuel costs, and also on fuel surcharges the company levies on shipments from time to time.

SECTOR: **Transportation**
BETA COEFFICIENT: **1.13**
10-YEAR COMPOUND EARNINGS PER SHARE GROWTH: **16.5%**
10-YEAR COMPOUND DIVIDENDS PER SHARE GROWTH: **14.5%**

	2005	2006	2007	2008	2009	2010	2011	2012
Revenues (mil)	8,527	9,407	9,432	10,661	7,969	9,516	11,172	11,040
Net income (mil)	1,161	1,481	1,464	1,716	1,034	1,498	1,853	1,749
Earnings per share	2.82	3.58	3.68	4.52	2.76	4.00	5.27	5.37
Dividends per share	0.48	0.68	0.96	1.22	1.36	1.40	1.68	1.94
Cash flow per share	4.72	5.58	5.90	6.88	5.07	6.48	8.22	8.49
Price: high	45.8	57.7	59.6	75.5	54.8	63.7	78.4	78.5
low	29.6	39.1	45.4	41.4	26.7	46.2	57.6	56.1

Norfolk Southern Corporation
Three Commercial Place
Norfolk, VA 23510–2191
(757) 629-2600
Website: www.nscorp.com

Otter Tail Corporation

❑ Ticker symbol: OTTR (NASDAQ) ❑ S&P rating: BBB- ❑ Value Line financial strength rating: B+
❑ Current yield: 3.8% ❑ Dividend raises, past 10 years: 5

Company Profile

Otter Tail Corporation is a holding company and a mini-conglomerate operating primarily in the upper Midwest. The conglomerate is centered on and stabilized by the Otter Tail Power Company, a regulated utility serving about 129,000 customers in rural Minnesota, North Dakota, and South Dakota. The utility accounted for about 32 percent of the total business in FY2011 and now accounts for about 41 percent as the company trims some of its noncore, nonutility assets.

Extensive use of wind generation and hydro power, and lower grades of coal available in the region, have driven fuel costs down to 13.4 percent of revenues, a very low figure for the industry. (By comparison, Xcel Energy, which supplies electricity to surrounding areas in North Dakota and Minnesota as well as other Great Plains locations, Colorado, and Texas, spends 50 percent of revenues on fuel.) Approximately 12 percent of power generation is from wind or hydro sources.

Beyond the utility, the company, which has sold 6 fairly good-sized businesses in the past 2 years, now operates in 3 other business segments, accounting for the other 60 percent of the business:

- The Manufacturing segment (now about 24 percent of revenues, up from 21 percent) houses 3 smaller businesses. BTD Manufacturing is a metal stamping, fabricating, and laser-cutting shop supplying custom parts for agriculture, lawn care, health and fitness, and the RV industry. T.O. Plastics supplies packaging and handling products for the horticultural industry. The ShoreMaster business, which produces and markets residential and commercial waterfront equipment—boat lifts, docks, and marinas—was sold in early 2013 and accounted for about 3 percent of the company's business.
- The Plastics segment (15 percent of revenues, up from 11 percent) has 2 operations supplying commercial and utility-grade PVC and other plastic pipe and accessories.
- Construction (about 17 percent, unchanged) is a

residential, commercial, and industrial installer of electric, fiber optic, HVAC, and water and wastewater systems primarily in the Midwest.

Otter Tail has been divesting itself of noncore businesses over the past 2 years and has exited the wind-power equipment business altogether. In 2011 it sold Idaho Pacific Holdings, a maker of dehydrated potato products for the snack food and food service industries; its Health Services Segment, known as DMS, which integrated and sold diagnostic medical imaging and patient monitoring equipment; and its specialty trucking business, E. W. Wylie, which specialized in moving wind power equipment. In FY2012, the company sold its DMI wind tower business, and in early FY2013 it completed the sale of ShoreMaster. Together these businesses had accounted for about 18 percent of the company's total.

Overall, the company has 2,231 employees, and most operations are centered in the upper Midwest.

Financial Highlights, Fiscal Year 2012

FY2012, like FY2011, was a transition year for the company highlighted by the sale of 2 more of its larger subsidiary businesses. Revenues, earnings, and per-share results are thus difficult to compare, but the business divestitures appears to be heading the company in the right direction. FY2012 earnings perked up to $1.05 per share from $0.45 the previous year and are projected in the $1.30–$1.55 range in FY2013, a notable improvement. The company raised its dividend modestly for the first time in a few years,

Reasons to Buy

When we first added Otter Tail to the 2012 *100 Best* stocks list, admittedly we were taken by its Berkshire Hathaway–like construct of basic business around a steady core, the electric utility. We also liked its commitment to the wind energy business. But aside from reducing energy input costs to the utility, the wind business wasn't working well, and the other businesses may have been a bit too far flung to manage effectively—so they retrenched, trimmed the branches, so to speak, and continued on with a company still more or less constructed around this model. No doubt, these were hard decisions, but if the numbers and projections are right (and if a strong share price performance is right, as well), the decisions were the right ones. In fact, the decision to jettison businesses that don't fit, or ones such as the wind energy business threatened by cheap natural gas, are hard to make, and the fact that this company makes them can be viewed as a plus. Otter Tail still appears to be a good way to participate in several well-managed businesses while getting a decent current return with solid cash flows and dividends. It is the only small-cap stock on our *100 Best* list, for those wanting to add a bit of small-cap flavor to their portfolios. It is indeed like a "small town" company in contrast to "big city" corporate America.

Reasons for Caution

The dividend hasn't been covered by current earnings and is only barely covered currently, a caution flag in any business, although it is amply covered by cash flow. The utility is stable but not likely to be helped along by population growth. Further business sales may continue to raise some questions about overall strategy, as well as create distractions. We compared Otter Tail to Berkshire Hathaway but should note that Berkshire is more diversified and has much larger anchor businesses.

SECTOR: **Utilities/Industrial**
BETA COEFFICIENT: **1.08**
10-YEAR COMPOUND EARNINGS PER SHARE GROWTH: **-9.5%**
10-YEAR COMPOUND DIVIDENDS PER SHARE GROWTH: **1.5%**

	2005	2006	2007	2008	2009	2010	2011	2012
Revenues (mil)	1,046	1,105	1,239	1,311	1,040	1,118	1,078	859.2
Net income (mil)	52.9	50.8	54.0	35.1	26.0	13.6	16.4	39.0
Earnings per share	1.78	1.88	1.78	1.09	0.71	0.38	0.45	1.05
Dividends per share	1.12	1.15	1.17	1.19	1.19	1.19	1.19	1.19
Cash flow per share	3.35	3.39	3.55	2.81	2.76	2.82	2.39	2.71
Price: high	32.0	31.9	39.4	46.2	25.4	25.4	23.5	25.3
low	24.0	25.8	29.0	15.0	18.5	18.2	17.5	20.7

Otter Tail Corporation
P.O. Box 496
Fergus Falls, MN 56538
(866) 410-8780
Website: www.ottertail.com

AGGRESSIVE GROWTH

Pall Corporation

❑ Ticker symbol: PLL (NYSE) ❑ S&P rating: BBB ❑ Value Line financial strength rating: A ❑ Current yield: 1.4% ❑ Dividend raises, past 10 years: 8

Company Profile

Okay, raise your hand if you've heard of Pall Corporation. Anyone? No? Well, neither had we until we found this company in 2010 in a search for quality industrial suppliers that were number 1 or 2 in their markets.

Pall supplies filtration, separation, and purification technologies for the removal of solid, liquid, and gaseous contaminants from a variety of liquids and gases. Its products are used in thousands of industrial and clinical settings: removal of contaminants from gas reagents in every semiconductor production facility in the world, removal of bacteria and virus spores from water in hospitals and other clinical settings, and detection of bacteria in blood samples. Its products range in scale from simple in-line filters, sold 100 to the carton, to entire graywater treatment systems with capacities up to 150,000 gallons/day.

Business segmentation remains much the same as last year, except for a 7 percent advance in the size of the Biopharma business, mostly at the expense of the General Industrial segment discussed below. Pall's product and customers fall into two broad categories: Life Sciences (47 percent of the FY2012 business) and Industrial (53 percent). The Life Sciences category breaks down further into Blood/Medical (16 percent) and Biopharma (31 percent). The company's Life Sciences technologies are used in the research laboratory, pharmaceutical and biotechnology industries, in blood centers, and in hospitals at the point of patient care. Certain medical products improve the safety of the use of blood products in patient care and help control the spread of infections in hospitals. Pall's separation systems and disposable filtration and purification technologies are critical to the development and commercialization of chemically synthesized and biologically derived drugs and vaccines.

The Industrial segment includes General Industrial (28 percent of sales), Aerospace and Transportation (12 percent), and Microelectronics (13 percent). Industrial markets include, but aren't limited to, consumer electronics, municipal and industrial water, fuels, chemicals, energy, and food and beverage markets. As an example, Pall sells filtration solutions to the wine, beer, soft drink, bottled water, and food ingredient markets. Additionally, the company sells filtration and fluid monitoring equipment to the aerospace industry for use on commercial and military aircraft, ships, and land-based military vehicles to help protect critical systems and components. Pall also sells filtration and purification technologies for the semiconductor, data storage, fiber optic, advanced display, and materials markets.

Pall is the leader in almost all of these markets. International sales account for 67 percent of the total.

Financial Highlights, Fiscal Year 2012

In the wake of the recession, both R & D and manufacturing activities have picked up, helping the overall results of the business. That said, the company sells products likely to be stocked at distributors and in a customer's inventory prior to use. As such, the company can experience inventory cycles; that plus softness in Europe put a bit of a filter on FY2012 results. After a 14 percent rise in revenues in FY2011, the company experienced a 2.5 percent sales drop in FY2012 with slightly lower margins to boot. But a lower effective tax rate and a modest share buyback boosted earnings anyway. For FY2013, the company appears to be ready to emerge from the inventory cycle, with management

guidance of $2.90–$3.05 per share for an increase of around 10 percent. The company boosted its dividend 25 percent in FY2012. Strong cash flows make further healthy incremental boosts, as well as additional share buybacks, likely.

Reasons to Buy

We like companies with a dominant position in their marketplaces or market niches. We also like industrials with a diversified customer base, and we like companies that have a strong and ongoing base of repeat business. Pall delivers on all 3 principles. The company sells into the medical, biopharma, energy, and water-process technologies; aerospace; and microelectronics spaces, among others. These sectors will continue to show consistency and strength over time. Further, Pall's products are consumables used consistently within the lab and manufacturing processes they sell into; they do not depend greatly on capital spending decisions and are relatively less sensitive to economic cycles, although they can be affected by inventory cycles as mentioned. Seventy-five percent of Pall's sales are repeat-purchased consumables; this makes the company a little more recession proof, and with a dominant market position, net profit margins in the 12 percent range are strong enough to generate healthy ongoing cash flow. We also like the company's strong international footprint.

Reasons for Caution

While its presence in the consumables side of the business attenuates the effects of economic cycles somewhat, the company is still sensitive to economic downturns. The recent strength in the business and business model has been noticed by others, too. This may attract more competition (or who knows, a takeover bid?) from the likes of 3M or a similar company. The strength continues to be reflected in the share price; new investors should look to buy on dips. While cash returns are on the increase, we would like to see even more accelerated dividend hikes and share repurchases.

SECTOR: **Industrials**
BETA COEFFICIENT: **1.19**
10-YEAR COMPOUND EARNINGS PER SHARE GROWTH: **10.5%**
10-YEAR COMPOUND DIVIDENDS PER SHARE GROWTH: **2.0%**

		2005	2006	2007	2008	2009	2010	2011	2012
Revenues (mil)		1,902	2,017	2,250	2,572	2,392	2,402	2,741	2,672
Net income (mil)		141	146	128	217	196	241	315	319
Earnings per share		1.12	1.16	1.02	1.76	1.64	2.03	2.67	2.71
Dividends per share		0.40	0.44	0.48	0.51	0.58	0.64	0.70	0.88
Cash flow per share		1.86	1.97	1.81	2.60	2.44	2.90	3.60	3.77
Price:	high	31.5	35.6	49.0	43.2	37.3	44.7	59.5	65.8
	low	25.2	25.3	33.2	21.6	18.2	31.8	39.8	50.0

Pall Corporation
2200 Northern Boulevard
East Hills, NY 11548
(516) 484-5400
Website: www.pall.com

AGGRESSIVE GROWTH

Patterson Companies, Inc.

❏ Ticker symbol: PDCO (NASDAQ) ❏ S&P rating: not rated ❏ Value Line financial strength rating: A ❏ Current yield: 1.5% ❏ Dividend raises, past 10 years: 3

Company Profile

Patterson Companies is a value-added distributor operating in 3 segments—Dental Supply, Veterinary Supply, and Medical Supply. Dental Supply (about 65 percent of sales) provides a complete range of consumable dental products, equipment, and software; turnkey digital solutions; office design and setup; and value-added services to dentists and dental laboratories primarily for the North American market. Veterinary Supply (20 percent) is the nation's second-largest distributor of consumable veterinary supplies, equipment, diagnostic products, vaccines, and pharmaceuticals to companion-pet veterinary clinics. Medical Supply (15 percent) distributes medical supplies and assistive products, primarily for rehabilitation and sports medicine, globally to hospitals, long-term-care facilities, clinics, and dealers.

Patterson has one-third of the dental supply market. Their main competitors are HSIC (Henry Schein), which also has about a one-third share, and Dentsply (a former *100 Best* stock). The remaining share is fragmented among a number of smaller players. As one of the lead dogs, Patterson has the clout to negotiate a number of exclusive distribution deals. It is sole distributor for the industry's most popular line of dental chairs, and also has an exclusive on the CEREC 3-D dental restorative system, an increasingly popular alternative to traditional dental crowns. Patterson is also the leading provider of digital radiography systems, which create instant images of dental work, superior to the images generated by traditional x-ray equipment.

Patterson's veterinary business, Webster Veterinary, is the second-largest distributor of consumable veterinary supplies to companion-pet veterinary clinics. Its line also includes equipment and software, diagnostic products, and vaccines and pharmaceuticals.

In FY2012, the company acquired the American Veterinarian Supply Company to enhance its presence in the veterinary segment and Orthoplast and Surgical Synergies Pty Ltd to expand in the rehabilitative surgical market, the latter with an international footprint in Australia and New Zealand.

Financial Highlights, Fiscal Year 2012

It's human nature to delay trips to the dentist as long as possible regardless of economic times, and the "dental lag" gets even longer in a recession. The soft economy gave patients plenty of reasons (and excuses) to defer elective and even not-so-elective procedures, and dentists, as a result, drew down their inventories and delayed capital purchases for things like dental chairs and digital imaging systems.

The dental industry seems to be one of the most lagging of many lagging industries after a recession. This scenario continues into early FY2013. Year-over-year sales growth continues to be very modest at about 4.7 percent, which still compares favorably to FY2011's 2.4 percent. We've commented on the strong recoveries enjoyed by a lot of other *100 Best* stocks businesses, but here "dental lag" still seems to carry the day. Net profits edged higher, but the company also reduced share counts a few percentage points and with a relatively low share count of 108 million and dropping, managed to eke out a 9.4 percent gain in earnings per share. The active share repurchase program may drop the share count again to 100 million (it was 123 million in 2009 and 139 million in 2006), delivering a far more solid EPS growth projection for FY2013 to $2.60, a nearly 24 percent gain.

Reasons to Buy

We think that dental lag will subside sooner or later, and dental procedures, capital investment, and inventory replenishment will all return to more normal levels. While there have been some improvements in the art of long-term dental care, such as more widespread fluoride use, we see the need for replacement crowns as well as more expensive and material-intensive implant restorations continuing, if not growing, as the population ages and as dental care becomes a bigger industry overseas.

The aforementioned CEREC 3-D is an imaging and milling system that allows the dentist to take an image of the area to be restored and in less than 30 minutes produce a crown, inlay, or other device that is then fitted to the patient's existing dental structure. It's a compelling proposition for high-volume offices where patient throughput is at a premium and the equipment can be fully utilized. Sales of this high-ticket item have been very good and generate ongoing supplies revenue. Patterson's exclusive license to this product is a powerful foot in the door for new accounts.

We like the company's moves into the companion-pet veterinary and rehabilitative markets, both of which are driven by a growing and profitable demographic. Today the company is primarily focused on the North American market, with promised 24- to 48-hour delivery for most items. They have established an international beachhead with the Patterson Medical group in the U.K. and France and intend to leverage this presence to expand the dental and veterinary businesses; thus far international expansion remains more an opportunity—a good one—than a reality. The company continues to aggressively invest in its investors, making significant share repurchases and decent dividend increases. Patterson is one of a small handful of mid-cap companies on our *100 Best* stocks list, so it may be of interest to investors looking for something in that size range to complement our mostly large-cap-dominated

list. Notably, the company was once again named to the *Forbes* list of America's 100 Most Trustworthy Companies.

Reasons for Caution

Competition in this arena is strong, and the company will have to stay sharp to take advantage once dental lag subsides; otherwise, it could lose share to competitors. We believe that the number of companies offering good dental insurance is declining, and any factor that makes dental procedures more "elective" will likely work against Patterson. Some of the expected recovery from dental lag may already be priced into the stock, so entry points should be chosen carefully, although this stock has proven to be fairly stable.

SECTOR: **Health Care**
BETA COEFFICIENT: **0.86**
10-YEAR COMPOUND EARNINGS PER SHARE GROWTH: **12.5%**
10-YEAR COMPOUND DIVIDENDS PER SHARE GROWTH: **NM**

	2005	2006	2007	2008	2009	2010	2011	2012E
Revenues (mil)	2,615	2,798	2,998	3,094	3,237	3,415	3,536	3,655
Net income (mil)	198	208	225	200	212	225	213	210
Earnings per share	1.43	1.51	1.69	1.70	1.78	1.91	1.92	2.05
Dividends per share	—	—	—	—	0.10	0.42	0.50	0.58
Cash flow per share	1.68	2.05	1.88	2.00	2.04	2.20	2.31	2.60
Price: high	53.8	38.3	40.1	37.8	28.3	32.8	39.9	37.6
low	33.4	29.6	28.3	15.8	16.1	24.1	26.2	34.3

Patterson Companies, Inc.
1031 Mendota Heights Road
St. Paul, MN 55120–1419
(651) 686-1775
Website: www.pattersoncompanies.com

AGGRESSIVE GROWTH

Paychex, Inc.

❑ Ticker symbol: PAYX (NASDAQ) ❑ S&P rating: not rated ❑ Value Line financial strength rating: A ❑ Current yield: 3.0% ❑ Dividend raises, past 10 years: 8

Company Profile

Paychex, Inc. provides payroll, human resource, and benefits outsourcing solutions for small- to medium-sized businesses with 10–200 employees. Founded in 1971, the company has more than 100 offices and serves over 567,000 clients in the United States, and an additional 2,000 clients in Germany. The company has 2 sources of revenue: service revenue, paid by clients for services, and interest income on the funds held by Paychex for clients.

Paychex offers a portfolio of services and products, including:

- Payroll processing
- Payroll tax services
- Employee payment services, including expense reporting, reimbursements, etc.
- Regulatory compliance services (new-hire reporting and garnishment processing)
- Comprehensive human resource outsourcing services
- Retirement services
- Workers' compensation insurance services
- Health and benefits services
- Time and attendance solutions
- Medical deduction, state unemployment, and other HR services and products

The company's products are marketed primarily through its direct sales force, the bulk of which is focused on payroll products. In addition to the direct sales force, the company uses its relationships with existing clients, CPAs, and banks for new client referrals. Approximately two-thirds of its new clients come via these referral sources.

Larger clients can choose to outsource their payroll and HR functions or to run them in-house using a Paychex platform. For those clients, the company offers "Major Market Services" (MMS) products, which can be run locally or on a web-hosted environment.

In addition to traditional payroll services, Paychex offers full-service HR outsourcing solutions; custom-built solutions including payroll, compliance, HR, and employee benefits sourcing and administration; outsourcing management; and even professionally trained onsite HR representatives. The company also manages retirement plans and other benefits, including pretax "cafeteria" plans, and has a subsidiary insurance agency offering property and casualty, workers' comp, health, and auto policies to an employer's employee base. About 21,000 of the 567,000 clients use the full Human Resource Services offering. The company has recently made a push to implement web-based and mobile versions of its key products, adding to convenience and reducing paperwork for its clients.

Financial Highlights, Fiscal Year 2012

As the global economy emerges from recession, the expansion in employment helps Paychex's business. Thus, the revenue gain for FY2012 far exceeded that for FY2011, with a gain of 7 percent compared to 4.3 percent in FY2011 after a bottoming year in FY2010. The company's revenues are driven by payroll numbers, payroll activity, and the float—the interest earned on money held before paychecks are cashed and before tax payments are made to tax collecting authorities—which can be 30–90 days depending on the type of tax and the arrangement with the employer. Low interest rates on cash deposits continue to attenuate what might otherwise be stronger profit numbers, but even with that, net profits rose almost in line with revenues at 6.4 percent.

The generous dividend continues to consume more than 80 percent of earnings, so there wasn't much left over for share buybacks or even dividend increases during the past few years. The company has 3 primary growth strategies: first, offer a more complete service, such as HR; second, acquire other smaller companies offering similar local services; and third, create more cloudlike services to enable clients to switch from homegrown to Paychex solutions. The company made a few small acquisitions during the year and may continue to do so. Company projections are for a net income increase in the 5–7 percent range in FY2013.

Reasons to Buy

A bet on Paychex is a bet on two things: continued improvement in the economy and an eventual increase on interest rates (so they can make money on the float). In the meantime, you get a pretty decent yield and little downside risk if you own the stock.

Paychex's primary market is companies with fewer than 100 employees. This is one of the primary reasons that Paychex lost clients—many small businesses went out of business during the recession. That trend has turned around with the economy, and beyond that, the cost of switching and a generally good client relationship has made for a loyal client base. We continue to think the trend to outsource payroll and HR activities will not only continue but accelerate as easier Internet-based solutions come more into favor. The company is conservatively run and is well financed. It carries no long-term debt and should have little difficulty funding the generous dividend, even at its current payout level of 80–90 percent of earnings. Fragmentation in the market and Paychex's extremely strong financial position will allow the company to continue to grow market share through acquisition. As business activity has heated up and competition waned, the company has been able to tack on a few small price increases. Finally, sooner or later short-term interest rates must tick upward; then the company will once again be able to profit from the float. We would expect dividend increases—and share repurchases—to resume at that point if not before.

Reasons for Caution

This company will always be vulnerable to economic swings, and did hit the slow-growth wall in 2009 with only a slow recovery. The company's acquisition strategy makes sense, as those acquisitions will increase market share, but they do come with costs and risks. Finally, while most analysts consider the dividend payout secure, it does account for a substantial fraction of the company's cash flow, and increases may be hard to come by for the immediate future. Also, with such a high yield and relatively low growth, near-term share appreciation might be difficult.

SECTOR: **Information Technology**
BETA COEFFICIENT: **0.85**
10-YEAR COMPOUND EARNINGS PER SHARE GROWTH: **10.5%**
10-YEAR COMPOUND DIVIDENDS PER SHARE GROWTH: **18.0%**

	2005	2006	2007	2008	2009	2010	2011	2012
Revenues (mil)	1,445	1,675	1,887	2,066	2,083	2,001	2,084	2,230
Net income (mil)	369	465	515	576	534	477	516	548
Earnings per share	0.97	1.22	1.35	1.56	1.48	1.32	1.42	1.51
Dividends per share	0.51	0.61	0.79	1.20	1.24	1.24	1.24	1.27
Cash flow per share	1.14	1.40	1.54	1.82	1.72	1.56	1.67	1.78
Price: high	43.4	42.4	47.1	37.5	32.9	32.8	33.9	34.7
low	28.8	33.0	36.1	23.2	20.3	24.7	25.1	29.1

Paychex, Inc.
911 Panorama Trail South
Rochester, NY 14625–0397
(585) 385-6666
Website: www.paychex.com

CONSERVATIVE GROWTH

PepsiCo, Inc.

◻ Ticker symbol: PEP (NYSE) ◻ S&P rating: A ◻ Value Line financial strength rating: A++
◻ Current yield: 2.8% ◻ Dividend raises, past 10 years: 10

Company Profile

PepsiCo is a global beverage, snack, and food company. It manufactures, markets, and sells a variety of salty, convenient, sweet, and grain-based snacks; carbonated and non-carbonated beverages; and foods in approximately 200 countries, with its largest operations in North America (United States, Canada, and Mexico), the United Kingdom, and now Russia. Most of the major PepsiCo brands, such as the familiar Pepsi Cola, are likely to show up in abundance in your refrigerator and kitchen cupboard at any time.

PepsiCo is organized into 4 business units, as follows:

■ Pepsico Americas Foods (37 percent, 52 percent), which includes two major foods groups, formerly reported as separate operating segments. The first is the familiar Frito-Lay, which makes and distributes the too-familiar snack brands—Fritos, Doritos, Lay's, Cheetos, Tostitos, Ruffles, SunChips, and various dips and spreads to go with these products. The second is Quaker Foods which came to

Pepsi in 2001 and sells Quaker Oats, Aunt Jemima, Cap'n Crunch, Life cereal, Rice-A-Roni, Mother's Cookies, and Near East, to name a few.

■ PepsiCo Americas Beverages (33 percent, 28 percent), the flagship business, includes PepsiCo Beverages North America and all of the Latin American beverage businesses, and brings to market Tropicana and Gatorade products, Lipton teas, Aquafina bottled water, SoBe, and Naked juices, in addition to several familiar soft drink brands like Pepsi, Mountain Dew, Sierra Mist, and 7UP outside the United States. The Beverages unit also distributes Dr Pepper, Crush, and Rockstar energy drinks, and handles all beverage distribution in the Latin American market, including specialized local brands like Sabritas and Gamesa in the Mexican market.

■ PepsiCo Europe (20 percent, 13 percent) includes all PepsiCo businesses in the United Kingdom and the rest of Europe. The Europe and "AMEA" (Asia, Middle East, and Africa) explained next, distribute not only U.S.-branded products but also many that are formulated and branded for local markets, similar to the Sabritas and Gamesa examples cited above.

- AMEA—Asia, Middle East, and Africa (10 percent, 7 percent) handles distribution of Pepsico products in these regions as just described.

Many of PepsiCo's brand names are more than 100 years old, but the corporation is relatively young. PepsiCo was founded in 1965 through the merger of Pepsi-Cola and Frito-Lay. PepsiCo now has at least 18 brands that generate over $1 billion in retail sales. The top 2 brands are Pepsi-Cola and Mountain Dew, but beverages constitute less than half of Pepsi's sales. It is primarily a snack company, with beverages coming in second. Frito-Lay brands alone account for more than half of the U.S. snack chip industry. Note also that the snack businesses are relatively more profitable and contribute a larger share of the company's total profits.

PepsiCo began its international snack food operations in 1966. Today, with operations in more than 40 countries, it's the leading multinational snack chip company, with more than a 25 percent market share of international retail snack chip sales. Brand Pepsi and

other Pepsi-Cola products—including Diet Pepsi, Pepsi-One, Mountain Dew, Slice, Sierra Mist, and Mug brands—account for nearly one-third of total soft drink sales in the United States, a consumer market totaling about $60 billion. Pepsi-Cola also offers a variety of noncarbonated beverages, including Aquafina bottled water, Lipton ready-to-drink tea, and Frappuccino ready-to-drink coffee through a partnership with Starbucks.

PepsiCo acquired Tropicana, including the Dole juice business, in August 1998 and now markets these products in 63 countries. Tropicana Pure Premium is the third-largest brand of all food products sold in grocery stores in the United States. Gatorade, acquired as part of the Quaker Oats Company merger in 2001, is the world's leading sports drink.

Financial Highlights, Fiscal Year 2012

Strategic shifts, new investments, and rising commodity costs continued to keep the fizz out of Pepsi's earnings in FY2012. The company implemented a series of price increases to recover increasing commodity costs, and those may not have gone over well with customers—a bag of Doritos can now set you back more than $4. Revenues actually dropped slightly to just under $66 billion. Although price increases did improve margins slightly to better than 20 percent, total operating profits also declined slightly largely due to continued investments in supply chain and other cost-containment programs. Per-share earnings did eke out another 2 percent gain, similar to last year, based mostly on a continued aggressive reduction in share count. To offset the higher costs of those Doritos, the company did hand out a 4.4 percent dividend increase, and appears poised to continue strong cash returns to shareholders, with a $10 billion buyback authorization in early 2013. Although currency translation is still a headwind, and there is still some restructuring going on, the company is guiding growth in the mid-single digits, which it considers its long-term target.

Reasons to Buy

PepsiCo continues to offer a compelling combination of steady and predictable earnings, dividend, and cash flow growth with a strong measure of safety as the low beta of 0.47 suggests. The food business adds some diversification, channel strength, and profitability that rival Coke does not have.

The company is taking an aggressive approach to geographical expansion and brand recognition, and it expects continued solid growth in international markets. Recently, for example, the company opened a food and beverage R & D center in Shanghai to address the Asian market. International growth combined with new operational efficiencies should bode well for the long term; in the meantime, the current flat spot may be a good time to invest with a nice dividend yield to hold investors over until these initiatives bear fruit.

Reasons for Caution

The puck is still moving to more innovative and health-conscious drinks and food products, and PepsiCo will need to invest aggressively in this area. They have many new and reformulated products in the works that use healthier ingredients and reduced levels of sodium and trans fats, but the competition for this segment is intense. The newly formed Global Nutrition Group is addressing this challenge, as a recent release of Tropicana Farmstand 100 percent fruit and vegetable drinks exemplifies (if you haven't tried their pomegranate blueberry juice—do so; it's brain food). While Pepsi is investing heavily in international markets, there is no guarantee that they will displace Coke, although the food offering will help get attention and valuable shelf space. Finally, the food business may be a drag depending on which way commodity prices run; for instance, most snack products are heavily influenced by corn prices.

SECTOR: **Consumer Staples**
BETA COEFFICIENT: **0.47**
10-YEAR COMPOUND EARNINGS PER SHARE GROWTH: **10.5%**
10-YEAR COMPOUND DIVIDENDS PER SHARE GROWTH: **13.0%**

	2005	**2006**	**2007**	**2008**	**2009**	**2010**	**2011**	**2012**
Revenues (mil)	32,562	35,137	39,474	43,251	43,232	57,938	66,504	65,492
Net income (mil)	4,078	5,065	5,543	5,142	5,946	6,320	6,379	6,178
Earnings per share	2.39	3.00	3.34	3.21	3.77	3.91	3.98	3.92
Dividends per share	1.01	1.16	1.43	1.60	1.75	1.89	2.03	2.13
Cash flow per share	3.65	3.95	4.38	4.30	4.84	5.47	5.83	5.74
Price: high	60.3	66.0	79.0	79.8	64.5	68.1	71.9	73.7
low	51.3	56.0	61.9	49.7	43.8	58.8	58.5	62.2

PepsiCo, Inc.
700 Anderson Hill Road
Purchase, NY 10577–1444
(914) 253-3055
Website: www.pepsico.com

AGGRESSIVE GROWTH

Perrigo Company

❑ Ticker symbol: PRGO (NASDAQ) ❑ S&P rating: not rated ❑ Value Line financial strength rating: B++ ❑ Current yield: 0.3% ❑ Dividend raises, past 10 years: 10

Company Profile

Perrigo is the world's largest manufacturer of over-the-counter pharmaceutical products for the store-brand market. They also manufacture generic prescription pharmaceuticals, nutritional products, and active pharmaceutical ingredients (APIs).

The company operates in four segments: Consumer Healthcare, Nutritionals, Rx Pharmaceuticals, and API. Consumer Healthcare is by far the largest segment, generating about 57 percent of Perrigo's revenue in 2012, while Nutritionals brings in 16 percent, Rx Pharma 20 percent, and APIs 5 percent.

The company's success depends on its ability to manufacture and quickly market generic equivalents to branded products. It employs internal R & D resources to develop product formulations and manufacture in quantity for its customers. It also develops retail packaging specific to the customer's needs.

If you have bought a store-branded over-the-counter medication such as ibuprofen, acetaminophen, skin remedies, or cough medicine in the past year, there's a good chance (a 75 percent

chance, in fact) that it was made by Perrigo. The company's Consumer Healthcare business produces and markets over 21,800 store-brand products in 8,300 individual SKUs to approximately 700 customers, including Walmart, CVS, Walgreens, Kroger, Target, Safeway, Dollar General, Costco, and other national and regional drugstores, supermarkets, and mass merchandisers. Walmart is its single largest customer and accounts for 20 percent of Perrigo's net sales. The retail market for the branded equivalents of Perrigo's most widely used products is over $12 billion.

The Nutritionals segment is relatively new as a standalone segment and includes store-brand infant formula, vitamins, and minerals. The segment distributes 400 store-brand products in 2,500 SKUs to more than 150 customers. This operation moved forward with a recent distribution partnership for U.S.-manufactured baby formula to be distributed in China. The company is pursuing similar partnerships in other regions.

The Rx Pharma operations produce generic prescription drugs (in contrast to the over-the-counter drugs produced in the Consumer Healthcare segment), obviously benefiting when key patented drugs run past their patent protection. Rx Pharma markets approximately 300 generic prescription products, many of them topicals and creams, with over 760 SKUs, to approximately 120 customers, while the API division markets an assortment of active ingredients to other drug manufacturers as well as for the company's own products, including a number of active ingredients that we'd have trouble spelling correctly, so won't even try. The company's products are manufactured in 9 facilities around the world. Its major markets are in North America, Mexico, the U.K., and China. About 33 percent of sales are overseas

Financial Highlights, Fiscal Year 2012

Perrigo posted another healthy year in FY2012, with sales, earnings, and cash flows all up 15–20 percent. The company did well in all markets and projects significant new store-branded products; that combined with its high market share and relative pricing power is projected to drive operating margins from 21.5 percent in FY2011 to almost 24 percent in FY2013. As a result, management is guiding for another 12–15 percent gain in revenues and raised guidance to call for a 29 percent increase in per-share earnings.

Reasons to Buy

Perrigo is a real success story of solid niche dominance (store-branded medications) with a couple of high-growth, high-margin businesses mixed in. Steady growth in sales combined with a steady growth in margins have a multiplicative effect, and the company has enjoyed well-above-average profit growth in this industry.

Not only does the company dominate a niche, it is a growing niche. People are becoming more sensitive to their own health-care costs and spending in general and are opting more often for the store brand; after all, 200 mg of ibuprofen is 200 mg of ibuprofen. And this all sits on top of the demographic tailwind of the aging population.

The company continues to successfully bring both new generic over-the-counter and generic prescription drugs to market. New generics for Prevacid, Mucinex, the Nicorette Mini-Lozenge, and a store-branded version of Allegra will help, as will the new ventures for baby formula and other products in China. With its 75 percent market share of the private-label OTC market, Perrigo is in a position to capture the larger share of any future generic rollout opportunities.

Reasons for Caution

There are some risks in the generic pharmaceutical industry; among them are patent infringement lawsuits and manufacturing problems. The company has had a few lawsuits but fortunately none of the manufacturing problems experienced by rival Johnson & Johnson; a major hiccup could put a dent in the company's business. Competition has been heating up as others see the niche opportunities. Also, the stock price has followed the story upward, which makes investors vulnerable to any short-term hiccup in the growth story. That said, the stock price momentum has slowed in recent months, and the P/E ratio looks reasonable in light of earnings growth.

SECTOR: **Health Care**
BETA COEFFICIENT: **0.69**
10-YEAR COMPOUND EARNINGS PER SHARE GROWTH: **22.5%**
10-YEAR COMPOUND DIVIDENDS PER SHARE GROWTH: **9.5%**

	2005	2006	2007	2008	2009	2010	2011	2012
Revenues (mil)	1,024	1,366	1,447	1,822	2,007	2,269	2,765	3,173
Net income (mil)	37.9	74.1	78.6	150	176	263	341	411
Earnings per share	0.49	0.79	0.84	1.58	1.87	2.83	3.64	4.37
Dividends per share	0.16	0.17	0.18	0.21	0.22	0.25	0.27	0.32
Cash flow per share	0.77	1.41	1.46	2.35	2.67	3.69	4.78	5.84
Price: high	19.9	18.7	36.9	43.1	61.4	67.5	104.7	120.8
low	12.8	14.4	16.1	27.7	18.5	37.5	62.3	90.2

Perrigo Company
515 Eastern Avenue
Allegan, MI 49010
(269) 673-8451
Website: www.perrigo.com

CONSERVATIVE GROWTH

Praxair, Inc.

❑ Ticker symbol: PX (NYSE) ❑ S&P rating: A ❑ Value Line financial strength rating: A ❑ Current yield: 2.1% ❑ Dividend raises, past 10 years: 10

Company Profile

Praxair, Inc. is the second-largest supplier of industrial gases in the world. The company, which was spun off to Union Carbide shareholders in June 1992, supplies a broad range of atmospheric, process, and specialty gases; high-performance coatings; and related services and technologies.

Praxair's primary products are atmospheric gases—oxygen, nitrogen, argon, and rare gases (produced when atmospheric air is purified, compressed, cooled, distilled, and condensed) and process and specialty gases—carbon dioxide, helium, hydrogen, and acetylene (produced as by-products of chemical production or recovered from natural gas). Customers include makers of primary metals, metal fabricators, petroleum refiners, and producers of chemicals, health-care products, electronics, glass, pulp and paper, and environmental products.

The gas products are sold into the packaged-gas market and the merchant market. In the packaged-gas market, bulk gases are packaged into high-pressure cylinders and either delivered to the customer or to distributors. In the merchant market, bulk gases are liquefied and transported by truck to the customer's facility.

The company also designs, engineers, and constructs cryogenic and noncryogenic gas supply systems for customers who choose to produce their own atmospheric gases on-site. This is obviously a capital-intensive delivery solution for Praxair but results in lower delivered cost to the customer and higher returns for Praxair, as all operational costs are paid by the customer. Contracts for these installations can run to 20 years.

Praxair Surface Technologies is a subsidiary that applies wear, corrosion, and thermal-resistant metallic and ceramic coatings and powders to metal surfaces in order to resist wear, high temperatures, and corrosion. Aircraft engines are a primary market, but it serves others, including the printing, textile, chemical, and primary metals markets, and provides aircraft engine and airframe component overhaul services. About 62 percent of Praxair's sales come from outside the U.S.

Financial Highlights, Fiscal Year 2012

Softness in Europe and Brazil and strength in the dollar tempered Praxair's FY2012 results, a bit more than we expected. Sales, net profits, and earnings per share were essentially flat, taking some of the air out of what had been a pretty nice post-recession recovery. The international effects disguised a 5 percent sales gain and a 10 percent profit gain in North America. That said, in total it was nothing more than a "golf clap" year as we suggested in last year's edition. These issues will continue to affect the company, although they are more optimistic about FY2013 and have issued guidance for high single-digit growth for the year.

Reasons to Buy

It's nice to own a few "golf clap" stocks in companies that show high margins, steady growth, and no surprises. Par, par, birdie, par—not a bad round, and Praxair is the sort of company that can deliver that. The name Praxair, after all, is derived from the Greek *praxis*, meaning "practical"—so "practical air."

Praxair is the largest gas provider in the emerging markets of China, India, Brazil, Mexico, and Korea and continues to invest heavily in plants in these regions. The company is a big player in the petroleum industry and especially the heavy crude segment and is seeing stronger demand in its U.S. heavy manufacturing segments as well. The company also bought NuCO2—a major supplier of carbonating gas for soda fountains—and will likely continue to make small acquisitions through the year. We especially like the company's high margins (31 percent) and cash flow generation—and the willingness to share it with shareholders, with steady 10 percent dividend increases over the past 5 years and likely in years to come, with some share repurchases thrown in for good measure.

Reasons for Caution

Competitors are strong, and getting stronger with the recent Air Products–Airgas merger and a consolidation of smaller players in the industry. As hydrocarbon energy products are feedstock for many of Praxair's products, the company is sensitive to increases in energy prices, although the recent decline in natural gas prices—an important feedstock—bodes well shorter term. Results are sensitive to currency headwinds, but those headwinds may subside or even turn into tailwinds. Finally, the markets have recognized Praxair's recent score card and are still giving a low handicap in the form of a high share price approaching 20 times earnings, difficult to sustain for a high single-digit growth rate. New investors should thus look for favorable entry points.

SECTOR: **Materials**
BETA COEFFICIENT: **0.84**
10-YEAR COMPOUND EARNINGS PER SHARE GROWTH: **12.0%**
10-YEAR COMPOUND DIVIDENDS PER SHARE GROWTH: **19.0%**

	2005	2006	2007	2008	2009	2010	2011	2012
Revenues (mil)	7,656	8,324	9,402	10,796	8,956	10,118	11,252	11,224
Net income (mil)	726	988	1,177	1,335	1,254	1,195	1,672	1,692
Earnings per share	2.20	3.00	3.62	4.19	4.01	3.84	5.45	5.61
Dividends per share	0.72	1.00	1.20	1.50	1.60	1.80	2.00	2.20
Cash flow per share	4.61	5.25	6.18	8.63	6.85	6.95	8.95	9.10
Price: high	54.3	63.7	92.1	77.6	86.1	96.3	111.7	116.9
low	41.1	50.4	58.0	53.3	53.3	72.7	88.6	100.0

Praxair, Inc.
39 Old Ridgebury Road
Danbury, CT 06810–5113
(203) 837-2354
Website: www.praxair.com

CONSERVATIVE GROWTH

The Procter & Gamble Company

❑ Ticker symbol: PG (NYSE) ❑ S&P rating: AA- ❑ Value Line financial strength rating: A++
❑ Current yield: 2.9% ❑ Dividend raises, past 10 years: 10

Company Profile

Procter & Gamble dates back to 1837, when William Procter and James Gamble began making soap and candles in Cincinnati, OH. The company's first major product introduction took place in 1879 when it launched Ivory soap. Since then, P&G has continually created a host of blockbuster products, added some key acquisitions, exited the food business and a few others, and, in total, has some of the strongest, most recognizable consumer brands in the world.

P&G is a uniquely diversified consumer products company with a strong global presence. P&G markets its broad line of products to nearly 5 billion consumers in more than 180 countries.

The company is a recognized leader in the development, manufacturing, and marketing of quality laundry, cleaning, paper, personal care, food, beverage, and health-care products, including prescription pharmaceuticals.

To understand Procter, it's worth a look at how the company is now organized. As of mid-FY2011, there are 2 Global Business Units: Beauty and Grooming and House-hold Care. Within these 2 units

are 5 reportable segments: Beauty (24 percent of sales, 22 percent of profits), Grooming (10 percent, 16 percent), Health Care (14 percent, 16 percent), Fabric Care & Home Care (32 percent, 26 percent), and Baby Care & Family Care (19 percent, 19 percent). The 300 brands sold under these segments are eminently familiar but too numerous to list and categorize; here are a few: Gillette, Tide, Always, Whisper, Pro-V, Olay, Duracell, Ariel, Crest, Pampers, Pantene, Vicks, Bold, Dawn, Head & Shoulders, Cascade, Zest, Bounty, Braun, Comet, Scope, Old Spice, Charmin, Tampax, Downy, Cheer, and Prell. If these brands sound a bit "slow lane" for you, try the new Dolce & Gabbana, Gucci, and Hugo Boss fragrance brands recently added to the mix.

The company has a huge international presence, with 65 percent of sales originating outside the U.S. The company also manufactures locally for the largest international markets.

Financial Highlights, Fiscal Year

Despite strong currency headwinds, which created a 6 percent unfavorable currency translation, and despite the closing of a deal to sell Pringles to Kellogg, Procter washed out a 1.4 percent sales gain for FY2012. Operating and restructuring expenses, including a rare staff cut that eliminated 1,600 positions during the year, and higher commodity costs stained net earnings just a bit to a level almost 4 percent lower than the record of $11.8 billion in FY2011. While many in the industry were concerned about generic competition, Europe, and an increased dependence on more trendy cosmetic products, the company and most analysts now expect greater efficiencies and a return of pricing power to lead to a good FY2013 with net earnings in the $3.97–$4.07 per share range, with comparable growth in revenues, cash flow, and dividends. The company also increased the share repurchase commitment 50 percent to $6 billion, and has retired 400 million shares, or 15 percent of its stock since 2006.

Reasons to Buy

Regardless of developments in the world economy, people will continue to shave, bathe, do laundry, and care for their babies, and P&G is the global leader in baby care, feminine care, fabric care, and shaving products. Everyone should consider at least one defensive play in their portfolio, and P&G deserves to be at the top of the list.

P&G is extending its reach to capture share in channels and markets that are currently underserved. Developing markets are a huge opportunity, representing 86 percent of the world's population, and P&G feels it can be a leader in many product categories. Emerging markets already represent 32 percent of their revenue, up from 20 percent in 2002. P&G is also broadening its distribution channels to pursue opportunities in drug and pharmacy outlets, convenience stores, export operations, and even e-commerce.

In a move that will reduce operating and some marketing and advertising costs significantly, the company has departed from its traditional model of managing brands as wholly separate businesses with brand-specific advertising budgets, product research labs, and so forth. Synergies from combining ads and ad strategies alone should reduce total costs across the company's many portfolios. Recent cost-cutting moves (which are expected to save $10 billion annually by 2016) will grow the profit base faster than the moderately strong growth in the sales base—all a good combination. Recently, the company brought back former CEO A. G. Lafley for what appears to be a short term assignment to groom his successor and to tune up the innovation machine; this move bodes well long term although adds a measure of short term uncertainty. In short, we continue to like the brand, marketplace, and financial strength; sure and steady dividend growth; and short- and long-term prospects.

Reasons for Caution

The recent recession made consumers much more price conscious, and many switched to generics. That switch has reversed to a degree, but it may take a long time to get everybody back on board, if the company can do it at all. The company has dealt with that to a degree by introducing some low-end sub-brands to its mix. Rising commodity costs can affect P&G, and the expansion into the health and beauty business brings more exposure to often-fickle consumer tastes and shorter brand life than the company may be used to. Additionally, the return of Mr. Lafley could signal some larger underlying problems, but we think it's more of a plus than a negative. Finally, while the stock price had remained relatively flat for a while even after results started to improve, recent quotes suggest you might want to clip a few coupons or wait for a sale to get a better entry price.

SECTOR: **Consumer Staples**
BETA COEFFICIENT: **0.46**
10-YEAR COMPOUND EARNINGS PER SHARE GROWTH: **9.0%**
10-YEAR COMPOUND DIVIDENDS PER SHARE GROWTH: **11.0%**

	2005	2006	2007	2008	2009	2010	2011	2012
Revenues (mil)	56,741	68,222	76,476	83,503	79,029	78,938	82,559	83,680
Net income (mil)	7,257	8,684	10,340	12,075	11,293	10,946	11,797	11,344
Earnings per share	2.53	2.64	3.04	3.64	3.58	3.53	3.93	3.85
Dividends per share	1.03	1.15	1.28	1.45	1.64	1.80	1.97	2.14
Cash flow per share	3.51	3.51	4.25	4.97	4.65	4.87	5.21	5.20
Price: high	59.7	64.2	75.2	73.8	63.5	65.3	67.7	71.0
low	51.2	52.8	60.4	54.9	43.9	39.4	57.6	59.1

The Procter & Gamble Company
1 Procter & Gamble Plaza
Cincinnati, OH 45202
(513) 983-1100
Website: www.pg.com

Quest Diagnostics Inc.

❏ Ticker symbol: DGX (NYSE) ❏ S&P rating: BBB+ ❏ Value Line financial strength rating: B++
❏ Current yield: 2.1% ❏ Dividend raises, past 10 years: 4

Company Profile

If you have gone for any kind of medical test, either at the recommendation of a doctor or as required by an employer or an insurance company, chances are you got that test in a lab operated by Quest Diagnostics. Quest is the world's leading provider of diagnostic testing, information, and services to support doctors, hospitals, and the care-giving process.

The company operates more than 2,000 labs and patient service centers and about 150 smaller "rapid-response" labs in the U.S. and has facilities in India, Mexico, the U.K., Ireland, and Sweden. It provides about 150 million lab test results a year and serves physicians, hospitals, employers, life and healthcare insurers, and other health facilities. The company estimates that it serves more than half the hospitals and physicians in the U.S.

The company offers diagnostic testing services covering pretty much the gamut of medical necessity in its testing facilities, and also offers a line of diagnostic kits, reagents, and devices to support its own labs, home and remote testing, and other labs. The company offers a series of "wellness and risk management services," including tests, exams, and record services for the insurance industry. The company also does tests and provides other support for clinical research and trials, and finally, through its information technology segment, offers a Care360 platform to help physicians maintain charts and access data through its network, which has about 200,000 physicians enrolled.

The company has begun to provide "insourced" solutions to hospitals that formerly ran their own labs. More progressive hospitals and hospital systems have been trying to cut costs and are starting to look at independent labs to run some of their in-house functions. The company recently acquired parts of the UMass Memorial Medical Center and California's Dignity Health's (formerly Catholic Healthcare West) "outreach" lab business; that is, its labs located off hospital premises.

Financial Highlights, Fiscal Year 2012

Medicare cutbacks and competition in the lab diagnostic business have softened results, especially in

FY2012 and early FY2013. Revenues have been essentially flat during the period, and margins and earnings have declined slightly and are projected to do so again in FY2013. Cash flows have been strong, and moderate share buybacks and an especially large one (9 percent in 2011) have kept the per-share earnings on a growth track. Share counts have dropped from 214 million in 2004 to 158 million recently. The company has announced a near doubling of the dividend for FY2013. For the year the company projects earnings at about $4.45 per share, flat from last year, on revenues up 0–1 percent.

Reasons to Buy

Granted, increased utilization initiatives, particularly on the Medicare front, have softened results. But we believe, going forward and especially into FY2014, the company stands to benefit substantially from the Affordable Care Act ("Obamacare") as 30 million more patients get access to "free" or subsidized health care. Additionally, an ever greater emphasis on wellness and preventative care is likely to send more people for routine checkups, particularly if insurance carriers offer benefits (like free tests or lower coinsurance) to motivate such preventative care. We also like the ancillary businesses—clinical trials, insurance qualifications, employer testing, and IT services—which all should do well in an environment favoring greater cost control and outsourcing of distinct services as Quest provides. The company is a leader in its industry and recently was priced favorably against its relatively predictable earnings and especially its cash flows, and has a beta of 0.61, indicating relative safety. Finally, shareholder returns have become quite a bit more attractive in the past few years and are likely to improve further going forward.

Reasons for Caution

The company has been forced to reach for growth through acquisitions, which don't always work out, and through hospital partnerships, which can lead to some revenue sharing and thus pressure on margins. Medicare cuts are likely to continue, although we see that trend stabilizing and perhaps reversing in favor of wellness and preventative care. The company may also face more competition as large group physician practices get larger and bring some of their lab operations in house—although that trend may be countered by hospitals and other large organizations getting out of this relatively easily outsourced business.

SECTOR: **Health Care**
BETA COEFFICIENT: **0.61**
10-YEAR COMPOUND EARNINGS PER SHARE GROWTH: **21.5%**
10-YEAR COMPOUND DIVIDENDS PER SHARE GROWTH: **8.5%**

	2005	2006	2007	2008	2009	2010	2011	2012
Revenues (mil)	5,504	6,269	6,705	7,249	7,455	7,400	7,511	7,468
Net income (mil)	546.3	641.4	553.8	640.0	730.3	720.9	728.7	700.0
Earnings per share	2.66	3.22	2.84	3.27	3.88	4.05	4.53	4.43
Dividends per share	0.36	0.40	0.40	0.40	0.40	0.40	0.47	0.68
Cash flow per share	3.64	4.32	4.08	4.75	5.52	5.00	6.42	6.25
Price: high	54.8	64.7	58.6	59.9	62.8	61.7	61.2	64.9
low	44.3	48.6	48.0	38.7	42.4	40.8	45.1	53.3

Quest Diagnostics Inc.
3 Giralda Farms
Madison, NJ 07940
(973) 520-2700
Website: www.questdiagnostics.com

AGGRESSIVE GROWTH

Ross Stores, Inc.

❑ Ticker symbol: ROST (NASDAQ) ❑ S&P rating: BBB+ ❑ Value Line financial strength rating: A
❑ Current yield: 1.2% ❑ Dividend raises, past 10 years: 10

Company Profile

Ross Stores is the second-largest off-price retailer in the United States. Ross and its subsidiaries operate 2 chains of apparel and home accessories stores. As of 2011 the company operated a total of 1,055 stores, of which 988 were Ross Dress for Less locations in 27 states and Guam and 67 were dd's DISCOUNTS stores in four states. Just over half the company's stores are located in 3 states—California, Florida, and Texas.

Both chains target value-conscious women and men between the ages of 18 and 54. Ross's target customers are primarily from middle-income households, while the dd's DISCOUNTS target customers are typically from lower- to middle-income households. Merchandising, purchasing, pricing, and the locations of the stores are all aimed at these customer bases. Ross and dd's DISCOUNTS both offer first-quality, in-season, name-brand and designer apparel, accessories, and footwear for the family at savings typically in the 20–60 percent range off department store prices (at Ross) or 20–70 percent off (at dd's DISCOUNTS). The stores also offer discounted home fashions and housewares, educational toys and games, furniture and furniture accents, luggage, cookware, and (at some stores) jewelry.

Ross's strategy is to offer competitive values to target customers by offering a well-managed mix of inventory with a strong percentage of name brands and items of local and seasonal interest at attractive prices.

Financial Highlights, Fiscal Year 2012

The Great Recession was nothing but good news for this company, bringing newly cost-conscious customers by the busload. The question was—what would happen after that? Would people feel they were on more solid footing and abandon Ross in droves for more fully priced favorites? The answer, so far, appears to be a pretty solid no. Sales and earnings continue to grow in the mid-teens, albeit with a 5 percent growth in the store base. Sales are fully 33 percent ahead of their FY2009 low. Earnings per share, helped by an aggressive buyback policy and operational improvements, advanced 23 percent in

FY2012 to $3.53 per share, a very good performance for a mature retail player. The company projects EPS growth around 11 percent for FY2013. From 2003 forward, the company has reduced share counts some 28 percent from 302 million to 220 million, and has raised its dividend by a factor of 10 over the same period.

Reasons to Buy

The recession apparently helped Ross gain mainstream appeal across a wider set of customers. While some of those customers defected back to full-price retail stores as things improved, a greater number have shown that they will continue to shop at the stores. At the same time, the company was successful with operational changes begun in 2009 to improve merchandising and inventory management, which led to better stocking of a more favorable mix of goods and better inventory turnover. These marketplace and operational changes have led to the financial success one would expect and then some, and the company continues to improve its inventory management and should see greater profitability almost regardless of the economic environment.

The company plans to expand the formula into the Midwest and other regions, which should be a good match for the offering. The

company operates in only 27 states, suggesting in itself a growth opportunity. As mentioned, the company has done plenty for its shareholders. There is plenty of room in the cash flow to increase the payout, and the company has almost no long-term debt. The emergence of the recession and the demand and supply shifts we had expected caused us to rethink the long-term future of Ross as a *100 Best* stock, but after we looked at the growth and cash flow numbers, as you can see, it's still on the list.

Reasons for Caution

The stock was split two-for-one at the end of 2011, and we expected—and got—the typical price surge on the good news, which lasted to meet an all-time high just over $70, only to pull back to a more normal growth curve. So recent price performance has been mediocre, and there were probably more than a few who thought customer defections would be larger. There are still questions about Ross's ability to acquire the same quantity and quality of merchandise as the economy picks up and full-price retailers begin to see higher levels of foot traffic. Such inventory follows a cycle, and if full-price retailers cut back on orders, there is less for everyone—and if the economy picks up, they will sell more, so less for Ross. Upshot: Inventory management improvements at full-price retailers could make things tougher for the company. On top of that, the company still depends to a degree on store expansion, which could make supply constraints hurt even more. That said, the company seems to have effective inventory and procurement practices in place; that should help neutralize the effect.

SECTOR: **Retail**
BETA COEFFICIENT: **0.75**
10-YEAR COMPOUND EARNINGS PER SHARE GROWTH: **17.5%**
10-YEAR COMPOUND DIVIDENDS PER SHARE GROWTH: **25.0%**

	2005	**2006**	**2007**	**2008**	**2009**	**2010**	**2011**	**2012**
Revenues (mil)	4,944	5,570	5,975	6,486	7,184	7,866	8,608	9,721
Net income (mil)	200	241	261	305	443	555	657	787
Earnings per share	0.68	0.85	0.95	1.77	1.77	2.32	2.84	3.53
Dividends per share	0.11	0.13	0.16	0.20	0.25	0.35	0.47	0.56
Cash flow per share	1.08	1.26	1.42	1.76	2.45	3.03	3.65	4.42
Price: high	15.7	15.9	17.6	20.8	25.3	33.3	49.2	70.8
low	11.2	11.1	12.2	10.6	14.0	21.2	30.1	47.1

Ross Stores, Inc.
4440 Rosewood Dr.
Building 4
Pleasanton, CA 94588–3050
(925) 965-4400
Website: www.rossstores.com

AGGRESSIVE GROWTH

Schlumberger Limited

❑ Ticker symbol: SLB (NYSE) ❑ S&P rating: A+ ❑ Value Line financial strength rating: A++
❑ Current yield: 1.6% ❑ Dividend raises, past 10 years: 7

Company Profile

Schlumberger Limited is the world's leading oilfield services company. It provides technology, information solutions, and integrated project management services with the goal of optimizing reservoir performance for its customers in the oil and gas industry. Founded in 1926, today the company has a large international footprint, employing more than 113,000 people in 80 countries. The company operates in 2 business segments:

Schlumberger Oilfield Services is, at 93 percent of revenues and 99 percent of profits, by far the largest segment and supplies a wide range of products and services. Within the Oilfield Services segment, 3 groups broadly characterize the deliverables of the segment. The Reservoir Characterization Group is mostly a consulting service, applying technologies toward finding, defining, and characterizing hydrocarbon deposits. The Drilling Group, not surprisingly, does the actual drilling and creation of wells for production, while the Reservoir Production Group completes and services the well for production, maintaining and enhancing productivity

through its life. The company not only provides physical on-site services but also substantial consulting, modeling, information management, and project management around these activities. In short, SLB Oilfield Services offers a full outsourcing supply chain for oil and gas field development and production.

The smaller Distribution Operations segment operates in the refining, petrochemical mining, and power generation industries. Schlumberger manages its business through 28 GeoMarket regions, which are grouped into 4 geographic areas, fairly evenly split according to the pretax profits delivered: North America (31 percent); Latin America (14 percent); Europe, Commonwealth of Independent States, and Africa (26 percent); and Middle East and Asia (26 percent). The GeoMarket structure provides a single point of contact at the local level for field operations and brings together geographically focused teams to meet local needs and deliver customized solutions.

The company made the big-ticket acquisition of oil services

giant Smith International, which was integrated into the operations and financials during FY2011.

Financial Highlights, Fiscal Year 2012

Beyond the Smith acquisition, which added about $12 billion to a $27 billion revenue base in FY2011, Schlumberger continues to ring up decent growth numbers. FY2012 revenues advanced 6.6 percent to just over $42 billion; net earnings, helped along by a lower tax rate, increased over 13 percent; and per-share earnings advanced at a 15 percent clip, helped along by a 6 million share reduction in share count.

This is an interesting time for diversified oil field service companies. On one hand, oil prices continue to be strong, although not as strong as during the 2008 spike. On the other hand, natural gas prices have dropped significantly, cutting into exploration. New domestic resources and fracking technologies have created an oil and gas boom in the U.S., a 22 percent increase in domestic production, and a fertile ground for oil field expansion. On the other hand, on-shore, land-based exploration isn't as large or as profitable an undertaking as offshore, deepwater, and international operations. On that same hand, worldwide oil demand has softened, with Europe and China leading the way.

You get the idea—there are a lot of crosscurrents out there affecting the company. It appears that higher oil prices and the exploration boom will win out. Sorting all of that out, the company in FY2013 expects to wind up with revenues some 9 percent ahead of FY2012, net profits ahead 16 percent, and per-share earnings ahead 17.3 percent. Consistent with that, the company announced a 16 percent dividend increase to $1.25 annually in early 2013.

Schlumberger issued some 175 million shares to buy Smith; unlike most companies we select, SLB's share count has actually risen since mid-decade. However, they have since bought back shares aggressively, about 45 million of the 175 million issued, in just 2 years. We applaud that effort to essentially pay off the acquisition and clean up the dilution of existing shareholders. If SLB can add $12 billion in revenue and a billion in profit on the pre-existing share base, that would be a big win. They have about 130 million shares to go.

Reasons to Buy

The first page of Schlumberger's 2009 annual report began with: "The age of easy oil is over." The sentence seems prescient and, along with its size and complete offering to the exploration and production industry, it is perhaps the most succinct statement of Schlumberger's advantages in the E&P business. Its expertise is most valuable in the most technically challenging projects, such as the several recent subsalt offshore finds in Brazil, West Africa, and the Gulf of Mexico.

We were concerned about some of the crosscurrents mentioned above, especially what seems like a long-term softening of natural gas prices. But when you look at the results, it's clear that the company manages such crosscurrents well and performs strongly even during down cycles. That, combined with the strong and likely growing imperative for big oil companies to replace reserves, should benefit the company over the long haul. So, while business conditions aren't perfect, and there are some large shifts afoot in the marketplace, we continue to like SLB for the long term.

Reasons for Caution

The large shifts just mentioned could get larger, and that plus competition could put a bigger dent in the oil service industry. The current dip in natural gas prices—if it starts to really eat into production—could become a firm "down" story. The company also faces the traditional risks of oil drilling—particularly offshore drilling—that culminated in the BP disaster of 2010.

SECTOR: Energy
BETA COEFFICIENT: 1.41
10-YEAR COMPOUND EARNINGS PER SHARE GROWTH: 17.5%
10-YEAR COMPOUND DIVIDENDS PER SHARE GROWTH: 9.0%

	2005	2006	2007	2008	2009	2010	2011	2012
Revenues (mil)	14,309	19,230	23,277	27,163	22,702	27,447	39,540	42,149
Net income (mil)	2,022	3,747	5,177	5,397	3,142	3,408	3,954	5,439
Earnings per share	1.67	3.04	4.18	4.42	2.61	2.70	3.51	4.06
Dividends per share	0.41	0.48	0.70	0.81	0.84	0.84	1.00	1.10
Cash flow per share	2.86	4.51	5.94	6.42	4.70	4.55	6.05	6.75
Price: high	51.5	74.8	114.8	112.0	71.1	84.1	95.6	80.8
low	31.6	47.9	56.3	37.1	35.1	54.7	54.8	59.1

Schlumberger Limited
5599 San Felipe, 17th Floor
Houston, TX 77056
(713) 375-4300
Website: www.slb.com

Seagate Technology

◻ Ticker symbol: STX (NASDAQ) ◻ S&P rating: BB+ ◻ Value Line financial strength rating: B+
◻ Current yield: 4.4% ◻ Dividend raises, past 10 years: 7

Company Profile

About 30 years ago, you could buy a 5 megabyte hard disk drive from a major computer manufacturer like IBM or HP. It was about the size of a washing machine, cost several thousand dollars, and made little grunting noises as it operated. Today, you can store about 200,000 times the information on an inexpensive hard drive measuring about 2.5 by 3 inches, about 7mm thick.

At the heart of the evolution and production of these devices is Seagate Technology—the world's largest producer of computer hard disk drives and related storage media. Seagate offers a range of internal and external drive devices for enterprise, client, and noncomputer environments, such as DVRs, and video game consoles.

Computer hard disk drives have become a high-volume commodity. Seagate will ship somewhere around 235 million drives in FY2013. Roughly 70 percent of those are for client applications—PCs, notebooks, external storage for PCs, and workstations. About 18 percent are for the noncomputer market—DVRs, video game consoles, and so forth—leaving about 12 percent for enterprise storage applications.

So why would we be interested in a commodity business? First—as has happened with other commodity industries in the past—the industry eventually consolidates from many smaller players into a few larger, more powerful ones. During the PC boom, numerous small, nameless, mostly Asian manufacturers got on the bandwagon, creating oversupply and driving prices down. As prices dropped and profits disappeared, and as OEMs like HP and Dell wanted more reliable sourcing, the weak hands left the market. Now—particularly after Seagate's 2011 purchase of Samsung's hard drive business—2 companies control the market: Seagate and Western Digital.

The second factor driving long-term profitability is the forthcoming change in the computing landscape toward cloud computing. While the cloud may temper client demand somewhat, those cloud server centers will need huge amounts of larger, more profitable storage devices. Innovation will once again drive this business, and Seagate is in a good position to lead. Seagate is also leading the way in hybrid drive (a hard disk plus a solid-state memory array) and solid-state hard drive (SSHD) technology, which will replace mechanical drives in many applications with simpler, more energy-efficient units. The company, in all, sells 10 lines of disk drives, ranging from larger-capacity high-performance 3.5" Cheetah drives for high-performance data warehousing environments down to its 2.5" Pipeline Mini drives used in gaming consoles and home entertainment devices—with the gamut of data center, PC, notebook, tablet, gaming, DVR, and other devices covered in between. The technology continues to improve, with the attainment of 1 terabit (1 trillion bits or 1,000 gigabytes) per inch storage capacity through new recording technology announced during FY2012. The company projects 3.5" 60 terabyte drives to be available within 10 years.

About 72 percent of the business is done directly with OEMs such as PC and storage manufacturers under long-term contracts—HP and Dell accounted for about 30 percent of the business—and these contracts tend to add some stability. As 1 of 2 major players in its market, the company has more pricing power than was inherent in the industry just a few years ago. With 224 million units shipped in a market of approximately 600 million annual, market share is approximately 37 percent. The largest concentrations of manufacturing capacity are in Thailand, Singapore, and China, respectively, and about 55 percent of sales are to Asian customers.

Financial Highlights, Fiscal Year 2012

Although supply shortages (and price bulges) related to the 2011 Thailand floods have largely played out, Seagate continues to post excellent results. Sales jumped to $14,939 million during the year, and with some price softening are projected to total $14,100 million for FY2013, which actually ends on July 1, 2013. FY2013 earnings are expected to dip to $1,940 million as lower prices drop the gross margin to just over 20 percent from the record 27.2 percent in FY2012. Earnings per share are expected at $5.20, lower than FY2012's $6.75 rate, but still quite healthy and, we believe, more representative of long-term performance. Cash flows are strong, sizably above the reported per-share earnings, and have funded dramatic dividend increases and share buybacks. Dividends for 2013 are indicated in the $1.52 range, while the company also authorized another $2.5 billion share buyback. The share count has dropped from 575 million to an estimated 380 million by the end of FY2013.

Reasons to Buy

Seagate is one of the more volatile and aggressive stocks on our *100 Best* list, but we think the future is bright and probably more stable. We've already shared most of the "buy side" story—a shift to a suppliers market with Seagate and Western Digital in charge, larger long-term contracts, higher-value-add technology, and an evolving computing and network architecture that should drive more high-value demand. The company seems to be capitalizing on these trends well, is improving its technology, and over time will achieve a healthy and profitable steady state. In the meantime, it is returning substantial cash to shareholders both through dividends and buybacks.

Reasons for Caution

This industry is noted for its "dreaded diamonds"—where scant supply triggers over-ordering, which eventually triggers overproduction into a softening market; on top of that, the excess orders get cancelled, supply balloons, and prices drop. With only 2 suppliers and a healthy and broadening technology demand, most don't see this happening in the near future. But one must always question the "it's different this time" viewpoint. We're also concerned about the fact that its largest customers are PC makers but also see that no matter what the device, data will have to be stored in ever increasing volumes with greater miniaturization—Seagate will play well no matter where this puck goes. This will, by nature, be a more volatile play than most on the *100 Best Stocks* list (the beta of 2.39 serves as evidence), but we do think that volatility will decline from years past and is offset by the strong cash flows paid to investors.

SECTOR: **Information Technology**
BETA COEFFICIENT: **2.39**
10-YEAR COMPOUND EARNINGS PER SHARE GROWTH: **26.5%**
10-YEAR COMPOUND DIVIDENDS PER SHARE GROWTH: **NM**

	2005	2006	2007	2008	2009	2010	2011	2012
Revenues (mil)	7,553	9,208	11,380	12,708	9,805	11,395	10,971	14,939
Net income (mil)	707	840	822	1,415	(231)	1,609	578	2,977
Earnings per share	1.41	1.60	1.40	2.63	(0.47)	3.14	1.09	6.75
Dividends per share	0.26	0.32	0.40	0.42	0.27	—	0.18	0.86
Cash flow per share	2.46	2.52	3.13	4.63	1.42	5.08	3.14	6.57
Price: high	21.5	28.1	28.9	25.8	18.5	21.6	18.5	35.7
low	13.8	19.2	20.1	3.7	3.0	9.8	9.0	16.2

Seagate Technology
38/39 Fitzwilliam Square
Dublin 2, Ireland
(353)(1) 234-3136
Website: www.seagate.com

AGGRESSIVE GROWTH

Sigma-Aldrich Corporation

◻ Ticker symbol: SIAL (NASDAQ) ◻ S&P rating: A+ ◻ Value Line financial strength rating: A+
◻ Current yield: 1.1% ◻ Dividend raises, past 10 years: 10

Company Profile

Sigma-Aldrich is a manufacturer and reseller of the world's broadest range of high-value-add chemicals, biochemicals, laboratory equipment, and consumables used in research and large-scale manufacturing activities. The company sells over 185,000 chemicals and manufactures about a third of the items itself, comprising about 60 percent of sales. It also stocks more than 45,000 laboratory equipment items. Most of the company's 97,000 customer accounts are research institutions that use basic laboratory essentials such as solvents, reagents, and other supplies, mostly in small but repeated quantities. Sigma-Aldrich products support a range of activities, including R & D, diagnostics, pilot plant, and small-scale high-tech manufacturing. The company also sells chemicals in large quantities to pharmaceutical companies, but no single account provided more than 2 percent of Sigma-Aldrich's total sales. Sigma-Aldrich's business model is to provide its generic and specialized products with expedited (in most cases, next day) delivery. The company sells in 166 countries and obtains about 66 percent of its sales internationally.

Sigma-Aldrich operates 4 business units, each catering to a separate class of customer and product. Research Essentials sells common lab chemicals and supplies such as biological buffers, cell culture reagents, biochemicals, solvents, reagents, and other lab kits to customers in all sectors. Research Specialties sells organic chemicals, biochemicals, analytical reagents, chromatography consumables, reference materials, and high-purity products. Research Biotech provides "first to market products" to high-end biotech labs, selling immunochemical, molecular biology, cell signaling, genomic, and neuroscience biochemicals. Fine Chemicals fills large-scale orders of organic chemicals and biochemicals used for production in the pharmaceutical, biotechnology, and high-tech electronics industries.

The company's biochemical and organic chemical products and kits are used in scientific and genomic research, biotechnology, pharmaceutical development, the diagnosis of disease, and as key components in pharmaceutical and other high-technology manufacturing. Research applications account for about 70 percent of sales. Most of Sigma-Aldrich's customers are life science companies, university and government institutions, hospitals, and general manufacturing industry.

Financial Highlights, Fiscal Year 2012

Sigma-Aldrich continues on a mid- to high-single-digits growth trajectory. With 41 percent of its sales going to Europe, and 66 percent overall international, one would expect soft results, especially with currency translation. Yet, the top line grew 4.7 percent and is projected for similar growth in FY2013. Earnings and EPS growth took a bit of a breather in FY2012, both rising under 2 percent, but FY2013 is projected to resume the growth train, with EPS guided in the range of $4.10–$4.20, the midpoint of which would represent a 10 percent advance over FY2012. The company does face some headwinds with the recent federal government sequestration (which may cut into research activities) and a soft academic environment. But the company has shown resilience in the face of much worse. International expansion continues into Latin America and with a recent joint venture agreement with a local company in Korea to supply chemical technologies into the flat-panel display and semiconductor market. The company has also been active in signing international distribution agreements for its products.

Reasons to Buy

Sigma has been a very steady performer in a high-value-add segment of the chemical and health-care business. The company is big enough and broad enough to maintain its top-dog position in this lucrative niche, and has a good brand and sterling reputation both in domestic and international markets. For investors, it is a safe, steady grower in a solid business in a solid industry, and the stock price trajectory is about as even-up-and-to-the-right as any we've researched.

Reasons for Caution

The company's growth is tied to the state of research in the chemical and bio/pharmaceutical industries, and while steady, economic and political factors can create doubts from time to time. Rapid growth in existing businesses isn't likely; when a company depends on acquisitions to grow, that brings some risks with it. While Sigma gets high marks for regular dividend raises, we still feel that a company in this industry with such a steady business and cash flow could pay out a little more to shareholders. Share buybacks have stalled at near zero over the past 5 years after steady activity up until 2008. Who knows—maybe that will change.

SECTOR: **Industrials**
BETA COEFFICIENT: **0.92**
10-YEAR COMPOUND EARNINGS PER SHARE GROWTH: **14.5%**
10-YEAR COMPOUND DIVIDENDS PER SHARE GROWTH: **15.5%**

	2005	2006	2007	2008	2009	2010	2011	2012
Revenues (mil)	1,667	1,798	2,039	2,201	2,148	2,271	2,505	2,623
Net income (mil)	258	276	311	342	347	384	457	460
Earnings per share	1.88	2.05	2.34	2.65	2.80	3.12	3.72	3.77
Dividends per share	0.38	0.42	0.46	0.52	0.58	0.64	0.72	0.80
Cash flow per share	2.55	2.74	3.09	3.60	3.61	3.95	4.59	4.89
Price: high	33.6	39.7	56.6	63.0	56.3	67.8	76.2	78.3
low	27.7	31.3	37.4	34.3	31.5	46.5	58.2	61.7

Sigma-Aldrich Corporation
3050 Spruce Street
St. Louis, MO 63103
(314) 771-5765
Website: www.Sigma-Aldrich.com

The Southern Company

◻ Ticker symbol: SO (NYSE) ◻ S&P rating: A ◻ Value Line financial strength rating: A ◻ Current yield: 4.4% ◻ Dividend raises, past 10 years: 10

Company Profile

Through its 4 primary operating subsidiaries—Georgia Power, Alabama Power, Mississippi Power, and Gulf Power—Southern Company serves some 4.4 million customers in a large area of Georgia, Alabama, Mississippi, northern Florida, and parts of the Carolinas. The company also wholesales power to other utilities in a wider area.

The revenue mix is balanced: 35 percent residential, 30 percent commercial, 19 percent industrial, 11 percent wholesale, and 5 percent other. The service area includes the Atlanta metropolitan area and a large base of modern manufacturing facilities in the region such as the many Asian-owned manufacturing facilities, including large auto plants. The fuel mix is more diverse and less vulnerable to price fluctuations than some, with 49 percent coal, 28 percent oil and gas, 15 percent nuclear, 2 percent hydroelectric, and 6 percent purchased. The company followed the industry trend of converting some coal plants to natural gas, dropping the percentage of coal generation to 49 percent from 55 percent last year. (Even so, with its high percentage of coal-fired plants,

SO must work to stay up with environmental regulations and pay close attention to transportation costs.) Additionally, the company plans to deploy 2 of 40 worldwide copies of the new and more efficient Westinghouse AP1000 nuclear reactors for its massive Vogtle power station in Georgia, purchased with an $8.3 billion loan guarantee from the U.S. Department of Energy. These plants, which serve as a showcase for the industry, are under construction and on track and received their operating license from the Nuclear Regulatory Commission in February 2012. They will add 1,000 megawatts of capacity to a 43,555 mW generating base and are expected to come on line in 2016. The company is also investing in alternative energy, along with partner Ted Turner's Turner Renewable Energy, most recently in an already-built 20mW photovoltaic grid project in Nevada purchased during 2012. SO is also building a coal gasification plant in Mississippi.

The company also has engaged in telecommunications services, operating as a regional wireless carrier in Alabama, Georgia, southeastern Mississippi, and northwest Florida and operating some fiber-optic networks co-located on company rights of way. The company also provides consulting services to other utilities.

Financial Highlights, Fiscal Year 2012

A slow return to prosperity in the manufacturing-intensive service area continues. Net earnings (a better measure of performance for utilities than revenues, since revenues are controlled) advanced 6.5 percent to $2.4 billion, while earnings per share advanced a slightly lower 5.1 percent (unlike many of our picks, SO has been issuing a modest number of shares lately). The majority of the business depends on regular, and typically formulaic, rate relief, and the regulatory environment in all 4 states it operates in remains favorable. So the slow, steady pace of revenue and earnings growth will likely continue. FY2013 EPS is now guided at $2.76, which, especially with the strong cash flow of almost double that, adequately supports the dividend and the typical 7-cents-per-year raise. We expect this well-entrenched pattern to continue.

Reasons to Buy

Southern serves a growing, diverse, and economically stable customer base and operates in a cooperative regulatory environment. The main appeal of this stock lies almost entirely in its dividend, which has been raised slowly but steadily for years. The return won't put you into a yacht, but if you've already got one, it will certainly help you keep it. The solid history and relationship with local regulatory bodies makes the dividend and its annual raises look secure for the future. The stock price, too, has been very stable over time with one of the lowest beta coefficients on our list at 0.25.

In today's environment the new nuclear facilities do add some risk, but we feel this is a good economic move for the future. We do like the decreased reliance on coal and believe that the current energy source mix is a good one for the long haul, especially with its experiments in alternative energy projects.

Reasons for Caution

Electric utilities are always subject to rate and other forms of regulation, and one never knows what will happen in that arena. Additionally, utilities are always vulnerable to capital costs and the attractiveness of alternative fixed-income investments and are sensitive to rising interest rates, especially if they rise quickly. SO is more exposed to coal prices and rail freight rates for its transport than most, although today coal and rail freight may get cheaper due to softer demand. Recently, the stock price has hit new highs, adding to risk should interest rates rise; new investors should pick good entry points.

SECTOR: **Utilities**
BETA COEFFICIENT: **0.25**
10-YEAR COMPOUND EARNINGS PER SHARE GROWTH: **3.0%**
10-YEAR COMPOUND DIVIDENDS PER SHARE GROWTH: **3.0%**

	2005	2006	2007	2008	2009	2010	2011	2012
Revenues (mil)	13,554	14,356	15,353	17,127	15,743	17,456	17,657	16,537
Net income (mil)	1,621	1,608	1,782	1,807	1,912	2,040	2,268	2,415
Earnings per share	2.13	2.10	2.28	2.25	2.32	2.37	2.57	2.68
Dividends per share	1.48	1.54	1.60	1.66	1.73	1.80	1.87	1.94
Cash flow per share	4.03	4.01	4.22	4.43	4.25	4.30	4.85	5.20
Price: high	36.5	37.4	39.3	40.6	33.8	38.6	46.7	48.5
low	31.1	30.5	33.2	29.8	30.8	30.8	35.7	41.8

The Southern Company
30 Ivan Allen Jr. Boulevard NW
Atlanta, GA 30308
(404) 506-5000
Website: www.southerncompany.com

AGGRESSIVE GROWTH

Southwest Airlines Co.

❑ Ticker symbol: LUV (NYSE) ❑ S&P rating: BBB- ❑ Value Line financial strength rating: B+
❑ Current yield: 0.3% ❑ Dividend raises, past 10 years: 2

Company Profile

Southwest Airlines provides passenger air transport mainly in the United States, all within North America. At the end of FY2012, the company served 97 cities in 41 states, and with the acquisition of AirTran it also served Mexico and the Caribbean with point-to-point, rather than hub-and-spoke, service. The company uses 694 Boeing 737 aircraft.

The company is one of the largest in the United States and is the world's largest by number of passengers flown, which should give an idea of their business model—low-cost, shorter flights, and maximum passenger loads. Indeed, the average trip is 939 miles and the average one-way fare is $141.72, one of the lowest in the industry. The business model is one of simplicity—no-frills aircraft, no first-class passenger cabin, limited interchange with other carriers, no on-board meals, simple boarding and seat assignment practices, direct sales over the Internet (84 percent of revenues are booked this way), no baggage fees—all designed to provide steady and reliable transportation, with one of the best on-time performances in the industry, and to maximize asset utilization with minimal downtime, crew disruptions, and other upward influences on operating costs. The company has long used secondary airports—such as Providence, RI, and Manchester, NH, to serve Boston and the New England area—to reduce delays and costs. This strategy has worked well.

Most of what we have just said reflects the business of the original Southwest Airlines. In 2012 the company completed the integration of AirTran Holdings, a medium-sized, Florida-based discount carrier. With 140 aircraft, again mostly 737s, AirTran brings a similar operational footprint but expands service to eastern airports, particularly Atlanta, Orlando, the D.C. area, and Mexico and the Caribbean.

We expect the carrier to continue the simple, straightforward value proposition that has been a customer favorite for years. Recently Southwest has embarked on a few initiatives to squeeze out some extra revenue without alienating the core passenger group, mostly targeted to business travelers. One is Business Select, which offers priority boarding, priority security, bonus frequent flyer credit, and a free beverage for an upgrade fee. The company also sells "one-off" early boarding for a small fee. The company is also tinkering with baggage fees, raising fees for overweight or excess bags, though leaving the basic two-bag limit free for now (we applaud that move).

Financial Highlights, Fiscal Year 2012

With the continued economic recovery and Southwest's reputation and inherent competitive advantages, the airline enjoyed another strong year from a revenue perspective, with total FY2012 revenues up another 9 percent moved along by a record-high load factor (that is, the percent of seats filled) of 80.9 percent and a series of modest price increases. While demand continues strong, fuel prices and other costs are also high, so operating margins remained in the subpar 9.5 percent range for FY2012 but are expected to rise to the 12.0 percent range in FY2013 with fare and fee increases and a leveling off of fuel prices. With softer margins and higher volumes, the company still rang up an 18 percent increase in net earnings, and with a massive 40 million share buyback, grew EPS by over 30 percent. With a favorable pricing environment, the AirTran addition, and some likely indigestion with the merger of American and U.S. Airways, FY2013 looks like a good one for the top line (5 percent growth)

and especially the bottom line with a forecasted growth of 63 percent in earnings per share.

Reasons to Buy

Those who have read 100 Best Stocks over the years have heard us say we'd never put an airline on the list because airlines are extremely competitive with little to no control over prices, and with the major cost components of fuel, airport fees, and union labor, they have almost no control over their costs.

However, Southwest has continually proved to be the exception. The value proposition is the envy of the industry, and we're frankly surprised that no one else has been able to emulate it (United and Delta, among others, have tried). The airline realizes that what customers want is no-hassle transportation at best-possible prices—and yes, no bag fees—and has been able to do that better than anyone else for years. Good management, efficient operation, and excellent marketing make it possible. Larger market share in a larger market— we like that. When that happens, not being able to control price becomes more of a problem for the competition than it is for Southwest. We think this is a stock people have forgotten about after its glory days decades ago. Now, with margins, earnings, and share buybacks on a strong ascent, and little in the way of competitive threats, all with the tailwind of an improving economy, it looks like time to hop on board. We also changed the category from Conservative Growth to Aggressive Growth, feeling that a climb to higher altitudes may be in the offing.

Reasons for Caution

The acquisition of AirTran and a modest de-simplification of the Rapid Rewards frequent flyer program to provide international rewards and sell points to third parties gave us some pause, but both have gone well and the core business model still seems intact. Fuel prices are still a wild card, but increasing domestic supply should hold that in line for the time being. We, too, would like to see a bit more cash return, although aggressive buybacks would be a good substitute; we're watching closely what the company does in 2013 after buying back more than 5 percent of itself in 2012. We still worry that Southwest may forget what got it this far (there's no sign of this, although the AirTran acquisition did cause us to grab our armrest a bit tighter, and likewise, broad implementation of baggage fees would cause us to grab the airsick bag). Investors should watch for any sign that Southwest is straying from its successful, industry-leading business model.

SECTOR: **Transportation**
BETA COEFFICIENT: **1.13**
10-YEAR COMPOUND EARNINGS PER SHARE GROWTH: **-3.5%**
10-YEAR COMPOUND DIVIDENDS PER SHARE GROWTH: **2.0%**

		2005	2006	2007	2008	2009	2010	2011	2012
Revenues (mil)		7,584	9,086	9,861	11,023	10,350	12,104	15,658	17,088
Net income (mil)		469	592	471	294	140	550	330	421
Earnings per share		0.57	0.72	0.81	0.40	0.19	0.73	0.42	0.58
Dividends per share		0.02	0.02	0.02	0.02	0.02	0.02	0.03	0.04
Cash flow per share		1.18	1.41	1.40	1.41	1.21	1.02	1.35	1.73
Price:	high	17.0	18.2	17.0	16.8	11.8	14.3	13.9	10.6
	low	13.0	14.6	12.1	7.1	4.0	10.4	7.1	7.8

Southwest Airlines Co.
P.O. Box 36611
2702 Love Field Drive
Dallas, TX 75235
(214) 904-4000
Website: www.southwest.com

AGGRESSIVE GROWTH

St. Jude Medical, Inc.

❑ Ticker symbol: STJ (NYSE) ❑ S&P rating: A ❑ Value Line financial strength rating: A ❑ Current yield: 2.3% ❑ Dividend raises, past 10 years: 2

Company Profile

St. Jude Medical, Inc. designs, manufactures, and distributes cardiovascular medical devices for cardiology and cardiovascular surgery, including pacemakers, implantable cardioverter defibrillators (ICDs), vascular closure devices, catheters, neuromodulation devices, and heart valves. The company has 4 main business segments:

■ The Cardiac Rhythm Management (CRM) portfolio (responsible for about 52 percent of sales) includes products for treating heart rhythm disorders as well as heart failure. Its products include ICDs, pacemaker systems, and a variety of diagnostic and therapeutic electrophysiology catheters. The company also develops catheter technologies for the Cardiology/Vascular Access therapy area. Those products include hemostasis introducers, catheters, and a market-leading vascular closure device. Many products in this portfolio use RF (radio frequency) and other leading technologies for rhythm management, ablation, and other advanced cardiovascular problems.

■ The Cardiovascular segment (24 percent) has been the leader in mechanical heart valve technology for more than 25 years. St. Jude Medical also develops a line of tissue valves, vascular closures, and valve-repair products for various cardiac surgery procedures.

■ The company's Neuromodulation segment (8 percent) produces implantable devices and drug delivery systems for use primarily in chronic pain management and in treatment for certain symptoms of Parkinson's disease and epilepsy.

■ The Atrial Fibrillation business (16 percent) markets a series of products designed to map and treat atrial fibrillation and other heart rhythm problems.

St. Jude Medical products are sold in a highly targeted niche market in more than 100 countries.

Financial Highlights, Fiscal Year 2012

The cardiac care business is by nature really 2 businesses. The cardiac surgery business is critical and almost completely immune to economic cycles; when you need it, you need it. The largest segment, Cardiac Rhythm Management, which essentially makes pacemakers and related products, is a bit more discretionary and vulnerable to expense cuts on the part of patients and care providers and contractions in the inventory pipeline. As a result, CRM segment revenue actually declined for FY2012, which weighed on total revenues for the year, which dropped nearly 2 percent for the year. However, slightly stronger margins and a solid performance in the cartioverter defibrillator, pacemaker, and the Atrial Fibrillation businesses brought a modest 2 percent increase in net profits, and that plus a healthy 4 percent stock buyback led to a 6 percent earnings per share increase. On top of the buyback, the company, which paid no dividends prior to 2011, anted up another healthy dividend increase to 92 cents and just announced another increase to $1.00 per share. The company is targeting a similar increase in per-share earnings to the $3.68–$3.73 range, with more modest buyback activity still a factor.

Reasons to Buy

St. Jude is a market leader in the heart rhythm and vascular surgery niche. Both the Neuromodulation and Atrial Fibrillation segments have grown rapidly and seem well positioned for growth in at least the 15 percent range. The techniques employed in neuromodulation are growing quickly in the field as a preferred treatment for long-term pain management. St. Jude (and others) see this as a disruptive technology, potentially replacing drug and physical therapy regimens and offering improved lifestyle at a reduced cost. These 2 businesses serve as solid growth kickers, complementing the flatter CRM and cardiovascular segments.

St. Jude has a consistent track record of steady growth and relative earnings and share-price stability. The company easily scores a triple play with double-digit 10-year compounded growth in sales, earnings, and cash flows, and we expect this to continue—and it has gotten on the dividend bandwagon to boot.

Reasons for Caution

St. Jude has experienced a few product problems in the past year, including a technical flaw in a line of implantable defibrillator leads. This issue caused a bit of a panic in the stock and served as a reminder of the risks that advanced surgical and cardiac equipment providers face. Also there is open discussion about the real need for some of the procedures St. Jude products support, and in today's era of cost containment, such discussions should be watched closely.

SECTOR: **Health Care**
BETA COEFFICIENT: **0.84**
10-YEAR COMPOUND EARNINGS PER SHARE GROWTH: **19.5%**
10-YEAR COMPOUND DIVIDENDS PER SHARE GROWTH: **NM**

	2005	2006	2007	2008	2009	2010	2011	2012
Revenues (mil)	2,915	3,302	3,779	4,363	4,681	5,165	5,612	5,503
Net income (mil)	394	548	652	807	838	995	1,074	1,095
Earnings per share	1.04	1.47	1.85	2.31	2.43	3.01	3.28	3.48
Dividends per share	—	—	—	—	—	—	0.84	0.92
Cash flow per share	1.42	2.05	2.48	2.92	3.24	3.70	4.35	4.50
Price: high	52.8	54.8	48.1	48.5	42.0	43.0	54.2	44.8
low	34.5	31.2	34.9	25.0	28.9	34.0	32.1	30.3

St. Jude Medical, Inc.
One St. Jude Medical Drive
St. Paul, MN 55117
(651) 766-3029
Website: www.sjm.com

AGGRESSIVE GROWTH

Starbucks Corporation

❑ Ticker symbol: SBUX (NASDAQ) ❑ S&P rating: A- ❑ Value Line financial strength rating: A+
❑ Current yield: 1.5% ❑ Dividend raises, past 10 years: 3

Company Profile

Starbucks Corporation, formed in 1985, is the leading retailer, roaster, and brand of specialty coffee in the world. The company sells whole-bean coffees through its retailers, its specialty sales group, and supermarkets. The company has 7,857 company-owned stores in the Americas and 1,548 in international markets, in addition to 8,661 licensed stores worldwide. Retail coffee shop sales constitute about 86 percent of its revenue. These figures reflect the effects of a modest downsizing campaign in 2010 and 2011, in which a number of poor-performing stores were closed, but in 2012 the company resumed its store growth, adding some 223 domestic stores, 87 international stores, and a significant number of licensees. Unlike many in the restaurant sector, the company does not franchise its stores—all are either company owned or operated by licensees in special venues such as airports, college campuses, and other places where access is restricted.

The company continues to expand overseas, usually at first through partnerships and joint ventures; sometimes they buy out the partner as they did in China in 2011. The company announced plans to open 300 stores in China in 2013 and signed an agreement to expand into Vietnam. Starbucks also has joint ventures with PepsiCo and Dreyer's to develop bottled coffee drinks and coffee-flavored ice creams. All channels outside the company-operated retail stores are collectively known as specialty operations.

The company's retail goal is to become the leading retailer and brand of coffee in each of its target markets through product quality and by providing a unique Starbucks experience, which the company defines as a third place beyond home and work. The "experience" is built upon superior customer service and a clean, well-maintained retail store that reflects the personality of the community in which it operates, thereby building a high degree of customer loyalty.

The company's specialty operations strive to develop the Starbucks brand outside the company-operated retail store environment through a number of channels, with a strategy to reach customers where they work, travel, shop, and dine. The strategy employs various models, including licensing arrangements, foodservice accounts, and other initiatives related to the company's core businesses.

The company has successfully introduced a line of K-Cup single-serve coffees and brewers in conjunction with industry leader Keurig (owned by Green Mountain Coffee Roasters). It shipped some 500 million single-serve packs and estimates that it owns 16 percent of that market. It is also gradually moving into the tea market with its line of Tazo teas and the recent acquisition of Teavana Holdings, a supplier of over 100 varieties of loose-leaf teas. The company also introduced a line of Evolution Fresh juices and La Boulange bakery items, both of which are doing well.

Financial Highlights, Fiscal Year 2012

FY2012 brewed up very strong results in all parts of the business. Revenues advanced 11.1 percent with U.S. same-store sales up a full 7 percent. Margins and earnings have both recovered from a sharp 2009 lull, and net profits and earnings per share advanced 18 percent. FY2013 guidance calls for revenue growth in the 10–13 percent range on comparable store growth in the "mid single digits;" strong China growth obviously figures in here. Margins should improve a bit with

lower coffee prices, and earnings per share are projected in the $2.08–$2.15 range, the midpoint of which would continue the 18 percent growth rate. The company has also become more aggressive with stock buybacks, authorizing a 25 million share (3 percent) repurchase at the end of FY2012.

Reasons to Buy

Howard Schultz is back, and Starbucks is hitting on all cylinders again. We never thought the company's slow spot in 2009–2010 was permanent; the company's stores continue to be more than coffee shops and are really that "third place" where professionals, students, moms, and other prosperous people will meet and dole out a few bucks for quality drinks. The "third place" aura creates a lot of the brand strength and, in our view, represents the company's true strength—well beyond the quality of the coffee itself. The company has a steadily (and profitably) growing presence in Europe, Japan, and China, although not surprisingly, Europe has been a soft spot of late. New single-cup ventures and the new Blonde light-roast products are broadening appeal to larger customer segments, as we thought would happen; the single-cup market has huge potential. We expect margins to continue to improve as such specialty products catch on and as the company continues to learn generally how to earn more money selling high-end products. The company is well managed, has an extremely strong brand, has solid financials, and, once again, a steady growth track record, and it is carving out an ever-stronger international footprint. If this wasn't enough, new focus on cash returns for investors has brought generous dividend increases and, finally, a substantial share repurchase.

Reasons for Caution

There is continued fear—although little has happened to justify it— that coffee drinkers may learn to get along without the $5 latte and become just $1.50 drippers. As we saw at the end of the 2000 decade, oversaturation is also a risk. Competitors Peet's and Caribou Coffee have been acquired by deep pockets, and Dunkin' Donuts is making a strong play in the lower high-end segment as McDonald's did a few years ago with mixed success, but overall we don't see much change in the competitive landscape in the near term. The biggest threat is that the stock price, with the P/E in the 30 range, may prove to be too hot to handle—but detractors have been saying that for years. While Starbucks is an exceptional story for the long term, it's worth waiting for an attractive price.

SECTOR: **Restaurants**
BETA COEFFICIENT: **1.18**
10-YEAR COMPOUND EARNINGS PER SHARE GROWTH: **21.0%**
10-YEAR COMPOUND DIVIDENDS PER SHARE GROWTH: **NM**

		2005	2006	2007	2008	2009	2010	2011	2012
Revenues (mil)		6,369	7,787	9,412	10,383	9,774	10,707	11,701	13,299
Net income (mil)		495	519	673	525	598	982	1,174	1,385
Earnings per share		0.61	0.73	0.87	0.71	0.80	1.28	1.52	1.79
Dividends per share		—	—	—	—	—	0.23	0.52	0.68
Cash flow per share		1.09	1.28	1.54	1.46	1.53	2.00	2.28	2.58
Price:	high	32.5	40.0	36.6	21.0	24.5	31.3	46.5	62.0
	low	22.3	28.7	19.9	7.1	21.3	21.3	30.8	43.0

Starbucks Corporation
2401 Utah Avenue South
Seattle, WA 98134
(206) 447-1575
Website: www.starbucks.com

CONSERVATIVE GROWTH

State Street Corporation

❑ Ticker symbol: STT (NYSE) ❑ S&P rating: A+ ❑ Value Line financial strength rating: B++
❑ Current yield: 1.8% ❑ Dividend raises, past 10 years: 8

Company Profile

Are you afraid of SPDRs? Not the eight-legged kind, but the original and 1 of 3 leading brands of exchange-traded funds (ETFs) out there rapidly gaining ground on the "traditional" fund industry? If you aren't afraid of SPDRs, and you aren't too afraid of financial stocks in general, we may have something for you here in State Street.

Like many financial power-houses, State Street has a number of businesses under its umbrella. But unlike many, its core products are concentrated on offering services to other financial services firms, and on offering the relatively new and growing ETF investment package to investors.

The company operates with 2 main lines of business: Investment Servicing and Investment Management:

■ Investment Servicing (88 percent of revenues) provides administrative, custody, analytic, and other value-add functions to investment companies—mainly mutual funds, hedge funds, and pension funds, including settlement and payment services, transaction management, and setting the NAV (net asset value, or price) of about 40 percent of U.S.-based mutual funds on a daily basis.

■ Investment Management (about 12 percent of revenues) provides investment vehicles and products through its State Street Global Advisors, or SSGA, subsidiary, including the well-known SPDR ETFs and some of the analytic tools and indexes supporting these products.

About 74 percent of total State Street revenues come from non-interest-related sources; the rest from interest and related income. The company has operations in 29 countries, and about 28 percent of revenues come from overseas operations, mostly in Europe.

Financial Highlights, Fiscal Year 2012

With its new ETF products on top of a booming global investment business, State Street enjoyed considerable prosperity during the boom years. Steady gains in revenues, earnings, cash flows, and dividends were the norm. And then 2008 happened. Earnings and revenues declined; that combined with fear and regulatory scrutiny almost destroyed the dividend. Now that period has pretty much passed, and the investment industry is booming once again. In 2012, the company added a new asset-servicing business mostly targeting hedge funds. Total assets, revenues, and especially earnings all grew at a healthy clip—and the latter would have been better without the 46-cent-per-share charge related to the Lehman Brothers collapse. Without that charge, earnings would have increased some 23 percent; even without it they were up some 11 percent with the help of a substantial 29 million share buyback. The dividend finally exceeded levels achieved before the financial crisis. For FY2013 the picture isn't completely clear. The new hedge fund custody business, a greater portion of investments going into equities, and some operational improvement programs will help, but these will be offset to a degree by the low interest rate climate and a relatively flat traditional mutual fund base. FY2013 revenues and earnings are projected to grow at about 3 percent, with an 8 percent growth in the dividend.

Reasons to Buy

When there's a gold rush, the people who sell picks, shovels, and maps usually win. That's sort of the case with State Street. They make a lot of steady money on selling services to other financial service firms. It's a steadier income stream absent some of the risks facing its other financial brethren. We think that State Street has a steady business with an innovative growth path in the ETF business, and we like the SPDR brand. We also like the fact that, unlike most financials, their income is more heavily based on fees and services than on interest margins and investment gains. It seems that, as much out of fear as anything else, the stock price hasn't appreciated as much as the earnings growth might suggest—translation: Upside potential plus decent dividend growth and share buybacks should lie ahead.

Reasons for Caution

Like other financial firms, State Street is enormously complex and hard to understand—we almost gave up. If you insist on fully understanding how a business works, what it sells, how it delivers, and so forth, this one might not be for you. It's a bit murky, though it is easier to see how they make money on the ETF business. Although the business is different than most financials, it could be swept up in another financial crisis. Likewise, a major market pullback and a decline in public interest could hurt. For all of these reasons, State Street is far from the least risky stock on our *100 Best Stocks* list, but it deserves a look if you like financials; there are only 2 others (Cincinnati Financial and Wells Fargo) on the list.

SECTOR: **Financials**
BETA COEFFICIENT: **1.48**
10-YEAR COMPOUND EARNINGS PER SHARE GROWTH: **7.0%**
10-YEAR COMPOUND DIVIDENDS PER SHARE GROWTH: **-2.5**

	2005	2006	2007	2008	2009	2010	2011	2012
Assets (bil)	98.0	107.3	142.5	173.6	157.9	160.5	216.8	222.6
Revenues (mil)	5,473	6,311	8,336	10,693	8,640	8,953	9,594	9,649
Net income (mil)	945	1,096	1,231	1,811	1,803	1,559	1,920	2,061
Earnings per share	2.82	3.26	3.45	4.30	3.46	3.09	3.79	4.20
Dividends per share	0.72	0.80	0.88	0.95	0.04	0.04	0.72	0.96
Price: high	59.8	68.6	82.5	86.6	55.9	48.8	50.3	47.3
low	40.6	54.4	59.1	28.1	14.4	32.5	29.9	38.2

State Street Corporation
One Lincoln Street
Boston, MA 02110
(617) 786-3000
Website: www.statestreet.com

AGGRESSIVE GROWTH

Stryker Corporation

❑ Ticker symbol: SYK (NYSE) ❑ S&P rating: A+ ❑ Value Line financial strength rating: A++
❑ Current yield: 1.6% ❑ Dividend increases, past 10 years: 10

Company Profile

Stryker Corporation was founded as the Orthopedic Frame Company in 1941 by Dr. Homer H. Stryker, a leading orthopedic surgeon and the inventor of several orthopedic products. The company now ranks as a dominant player in the global orthopedics industry with more than 59,000 products in its catalog and a strong innovation track record, with over 5 percent of sales invested in R & D.

The Reconstructive segment, formerly known as Orthopedic Implants, comprising about 45 percent of sales, has a significant market share in such "spare parts" as artificial hips, prosthetic knees, implant products for other extremities, and trauma products.

The MediSurg unit, about 38 percent of sales, develops, manufactures, and markets worldwide powered and computer-assisted surgical instruments, endoscopic surgical systems, hospital beds, and other patient care and handling equipment.

The Neurotechnology & Spine segment, a large part of which was acquired from Boston Scientific in 2010, accounts for 17 percent of sales and sells spinal reconstructive and surgical equipment, neurovascular surgery, and craniomaxillofacial products. This is the smallest but fastest-growing segment in the company.

Stryker acquired Trauson Holdings in 2012, giving it a strong and profitable presence in the Chinese market, as well as the rest of Asia. Stryker's revenue is split roughly 60/40 among implants and equipment and 65/35 domestic and international.

Financial Highlights, Fiscal Year 2012

Stryker reported FY2012 sales of $8.65 billion, about 4 percent ahead of FY2011 despite a fairly strong currency headwind and a soft Europe environment. Per-share earnings came in at $3.72, a 9.4 percent increase over FY2011. For FY2013, the company is expecting revenue to increase 3–5.5 percent excluding foreign exchange and acquisitions, with EPS ahead 4–8 percent to the $4.25–$4.40 range. Cash flows remain strong and annual dividend increases are in the 20 percent range; the dividend is more than double its previous 2008 high and appears likely to go higher. The company just announced a $250 million "accelerated" share repurchase program.

Reasons to Buy

Stryker's top line is driven largely by elective surgeries, and the Great Recession years turned out to be years for delaying whatever medical procedures could be delayed. Many consumers decided to wait and see how the medical care legislation would turn out, and some were simply deciding to hold on to their cash until economic conditions improved. That's all over now, and a resumed surgical calendar and international expansion bode well for the near-term future. We continue to see Stryker as an innovative health-care products company with relatively less entrenched competition than many others. We also see an acceleration in shareholder returns through dividends and buybacks.

Reasons for Caution

Ongoing scrutiny of health-care costs and continued reliance on acquisitions to fuel growth bring risks to the company, but we don't think the risks are excessive. The company makes fairly high-tech medical products and as such is exposed to legal, regulatory, and manufacturing risks, as evidenced by a recent letter from the FDA raising quality concerns at one of its plants. Finally, ongoing efforts to contain medical costs could hurt the more elective orthopedic procedures.

SECTOR: **Health Care**
BETA COEFFICIENT: **0.92**
10-YEAR COMPOUND EARNINGS PER SHARE GROWTH: **19.5%**
10-YEAR COMPOUND DIVIDENDS PER SHARE GROWTH: **30.5%**

		2005	2006	2007	2008	2009	2010	2011	2012
Revenues (mil)		4,872	5,406	6,001	6,718	6,723	7,320	8,307	8,656
Net income (mil)		644	778	1,017	1,148	1,107	1,330	1,448	1,561
Earnings per share		1.57	1.89	2.44	2.78	2.77	3.30	3.72	4.08
Dividends per share		0.11	0.11	0.22	0.33	0.50	0.63	0.72	0.85
Cash flow per share		2.49	2.85	3.33	3.87	3.75	4.40	5.05	5.40
Price:	high	56.3	55.9	76.9	74.9	52.7	59.7	65.2	64.1
	low	39.7	39.8	54.9	35.4	30.8	42.7	43.7	55.2

Stryker Corporation
P.O. Box 4085
Kalamazoo, MI 49002
(616) 385-2600
Website: www.stryker.com

Suburban Propane Partners, L.P.

❑ Ticker symbol: SPH (NYSE) ❑ S&P rating: BB ❑ Value Line financial strength rating: B+
❑ Current yield: 7.9% ❑ Dividend raises, past 10 years: 9

Company Profile

You probably know this company best for its propane distribution business and the white sausage-shaped tanks dotting the landscape, especially in rural areas, and for the trucks serving them. Suburban Propane Partners, L.P., through its subsidiaries, engages in the retail marketing and distribution of propane, fuel oil, and refined fuels, and to a lesser extent, in the marketing of natural gas and electricity in the United States.

At about 70 percent of the business, the Propane segment is the largest part of the company and engages in the retail distribution of propane to residential, commercial, industrial, and agricultural customers, as well as wholesale distribution to large industrial end users. The Fuel Oil and Refined Fuels segment engages in the retail distribution of fuel oil, diesel, kerosene, and gasoline to residential and commercial customers for use primarily as a source of heat in homes and buildings, primarily in the East, while the Natural Gas and Electricity segment markets those commodities to residential and commercial customers in the deregulated energy markets of New York and Pennsylvania.

The company took a big step forward in 2012 with the acquisition of competitor Inergy L.P.'s retail business, which effectively doubled the size of Suburban's propane customer base and gave it an important position in the Midwest. Previously, Suburban's footprint was largest in the eastern and western regions of the country. The Inergy acquisition took its toll on 2012 financial performance but will solidify results moving forward.

As of September 2012, the company served approximately 1,135,000 residential, commercial, industrial, and agricultural customers, up from 750,000, through approximately 750 locations in 41 states (up from 300 locations in 30 states). The company is also involved in selling and servicing heating, ventilation, and air conditioning (HVAC) units that consume its fuels.

Financial Highlights, Fiscal Year 2012

As far as basic financial performance is concerned, you could call 2012 a

THE 100 BEST STOCKS TO BUY IN 2014

perfect storm, which is quite evident from the following numbers—no need to elaborate. Two primary factors almost wiped out net earnings, and one of them took its toll on the top line as well. The direct costs of the Inergy acquisition and related administrative costs hit earnings—that's a done deal moving forward. More interesting to watch for the future was the unusually warm weather of 2012, which caused a 15 percent shortfall in unit volumes of propane (23 percent for fuel oil, if you're curious), and as you'd expect in this environment, softer pricing. Revenues fell 11 percent with some helpful offset from the Inergy acquisition later in the year. The company cites a report from the National Oceanic and Atmospheric Administration (NOAA) stating that average temperatures in Suburban's service territories were 14 percent above normal and 13 percent above FY2011.

All of this seems to be behind the company for now. Cold weather has returned, as have unit volumes, and Inergy is fully on board. For the first quarter of FY2013, the company earned $1.04 per unit (SPH is a "master limited partnership," not a stock per se, so you own units, avoiding corporate taxes so long as most earnings are paid out to holders, but this creates some tax consequences for individuals as these are not "qualified" dividends; consult a tax advisor). That $1.04 compared to only $0.65 in the comparable 2012 quarter, and the company is projecting earnings of $155 million, or $2.60 per unit, on a record $1.6 billion in sales for all of FY2013. The company issued about 20 million units to make the acquisition, hence the dilution, but fully expects to support and even raise the FY2013 distribution and beyond through cash flow. As a sign of confidence, the company raised the distribution in early FY2013.

Reasons to Buy

The main draw with companies like Suburban Propane is the high, steady, and often growing payout. The current yield of 7.9 percent, with relatively little volatility in what is usually a fairly steady business, is extremely attractive in an environment where a 2–4 percent yield is considered decent. The company must pay out almost all of its earnings and is willing to dip into assets to sustain the payout when necessary, indicating the true priority of owner interests.

The question, of course, is whether the cash payout is sustainable. We think the core business model is still relatively safe, and any upside (lower temperatures, higher natural gas prices) should stabilize the cash flow situation. Moreover, even if the company cuts the distribution, say by a third, it would still be paying about $2.30 a unit, which would be less than annual per-unit earnings and a healthy 5.2 percent yield at today's unit price. So while there is risk, we don't think the downside risk is too severe—and those who embraced this risk were rewarded with a 15 percent stock price appreciation last year. We think the ongoing risks are worth taking in the interest of achieving above-market yields from a company with utility-like fundamentals.

Reasons for Caution

The concern, of course, is whether warm weather is here to stay (we're not so sure) and whether natural gas prices will continue to stay so low (we don't think so, at least in the long term). SPH is tied somewhat to the new housing construction industry, particularly in outlying areas, but that industry has shown some strength lately. If the weather were to warm up again, we're concerned, of course, about how long Suburban can maintain its business model and its payout. All said, even after a possible large cut in the payout in unfavorable circumstances, the company still appears to be a worthwhile candidate.

SECTOR: **Energy**
BETA COEFFICIENT: **0.46**
10-YEAR COMPOUND EARNINGS PER SHARE GROWTH: **-1.0%**
10-YEAR COMPOUND DIVIDENDS PER SHARE GROWTH: **4.5%**

	2005	2006	2007	2008	2009	2010	2011	2012
Revenues (mil)	1,620	1,662	1,440	1,574	1,143	1,137	1,191	1,064
Net income (mil)	(9.1)	90.7	123.3	111.2	165.2	115.2	115.0	2.0
Earnings per share	(0.29)	2.84	3.79	3.39	4.99	3.26	3.24	0.05
Dividends per share	2.45	2.50	2.69	3.14	3.28	3.37	3.41	3.41
Cash flow per share	0.92	4.09	4.66	4.26	5.55	4.13	4.25	1.25
Price: high	37.4	39.2	49.6	42.6	47.7	57.2	59.0	48.3
Low	23.5	26.0	35.1	20.4	31.0	39.2	40.3	34.6

Suburban Propane Partners, L.P.
240 Route 10 West
Whippany, NJ 07981
(973) 887-5300
Website: www.suburbanpropane.com

CONSERVATIVE GROWTH

Sysco Corporation

◻ Ticker symbol: SYY (NYSE) ◻ S&P rating: A+ ◻ Value Line financial strength rating: A++
◻ Current yield: 3.3% ◻ Dividend raises, past 10 years: 10

Company Profile

Sysco is the leading marketer and distributor of food, food products, and related equipment and supplies to the U.S. foodservice industry. The company distributes fresh and frozen meats, prepared entrées, vegetables, canned and dried foods, dairy products, beverages, and produce, as well as paper products, restaurant equipment and supplies, and cleaning supplies. The company might be familiar for its "institutional" number-ten-sized cans of food found in many high-volume kitchens, but the product line and customer base is much larger, including many specialty and chain restaurants, lodges, hotels, hospitals, schools, and other distribution centers across the country. Restaurants account for about 63 percent of the business; these "other" categories make up the rest. You see their lift-gated "bobtail" delivery trucks continuously, but you may not notice them delivering and unloading a pallet or two of goods at a time for a broad assortment of foodservice venues in your area. If you eat out at all, you've most likely consumed Sysco-distributed products, and their slogan, "Good Things Come from Sysco," is classic.

Sysco was founded in 1969 with the goal of becoming a national foodservice network. By 1977, the company had become the largest foodservice supplier in North America, a position they have retained for more than 30 years. They have over 400,000 customers and conduct business in more than 100 countries.

Sysco operates 185 distribution facilities across the United States, Canada, and Ireland and distributes 1.3 billion cases of food annually. These facilities include their 90 Broadline facilities, which supply independent and chain restaurants and other food preparation facilities with a wide variety of food and nonfood products. They have 14 hotel supply locations, 31 specialty produce facilities, 21 SYGMA distribution centers (specialized, high-volume centers supplying to chain restaurants), 17 custom-cutting meat locations, and 2 distributors specializing in the niche Asian foodservice market.

The company also supplies the hotel industry with guest amenities, equipment, housekeeping supplies, room accessories, and textiles.

Sysco is by far the largest company in the foodservice distribution industry, and has made several small acquisitions of late, including Ohio Central Seafood Company, Buchy Food Service, and Appert's Foodservice—you can see the strategy of bolting on smaller competitors. The company estimates that it serves 18 percent of a $235 billion market, and is more than twice the size of the nearest competitor.

Financial Highlights, Fiscal Year 2012

The restaurant industry got clobbered in the 2009 recession but is well along in its rebound, with a 6.8 percent rise in the size of the overall restaurant market in 2012. Sysco more than kept pace with a 7.8 percent rise in sales, although some of this may have been food price inflation. Unfortunately, not enough inflation was passed on to customers, and increased food and delivery costs caused margins to decline slightly in this margin-sensitive business, and earnings came in slightly below last year's $1.15 billion at $1.13 billion, or $1.90 per share. For FY2013, top-line strength, the completion of certain acquisitions and restructurings, and a more favorable food price environment should lead to a healthier 6–7 percent gain in per-share earnings, helped along by a modest 2 percent share buyback. Cash flow is strong,

and the company continues to raise dividends and looks positioned to do so well into the future.

Reasons to Buy

Sysco continues to be a dominant player in a niche that won't go away anytime soon. While near-term commodity prices may add some cost pressure, the value of the franchise and near-term sales should remain unchanged or even improve as the restaurant market gradually strengthens.

Sysco's recent investments in technology continue to bear fruit, and we like to see innovation in an industry not known for innovation. Improvements in routing and inventory management have allowed the company to increase its shipment frequency by 10 percent with 4 percent fewer people, all while using 10 percent less fuel. There is now even a Sysco app for tech-driven restaurant owners and managers. The company dominates a highly fragmented industry and could increase that domination through acquisition; it has the financial strength to do so. In sum, this is a steady and safe company with a pretty good track record for shareholder payouts.

Reasons for Caution

Although the trend is slowly reversing, the recession got many folks away from the habit of eating out, and many restaurants disappeared altogether during this period. The steady climb in food and ingredient prices, and the resulting margin pressure, is a cause for concern.

This is a "sleep at night" kind of investment; investors seeking rapid growth might want to look somewhere outside of this steady and rather unsexy business.

SECTOR: **Consumer Staples**
BETA COEFFICIENT: **0.70**
10-YEAR COMPOUND EARNINGS PER SHARE GROWTH: **8.5%**
10-YEAR COMPOUND DIVIDENDS PER SHARE GROWTH: **13.5%**

	2005	2006	2007	2008	2009	2010	2011	2012
Revenues (mil)	30,282	32,628	35,042	37,522	36,853	37,243	39,323	42,381
Net income (mil)	961	855	1,001	1,106	1,056	1,181	1,153	1,122
Earnings per share	1.47	1.35	1.60	1.81	1.77	1.99	1.96	1.90
Dividends per share	0.58	0.66	0.72	0.82	0.93	0.99	1.03	1.07
Cash flow per share	2.03	1.92	2.23	2.46	2.44	2.67	2.62	2.63
Price: high	38.4	37.0	36.7	35.0	29.5	32.6	32.6	32.4
low	30.0	26.5	29.9	20.7	19.4	27.0	25.1	27.0

Sysco Corporation
1390 Enclave Parkway
Houston, TX 77077–2099
(281) 584-1458
Website: www.sysco.com

AGGRESSIVE GROWTH

Target Corporation

❏ Ticker symbol: TGT (NYSE) ❏ S&P rating: A+ ❏ Value Line financial strength rating: A ❏ Current yield: 2.1% ❏ Dividend raises, past 10 years: 10

Company Profile

Target is the nation's second-largest general merchandise retailer and specializes in general merchandise at a discount in a large-store format. The company now operates 1,763 stores in 49 states, including 251 Super Targets, which also carry a broad line of groceries. The greatest concentration of Target stores is in California (14 percent), Texas (8 percent), and Florida (7 percent), with a combined total of about 30 percent of the stores. There is another concentration in the upper Midwest. With the sale of Marshall Field and Mervyn's in 2004, the company has focused completely on discount retail in store locations and on the Internet.

Target positions itself against its main competitor, Walmart, as a more upscale and trend-conscious "cheap chic" alternative. The typical Target customer has a higher level of disposable income, which the company courts by offering brand-name merchandise in addition to a series of largely successful house brands such as Michael Graves and Archer Farms. The company's revenues come from retail pretty much exclusively; it sold its credit card operations to TD Bank and will most likely use the proceeds to repurchase stock and to pay off debt incurred to achieve the 50 million shares already repurchased in the past 2 years.

Target is in the midst of a 125-store expansion into Canada, which should be completed in 2014, leveraging the acquisition of a series of store sites there. The company is also investing domestically in its food lines, which now account for 19 percent of total sales; up from 17 percent last year. Food is sold in about 70 percent of stores, up from 50 percent last year. To complement the food foray, the company announced the acquisition of CHEFS Catalog and cooking.com to bolster kitchenware offerings.

Financial Highlights, Fiscal Year 2012

Target took some lumps during the recession, but the strong value proposition of quality for less resonated well with most customers. Revenues logged about a 5.1 percent gain on top of last year's 4 percent gain on a relatively constant (up less than 1 percent) store base. Earnings per share only rose 2.8 percent, but the

Canada expansion cost about 40 cents a share as expected; without this charge EPS would have risen just over 12 percent on somewhat stronger margins and a 19 million (3 percent) share count reduction. Per-share earnings are guided at $4.80, a 9 percent increase, on a 5 percent revenue increase; both figures are expected to accelerate notably in FY2014 with the Canada expansion. Cash flow looks very strong at a projected $8.60 per share, easily supporting future buybacks and dividend increases.

Reasons to Buy

Target is a classic positioning success story. Customers understand and appreciate Target, and it has some of the highest customer satisfaction numbers in the industry. The company continues to take share away from specialty retailers in home lines, clothing, children's items, and other areas. People like the Target brand and associate it with well-managed stores and quality and good taste at a reasonable price with good locations. More recently they appear to be making more regular and frequent visits to the store because of the grocery department.

Better economic conditions and more spending on home and domestic goods should improve Target's market share. Trend data indicates that Target performs better than its competitors during periods of economic growth. We also feel that the Canada expansion should work well, and may provide some learning and impetus for future international expansion. Share counts have dropped from 911 million in 2003 to about 650 million recently. The dividend rose 20 percent again in FY2012, and the company still "targets" a $3 dividend by 2017, suggesting a 22 percent dividend growth rate between now and then.

Reasons for Caution

Target is up against some very tough competitors: Walmart, Costco, and others. Also, these two competitors are growing their international presence, while Target, other than Canada, has none and has no current plans for growth outside the United States. We still see some risk in the grocery business, as groceries are very low margin and the company hasn't really figured out how to make the grocery offering complete with meats and fresh produce. Gross margins have dipped slightly recently, probably a result of the larger grocery footprint, although groceries do attract customers and increase the frequency of store visits.

SECTOR: Retail
BETA COEFFICIENT: 0.92
10-YEAR COMPOUND EARNINGS PER SHARE GROWTH: 10.5%
10-YEAR COMPOUND DIVIDENDS PER SHARE GROWTH: 15.0%

	2005	2006	2007	2008	2009	2010	2011	2012
Revenues (mil)	52,620	59,490	63,367	64,948	63,435	67,390	69,865	73,301
Net income (mil)	2,408	2,787	2,849	2,214	2,488	2,830	2,829	2,925
Earnings per share	2.71	3.21	3.33	2.86	3.30	3.88	4.28	4.38
Dividends per share	0.38	0.42	0.56	0.60	0.66	0.84	1.10	1.32
Cash flow per share	4.37	4.98	5.51	5.37	5.90	6.98	7.46	7.82
Price: high	60.0	60.3	70.8	59.6	51.8	60.7	61.0	65.5
low	45.6	44.7	48.8	25.6	25.0	46.2	45.3	47.3

Target Corporation
1000 Nicollet Mall
Minneapolis, MN 55403
(612) 370-6735
Website: www.target.com

Tiffany & Co.

❏ Ticker symbol: TIF (NYSE) ❏ S&P rating: not rated ❏ Value Line financial strength rating: A
❏ Current yield: 1.9% ❏ Dividend raises, past 10 years: 10

Company Profile

As a variant on the old cliché goes, "If you have to ask who they are, you can't afford them." But when it comes to investing, it's perfectly okay to ask, and we're here to provide the answer, so here goes . . .

Tiffany is a jeweler and specialty retailer principally offering jewelry (accounting for 91 percent of FY2011 sales) but also timepieces, sterling silver goods (e.g., silver spoons), china, crystal, fragrances, stationery, leather goods, and other personal items. The design of both product and packaging is distinctive, with a historic tradition and elegant simplicity that sets it apart. Ditto for the stores and catalog. Tiffany is probably the world's most recognized general jewelry brand (aside from Rolex and similar brands in the watch business), and the company has a sizeable presence in other countries.

In fact, some 50 percent of sales are from outside the Americas. Just to give some figures, there are 87 stores in the United States, 7 in Mexico, 5 in Canada, and 3 in Brazil. Notably, the multistory flagship store on Fifth Avenue in New York City accounts for about 10 percent of Tiffany's business alone, albeit much of it from visiting foreign tourists craving the experience (and what is still a relatively weak dollar).

Now, moving to Asia, which accounts for 21 percent of sales, there are 16 stores in China, 14 in Korea, 7 in Taiwan, 5 in Australia, 4 in Singapore, 2 in Macau, and 2 in Malaysia. Oh, yes—what about Japan? Japan is so large it is accounted for as a separate region, with 17 percent of the business and 51 stores. Do the Japanese appreciate quality and elegant simplicity? You bet!

Finally, we come to Europe, which represents 12 percent of sales with 10 stores in the U.K., 6 in Germany, 3 in France, 2 in Spain, 2 in Switzerland, and 1 each in 4 other countries. Beyond Europe, the company also does business in the Middle East, Russia, and elsewhere through distributors. The Middle East and the BRIC countries (Brazil/Russia/India/China) are the most important growth areas and—oh, by the way—the sovereign wealth fund of Qatar apparently sees Tiffany as a crown jewel, recently making two large purchases to bring its holdings up to more than 11 percent of the company.

In addition to retailing a broad line of luxury goods, Tiffany also designs and manufactures much of its branded jewelry. The Tiffany cachet raises margins on these items without significantly diluting brand strength, while at the same time driving store visits higher. Clearly, the company is a bastion for wealthy consumers, but it also works hard to attract so-called "aspirational" consumers seeking moderately priced, say, $100–$300, items with that Tiffany cachet and experience. Internationally, and particularly in Asia, Tiffany appeals to the very wealthy, and the average selling price of items in Asia runs 8 to 10 times the average price of items sold in the Americas.

Financial Highlights, Fiscal Year 2012

Most would have expected stronger sales and profits in FY2012 as the world emerged from the recession and resumed its buying habits, and we were among them, which, along with its unique brand cachet, is why we put Tiffany on our *100 Best Stocks* list last year. Well, all that glitters isn't gold; in fact, it was really silver that didn't glitter so much last year. Sales improved 10.6 percent to $3.83 billion, a healthy figure, considering currency headwinds. But relatively weak demand in the lower-end products—mainly made of silver and especially in

Europe and Japan—and new costs to expand into smaller markets reduced operating margins from 24.6 percent to 22.5 percent and caused the company to miss earnings targets. Surprisingly, the silver-based, under-$500 product segment is among the most profitable and typically accounts for 25 percent of the business. Earnings per share fell from $3.61 to $3.22 for the period. For FY2013, the company expects a limited recovery in this segment and more strength in the higher-end segments, especially diamonds. Lower precious metal costs will also help. Tiffany expects earnings in the $3.55 per share range with sales up about 6 percent.

Reasons to Buy

Tiffany is a classic branding story, where brand image supports the product and the product supports the brand image. People buy Tiffany because it is Tiffany and because they are attracted to the distinctive cachet and elegant simplicity. While the company is working to offer more moderately priced items for the "aspirational" market, we don't expect it to lower quality and damage the brand prestige—although this is always a risk and, as discussed in the next section, our concerns about it have escalated. We are very strong on the company's international footprint and the ability to grow sales and leverage the brand, particularly in Asia. The company is also introducing a new smaller-footprint store format to cover moderately sized markets. Dividend raises have been steady and growing, although share buybacks have pretty much stalled over the last few years on a total share count basis.

Reasons for Caution

Last year we suggested that there was some risk in going too far to cater to the aspirational base with less expensive, and perhaps lower-quality and less "elegantly simple" items. Given last year's results, we may have been right, and it will be interesting to see what Tiffany

does now in this low-end market. Lose the cachet, and Tiffany is just another corner jeweler. If the low-end segment doesn't improve (or get downsized as a result), Tiffany may stay on Fifth Avenue but may not stay on our list next year.

Naturally, the company is somewhat exposed to economic cycles, particularly economic circumstances that affect the rich, as the last recession clearly did. It is also exposed to the volatility of gold and silver—although this volatility actually creates some demand as buyers, particularly in Asia, look at fine jewelry and its precious metals as a store of value.

SECTOR: **Retail**
BETA COEFFICIENT: **1.79**
10-YEAR COMPOUND EARNINGS PER SHARE GROWTH: **10.0%**
10-YEAR COMPOUND DIVIDENDS PER SHARE GROWTH: **20.5%**

	2005	2006	2007	2008	2009	2010	2011	2012
Revenues (mil)	2,395	2,648	2,938	2,860	2,709	3,085	3,643	3,794
Net income (mil)	254	254	322	294	266	378	465	416
Earnings per share	1.75	1.60	2.33	2.33	2.12	2.93	3.61	3.25
Dividends per share	0.30	0.38	0.52	0.66	0.68	0.95	1.12	1.25
Cash flow per share	2.56	2.74	3.50	3.44	3.21	4.13	4.82	4.57
Price: high	43.6	41.3	57.3	50.0	44.5	65.8	84.5	74.2
low	28.6	29.6	38.2	18.8	16.7	35.6	54.6	49.7

Tiffany & Co.
727 Fifth Ave.
New York, NY 10022
(212) 755-8000
Website: www.tiffany.com

Time Warner Inc.

❑ Ticker symbol: TWX (NYSE) ❑ S&P rating: BBB ❑ Value Line financial strength rating: B++
❑ Current yield: 2.1% ❑ Dividend raises, past 10 years: 7

Company Profile

We'd be willing to bet that all of you, our readers, have made a big, glaring goof at one time during your lives. A mistake that caused pain, grief, embarrassment, and startled looks from the people around you. Anything from a bad investment to a drinking binge to a big traffic ticket. It took a while to recover. But you did; you learned from the mistake and moved on to do much bigger, better things and to laugh about your mistake in the end. It's a common human experience.

Time Warner, too, proved itself to be quite human in the late 1990s. It tried to buy the Internet. It bought Netscape, then followed this gaffe by buying America Online (AOL) in what at the time amounted to David buying Goliath. It changed its name to AOL Time Warner and proceeded to destroy one of history's largest chunks of shareholder value. Finally, in 2009, Time Warner spun off AOL (and Time Warner Cable, too) and cleaned house with an extraordinary (for our *100 Best* list, anyway) one-for-three reverse split—and went back to being a premier media and content company. The struggle to control the last mile of distribution was, fortunately, over.

So now we have a focused $29 billion media giant (okay, so that's down from $47 billion in AOL and cable days) aimed squarely at producing and distributing media in both traditional and innovative ways. The newly downsized company was back to working in the areas it knows best—content—and working on new ways to make more money producing and delivering that content. It was a good story, and we had no entertainment stocks on the list, so we bought a ticket . . . and were pleasantly surprised, to say the least. And the story of change apparently has an interesting epilogue, with a recent announcement to spin off (or sell) Time Inc.—the print portion—of this strengthening media conglomerate.

The company operates in three main segments:

■ Film and TV Entertainment (44 percent of revenues), including Warner Bros. Pictures and New Line Cinema. Warner Bros. produces about 22 feature films a year and distributes hundreds of others.

- Networks (47 percent), which feeds a variety of content to an assortment of media devices including some of the best brands in the business, mainly delivered through the Turner Broadcasting System (CNN, TNT, Turner Classic, Cartoon Network, Adult Swim, Boomerang, digital sports networks including NBA.com and PGA.com, and others), and the HBO and Cinemax networks.
- Publishing (13 percent), which includes legacy magazine businesses such as *Time*, *Sports Illustrated*, *People*, and others—21 magazines in the United States and 70 magazines internationally in all. This is the portion of the business currently on the block.

The details of these businesses and sub-businesses expands far beyond what is described here; suffice it to say TWX has a huge presence in the creation and distribution of many forms of media. The company is quite dedicated to innovation, and the use of innovations to get more content to more people in more places at more times than ever before. A new "TV Everywhere" initiative is one example. The company lists its innovations right behind its home page (tabs "Our Content," "Our Company," and "Our Innovations" speak to the importance of finding new ways to do things). Platforms like HBO GO are designed to deliver content to tablets and smartphones as well as traditional devices.

Financial Highlights, Fiscal Year 2012

Time Warner continues to rightsize after the AOL debacle with spinoffs and restructurings; this makes yearly revenue and profit comparisons tricky. What we do know is that net profit margins have been growing into the 10 percent range, up from the 6–8 percent range mid-decade. Sales declined from $47 billion to $25 billion after the AOL and cable separation but are up about $5 billion since then. That figure will change again, by approximately $4 billion, with the Time Inc. spinoff. Earnings per share rose a modest 5.2 percent for FY2012, mainly on a 34 million reduction in share count (about 4 percent). As we said last year, the buybacks may slow a bit, but the company also raised its dividend 10 percent. For FY2013, including the Time Inc. spinoff, the company projects a mid–double-digit earnings per share growth.

Reasons to Buy

Time Warner has taken its medicine, and we think it is unlikely to repeat past mistakes. As the Internet universe expands, and as people have smart devices capable of receiving anything anywhere anytime, we think the demand for content will only go up, and TWX has some of the great properties and brands, such as CNN, HBO, and TBS, to leverage as platforms to develop and deliver this content. Last year we thought that once TWX regained focus and investors started to "get" the story, good things could happen. Apparently that wish has come true. Additionally, the company is working hard on new programming, new delivery, new channels for its content library, cost structure, and profitability. We think the growth in earnings and cash flow will accelerate. The spinoff of *Time* as a separate stock could help shareholders, too—while we're not that excited by magazines at this time, the *People*

and *Sports Illustrated* brands in particular are golden. This is a cash-generating business, and we like the cash returns to investors.

Reasons for Caution

The good news is also the bad news—investors have "gotten" this branding and rightsizing story and have sent the stock up almost 60 percent since we selected it last year. The business remains competitive, and TWX does not possess some of the industry's edgiest, most contemporary brands, like Comedy Central (Viacom), but we're okay with that. Finally, we're not sure how the "TV Everywhere" idea will play out, and we'd probably frown on any other big acquisitions, especially outside the core industry.

SECTOR: **Entertainment**
BETA COEFFICIENT: **1.17**
10-YEAR COMPOUND EARNINGS PER SHARE GROWTH: **3.4**
10-YEAR COMPOUND DIVIDENDS PER SHARE GROWTH: **NM**

		2005	2006	2007	2008	2009	2010	2011	2012
Revenues (mil)		43,652	44,224	46,482	46,894	25,785	26,888	28,944	29,450
Net income (mil)		2,905	5,114	4,051	3,574	2,079	2,578	2,886	2,780
Earnings per share		1.86	3.63	2.97	2.88	1.74	2.25	2.71	2.85
Dividends per share		0.30	0.63	0.71	0.75	0.75	0.85	0.94	1.04
Cash flow per share		4.12	6.75	7.07	6.83	2.66	3.20	3.91	4.10
Price:	high	58.9	66.8	69.5	50.7	33.5	34.1	38.6	48.5
	low	45.3	47.1	45.5	21.0	17.8	26.4	27.6	33.5

Time Warner Inc.
One Time Warner Center
New York, NY 10019
(212) 484-6000
Website: www.timewarner.com

GROWTH AND INCOME

Total S.A. (ADR)

❑ Ticker symbol: TOT (NYSE) ❑ S&P rating: AA- ❑ Value Line financial strength rating: A++
❑ Current yield: 6.0% ❑ Dividend raises, past 10 years: 6

Company Profile

Total S.A. (S.A. is short for Société Anonyme, which is the French equivalent of "incorporated") is the fifth-largest publicly traded oil and gas company in the world. Headquartered in France and primarily traded on the French CAC stock exchange, the company has operations in more than 130 countries. Total is vertically integrated with upstream operations engaged in oil and gas exploration and downstream operations engaged in refining and distribution of petroleum products; the company also has a chemicals subsidiary.

Upstream activities are geographically well diversified, with exploration occurring in 40 countries and production happening in 30 of them. Many of the E&P projects are done through partnerships to spread risk. The largest production regions are (in production-volume sequence) in the North Sea, North Africa, West Africa, and the Middle East, with smaller operations in Southeast Asia and North and South America. Liquids (oil) account for about 61 percent of production, while natural gas is 39 percent. The company is a leader in the emerging liquefied natural gas (LNG) market for export. The company has had good results in the exploration and production side, somewhat better than the industry, with production up 6 percent, led by a 19 percent increase in gas output.

Downstream operations are also worldwide and centered in Europe. Operations include interests in 25 refineries worldwide, with 11 refineries and 85 percent of total refining capacity in Europe. Total also operates 16,425 service stations, again weighted toward Europe and North Africa. The downstream presence is also growing in Asia Pacific (including China), Latin America, and the Caribbean. The new Saudi Arabia refinery, coming on line in 2013, will help longer-term results as the company diversifies its processing and marketing capacity into the faster growing Middle East and Asian regions. Total also has ventures in alternative energy, notably solar. With 2 major partners it brought on line in 2013 what is thought to be the world's largest concentrated solar power plant at 100 megawatts in Abu Dhabi.

Financial Highlights, Fiscal Year 2012

A number of mostly small and temporary events produced mixed sales and reserve replacement results in FY2012. Those events included floods in Nigeria and political disruptions in Syria and Yemen—while these events and a 2011 North Sea spill are past, they can certainly occur again. Liquids production was flat compared to FY2011, while natural gas dropped 4 percent. Because of their geography, Total realizes better prices than some of the bellwether markets for their products—about $108 per barrel for its crude and $6.74 per million BTU for natural gas. As a result, and with slightly favorable currency translation, the company realized a healthy 11 percent revenue gain; North Sea and exploration costs kept earnings largely flat. The company intends to boost both oil and gas production into the 2–3 percent range in 2013 and ongoing, and anticipates similar gains in sales and earnings into the period. Most likely the company will make both some small acquisitions and divestitures to optimize its mix and diversify a bit geographically, but none big enough to substantially affect results. Currency translation will continue to challenge yearly comparisons, as well as following the progress of the dividend—which was recently raised about 3 percent

on an already strong 6 percent yield base. Share buybacks have been stilled for a few years, but we could see them starting up again with the strong cash flows.

Reasons to Buy

Total S.A. is a solid energy sector play with many of the features that make "big energy" attractive—namely, strong cash flows, high dividend yields, and demand that isn't going away anytime soon. Companies with a price-to-cash-flow ratio under 5, implying a 20 percent annual cash return, aren't easy to find. The dividend is one of the best in the industry. In addition, Total provides a stronger international play than other energy picks on our list. The company has a dominant position in Europe, which, albeit not growing, is a steady market, producing plenty of cash flow while allowing the company to dabble in more promising markets such as China and others in Asia Pacific and Latin America. Total is well positioned to take advantage of higher prices for their production as well as recent strength in the refining business. Finally, those believing that the dollar will weaken longer term, particularly against the euro, will like the fact that the dividend is paid in euros, which would translate favorably to ever-cheaper dollars.

Reasons for Caution

Continued European economic uncertainty and softness in its reserve replacement (oil reserves declined 2 percent in FY2012; gas was up 1 percent) have made this stock a "total"ly flat performer since the recession, while the rest of the market has marched upward. On a (ahem) total return basis, the dividend and international diversification keep the stock on our list, but without a bit more dynamic a growth strategy and some share buybacks to boost shareholder value, Total may soon prove to be a dry hole. We remain cautious on investing in foreign companies because of differences in management style and accounting rules; they aren't necessarily bad but are difficult to understand and follow. Antiquated European pension rules and other labor practices could also be a disadvantage. Typically, we prefer U.S. companies that do a lot of business overseas, but we still feel the strengths of Total overcome these concerns, and U.S.-based integrated oil and gas companies are already well represented on our *100 Best Stocks* list.

SECTOR: **Energy**
BETA COEFFICIENT: **1.02**
10-YEAR COMPOUND EARNINGS PER SHARE GROWTH: **12.0%**
10-YEAR COMPOUND DIVIDENDS PER SHARE GROWTH: **18.0%**

	2005	2006	2007	2008	2009	2010	2011	2012
Revenues (mil)	144,689	167,188	167,149	236,087	157,014	186,131	215,849	240,127
Net income (mil)	14,302	15,463	16,718	18,205	11,626	14,006	15,910	15,900
Earnings per share	6.41	6.82	7.35	8.55	5.31	6.24	7.05	7.01
Dividends per share	1.83	2.10	2.81	3.10	3.28	2.93	3.12	2.98
Cash flow per share	9.72	9.60	10.73	12.42	9.49	11.25	11.37	12.45
Price: high	69.0	73.8	87.3	91.3	66	67.5	64.4	57.1
low	51.9	58.1	63.9	42.6	42.9	43.1	40.0	41.8

TOTAL S.A. (ADR)
2, Place de la Coupole
La Defense 6 92400 Courbevole, France
(713) 483-5070 (U.S.)
Website: www.total.com

AGGRESSIVE GROWTH

Tractor Supply Company

❑ Ticker symbol: TSCO (NASDAQ) ❑ S&P rating: not rated ❑ Value Line financial strength rating: A+ + ❑ Current yield: 0.7% ❑ Dividend raises, past 10 years: 3

Company Profile

Tractor Supply Company is the largest operator of retail farm and ranch stores in the United States. Their focus is on the needs of recreational farmers and ranchers and those who enjoy the rural lifestyle, as well as tradesmen and small businesses. They operate retail stores, many in a "big box" format, under the names Tractor Supply Company and Del's Farm Supply. Their stores are located in towns outside major metropolitan markets and in rural communities, thus far mostly in the eastern two-thirds of the United States. Representative merchandise includes pet supplies, supplies for horses and other farm animals, equipment maintenance products, hardware and tools, lawn and garden equipment, and work and recreational clothing and footwear. They also offer online and other resources under the name Know-How Central and a magazine called *Out Here* to build community and help their customers use their products effectively. Tractor Supply is to farm, rural, and pet supply stores what Home Depot was once to lumber yards—a more complete, price-competitive, and convenient

big-box reformatting of the business—only TSCO thus far has no real competition.

Tractor Supply stores typically range in size from 15,500 square feet to 18,500 square feet of inside selling space and additional outside selling space. As of December 2012, they operated 1,176 retail farm and ranch stores in 45 states, up from 1,085 stores in 44 states at the end of FY2011. Del's Farm Supply operates 27 stores, primarily in the Pacific Northwest, offering a wide selection of products (primarily in the horse, pet, and animal category) targeted at those who enjoy the rural lifestyle. The company does not plan to grow Del's significantly beyond its current size.

For FY2012, sales were divided between the following segments, little changed from FY2011: livestock and pet products (42 percent); seasonal products like mowers and snow blowers (20 percent); hardware, tool, truck, and towing products (23 percent); clothing and footwear (9 percent) and agriculture (6 percent). Tractor Supply Company also sells a subset of its store goods online.

The company plans contin-
ued growth in store count to about
2,100, including about 300 new
stores in the West. There is also a new
initiative to create a series of higher-
margin, smaller-format stores.

Financial Highlights, Fiscal Year 2012

Tractor plowed ahead to another
in a long series of good years, with
sales up a little over 10 percent to
$4.67 billion and per-share earnings
up a stronger 26 percent to $3.80.
The big contributors: first, a 1.1
percent rise in the operating margin to 11.3 percent, driven by lower
input costs, price/mix optimization,
operational improvements, and
market pricing power; and second,
a 2.5 percent drop in share count to
about 69 million shares. This is the
second year in a row TSCO scored
a better than 1 percent gain in operating margins—a significant feat in
the retail world.

Fertile ground still lies ahead,
with a same-store sales growth projection in the 3–5 percent range,
despite the strong spring 2012 season brought on by milder weather.
Earnings are projected at $4.32–
$4.40 per share, the midpoint of
which would represent a 14.7 percent growth rate; annual earnings
growth is projected in the 14–16
percent range through 2017. Cash
flows are strong and growing and
should bring further dividend

increases—which the company targets at 15–20 percent—and share
repurchases of about 1 million per
year, significant for a company with
only 69 million shares outstanding.
The company has only $1.2 million
in long-term debt—miniscule for a
company of this size and type.

Reasons to Buy

TSCO serves a growing, specialized
niche in geographies often ignored
by other retailers. They carry a specialized mix of merchandise that
occupies a broad space—part big-
box hardware, part garden shop,
and part feed store. Their unique
target market nonetheless has
broad geographic distribution, giving TSCO room for growth, and
thus far, no real competition has
emerged in their niche to temper
that growth. The fact that TSCO's
biggest growth opportunity is in the
outdoor-oriented West also bodes
well.

TSCO carries a higher percentage of house brands than you
would find at a typical hardware
retailer. They earn higher gross margins on these products and build
loyalty in the process. The business
is unique, and for a retailer, has an
unusually wide moat. Not only do
they have the marketing and operational aspects of the business right,
they've also excelled financially,
funding almost all growth from
earnings and cash flow—a very

well-managed company. Last but not least, they've shared some of this success with shareholders and appear inclined to keep the shareholder troughs even fuller.

Reasons for Caution

TSCO's growth could eventually attract competition, just as Home Depot's success attracted Lowe's and others. The sooner they can build out to their target size, the better they will be able to protect margins—but then, a big growth and cost absorption driver goes away. Following the story, the stock has performed extremely well in the past 3 years, so investors may want to choose their entry points carefully.

SECTOR: **Retail**
BETA COEFFICIENT: **0.85**
10-YEAR COMPOUND EARNINGS PER SHARE GROWTH: **23.5%**
10-YEAR COMPOUND DIVIDENDS PER SHARE GROWTH: **NM**

	2005	2006	2007	2008	2009	2010	2011	2012
Revenues (mil)	2,068	2,370	2,703	3,008	3,207	3,638	4,232	4,664
Net income (mil)	85.7	91.0	96.2	81.9	115.5	168.0	223.0	277.0
Earnings per share	1.05	1.11	1.20	1.10	1.58	2.25	3.01	3.80
Dividends per share	—	—	—	—	—	0.28	0.43	0.72
Cash flow per share	1.52	1.65	1.97	1.99	2.52	3.27	4.25	5.26
Price: high	28.3	33.8	28.8	23.6	27.3	49.5	88.6	103.7
low	6.6	19.4	17.5	13.4	14.3	24.6	68.5	68.5

Tractor Supply Company
200 Powell Place
Brentwood, TN 37027
(615) 440-4000
Website: www.tractorsupply.com

CONSERVATIVE GROWTH

Union Pacific Corporation

□ Ticker symbol: UNP (NYSE) □ S&P rating: A- □ Value Line financial strength rating: A □ Current yield: 2.0% □ Dividend raises, past 10 years: 8

Company Profile

Union Pacific has been a familiar name and logo in the railroad business since its inception during the Civil War. With about 32,000 miles of track covering 23 states in the western two-thirds of the United States, today's Union Pacific Railroad, the primary subsidiary of the Union Pacific Corporation, describes itself as "America's Premier Railroad Franchise."

With 25,000 customers, a large number in today's era of trainload-sized shipments, UNP has a more diversified customer and revenue mix than the other rail companies, including the other 3 of the "big 4" railroads: BNSF, Norfolk Southern, and CSX. Energy (mainly Powder River Basin and Colorado) accounts for 19 (22) percent of revenues; Intermodal (trucks or containers on flatcars), 20 (17) percent; Agricultural, 16 (18) percent; Industrial, 17 (17) percent; Chemicals, 15 (16) percent; and Automotive, 9 (8) percent of FY2012 revenues.

And what were those numbers in parentheses? They represent the revenue mix in FY2011, just a single year before, and are something of a switch for a business not known for

big switches in business. Indeed, there has been a revenue shift away from coal and corn (agriculture) dictated by the recent expansion of natural gas production and gas-fired generation plants, and the agricultural slowdown of 2012 due to the drought. The company is handling it well, as we'll see in the financial results.

The company has long been an innovator in railroad technology, including motive power, communications and technology automation, physical plant, community relations, and marketing. The company operates with one of the lowest operating ratios in the industry, 70.6 percent, meaning that operating costs account for 67.8 (70.6 percent in FY2011) percent of total costs. This allows a good contribution to the substantial fixed costs of owning and running a railroad. This success has translated to continued strong operating margins, which of course have helped earnings and cash flows.

The company also invests a lot in marketing and community relations. One example is the steam-powered excursion train program, through which the company operates excursions on selected lines. Such public relations efforts may seem fairly ordinary for a major U.S. corporation, but for the railroad industry, these well-executed activities stretch the envelope, hence our noting them here.

Railroads have quietly been learning to use technology to improve operations and deliver better customer service. New tools can track shipments door to door using GPS-based technology, and the railroad will accept shipments and manage them door to door, even over other railroads or with other kinds of carriers. Customers can check rates and route and track shipments online. These services, combined with high fuel prices, have led to a continuing migration from trucks back to rail and intermodal rail services.

Financial Highlights, Fiscal Year 2012

It was almost as if the company knew the drought and coal slowdown was coming years before; it invested heavily in physical plants to speed the movement of intermodal (translation: trucks and containers) to all parts of the system. The drop in operating ratio in one year from 70.6 percent to 67.8 percent is remarkable and probably an industry first—and it pretty much dropped to the bottom line. Revenues were up a decent 7 percent, but this wasn't the real story. Net earnings rose almost 20 percent on top of a 33 percent gain in FY2011,

and earnings per share, helped along a little by buybacks, chugged ahead 23 percent. Operating margin rose 3 percent to 40 percent just year to year and is up from the 20 percent range in the early part of last decade. Cash flow per share has more than tripled since 2005, the dividend has quadrupled, and the company has bought back about a quarter of its shares since 2006. FY2013 has a bright headlight, too, with strong revenue flows for all business besides coal (we figure agriculture will come back) and new oil- and gas-related shipments. The Keystone pipeline could eventually change this, but right now there are trainloads of oil headed to Gulf Coast and East Coast refineries on the system (and on competing BNSF railways, too, we should add). Shipments of materials and supplies for the new oil and gas boom will also be strong, and FY2013 earnings per share are likely to speed up the track to $9.40, a 14 percent increase.

Reasons to Buy

Put simply—whether you enjoy watching trains or not—this company has been as exciting as any tech stock, and it is also returning plenty of cash to shareholders. UNP is an extraordinarily well-managed company and has managed its business well to become more efficient and at the same time more user friendly to its customers and to the general public. The company continues to make gains at the expense of the trucking industry, and new short- and long-distance intermodal services move higher-valued goods more quickly and cost-effectively; we see a steady shift toward this business. The company has a solid and diverse traffic base, and continues to have a good brand and reputation in the industry.

Reasons for Caution

Railroads are and will always be economically sensitive because of commodity revenue and their high fixed-cost structure. They also have significant headline risk—a single event like a derailment or spill can put them in a bad public eye, or worse, tangle them up in regulation and unplanned costs. Regulation and mandates for Positive Train Control and other safety features can be expensive. More recently, longtime CEO Jim Young was diagnosed with pancreatic cancer; as of this writing a veteran from the company has taken over day-to-day responsibility while Young stays on as chairman—okay for now but the signal down the track suggests management changes. Another longer-term factor may be the widening of the Panama Canal, which may shift some Asian import/export traffic to southern and eastern ports and away from the West Coast. Finally, the increase in profitability has been reflected "full throttle" in the share price, and further gains may be hard to come by, particularly if coal and agriculture remain soft or some other traffic segment runs into problems.

SECTOR: **Transportation**
BETA COEFFICIENT: **1.16**
10-YEAR COMPOUND EARNINGS PER SHARE GROWTH: **13.5%**
10-YEAR COMPOUND DIVIDENDS PER SHARE GROWTH: **17.0%**

	2005	2006	2007	2008	2009	2010	2011	2012
Revenues (mil)	13,578	15,578	16,283	17,970	14,143	16,965	19,557	20,926
Net income (mil)	809	1,606	1,856	2,338	1,826	2,780	3,292	3,943
Earnings per share	1.70	2.96	3.46	4.54	3.61	5.53	6.72	8.27
Dividends per share	0.60	0.60	0.68	0.93	1.08	1.31	1.93	2.49
Cash flow per share	3.78	5.15	6.09	7.40	6.47	8.68	10.23	12.15
Price: high	40.6	48.7	68.8	85.8	66.7	95.8	107.0	129.3
low	29.1	38.8	44.8	41.8	33.3	60.4	77.7	104.1

Union Pacific Corporation
1416 Dodge St.
Omaha, NE 68179
(402) 271-5777
Website: www.up.com

AGGRESSIVE GROWTH

UnitedHealth Group Inc.

❑ Ticker symbol: UNH (NYSE) ❑ S&P rating: A- ❑ Value Line financial strength rating: A+
❑ Current yield: 1.5% ❑ Dividend raises, past 10 years: 4

Company Profile

UnitedHealth Group is the parent company of a number of health insurers and service organizations. They are the second-largest publicly traded health insurance company in the United States, with over $110 billion in revenue reported in 2012.

The company has reorganized part of its business and now operates in 2 major business segments: UnitedHealthcare and Optum. UnitedHealthcare provides traditional and Medicare-based health benefit and insurance plans for individuals and employers, covering approximately 27 million Americans with about 400 national employer accounts and many other smaller employer accounts. The company estimates that it serves over half of the *Fortune* 100 companies list. The company, mainly through this unit, has been an active acquirer of other familiar health-care and insurance brands, including AIM Healthcare Services in 2009, and more recently an assortment of small, mostly Medicare-related providers. The UnitedHealthcare Medicare and Retirement business, formerly known as Ovations, serves about 9 million seniors—1 in 5 Medicare

beneficiaries. Taken together, these operations generated approximately 78 percent of UNH's overall revenue in 2012 and 84 percent of profits.

The remainder of the company's revenue comes from its health services businesses, which it markets under the Optum brand umbrella. This segment, which touches some 60 million customers, delivers service through 3 separate businesses. OptumHealth is an "information and technology"–based health solution, deploying mostly remote telesupport for well care, mental health, ongoing disease management, and substance abuse programs. The OptumRx business is a pharmacy benefits provider serving 14 million customers with about 350 million prescriptions annually, while OptumInsight is a relatively new management information, analytics, and process-improvement arm providing an assortment of services for health plans, physicians, hospitals, and life science research, formerly marketed under the Ingenix brand. Of the total Optum-branded business of $29.3 billion, Rx accounts for the lion's share at $18.4 billion, while OptumHealth, which grew some 22 percent last year, weighs in at $8.1 billion and OptumInsight at $2.9

billion. Although these numbers may seem small in the context of UNH's total $111 billion annual revenue footprint, they are sizeable businesses when looked at individually. Together, the 2 business units serve about 80 million individuals in the United States and in 18 other countries.

UnitedHealthcare has been a leader in process, delivery, and cost improvement and a recognized innovator in the industry. In 2012, using its own analytics, it launched myHealthcare Cost Estimator, a real-time tool designed to help doctors estimate treatment costs and for administrators to see cost differences between doctors and care providers. A new mobile app, Health4Me, helps individuals get access to nursing care and other information. The company sits on top of a mountain of health-care data, and is putting it to good use. For these and other reasons, the company was voted the World's Most Admired Company in the insurance and managed care sector—and number one in innovation—in 2012 by *Fortune* magazine. The company was also added to the Dow 30—the Dow Jones Industrial Average—during the year, signaling the importance of health care as a component of the overall economy.

Financial Highlights, Fiscal Year 2012

United posted solid results again in FY2012, well ahead of FY2011.

Revenues grew 8.6 percent to $110.7 billion, while per-share earnings, helped along by utilization and other cost management efforts, rose a healthy 11.3 percent to $5.28 per share. For FY2013, the company is guiding revenues in the $123–$124 billion range and earnings of $4.25–$5.50 per share. The company bought back some 45 million shares—about 4 percent of its float—during 2012, and posted another large dividend increase after a previous history of almost insignificant dividends.

Reasons to Buy

The company is one of the most solid and diverse enterprises in the health insurance industry. Health insurers such as Aetna, included on our *100 Best* list, seem to be getting past many of the fears of reform. These companies simply pass costs through but are doing more to control and reduce costs through utilization management and other initiatives, and these efforts are paying off. Meanwhile, like Aetna, UNH brings a fair amount of innovation to the marketplace, primarily through its Optum offerings. We like their initiatives to make use of their own "big data" with analytics; the size of their database and the tools they possess can deliver efficiency improvements, and even slight efficiency improvements can help the bottom line substantially. If price competition dictates lower premiums, those adjustments will lag cost-side improvements.

The scale of UNH's operation gives it tremendous leverage when negotiating for the services of health-care providers. Hospitals and physicians are motivated to join UNH's network, as doing so will provide assurance of steady referrals.

UnitedHealth has easily scored the quintuple play, with 10-year compounded growth in revenues, earnings, cash flow, dividends, and book value well into double digits; in fact, each has grown over 20 percent. True, a lot of that results from acquisitions, which we don't expect (or hope) to continue at this pace ongoing—but it gives an idea of the growth potential of the issue. And cash returns haven't been too bad, either—through increased dividends and share buybacks, the company is growing its cash returns to shareholders. Finally, the recent price-to-earnings ratio in the 10–11 range give a good margin for error.

Reasons for Caution

The impending mandates of the Affordable Care Act ("Obamacare") and particularly its initiatives and reforms to reduce Medicare and Medicaid payments may dampen the company's recent upward momentum. The company is vulnerable to shifts in public opinion and to new regulation, as well as economic downturns, which can hurt employer participation. The company also has demonstrated a fairly aggressive acquisition strategy—good, mostly so far, but it comes with risks.

SECTOR: **Health Care**
BETA COEFFICIENT: **0.89**
10-YEAR COMPOUND EARNINGS PER SHARE GROWTH: **22.5%**
10-YEAR COMPOUND DIVIDENDS PER SHARE GROWTH: **51.5%**

		2005	2006	2007	2008	2009	2010	2011	2012
Revenues (mil)		45,365	71,542	75,431	81,186	87,138	94,155	101,862	110,518
Net income (mil)		3,300	4,159	4,654	3,660	3,822	4,633	5,142	5,526
Earnings per share		2.48	2.97	3.42	2.95	3.24	4.10	4.73	5.28
Dividends per share		0.03	0.03	0.03	0.03	0.03	0.41	0.61	0.80
Cash flow per share		2.76	3.59	4.35	3.86	4.20	5.25	5.86	6.67
Price:	high	64.6	62.9	59.5	57.9	33.3	38.1	53.5	60.8
	low	42.6	41.4	45.8	14.5	16.2	27.1	36.4	49.8

UnitedHealth Group Inc.
9900 Bren Street
Minnetonka, MN 55343
(952) 936-1300
Website: www.unitedhealthgroup.com

CONSERVATIVE GROWTH

United Parcel Service, Inc.

❑ Ticker symbol: UPS (NYSE) ❑ S&P rating: AA- ❑ Value Line financial strength rating: A ❑ Current yield: 3.0% ❑ Dividend raises, past 10 years: 10

Company Profile

Back in 2011, we removed UPS from our *100 Best* stocks list in an early effort to weed out multiple companies on our list doing the same thing. We saw FedEx and UPS converging on the same business from different directions—FedEx being an air company getting ever more into the ground business; UPS being a ground business taking to the air. That convergence is still happening. Both companies continue to build international capabilities, invest in technology to track shipments, and provide logistics services beyond basic assortments of transportation services. Since being re-added, UPS delivered a nice reward, with a stock price up from the mid 60s to the mid 80s and a 21 percent increase in the dividend.

The time is also right for UPS because of the continued expansion of e-commerce and the gradual demise of the U.S. Postal Service, as well as the increased importance of the small package and document shipping business. Second, we liked the steady return to shareholders in the form of higher dividends and aggressive share buybacks, and the steadiness of the business. The third

reason at the time was the proposed acquisition of Dutch-based carrier and forwarder TNT, but that since has fallen apart due to anticompetitive sentiment in Europe and other issues. That may be just as well because of TNT's concentration in the soft international and especially European markets, and the apparently sufficient international capacity without TNT. With or without TNT, UPS is the world's largest air and ground package carrier. The company derives about 60 percent of revenues from U.S. package operations, 23 percent from international, and 17 percent from an assortment of bundled logistics and supply-chain services and solutions. The merger had been expected to increase the international contribution to about 36 percent of revenues, but the domestic business has turned out to be the stronger growth segment, as international dropped from 26 to 23 percent during the year.

The company operates 523 aircraft and almost 101,000 ground vehicles, most of the familiar brown "package car" variety. They serve more than 200 countries with an assortment of priority to deferred services. Once thought to be old fashioned and adverse to innovation, the company has invested in sophisticated package tracking systems and links for customers to tie into them. A new service called My Choice allows a customer to control the timing of deliveries midservice—so no more waiting half a day at home for a delivery that might come anytime (hallelujah!), a nice perk for a consumer waiting for an e-commerce shipment as well as a savings for the company, avoiding multiple delivery attempts.

Financial Highlights, Fiscal Year 2012

For FY2012, UPS total revenues rose a relatively modest 2 percent, as sluggish global trade, especially in Europe and some Asian lanes, and currency headwinds hurt international revenues. Volume in the domestic segment, driven mainly by e-commerce expansion and the modest rate increases it supported, made it a stronger year on the domestic side, although the company noted a lower margin mix (meaning, lower priority delivery and more ground transport) and less revenue from fuel surcharges. The company saw some increase in export traffic, always good news to balance capacity and avoid flying empty aircraft into international and especially Asian markets. Operating margins improved slightly

from 15.9 to 16.5 percent, and net and per-share earnings gained 7 percent. Share purchase continued at a moderate rate. The company has announced FY2013 guidance for earnings to increase in a fairly wide range of 6–12 percent—the pace of global economic recovery is obviously a big factor.

Reasons to Buy

The "fastest ship in the shipping business" continues to also be one of the most stable; UPS continues to position itself as the standard logistics provider of the world. The TNT merger failure may have hurt the company's ability to build volume and scale, but it will also make it a little less vulnerable to global headwinds, and we welcome the ability to focus more on the domestic e-commerce business. Improvements in U.S. export trade should also be a positive. We are also fans of its logistics and supply chain management businesses, as the push for many customers to optimize this part of their business will lead them to UPS's front door.

Reasons for Caution

Competition in this industry, particularly in lucrative Asia–U.S. lanes, is fierce. The demise of the U.S. Postal Service is a question mark and may be an opportunity, but what if Congress votes to subsidize more services, as they did with the recent resumption of funding for Saturday delivery and package delivery? Of about 400,000 employees, 62 percent are union, so labor relations and pension funding (which is in good shape now) both bear watching. Of course, fuel prices and the state of the global economy are big factors in UPS's success in any short-term scenario.

SECTOR: **Transportation**
BETA COEFFICIENT: **0.88**
10-YEAR COMPOUND EARNINGS PER SHARE GROWTH: **4.5%**
10-YEAR COMPOUND DIVIDENDS PER SHARE GROWTH: **11.0%**

	2005	2006	2007	2008	2009	2010	2011	2012
Revenues (mil)	42,58	47,547	49,692	51,466	45,297	49,545	53,105	54,127
Net income (mil)	3,870	4,202	4,369	3,581	2,318	3,570	4,213	4,389
Earnings per share	3.47	3.86	4.11	3.50	2.31	3.56	4.25	4.53
Dividends per share	1.32	1.52	1.64	1.77	1.80	1.88	2.08	2.28
Cash flow per share	5.03	5.56	5.91	5.42	4.09	5.43	6.60	6.90
Price: high	85.8	84.0	79.0	75.1	59.5	73.9	77.0	84.9
low	66.1	65.5	68.7	43.3	38.0	55.6	60.7	75.0

United Parcel Service, Inc.
65 Glenlake Parkway NE
Atlanta, GA 30328
(404) 828-6000
Website: www.ups.com

CONSERVATIVE GROWTH

United Technologies Corporation

❑ Ticker symbol: UTX (NYSE) ❑ S&P rating: A ❑ Value Line financial strength rating: A++
❑ Current yield: 2.4% ❑ Dividend raises, past 10 years: 10

Company Profile

United Technologies is a diversified provider of mostly high-technology products to the aerospace and building systems industries throughout the world. Major business lines, through the end of FY2011, were commercial and industrial businesses with 58 percent of sales, commercial aerospace at 22 percent, and military aerospace at 20 percent. But that stops well short of presenting a complete picture.

In 2012, the company made a significant $18.4 billion acquisition of Goodrich Corp. With that, the mix of businesses changed considerably and is still changing as the company completes the disposal of certain businesses mandated by regulators and exits a few others like wind turbines and rocket engines. At the end of FY2012, here is how UTX looks at its business, with approximate revenue and profit breakdowns:

■ Otis (21 percent of sales, 32 percent of profits), probably the most recognizable brand, designs and manufactures elevators, escalators, moving walkways, and shuttle systems, and performs related installation, maintenance, and repair services; it also provides modernization products and service for elevators and escalators.

■ Climate Controls and Security (29 percent, 30 percent), formerly known as Carrier, produces heating, ventilating, and air conditioning (HVAC) equipment for commercial, industrial, and residential buildings; HVAC replacement parts and services; building controls; and commercial, industrial, and transport refrigeration equipment. The Climate Controls and Security group now also includes the old UTC Fire and Security business, which provides security and fire protection systems; integration, installation, and servicing of intruder alarms, access control, and video surveillance and monitoring; response and security personnel services; and installation and servicing of fire detection and suppression systems.

The following 3 units are now part of the new Propulsion and Aerospace group, although reported separately for now. This group is still in transition as the Goodrich business is absorbed.

- Pratt & Whitney (24 percent, 20 percent) produces large and small commercial and military jet engines, spare parts, rocket engines and space propulsion systems, and industrial gas turbines, and it performs product support, specialized engine maintenance and overhaul, and repair services for airlines, air forces, and corporate fleets.
- Aerospace (14 percent, 8 percent), formerly known as Hamilton Sundstrand, produces aircraft electrical power generation and distribution systems; engine and flight controls; propulsion systems; environmental controls for aircraft, spacecraft, and submarines; auxiliary power units; space life support systems; and industrial products including mechanical power transmissions, compressors, metering devices, and fluid handling equipment. It also provides product support and maintenance, and offers repair services. Most of the Goodrich business was absorbed into this unit.
- Sikorsky (12 percent, 9 percent) designs and manufactures military and commercial helicopters and fixed-wing reconnaissance aircraft, and it provides spare parts and maintenance services

for helicopters and fixed-wing aircraft.

Financial Highlights, Fiscal Year 2012

FY2012 was a transition year, with the Goodrich acquisition closing in July of that year. The change in focus and organization as well as shifts in the business mix and business sales produced results that aren't easy to compare with previous years. Revenues declined slightly, mostly due to business sales, as did profits and earnings per share. The company signaled continued financial health with another in a long line of steady dividend increases and a fresh share repurchase authorization. For FY2013, the company is guiding revenues in the $65 billion range, which is incrementally higher by about the amount represented by the size of the Goodrich acquisition. Goodrich added about 75 cents a share in earnings; projections are in the $6–$6.10 range. The company authorized a massive $5.4 billion share repurchase—$1 billion each year, which figures to retire about 1 percent of shares over each of the next 5–6 years.

Reasons to Buy

UTX is a classic conglomerate play. The separate and loosely related or unrelated businesses buffer each other in line with what's happening in the economy, both in the private and public sectors, and the economic recovery should help most, if not all, of the businesses. Unlike many of its competitors, United Technologies maintains a global presence (60 percent of sales are from overseas), which benefits from global and emerging market infrastructure and other construction and even from defense spending by other countries. The company's brands, particularly Otis, are well known and very well supported worldwide, and a return of strength in global construction should help its 2 largest businesses. The company is focused on shareholder returns, and managed the Goodrich acquisition without increasing share count.

Reasons for Caution

The stability of the public sector portion of the business may diminish as Congress wrestles with the budget deficit and the Iraq and Afghanistan wars wind down. The company does supply a lot of materials for the new F-35 fighter program, as an example. The rest of the business is still sensitive to construction, and construction may not be out of the woods yet. While Goodrich was a good fit, we would hope the company doesn't get too aggressive in the acquisition space, for, like all conglomerates, UTX is a very complex business to manage. It can also be vulnerable to headline risk (like jet engine problems), hiccups in the airline industry, and public sector spending cuts.

SECTOR: **Industrials**
BETA COEFFICIENT: **1.06**
10-YEAR COMPOUND EARNINGS PER SHARE GROWTH: **12.5%**
10-YEAR COMPOUND DIVIDENDS PER SHARE GROWTH: **15.0%**

	2005	2006	2007	2008	2009	2010	2011	2012
Revenues (mil)	42,725	47,740	54,759	58,681	52,920	54,326	58,190	57,708
Net income (mil)	3,069	3,732	4,224	4,689	3,829	4,373	4,979	4,840
Earnings per share	3.03	3.71	4.27	4.90	4.12	4.74	5.49	5.34
Dividends per share	0.88	1.02	1.28	1.55	1.54	1.70	1.87	2.03
Cash flow per share	4.09	4.79	5.50	6.38	5.43	6.22	6.97	6.93
Price: high	58.9	67.5	82.5	77.1	70.9	79.7	91.8	87.5
low	48.4	54.2	61.8	41.8	37.4	62.9	66.9	70.7

United Technologies Corporation
One Financial Plaza
Hartford, CT 06103
(860) 728-7912
Website: www.utc.com

Valero Energy

❏ Ticker symbol: VLO (NYSE) ❏ S&P rating: BBB ❏ Value Line financial strength rating: B++
❏ Current yield: 1.8% ❏ Dividend raises, past 10 years: 9

Company Profile

Valero Energy is the largest independent oil refiner and marketer in the United States. The company owns 16 refineries and operates a network of 7,300 retail combined gasoline stations and convenience stores throughout the United States, the U.K. and Ireland, and Canada.

Most of the 16 Valero refineries are located in the United States, centered in the South and on the Texas Gulf Coast with others in Memphis, Oklahoma, and on the West Coast. Others are located in the Caribbean, Quebec, and Wales in the U.K. The refinery network was mostly assembled through a series of acquisitions from Diamond Shamrock in 2001; El Paso Corporation in the early 2000s; and, more recently, the Pembroke (Wales) refinery from Chevron in 2011. The refining operations produce the full gamut of hydrocarbon products—gasoline, jet fuel, diesel, asphalt, propane, base oils, solvents, aromatics, natural gas liquids, sulfur, hydrogen, and middle distillates. The company is strictly focused on downstream operations and owns no oil wells or production facilities. Instead, they purchase a variety of feedstocks on the open market and can adjust those purchases to market conditions while using contracts and hedging tools to manage input prices to a degree. About 63 percent of feedstocks are purchased under contracts, with the remainder on the spot market. Most of these refineries are legacy operations and have been in place for many years, as far back as 1908. The company has invested heavily in upgrading these refineries to improve capacity, efficiency, and environmental compliance.

The company operates about 7,300 stores under the Valero brand name in the U.S. and Canada through a mix of company-owned and franchise arrangements. Most are operated under franchise arrangements; in addition there are about 1,000 stores owned and operated by the company under the Corner Store brand and an upgraded assortment of merchandise and Valero-branded fuel. The company operates another 880 outlets under the Ultramar brand in Canada. The company also operates a network of wholesale and commercial product outlets and a network of 10 ethanol processing plants. Bulk sales to other retail, commercial distributors, and large end customers like airlines and railroads are also important.

Financial Highlights, Fiscal Year 2012

For 2012, the business remained largely unchanged from FY2011, including the financial results. The big story is what's ahead for 2013 and beyond. The shift in oil supply to relatively less expensive (but not always accessible) U.S. sources looks to increase refining profitability dramatically, while the company is also in talks to sell or spin off its vast retail business for $3.5 billion or more.

Revenues advanced about 10.5 percent, although a good portion of that was from price increases. Operating margins, which had been a big story last year, were only slightly up, and total and per-share earnings remained roughly flat. For FY2013, revenues are expected to rise less than 2 percent. But the effects of lower cost oil inputs will really be felt, with net profit margins expected to jump from 1.5 percent to 2.2 percent, and FY2013 per-share earnings from $3.79 to $5.60. It's a low-margin business, but when you do something to dramatically increase margins in a low-margin business, dramatic earnings increases will usually follow.

Possibly because of the advancing share price, the company has cut back on its share repurchase activity but continues to raise the dividend. Prospects from the sale of the retail business are unclear but should also enhance shareholder value, at least in the short term.

Reasons to Buy

The profitability of this business, like other refining businesses, depends on the supply and cost of feedstocks and the wholesale and retail prices of finished products. In addition, the availability of refining capacity is also a factor; when markets get tight, it is extremely difficult to put another refinery on the ground to handle demand. These two factors together work very favorably for Valero—lower input costs, no new competition—it's an oligopolist's dream and should bode well for profits for years to come. And, if the Keystone pipeline project or other projects come on line to make cheaper domestic crude more available, the company's fortunes should improve even more.

We like Valero's leading position in the refining business, and having 16 well-distributed and largely successful operating refineries on the ground already is a good thing. We also like the branding, abundance, look, and feel of the retail presence, and the focus this company has on the refining and marketing side of the business. The recent trend in the industry is to split large integrated companies into separate exploration and production (E&P) and downstream operations; ConocoPhillips (a *100 Best* stock) and Marathon (a former *100 Best* stock) have done it. Valero may be taking on the next step: to sell off the retail segment to focus on refining. How that works out for shareholders remains to be seen, but overall prospects for earnings growth and cash returns seem very bright.

Reasons for Caution

The refining business in particular is inherently volatile and complex, and what may appear today as an advantageous input and output pricing profile might disappear in a minute. Gross, operating, and net margins are very thin, typically in the 1–2 percent range—although as we've seen, Valero appears to be breaking out of that range for now. Refiners also endure the headline risk of refinery mishaps, a few of which have already come Valero's way in recent years.

Because of the strong branding, we're not sure we're on board with the idea of selling the retail business; we like some brand equity in this commodity business, and there is value in having a captive retail market for your product. In short, we like strength on the output side, not just the input side, of the business, so we have some strategic concerns about this one.

SECTOR: **Energy**
BETA COEFFICIENT: **1.53**
10-YEAR COMPOUND EARNINGS PER SHARE GROWTH: **2.5%**
10-YEAR COMPOUND DIVIDENDS PER SHARE GROWTH: **16.0%**

	2005	2006	2007	2008	2009	2010	2011	2012
Revenues (bil)	82.1	91.8	94.5	118.3	87.3	81.3	125.1	138.3
Net income (mil)	3,975	5,251	4,565	(1,131)	(352)	923	2,097	2,083
Earnings per share	6.75	8.30	7.72	(2.16)	(0.65)	1.62	3.69	3.75
Dividends per share	0.19	0.30	0.48	0.57	0.60	0.20	0.30	0.65
Cash flow per share	7.77	10.81	11.04	0.67	1.91	4.10	6.52	6.60
Price: high	58.6	70.8	75.7	71.1	26.2	23.7	31.1	34.5
low	21.0	46.8	47.7	13.9	16.3	15.5	16.4	16.1

Valero Energy Corporation
One Valero Way
San Antonio, TX 78249
(210) 345-2000
Website: www.valero.com

AGGRESSIVE GROWTH

Valmont Industries, Inc.

❑ Ticker symbol: VMI (NYSE) ❑ S&P rating: BBB- ❑ Value Line financial strength rating: B++
❑ Current yield: 0.6% ❑ Dividend raises, past 10 years: 10

Company Profile

Valmont Industries was founded in 1946 as a supplier of irrigation products and became one of the classic postwar industrial success stories, growing along with the need for increased farm output. They were early pioneers of the center-pivot irrigation system, which enabled much of that growth and now dominates the high-yield agricultural business. These machines remain a mainstay of its product line. But the company has expanded on that core expertise in galvanized metal to make such familiar infrastructure items as light poles, cell phone towers, and those familiar high-tension electric towers that crisscross the landscape.

Their corporate statement "Conserving Resources. Improving Life" says more than most and explains the company pretty well: "Wherever you live, whatever you do, chances are that Valmont is part of your life. Lighting and traffic poles guide your way. Utility poles bring power to your home and business. Communication poles and towers enable your wireless communications. Irrigation equipment brings much-needed water to cropland while conserving fresh water

resources. And our long-lasting finishes improve products around the world every day."

Valmont products and product lines now include:

■ Engineered Infrastructure Products (27 percent of FY2012 revenues)—lighting poles, including decorative lighting poles, guard rails, towers, and other metal structures used in lighting, communications, traffic management, wireless phone carriers, and other utilities. Products are available as standard designs and engineered for custom applications as needed for industrial, commercial, and residential applications. If you've ever sat at a stop light and wondered how a single cantilevered arm could support four 400-pound traffic signals, these are the folks to ask.
■ Utility Support Structures (27 percent)—This segment produces the very large concrete and steel substations and electric transmission support towers used by electric utilities. This has been Valmont's most

profitable operation over the last few years, due mainly to increased volumes in a period of declining costs.

- Irrigation (25 percent)— Under the Valley brand name, Valmont produces a wide range of equipment, including gravity and drip products, as well as its center-pivot designs, which can service up to 500 acres from a single machine. Valmont also sells its irrigation controllers to other manufacturers.

- Coatings (13 percent)— Developed as an adjunct to its other metal products businesses, the coatings business now provides services such as galvanizing, electroplating, powder coating, and anodizing to industrial customers throughout the company's operating areas.

There is also an "other" segment comprising about 10 percent of the business.

Financial Highlights, Fiscal Year 2012

As we had expected, an increase in electric grid investments, irrigation deployments, and the long lead time nature of Valmont's businesses and the economic recovery all led to a stellar FY2012. Revenues rose almost 14 percent after a 35 percent gain in FY2011. Margins increased

almost 2 full percentage points with stronger pricing and a more favorable product mix, leading to a 42 percent increase in earnings and a similar increase in earnings per share, well beyond the 25 percent increase predicted last year. Fortunately for our *100 Best Stock* annual results and for current investors, the stock price was also up a similar amount; the company was one of our best performers. For FY2013, the company is guiding revenue growth in the low teens and earnings growth in the high teens.

Reasons to Buy

We continue to view Valmont as a key infrastructure play. America's infrastructure needs to be replaced, as does infrastructure in much of the developed world. And as for the less-developed world, that infrastructure is needed in the first place. We think, long term, that Valmont is in the right place to capture a decent share of this replacement business, including electric utility infrastructure. The original irrigation business should also do well as agriculture, farmland, and farm commodity prices strengthen. Valmont has retained market share and remains the leader among the 4 dominant U.S.-based players in the large-scale irrigation market. The company's continued emphasis on growth into new geographies should pay dividends as India and China begin to build infrastructure and adopt more modern agricultural methods. So far, Valmont has had very little penetration in those 2 countries.

Reasons for Caution

Many Valmont products are purchased by public sector and government agencies, and these agencies will be scrutinizing purchases to a greater degree than in the past. Escalating raw materials costs may also hurt, especially in a reduced-demand, softer-pricing environment that might ensue from contracting government purchases. Indeed, the sectors that have showed strength sell to agriculture and utility interests, not government agencies. Finally, although the stock has done well, we would like to see a little more shareholder return; while dividends are raised regularly, they remain small with respect to the share price, and share buybacks haven't happened on a large scale. However, it should be noted that the company only has 26.5 million shares outstanding to begin with. The low share count may be part of the high stock price as institutions have bought in—any bad news could lead to a sharp downturn in the stock price if those investors flee. That said, the current and likely future results are too strong to suggest that scenario.

SECTOR: **Industrials**
BETA COEFFICIENT: **1.49**
10-YEAR COMPOUND EARNINGS PER SHARE GROWTH: **16.0%**
10-YEAR COMPOUND DIVIDENDS PER SHARE GROWTH: **8.5%**

	2005	2006	2007	2008	2009	2010	2011	2012
Revenues (mil)	1,108	1,281	1,500	1,907	1,787	1,975	2,661	3,029
Net income (mil)	40.2	61.5	94.7	132.4	155.0	109.7	158.0	225.0
Earnings per share	1.58	2.38	3.63	5.04	5.70	4.15	5.97	8.75
Dividends per share	0.34	0.37	0.41	0.50	0.58	0.65	0.72	0.80
Price: high	35.3	61.2	99.0	120.5	89.3	90.3	116.0	141.2
low	21.3	32.8	50.9	37.5	37.5	65.3	73.0	90.2

Valmont Industries, Inc.
1 Valmont Plaza
Omaha, NE 68154
(402) 963-1000
Website: www.valmont.com

GROWTH AND INCOME

Verizon Communications Inc.

❑ Ticker symbol: VZ (NYSE) ❑ S&P rating: A- ❑ Value Line financial strength rating: A+ ❑ Current yield: 4.2% ❑ Dividend raises, past 10 years: 7

Company Profile

Verizon operates 2 telecommunications businesses: Domestic Wireless, which provides wireless voice and data services, and Wireline, which provides voice, broadband data and video, Internet access, long-distance, and other services, and which owns and operates a large global Internet protocol network. The wireless business represents about 63 percent of the total; Wireline is about 37 percent of the total by revenues. As we'll get to shortly, the company's data and cloud computing business is one of the more exciting prospects.

In the consumer space, the Wireline segment also supplies Verizon's fiber-to-the-home (FiOS) broadband data infrastructure. One of Verizon's largest investments, FiOS provides a very high bandwidth link to the Internet, easily surpassing DSL and even cable. Over this network, Verizon can provide hundreds of HD video streams, high-speed data, and voice all simultaneously. This service competes head to head with AT&T's (a *100 Best* stock) U-verse and Comcast's (another *100 Best* stock) Xfinity services among others.

The Domestic Wireless segment is served by Verizon Wireless, which is a joint venture between Verizon Communications Inc. and Vodafone. Verizon Communications owns a 55 percent share in the business, and Vodafone 45 percent. Verizon Wireless is now the largest wireless carrier in the United States, and it operates in 19 countries outside the United States as well. The wireless side of the business has been rolling out their new LTE mobile broadband network, a leading-edge 4G network designed to be 10 times faster than the standard 3G network and now available in some 200 U.S. cities. Adding hardware products and wireless capacity hasn't been the only growth strategy employed at Verizon. The company continues to grow its footprint in advanced networking, private networks, and cloud computing, with the 2011 acquisition of IT and cloud services provider Terremark Worldwide, and a small but interesting partnership with a company called eMeter, which markets devices to automatically read and transmit energy usage for utilities using Verizon's wireless network. The company is leveraging its investment in the 4G LTE network for corporate customers to offer secure wireless private IP networks. In mid-2012, the company acquired Hughes Telematics, expanding its offerings in vehicle telematics (more popularly known as OnStar in GM cars) and other machine-to-machine communications.

Financial Highlights, Fiscal Year 2012

For a company its size, Verizon dialed in a pretty strong top-line growth in revenues, up just shy of 5 percent for the year, led by growth in FiOS, enterprise services, and the wireless business more generally. Earnings, and earnings per share, which had been held back by high subsidies for the Apple iPhone 5 rollout and strong competitive pressures in FY2011, advanced about 8 percent. The iPhone subsidy and costs of the LTE network rollout should diminish in FY2013 and years forward; as a result, earnings are projected to grow in the low double digits on mid-single-digit revenue growth. The company has also entered into talks with Vodafone about the future of the wireless partnership, which could result in Verizon buying out the partnership for complete control.

Reasons to Buy

Verizon offers a nice combination of stability and income with a play in the growth of the "new economy" and supporting technology. After a few years of lean profit growth as the company invested in infrastructure and iPhones, for the next few years, earnings growth will outpace top-line growth. We especially like the new cloud and wireless data services for the commercial market, which offer good promise and significant leverage of existing investments, and new services in the consumer space like the new video-on-demand venture, which also bears watching. The company has typically paid out a high portion of earnings as dividends and has increased its dividend regularly. Strong cash flows and advancing per-share earnings indicate likely future increases, and the company may be in a position to expand share repurchases, which have been modest lately. The high payout and low beta make the stock a safe core holding.

Reasons for Caution

The telecommunications business is always capital intensive, and Verizon, like others, must spend heavily just to keep up with technology and competition. Getting a solid return on new capital investments is thus critical, and one slipup could be costly for shareholders, especially with a high ratio of dividend payout to total earnings; a dividend cut could result. The business environment is extremely competitive, and Verizon's sheer size may hamper its flexibility to compete. Also, one shouldn't forget the substantial Vodafone stake in the wireless business, which may be up for sale; the buyout could be expensive short term but will also allow Verizon to control its own destiny.

SECTOR: **Telecommunications Services**
BETA COEFFICIENT: **0.45**
10-YEAR COMPOUND EARNINGS PER SHARE GROWTH: **-2.5%**
10-YEAR COMPOUND DIVIDENDS PER SHARE GROWTH: **2.0%**

	2005	**2006**	**2007**	**2008**	**2009**	**2010**	**2011**	**2012**
Revenues (mil)	74,910	88,144	93,469	97,354	107,808	106,585	110,875	115,846
Net income (mil)	7,151	6,021	6,854	7,235	6,805	6,256	6,087	6,535
Earnings per share	2.56	2.54	2.36	2.54	2.40	2.21	2.15	2.322
Dividends per share	1.62	1.62	1.65	1.78	1.87	1.93	1.96	2.02
Cash flow per share	7.24	7.07	7.40	7.65	7.70	7.60	7.96	7.80
Price: high	41.1	38.9	46.2	44.3	34.8	36.0	40.3	48.8
low	29.1	30.0	35.6	23.1	26.1	26.0	32.3	36.8

Verizon Communications Inc.
140 West Street
New York, NY 10007
(212) 395-1000
Website: www.verizon.com

Visa Inc.

❑ Ticker symbol: V (NYSE) ❑ S&P rating: A+ ❑ Value Line financial strength rating: A++ ❑ Current yield: 0.8% ❑ Dividend raises, past 10 years: 5

Company Profile

If we wrote about a company with a steady 37 percent net profit margin—uh, no, try 40 percent this past year—and a global brand that was in the business of collecting small fees on every one of the billions of transactions worldwide; a company that required almost no capital expenditures, plant, and equipment, or inventory; a company that brought in more than $1.2 million per employee in revenue and $494,000 per employee in net profit; a company growing earnings 20–30 percent a year; a company with a time-tested business model and absolutely 0 long-term debt—would you believe that it existed? Not to mention a company with a share price that rose from $74 to $118 in our standard one-year April 2011 to April 2012 measurement period—and again, to $168, in April 2013?

It's all true. And the company, formed in a 2007 reorganization and taken public in 2008, is Visa. Yes, the same Visa whose emblem has traditionally appeared on a majority of the world's credit cards—and now debit cards. In fact, there are about 2.1 billion such cards worldwide. The company operates the world's largest retail electronic payment network, providing processing services; payment platforms; and fraud-detection services for credit, debit, and commercial payments. The company also operates one of the largest global ATM networks with its PLUS and Interlink brands. In total, the company estimates it can process about 20,000 transactions per second.

For years, Visa has been synonymous with credit and credit cards, but in recent years it has become more of a digital currency company, stitching together consumers, retailers, banks, and other businesses in a giant global network. Really, Visa is a global payments technology business that not only develops and supplies the technology but also collects fees upon its use.

The shift from traditional cash and check forms of payment to debit cards and other digital forms is growing at about a 12 percent annual rate, driven by the security and convenience of these transactions as well as a shift away from consumer debt more to "paid for today" debit transactions. Debit transactions are projected to soon account for more than half the company's overall business volume. One interesting development on this front is a new strategic alliance with Intel to link internal mobile-device hardware with Visa's payWave mobile payment technology; the idea is to eventually (and we think sooner rather than later) enable fast, easy, secure "mobile wallet" transactions through individual mobile devices.

More than its rivals, Visa derives a significant percentage of transaction volume, about 35 percent, from overseas. International volumes are growing faster than in the United States, with global transaction volumes up some 14 percent in FY2011 as part of an overall 11.6 percent worldwide volume increase.

Financial Highlights, Fiscal Year 2012

Helped by international expansion and increased economic activity, Visa continued to hit on all cylinders in FY2012. Revenues advanced 13 percent; margin improvements drove a 15 percent increase in net earnings and earnings per share. For FY2013, the company expects revenue growth in the low double digits and earnings growth in the high teens, and it also approved a $1.75 billion share buyback.

Reasons to Buy

Simply, it would be hard to come up with a better business model—a company that develops and sells the network, and collects fees every time it's used. It would be like Microsoft collecting fees every time a file is created and saved, or a relatively unique e-mail platform that charges fees for every message. Visa is in a great position to not only capitalize on overall world economic growth, as most companies should be, but also to capitalize on a shift in this growth toward electronic payments. Even as debt-conscious consumers pull back on using credit cards, debit card usage continues to advance. This reinforces one of Visa's big strengths—unlike most other financial services businesses, Visa is relatively immune to downturns, as it makes its money by processing payments, not by extending credit. On the growth side, the company is expanding its footprint in emerging markets, and there is plenty of innovation opportunity in this business; the smartphone-driven "mobile wallet" concept, still a few years away, is a leading example. Overall, while Visa has competitors (MasterCard, American Express, and Discover), it has the strongest franchise, technology leadership, and pricing power at its back.

Reasons for Caution

The company has pricing power, but that power has come under government, merchant, and public scrutiny from time to time; the company must tread lightly or face possible consequences. As of early 2013 the company was faced with possibly having to buy its European licensee, currently owned by capital-starved European banks—this could hurt the balance sheet short term but is probably a long-term plus. Although Visa and others have driven payment technology for years, it is still possible that the mobile wallet opportunity may be capitalized on elsewhere in the industry, leaving credit card providers out of the loop. However, that doesn't look likely right now. Finally, the stock price has grown relentlessly as investors realize the positives; new investors should try for favorable entry points.

SECTOR: **Financials**
BETA COEFFICIENT: **0.76**
10-YEAR COMPOUND EARNINGS PER SHARE GROWTH: **NM**
10-YEAR COMPOUND DIVIDENDS PER SHARE GROWTH: **NM**

	2005	2006	2007	2008	2009	2010	2011	2012
Revenues (mil)	—	—	—	6,263	6,911	8,065	9,188	10,421
Net income (mil)	—	—	—	1,700	2,213	2,966	3,650	4,200
Earnings per share	—	—	—	2.25	2.92	3.91	4.99	6.20
Dividends per share	—	—	—	0.21	0.44	0.53	0.67	0.99
Cash flow per share	—	—	—	2.50	3.22	3.86	5.34	6.59
Price: high	—	—	—	89.6	89.7	97.2	103.4	152.5
low	—	—	—	43.5	41.8	64.9	67.5	98.3

Visa Inc.
P.O. Box 8999
San Francisco, CA 94128
(415) 932-2100
Website: www.visa.com

W. W. Grainger, Inc.

❏ Ticker symbol: GWW (NYSE) ❏ S&P rating: AA+ ❏ Value Line financial strength rating: A++
❏ Current yield: 1.5% ❏ Dividend raises, past 10 years: 10

Company Profile

Grainger is North America's largest supplier of maintenance, repair, and operating supply (MRO) products. They sell more than a million different products from more than 3,500 suppliers through a network of over 600 branches (400 in the U.S.), 15 distribution centers, and several websites, with a catalog containing some 307,000 items (a fascinating read if you like this sort of thing). Grainger also offers repair parts, specialized product sourcing, and inventory management supplies. Grainger sells principally to industrial and commercial maintenance departments, contractors, and government customers. The company has nearly 2 million customers, mostly in North America, and achieves overnight delivery to approximately 98 percent of them.

Their Canadian subsidiary is Canada's largest distributor of industrial, fleet, and safety products. They serve their customers through 172 branches and 5 distribution centers, and they offer bilingual websites and catalogs. Grainger, S.A. de C.V. is Mexico's leading facilities maintenance supplier, offering customers more than 84,000 products. The company also has important operations, through joint ventures, in Japan, China, and India and does business in 157 countries worldwide.

Grainger's customer base includes governmental offices at all levels; heavy manufacturing customers (typically textile, lumber, metals, and rubber industries); light manufacturing; transportation (shipbuilding, aerospace, and automotive); hospitals; retail; hospitality; and resellers of Grainger products. Grainger owns a number of trademarks, including Dayton motors, Dem-Kote spray paints, and Westward tools.

Many of Grainger's customers are corporate account customers, primarily *Fortune* 1,000 companies that spend more than $5 million annually on facilities maintenance products. Corporate account customers represent about 25 percent of Grainger's total U.S. sales. Both government and corporate account customer groups typically sign multiyear contracts for facilities maintenance products or a specific category of products, such as lighting or safety equipment. In 2009, the company averaged 95,000 transactions per day.

The Grainger strategy is centered on the idea of being easy to do business with. Customers can interact with a direct sales force, interact with one of the 400 distribution outlets in the United States, or order through an e-commerce website. Released quietly during the dot-com boom, *www.grainger.com* handles some $2.1 billion, or about 30 percent of the company's U.S. business each year, a solid e-commerce success story.

The business also depends a lot on reputation, and the company has earned numerous awards, including number one on *Fortune*'s America's Most Admired Companies list for diversified wholesalers and several prominent "best places to work" awards.

Financial Highlights, Fiscal Year 2012

It's hard to call an 11 percent increase in sales and a 5 percent increase in earnings a setback year, but for Grainger it almost feels like it. As the economy softened during the year, the company's recent record of sales increases tapered a bit, even as the company grew its e-commerce operations by 30 percent and increased the dividend by 20 percent.

It's worth noting that Grainger has reduced share count 25 percent since 2004, while doubling revenues and tripling profits in that same period. The company has raised its dividend 40 years in a row, and has raised it 50 percent over the past 2 years to $3.06 per share (if only you were receiving similar raises!). For FY2013, the company has offered guidance of 7 percent sales growth and EPS of $11.75, which would represent an increase of 24 percent.

Reasons to Buy

Grainger is far and away the biggest presence in the MRO world. Their only broad-line competitor is one-quarter their size, and the rest of the market is highly fragmented. They also have the deepest catalog by far. It's estimated that 40 percent of purchases in the MRO market are unplanned, so having the broadest inventory, fastest delivery, and friendliest service is a big advantage for Grainger. And if you doubt the value of a broad catalog, consider that this is primarily an industrial supplier that skated through the Great Recession practically untouched (just a 10 percent decline in sales).

Even with its size and scope, the company estimates that it still has less than 6 percent of the U.S. MRO market, leaving a large growth opportunity. The company has minimal debt and outstanding cash flow—we should not be surprised at all to see Grainger start leveraging its footholds in international locations with the purchase of existing distribution chains in Mexico, China, Japan, and Korea. The company has a larger presence in Canada (and 8 percent market share), and recently acquired Fabory Group, the largest MRO supplier in Europe (but still less than 1 percent market share). Especially with so much manufacturing relocated overseas, the international opportunity looks rich for Grainger.

The share repurchases and dividend increases reflect a better-than-average orientation to shareholder value, and shareholder value is indeed one of the stated goals of the company. To that end, the company has produced an average annual total shareholder return of over 20 percent for each of the past 5 years. We find it refreshing to see it not only stated but also delivered upon.

Reasons for Caution

Grainger will always be vulnerable to economic cycles and manufacturing displacement, especially so long as it remains concentrated on U.S. soil. International expansion should help alleviate this concern. Over the past 5 years, the share price has reflected most of the good news, mandating either careful price shopping for the stock or reliance on incremental growth opportunities in United States and especially overseas market share. Look for price pullbacks in times of greater macroeconomic concern.

SECTOR: **Industrials**
BETA COEFFICIENT: **0.95**
10-YEAR COMPOUND EARNINGS PER SHARE GROWTH: **14.5%**
10-YEAR COMPOUND DIVIDENDS PER SHARE GROWTH: **14.0%**

	2005	2006	2007	2008	2009	2010	2011	2012
Revenues (mil)	5,527	5,884	6,418	6,850	6,222	7,182	8,075	8,950
Net income (mil)	337	383	420	479	402	502	643	690
Earnings per share	3.78	4.25	4.94	6.09	5.25	6.81	9.04	9.52
Dividends per share	0.92	1.16	1.40	1.55	1.78	2.08	2.52	3.06
Cash flow per share	4.97	5.79	6.95	8.28	7.60	9.40	11.33	12.22
Price: high	72.4	80.0	98.6	94.0	102.5	139.1	193.2	221.8
low	51.6	60.6	68.8	58.9	59.9	96.1	124.3	172.5

W. W. Grainger, Inc.
100 Grainger Parkway
Lake Forest, IL 60045
(847) 535-0881
Website: www.grainger.com

CONSERVATIVE GROWTH

Wal-Mart Stores, Inc.

❑ Ticker symbol: WMT (NYSE) ❑ S&P rating: AAA ❑ Value Line financial strength rating: A ❑ Current yield: 2.4% ❑ Dividend raises, past 10 years: 10

Company Profile

Walmart is the world's largest retailer. It is also the world's largest private employer, ranked overall behind only the U.S. Department of Defense and the People's Liberation Army of China. So if on your next visit to the 'Mart the greeter gives you a snappy salute, don't say we didn't warn you about the upcoming move toward world domination. Better learn to speak Arkansas.

To clear up some confusion before it occurs, the Walmart company operates stores under the "Wal-Mart" brand, so if you feel like you're seeing two spellings of the same thing in error, that's the explanation (we expect they will clear this up soon by changing the corporate name). Wal-Mart Stores (10,800 at last count) is actually a collection of 69 different store banners in 27 countries. In the U.S., Walmart operates 3,150 Wal-Mart Supercenters, 620 Sam's Club stores, 561 Wal-Mart Discount Stores, and 286 Wal-Mart Neighborhood Markets. Rest-of-world retail locations total 6,148 medium and smaller footprint stores, mostly in Latin America, Canada, and the U.K. Nearly all of the stores are owned by the company, with the exception of those in India and China, which are mainly joint ventures.

Walmart operates in three business segments: the Walmart U.S. segment, the Walmart International segment, and the Sam's Club segment. In FY2012, the Walmart U.S. segment (which includes the online retail presence at Walmart.com) accounted for approximately 60 percent of revenue. The Walmart International segment accounted for 28 percent of sales in FY2012, while the Sam's Club segment and its online presence accounted for approximately 12 percent of net sales.

Walmart's mainline stores operate on an "everyday low price" philosophy. The idea is that customers need not wait for sale prices, as Walmart's normal price is at or near the bottom of the competitive market at all times. "Sale" prices are typically limited to seasonal and promotional goods, but there are occasional rollbacks on everyday items, typically staples.

The Sam's Club stores are focused on selling brand name and private label goods in larger quantities at "member" prices. The target competitors here are Costco and other warehouse merchandisers.

The Walmart U.S. segment does business in 6 merchandise units, including grocery, entertainment, health and wellness, apparel, and home. Grocery is typically available only at its superstore format, and the grocery section is quite large. Entertainment contains electronics, toys, cameras and supplies, cell phones, service plan contracts, and books. Hardlines consist of stationery, automotive accessories, hardware and paint, sporting goods, fabrics and crafts, and seasonal merchandise. Health and wellness includes pharmacy and optical services. Apparel includes apparel for women, girls, men, boys and infants, shoes, jewelry, and accessories. Home includes home furnishings, housewares and small appliances, bedding, home decor, outdoor living, and plants. The Walmart U.S. segment also offers financial services and related products, including money orders, wire transfers, check cashing, and bill payment. It has a private-label store credit card issued by a third-party provider and accepts online payments through PayPal. In addition, its pharmacy and optical departments accept payments for products and services through its customers' health benefit plans.

Financial Highlights, Fiscal Year 2013

Walmart turned in a workmanlike FY2013 with a 3.9 percent increase in sales (note that Walmart's fiscal 2013 closed in January 2013). Walmart International had the strongest performance, growing sales 7.9 percent and accounting for 30 percent of net sales. International also added 500 new stores. Overall, comps were up 1.8 percent, and the company opened just about 500 new stores during the fiscal year. Operating income rose 5.4 percent to $21.5 billion.

Reasons to Buy

Although FY2013 was less than impressive, improved domestic employment numbers and rapid growth in the International segment promise an improved FY2014. First quarter results from FY2014 show a year-over-year earnings growth of 4.6 percent, which is in line with estimates. The company has made progress against its cost goals and has reduced expenses just over 130 basis points (1.3 percent) since last year, and the company is on track to reduce operating costs a full percentage point by FY2017. This 1 percent may not sound like much, but at Walmart's scale it represents nearly $1 billion in continuous, ongoing savings.

Walmart U.S. plans to add another 16 million square feet of retail space this year, representing an incremental 230 units. There's no indication that saturation is in sight, and there have been very few store closings in the past few years.

The company's online businesses are growing well, with the first quarter of FY2014 showing a 30 percent growth over the same quarter last year. Amazon's decision to collect sales taxes on all transactions may lift a price ceiling on Walmart's online offerings.

Reasons for Caution

Recent events in the apparel production centers in Southeast Asia have some questioning whether cost-cutting pressures from Western buyers are having a deleterious effect on the industry. There is a lot more to be known in this area before anything definitive can be said, but it's an area that needs to be watched—Walmart relies on cost-cutting from its suppliers, probably more than most retailers, and if working conditions continue to deteriorate, it could affect the bottom line in Bentonville.

Some reports indicate that low stocking levels and long checkout wait times in Wal-Mart stores are having a material impact on the business. Walmart likes to cut cost through labor reduction, but you can't sell empty space and if the shelves aren't stocked, then sales are lost.

Remember that Walmart is one of the safest investments in the stock market with its enormous capitalization and terrific earnings predictability, so any "cautions" here should be viewed in that light.

SECTOR: **Retail**
BETA COEFFICIENT: **0.60**
5-YEAR COMPOUND EARNINGS PER SHARE GROWTH: **11.0%**
10-YEAR COMPOUND DIVIDENDS PER SHARE GROWTH: **18.0%**

	2006	2007	2008	2009	2010	2011	2012	2013 (FY)
Revenues (bil)	315.7	348.7	378.8	405.6	408.2	421.8	447.0	469.2
Net income (mil)	11.0	12.2	12.9	13.6	14.2	14.9	15.5	17.0
Earnings per share	2.63	2.92	3.16	3.42	3.66	4.07	4.45	5.02
Dividends per share	0.60	0.67	0.88	0.95	1.09	1.21	1.46	1.59
Cash flow per share	3.78	4.27	4.83	5.16	5.64	6.42	6.92	7.69
Price: high	54.6	52.2	51.4	63.8	57.5	56.3	60.0	77.6
low	42.3	42.3	42.1	43.1	46.3	47.8	48.3	57.2

Walmart Stores, Inc.
702 S.W. 8th St.
Bentonville, AR 72716
Website: www.Walmart.com

Waste Management, Inc.

❑ Ticker symbol: WM (NYSE) ❑ S&P rating: BBB ❑ Value Line financial strength rating: A
❑ Current yield: 3.7% ❑ Dividend raises, past 10 years: 9

Company Profile

You may refer to it as a "garbage company" if you want—we won't take offense. Waste Management is the largest and steadiest hand in the North American solid waste disposal industry. Like most large waste firms, WM has grown over time by assembling smaller, more local companies into a nationally branded and highly scaled operation with a notable amount of innovation on several fronts in the core business and especially in material recovery—translation, recycling.

The business is divided into 3 segments:

■ Collection, which accounts for 55 percent of the business, includes the standard dumpster and garbage truck operations. The company has over 600 collection operations, many of which have long-term contracts with municipalities and businesses. Innovations include a landfill-to-gas-liquefaction project that produces 13,000 gallons of fuel per day for WMI's trucks, online dumpster ordering, and the Bagster small-scale disposal units now sold through retail home-improvement outlets.

■ Landfill (17 percent of revenues). The company operates 266 landfills across North America, servicing its own collection operations and other collection service providers. Among these sites, there are 120 landfill-gas-to-energy conversion projects producing fuel for electricity generation—currently 540 megawatts of power, enough to power 400,000 homes.

■ Waste to energy, recycling and transfer (28 percent). These operations perform specialized material recovery and processing into useful commodities. There are 345 transfer stations set up for the collection of various forms of waste, including medical, recyclables, and e-waste. A wholly owned subsidiary, Wheelabrator Technologies, operates 17 waste-to-energy plants and 5 electricity-generating facilities producing electric power for about 1 million homes, in addition to the gasification projects at the landfills. The company has also pioneered single-stream recycling, where physical and optical sorting technologies sort out unseparated recyclable materials. Single-streaming has greatly increased recycling rates in municipalities where it is used, and provides a steady revenue stream in recovered paper, glass, metals, etc. for the company. The company also further refines these materials into industrial inputs, e.g., glass or plastic feedstocks in certain colors. The company recycles 8 million tons of commodities annually today and expects to grow that figure to 20 million by 2020.

Financial Highlights, Fiscal Year 2012

Results for FY2012 continued to be hampered by a soft recycled material market, especially in the paper and cardboard sector, and some of its energy contracts were renewed at lower rates. Revenues posted a modest 2 percent gain, while net profits dropped 4.1 percent. A moderate share repurchase held per-share earnings to a 2.9 percent drop. Neither the recycling nor the energy operations are core operations. There were acquisition costs, too—upshot: the base business was healthier. The company has guided for mainly flat earnings performance

again in 2013 but indicates better news ahead in 2014 as merger synergies and efficiency measures come into play and material prices start to improve. The company raised its dividend consistent with past policy and authorized another $500 million share repurchase. WM has steadily hauled off its share count from 570 million in 2004 to 455 million recently, representing about a 20 percent reduction.

Reasons to Buy

"Strategic" waste collection, particularly with the high-value-add material recovery operations that have become core to WM's business, is not only here to stay but also will only become more important to residential, industrial, and municipal customers as time goes on. WM exhibits a lot of innovation in an industry not particularly known for innovation. Additionally, the 4 percent dividend and share repurchase efforts make up for a relatively unexciting stock performance over the years; we feel that WM could break out of the doldrums as material recovery becomes an even more strategic and profitable enterprise. In the past 10 years, earnings have nearly doubled, while the share price is only up a third. The dividend has risen from 1 cent in 2003 to $1.45 expected in 2013; the company has clearly gotten the memo (on recycled paper, of course) about shareholder returns. This among other considerations makes WM a relatively safe bet, and indeed, the beta is only 0.57, a "sleep at night" stock in an economic storm. This may be a garbage company, but it is by no means a garbage stock.

Reasons for Caution

The company does rely on acquisitions for a lot of its growth. In this business, that might not be so bad, for existing companies have captive markets and disposal facilities, and can likely benefit from proven management processes and reduced overhead costs. The recycling operations, while cool and sexy, aren't always profitable, especially when competing material prices, like natural gas these days, are soft. The right combination of factors to drive improved recycling profitability may be close at hand or a ways off—you can have a clear environmental conscience (and collect your dividends) while you wait for better times. Additionally, any waste company runs the risk of going afoul of environmental regulations; WM has largely steered clear of trouble thus far, but there are no guarantees. Growth may be difficult to handle if regulations become more stringent.

SECTOR: **Business Services**
BETA COEFFICIENT: **0.57**
10-YEAR COMPOUND EARNINGS PER SHARE GROWTH: **4.0%**
10-YEAR COMPOUND DIVIDENDS PER SHARE GROWTH: **62%**

	2005	2006	2007	2008	2009	2010	2011	2012
Revenues (mil)	13,074	13,363	13,310	13,388	11,791	12,515	13,375	13,649
Net income (mil)	877	994	1,080	1,087	988	1,011	1,007	968
Earnings per share	1.55	1.82	2.07	2.19	2.00	2.10	2.14	2.08
Dividends per share	0.85	0.88	0.98	1.08	1.16	1.28	1.36	1.42
Cash flow per share	4.05	4.35	4.68	4.74	4.43	4.64	4.85	4.88
Price: high	31.0	35.6	41.2	39.3	34.2	37.3	36.7	36.3
low	26.8	30.1	32.4	24.5	22.1	31.1	27.8	30.8

Waste Management, Inc.
1001 Fannin, Suite 4000
Houston, TX 77002
(713) 512-6200
Website: www.wm.com

GROWTH AND INCOME

Wells Fargo & Company

❏ Ticker symbol: WFC (NYSE) ❏ S&P rating: AA- ❏ Value Line financial strength rating: A ❏ Current yield: 2.7% ❏ Dividend raises, past 10 years: 7

Company Profile

Wells Fargo & Company is a diversified financial services company, providing banking, insurance, investments, mortgages, and consumer finance from more than 11,000 offices and other distribution channels, including mortgage, investment management, commercial banking, and consumer finance branches across all 50 states, Canada, the Caribbean, and Central America.

The business is divided into 3 segments. First and largest is Community Banking, which provides traditional banking and mortgage services in all 50 states through a combination of branches, ATMs, and online services. Wholesale Banking provides commercial banking, capital markets, leasing, and other financing services to larger corporations. Wealth, Brokerage, and Retirement provides financial advisory and investment management services to individuals.

As of 2012, Wells Fargo had $1.42 trillion in assets, loans of $782 billion, and shareholder equity of $157 billion (this latter figure is up almost 25 percent from the end of 2010, a sign of health).

Based on assets, they are the third-largest bank holding company in the United States. They have 267,000 employees, or "team members," as they prefer to call them. The company expanded its footprint and market share—which is close to 10 percent of all U.S. banking services—considerably with the 2009 acquisition of Wachovia.

Financial Highlights, Fiscal Year 2012

Like all big banks, Wells took a big hit during the financial crisis with a substantial hit to earnings and concerns about asset quality. Since then the company has rebounded more successfully than its larger brethren. Loan losses and nonperforming assets have dropped significantly, and the so-called "tier 1" ratio, a measure of equity to total assets, has improved from 8.3 percent in 2010 to 9.5 percent in 2011 to 9.9 percent at the end of 2012, healthy by banking standards. The company also reported charge-offs for nonperforming assets of 1.05 percent compared to 1.36 percent in 2011; loan losses of 2.19 percent down from 2.56 percent, and nonperforming assets down to

3.07 percent from 3.37 percent. In line with these numbers, the loan loss reserve has dropped from $23 billion at the end of 2010 to $17 billion at the end of 2012, and the annual loan loss provision has dropped to about $7 billion from $21 billion in 2009. These figures all deliver a picture of improving financial health and asset quality.

These figures, while indicating health, also brought improved performance. Per-share earnings for FY2012 were $3.36, up 19 percent from FY2011, which was in turn up 28 percent from FY2010. The company raised its dividend substantially during the year, from 48 cents to 88 cents, and expects both the financial means and the regulatory support to move the dividend above a dollar by 2014. The company has begun to buy back shares, retiring 70 million during the year on a 5.2 billion share base; those buybacks should continue at least far enough to retire the billion or so shares issued to buy Wachovia. For FY2013, per-share earnings are expected in the $3.70 range.

Reasons to Buy

Wells Fargo seems to have learned its lessons from the financial crisis and the Wachovia purchase, has cleaned house, and seems ready to move forward with its solid, well-branded, universal banking business. We like its solid financial base, its growth in noninterest income (fees, etc.) that insulate it against possible interest rate hikes, its growth to become a more national bank, and its reputation in the marketplace. We also like what we believe to be a relatively minimal exposure to European debt and other events in Europe compared to its larger banking brethren.

Especially as the macroeconomic environment improves, we think WFC is well positioned to take advantage. We think shareholders will be rewarded with ample return in the form of dividends and buybacks as time goes on.

Reasons for Caution

Headline risk continues to abound in the banking industry. Any sign of trouble on the mortgage front will obviously hurt, although the recent settlement of the robosigning case reduces this risk somewhat. The company has been profiting from the difference between retail and wholesale interest rates, but if wholesale interest rates—i.e., deposits, Fed funds, and commercial paper—start to rise, the profit recovery could be jeopardized. The company (and others like it) is carrying a lot of low-interest-rate loans on its books.

SECTOR: **Financials**
BETA COEFFICIENT: **1.36**
10-YEAR COMPOUND EARNINGS PER SHARE GROWTH: **5.5%**
10-YEAR COMPOUND DIVIDENDS PER SHARE GROWTH: **11.5%**

		2005	**2006**	**2007**	**2008**	**2009**	**2010**	**2011**	**2012**
Loans (bil)		296.1	306.9	344.8	843.8	758	734	750	783
Net income (mil)		7,670	8,480	8,060	2,655	12,275	11,632	15,025	17,999
Earnings per share		2.25	2.49	2.38	0.70	1.75	2.21	2.82	3.36
Dividends per share		1.00	1.12	1.18	1.30	0.49	0.20	0.48	0.88
Price:	high	32.4	37.0	38.0	44.7	31.5	34.3	34.3	36.6
	low	28.8	30.3	29.3	19.9	7.8	23.0	22.6	27.9

Wells Fargo & Company
420 Montgomery Street
San Francisco, CA 94163
(415) 396-0523
Website: www.wellsfargo.com

CONSERVATIVE GROWTH

Whirlpool Corporation

❑ Ticker symbol: WHR (NYSE) ❑ S&P rating: BBB- ❑ Value Line financial strength rating: A
❑ Current yield: 1.7% ❑ Dividend raises, past 10 years: 3

Company Profile

Whirlpool is the world's leading home appliance manufacturer in a $120 billion global industry. The company manufactures appliances under familiar and recognized brand names in all major home appliance categories including fabric care (laundry), cooking, refrigeration, dishwashers, water filtration, and garage organization. Familiar brand names include Whirlpool, Maytag, Kitchen Aid, Amana, Jenn-Air, and international names Bauknecht, Brastemp, and Consul. The Whirlpool brand itself is the number one global appliance brand. About 48 percent of Whirlpool's sales come from overseas, a growth of 5 percent since 2008. Latin America has been the most dynamic player at 27 percent of sales, up from 19 percent in 2008, a gain that was offset by a 3 percent decline in the EMEA (Europe, Middle East, Africa) region.

In an industry not known for innovation, Whirlpool has striven to be an innovation leader in its industry. This has manifested itself both in new products and product platforms and in manufacturing and supply-chain efficiencies, such as a global platform design for local manufacture

of washing machine products, recalling similar achievements in the auto industry. Such gains are key in this competitive, price-sensitive industry. The company also has initiatives to build lifetime brand loyalty and product quality, improve energy efficiency, and to expand in key developing markets such as Brazil (where the Brastemp brand is sold) and India. The company is the number one appliance manufacturer in Latin America.

Financial Highlights, Fiscal Year 2012

Like most other manufacturing corporations, Whirlpool is enjoying the economic recovery. That isn't readily apparent in the numbers, however, as the expiration of a U.S. energy tax benefits program inflated results prior to the end of FY2011. Revenues, earnings, per-share earnings, and cash flows all showed a decline on this basis. Unit sales were also lower, but the company was able to enact some price increases and product mix improvements (to higher-end products) to offset higher material costs.

Despite what the numbers say, prospects are driven by an

improving economy and housing market and pent-up replacement demand for appliances, all at a time when the company has implemented structural and operational improvements to capitalize on the improved environment. Without the energy credits, the company expects to continue at an 8 percent operating margin and to generate $9.80–$10.30 in per-share earnings in FY2013 and per-share cash flows north of $16 (the company strongly believes in managing cash flow and especially free cash flow). Longer term, the company expects 5–7 percent revenue growth, 8-plus percent operating margins, and 10–15 percent annual earnings growth. When you have only 76 million shares outstanding, business improvements can bring sizable per-share gains; that's part of what's happening here. On top of that, the company is retiring approximately 1 million shares per year.

Reasons to Buy

Last year we added Whirlpool because we had a good feeling about the company, its management, its markets, and the health of the economy in general. We weren't disappointed; the stock almost doubled from the time of last year's analysis.

We like market leaders, particularly companies not content to sit on their laurels and reap increasingly lean cash flows while others

close in around them. Whirlpool has used the recession and ensuing recovery as a wake-up call and an opportunity to streamline its businesses and to put some real strategic thought into how to drive its brand assortment and international portfolio to achieve better results. As the company continues to innovate, tweak its operations, and build critical mass in overseas markets, we would expect it to resume a solid growth path in sales and especially earnings. Cash flows and investor returns are solid. More than most, the management team is a plus with a recognizable pragmatic and strategic approach to managing this business.

Reasons for Caution

By nature, the appliance business is highly competitive and cyclical. In addition, consumers with more disposable income have of late been opting for fancier, more expensive foreign brands, like Bosch and LG, a trend that could hurt if it continues. We believe that Whirlpool is countering this trend by adding elegance, advertising, and channel support for its top-tier brands and products; that plus a reversal of customer preferences toward American brands as seen to a degree in the auto industry should help. Commodity costs, labor issues, quality issues, and shifts in consumer preferences are perpetual risks. Finally, the share price has been relatively volatile for a mature business, probably reflecting differing views at differing times about the success of this economically sensitive company. You can see that in the high beta of 2.0, and recently high share prices may be a sign for caution for some investors.

SECTOR: Consumer Durables
BETA COEFFICIENT: 2.00
10-YEAR COMPOUND EARNINGS PER SHARE GROWTH: 3.0%
10-YEAR COMPOUND DIVIDENDS PER SHARE GROWTH: 2.5%

	2005	2006	2007	2008	2009	2010	2011	2012
Revenues (mil)	14,317	18,080	19,408	18,907	17,099	18,366	18,666	18,710
Net income (mil)	422	486	647	418	328	707	699	559
Earnings per share	6.19	6.35	8.10	5.50	4.34	9.10	8.95	7.05
Dividends per share	1.72	1.72	1.72	1.72	1.72	1.72	1.93	2.00
Cash flow per share	12.71	13.26	16.32	13.90	11.37	16.91	16.54	14.05
Price: high	86.5	96.0	118.0	98.0	85.0	118.4	92.3	104.2
low	60.8	74.1	72.1	30.2	19.2	71.0	45.2	47.7

Whirlpool Corporation
2000 M-63
Benton Harbor, MI 49022
(269) 923-5000
Website: www.whirlpoolcorp.com

▼ **Appendix A: Performance Analysis:** *100 Best Stocks 2013*

ONE-YEAR GAIN/LOSS, APRIL 1, 2012–APRIL 1, 2013, EXCLUDING DIVIDENDS; (*) = NEW FOR 2013

Company	Symbol	Price 4/1/2012	Price 4/1/2013	% change	Dollar gain/loss, $1,000 invested
3M Company	MMM	$86.92	$106.31	22.3%	$223.08
Abbott Laboratories	ABT	$61.29	$76.10	24.2%	$241.64
Aetna	AET	$50.16	$51.13	1.9%	$19.34
Allergan	AGN	$95.43	$111.63	17.0%	$169.76
Amgen	AMGN	$67.87	$102.51	51.0%	$510.39
Apple	AAPL	$599.55	$442.66	-26.2%	$(261.68)
Archer Daniels Midland	ADM	$31.23	$36.69	17.5%	$174.83
AT&T	T	$29.08	$35.27	21.3%	$212.86
Automatic Data Processing	ADP	$55.19	$65.03	17.8%	$178.29
Baxter	BAX	$57.11	$72.64	27.2%	$271.93
Becton, Dickinson	BDX	$77.65	$95.61	23.1%	$231.29
Bed Bath & Beyond	BBBY	$65.77	$64.42	-2.1%	$(20.53)
Campbell Soup	CPB	$33.85	$45.36	34.0%	$340.03
CarMax	KMX	$34.65	$41.70	20.3%	$203.46
Caterpillar	CAT	$106.52	$86.97	-18.4%	$(183.53)
Chevron	CVX	$107.21	$118.62	10.6%	$106.43
Church & Dwight	CHD	$49.19	$64.63	31.4%	$313.88
Cincinnati Financial	CINF	$34.51	$47.22	36.8%	$368.30
Clorox	CLX	$68.75	$88.53	28.8%	$287.71
Coca-Cola	KO	$36.00	$40.44	12.3%	$123.33
Colgate-Palmolive	CL	$97.78	$118.03	20.7%	$207.10
Comcast	CMCSA	$30.01	$41.98	39.9%	$398.87
ConocoPhillips	COP	$55.27	$60.10	8.7%	$87.39
Costco Wholesale	COST	$90.80	$106.11	16.9%	$168.61
CVS Caremark	CVS	$44.80	$54.99	22.7%	$227.46
Deere	DE	$80.90	$85.98	6.3%	$62.79
Dominion Resources	D	$51.21	$58.18	13.6%	$136.11

Company	Symbol	Price 4/1/2012	Price 4/1/2013	% change	Dollar gain/loss, $1,000 invested
Duke Energy	DUK	$60.17	$72.59	20.6%	$206.42
DuPont	DD	$52.90	$49.16	-7.1%	$(70.70)
Eastman Chemical (*)	EMN	$51.69	$69.87	35.2%	$351.71
Exxon	XOM	$86.73	$90.11	3.9%	$38.97
Fair Isaac	FICO	$43.90	$45.69	4.1%	$40.77
FedEx	FDX	$91.96	$98.20	6.8%	$67.86
Fluor Corporation	FLR	$60.04	$66.33	10.5%	$104.76
FMC Corporation	FMC	$52.50	$57.03	8.6%	$86.29
General Mills	GIS	$39.45	$49.31	25.0%	$249.94
Harman International (*)	HAR	$46.81	$44.63	-4.7%	$(46.57)
Heinz	HNZ	$53.55	$72.27	35.0%	$349.58
Honeywell	HON	$61.05	$75.35	23.4%	$234.23
IBM	IBM	$208.65	$213.30	2.2%	$22.29
Illinois Tool Works	ITW	$57.12	$60.94	6.7%	$66.88
Intel (*)	INTC	$28.12	$21.84	-22.3%	$(223.33)
International Paper	IP	$35.10	$46.58	32.7%	$327.07
Iron Mountain	IRM	$28.80	$36.31	26.1%	$260.76
Itron (*)	ITRI	$45.41	$46.40	2.2%	$21.80
J. M. Smucker	SJM	$81.36	$99.16	21.9%	$218.78
Johnson & Johnson	JNJ	$65.96	$81.53	23.6%	$236.05
Johnson Controls	JCI	$32.48	$35.07	8.0%	$79.74
Kellogg	K	$53.63	$64.43	20.1%	$201.38
Kimberly-Clark	KMB	$73.89	$97.98	32.6%	$326.03
Macy's (*)	M	$39.73	$41.84	5.3%	$53.11
Marathon Oil	MRO	$31.70	$33.72	6.4%	$63.72
McCormick	MKC	$54.43	$73.55	35.1%	$351.28
McDonald's	MCD	$98.10	$99.69	1.6%	$16.21
McKesson	MCK	$87.77	$107.96	23.0%	$230.03
Medtronic	MDT	$39.19	$46.96	19.8%	$198.26
Molex (*)	MOLX	$28.12	$29.28	4.1%	$41.25

Company	Symbol	Price 4/1/2012	Price 4/1/2013	% change	Dollar gain/loss, $1,000 invested
Monsanto	MON	$79.76	$105.63	32.4%	$324.35
Mosaic (*)	MOS	$55.21	$59.61	8.0%	$79.70
NextEra Energy	NEE	$61.08	$77.68	27.2%	$271.77
Nike	NKE	$53.40	$59.01	10.5%	$105.06
Norfolk Southern	NSC	$65.83	$77.08	17.1%	$170.89
Nucor	NUE	$42.95	$46.15	7.5%	$74.51
Otter Tail	OTTR	$21.70	$31.14	43.5%	$435.02
Pall Corporation	PLL	$59.63	$68.37	14.7%	$146.57
Patterson	PDCO	$33.40	$38.04	13.9%	$138.92
Paychex	PAYX	$30.99	$35.06	13.1%	$131.33
PepsiCo	PEP	$66.35	$79.11	19.2%	$192.31
Perrigo	PRGO	$103.31	$118.74	14.9%	$149.36
Praxair	PX	$114.64	$111.54	-2.7%	$(27.04)
Procter & Gamble	PG	$67.21	$77.06	14.7%	$146.56
Ross Stores	ROST	$58.10	$60.62	4.3%	$43.37
Schlumberger	SLB	$69.93	$74.89	7.1%	$70.93
Seagate Technology (*)	STX	$26.96	$36.56	35.6%	$356.08
Sigma-Aldrich	SIAL	$73.06	$77.65	6.3%	$62.83
Southern Company	SO	$44.93	$46.92	4.4%	$44.29
Southwest Airlines	LUV	$8.24	$13.48	63.6%	$635.92
St. Jude Medical	STJ	$44.31	$40.44	-8.7%	$(87.34)
Starbucks	SBUX	$55.89	$56.95	1.9%	$18.97
Stryker	SYK	$55.48	$65.24	17.6%	$175.92
Suburban Propane	SPH	$43.00	$44.50	3.5%	$34.88
Sysco	SYY	$29.86	$35.17	17.8%	$177.83
Target Corporation	TGT	$58.27	$68.45	17.5%	$174.70
Teva Pharmaceuticals	TEVA	$45.06	$39.68	-11.9%	$(119.40)
Tiffany (*)	TIF	$69.13	$69.54	0.6%	$5.93
Time Warner Inc. (*)	TWX	$37.75	$57.62	52.6%	$526.36
Total S.A.	TOT	$51.12	$47.98	-6.1%	$(61.42)

Company	Symbol	Price 4/1/2012	Price 4/1/2013	% change	Dollar gain/loss, $1,000 invested
Tractor Supply Company	TSCO	$90.56	$104.13	15.0%	$149.85
Union Pacific	UNP	$107.48	$142.41	32.5%	$324.99
UnitedHealth Group	UNH	$58.94	$57.21	-2.9%	$(29.35)
United Parcel Service (*)	UPS	$80.72	$85.90	6.4%	$64.17
United Technologies	UTX	$89.58	$79.80	-10.9%	$(109.18)
Valero (*)	VLO	$25.77	$45.49	76.5%	$765.23
Valmont Industries	VMI	$105.30	$118.06	12.1%	$121.18
Verizon	VZ	$37.78	$37.26	-1.4%	$(13.76)
Visa	V	$78.12	$123.16	57.7%	$576.55
W. W. Grainger	GWW	$214.81	$224.98	4.7%	$47.34
Waste Management (*)	WM	$34.96	$39.21	12.2%	$121.57
Wells Fargo	WFC	$29.11	$32.84	12.8%	$128.13
Whirlpool (*)	WHR	$76.86	$118.46	54.1%	$541.24

▼ Appendix B: *The 100 Best Stocks 2014*: Dividend and Yield, by Company

(*) = NEW TO LIST

		2012		2013 PROJECTED		
Company	Symbol	Dividend	Yield %	Dividend	Yield %	Dividend Raises, Past 10 Years
3M Company	MMM	$2.36	2.6%	$2.54	1.8%	10
Abbott Laboratories	ABT	$2.01	3.4%	$0.56	1.5%	10
Aetna	AET	$0.70	1.5%	$0.80	1.4%	4
Allergan	AGN	$0.20	0.2%	$0.20	0.2%	1
Amgen	AMGN	$1.44	2.1%	$1.88	1.8%	2
Apple	AAPL	$2.65	1.8%	$11.65	2.6%	2
Aqua America (*)	WTR			$0.70	2.2%	10
Archer Daniels Midland	ADM	$0.70	2.2%	$0.76	2.2%	10
AT&T	T	$1.76	5.7%	$1.80	4.7%	9
Automatic Data Processing	ADP	$1.55	2.9%	$1.70	2.5%	10
Baxter	BAX	$1.46	2.4%	$1.80	2.9%	10
Becton, Dickinson	BDX	$1.80	2.1%	$1.98	2.0%	10
Bemis (*)	BMS			$1.04	2.6%	10
Campbell Soup	CPB	$1.16	3.5%	$1.16	2.5%	9
CarMax	KMX					
Chevron	CVX	$3.51	3.0%	$3.76	3.2%	10
Church & Dwight	CHD	$0.96	2.0%	$0.96	1.8%	7
Cincinnati Financial	CINF	$1.62	5.7%	$1.64	3.1%	10
Clorox	CLX	$2.44	3.5%	$2.61	3.0%	9
Coca-Cola	KO	$1.02	2.8%	$1.12	2.6%	10
Colgate-Palmolive	CL	$2.44	2.5%	$2.66	2.3%	10
Comcast	CMCSA	$0.60	2.2%	$0.78	1.8%	5
ConocoPhillips	COP	$2.64	3.7%	$2.64	4.2%	9
Corning (*)	GLW			$0.40	2.7%	4

Company	Symbol	Dividend	Yield %	Dividend	Yield %	Dividend Raises, Past 10 Years
Costco Wholesale	COST	$1.00	1.2%	$1.14	1.1%	9
CVS Caremark	CVS	$0.65	1.5%	$0.90	1.5%	10
Deere	DE	$1.79	2.3%	$1.84	2.2%	10
Dominion Resources	D	$2.11	4.1%	$2.25	3.7%	10
Duke Energy	DUK	$3.03	4.8%	$3.09	4.2%	6
DuPont	DD	$1.70	3.1%	$1.76	3.3%	4
Eastman Chemical	EMN	$1.08	2.0%	$1.20	1.8%	2
Fair Isaac	FICO	$0.08	0.2%	$0.08	0.2%	2
FedEx	FDX	$0.52	0.6%	$0.56	0.6%	9
Fluor Corporation	FLR	$0.77	1.1%	$0.64	1.0%	2
FMC Corporation	FMC	$0.35	0.7%	$0.54	0.9%	5
General Mills	GIS	$1.22	3.1%	$1.32	3.0%	9
Harman International	HAR	$0.30	0.6%	$0.60	1.2%	2
Health Care REIT (*)	HCN			$3.06	4.1%	10
Honeywell	HON	$1.53	2.5%	$1.67	2.1%	9
IBM	IBM	$3.30	1.4%	$3.55	1.9%	10
Illinois Tool Works	ITW	$1.46	2.5%	$1.52	2.3%	10
International Paper	IP	$1.09	3.2%	$1.20	2.6%	3
Iron Mountain	IRM	$0.98	3.5%	$1.20	2.8%	4
Itron	ITRI					
J. M. Smucker	SJM	$2.04	2.4%	$2.08	2.0%	10
Johnson & Johnson	JNJ	$2.40	3.8%	$2.56	3.1%	10
Johnson Controls	JCI	$0.74	2.3%	$0.76	2.1%	9
Kellogg	K	$1.74	3.3%	$1.76	2.7%	8
Kimberly-Clark	KMB	$2.92	4.0%	$3.08	3.1%	10
Kroger (*)	KR			$0.65	1.7%	7
Macy's	M	$0.70	2.0%	$0.85	1.7%	7
McCormick & Co.	MKC	$1.24	2.3%	$1.36	1.9%	10
McDonald's	MCD	$2.87	2.9%	$3.15	3.0%	10

Company	Symbol	Dividend	Yield %	Dividend	Yield %	Dividend Raises, Past 10 Years
McKesson	MCK	$0.80	0.3%	$1.04	0.7%	4
Medtronic	MDT	$1.04	2.6%	$1.12	2.2%	10
Molex	MOLX	$0.80	3.6%	$0.88	3.3%	10
Monsanto	MON	$1.20	1.6%	$1.50	1.4%	8
Mosaic	MOS	$0.50	1.0%	$1.00	1.6%	2
NextEra Energy	NEE	$2.40	3.8%	$2.60	3.2%	10
Nike	NKE	$0.70	1.3%	$0.81	1.3%	10
Norfolk Southern	NSC	$1.88	2.8%	$2.00	2.6%	10
Otter Tail	OTTR	$1.19	5.4%	$1.30	3.9%	5
Pall Corporation	PLL	$0.80	1.4%	$0.88	1.5%	8
Patterson	PDCO	$0.58	1.7%	$0.66	1.7%	4
Paychex	PAYX	$1.24	4.2%	$1.27	3.6%	8
PepsiCo	PEP	$2.15	3.1%	$2.21	2.7%	10
Perrigo	PRGO	$0.32	0.3%	$0.34	0.3%	10
Praxair	PX	$2.20	1.9%	$2.40	2.1%	10
Procter & Gamble	PG	$2.14	3.1%	$2.29	3.1%	10
Quest Diagnostics(*)	DGX			$1.20	2.1%	5
Ross	ROST	$0.56	1.0%	$0.64	1.0%	10
Schlumberger	SLB	$1.10	1.6%	$1.25	1.6%	7
Seagate Technology	STX	$0.86	3.3%	$1.40	3.6%	7
Sigma-Aldrich	SIAL	$0.80	1.1%	$0.86	1.1%	10
Southern Company	SO	$1.94	4.3%	$2.02	4.3%	10
Southwest Airlines	LUV	$0.03	0.2%	$0.04	0.3%	1
St. Jude Medical	STJ	$0.92	2.4%	$1.00	2.4%	2
Starbucks	SBUX	$0.68	1.1%	$0.84	1.4%	3
State Street (*)	STT			$1.04	1.7%	8
Stryker	SYK	$0.85	1.2%	$1.06	1.6%	9
Suburban Propane	SPH	$3.41	7.8%	$3.50	7.3%	9
Sysco	SYY	$1.08	3.6%	$1.12	3.3%	10
Target Corporation	TGT	$1.32	2.1%	$1.50	2.0%	10

Company	Symbol	Dividend	Yield %	Dividend	Yield %	Dividend Raises, Past 10 Years
Tiffany	TIF	$1.25	1.7%	$1.28	1.7%	10
Time Warner Inc.	TWX	$1.04	2.9%	$1.08	1.9%	7
Total S.A.	TOT	$2.98	6.2%	$3.15	7.4%	5
Tractor Supply Company	TSCO	$0.72	0.5%	$0.92	0.9%	3
Union Pacific	UNP	$2.49	2.2%	$2.78	1.8%	8
UnitedHealth Group	UNH	$0.80	1.2%	$0.85	1.4%	5
United Parcel Service	UPS	$2.28	2.9%	$2.48	2.8%	10
United Technologies	UTX	$1.87	2.4%	$2.03	2.3%	10
Valero	VLO	$0.65	2.4%	$0.80	2.1%	9
Valmont Industries	VMI	$0.72	0.6%	$0.86	0.7%	10
Verizon	VZ	$2.02	5.5%	$2.06	3.9%	7
Visa	V	$0.99	0.7%	$1.32	0.7%	5
W. W. Grainger	GWW	$3.06	1.5%	$3.35	1.5%	10
Walmart (*)	WMT			$1.88	2.4%	10
Waste Management	WM	$1.42	4.2%	$1.46	3.5%	9
Wells Fargo	WFC	$0.88	2.5%	$1.00	3.1%	7
Whirlpool	WHR	$2.00	3.1%	$2.00	2.0%	3

▼ Appendix C: *The 100 Best Stocks 2014*: Dividend and Yield, by Descending Projected 2013 Yield (*) New to list

| Company | Symbol | 2012 | | 2013 PROJECTED | | Dividend Raises, Past 10 Years |
		Dividend	Yield %	Dividend	Yield %	
Total S.A.	TOT	$2.98	6.2%	$3.15	7.4%	5
Suburban Propane	SPH	$3.41	7.8%	$3.50	7.3%	9
AT&T	T	$1.76	5.7%	$1.80	4.7%	9
Southern Company	SO	$1.94	4.3%	$2.02	4.3%	10
ConocoPhillips	COP	$2.64	3.7%	$2.64	4.2%	9
Duke Energy	DUK	$3.03	4.8%	$3.09	4.2%	6
Health Care REIT (*)	HCN			$3.06	4.1%	10
Otter Tail	OTTR	$1.19	5.4%	$1.30	3.9%	5
Verizon	VZ	$2.02	5.5%	$2.06	3.9%	7
Dominion Resources	D	$2.11	4.1%	$2.25	3.7%	10
Paychex	PAYX	$1.24	4.2%	$1.27	3.6%	8
Seagate Technology	STX	$0.86	3.3%	$1.40	3.6%	7
Waste Management	WM	$1.42	4.2%	$1.46	3.5%	9
DuPont	DD	$1.70	3.1%	$1.76	3.3%	4
Molex	MOLX	$0.80	3.6%	$0.88	3.3%	10
Sysco	SYY	$1.08	3.6%	$1.12	3.3%	10
Chevron	CVX	$3.51	3.0%	$3.76	3.2%	10
NextEra Energy	NEE	$2.40	3.8%	$2.60	3.2%	10
Cincinnati Financial	CINF	$1.62	5.7%	$1.64	3.1%	10
Johnson & Johnson	JNJ	$2.40	3.8%	$2.56	3.1%	10
Kimberly-Clark	KMB	$2.92	4.0%	$3.08	3.1%	10
Procter & Gamble	PG	$2.14	3.1%	$2.29	3.1%	10
Wells Fargo	WFC	$0.88	2.5%	$1.00	3.1%	7
Clorox	CLX	$2.44	3.5%	$2.61	3.0%	9

Company	Symbol	Dividend	Yield %	Dividend	Yield %	Dividend Raises, Past 10 Years
General Mills	GIS	$1.22	3.1%	$1.32	3.0%	9
McDonald's	MCD	$2.87	2.9%	$3.15	3.0%	10
Baxter	BAX	$1.46	2.4%	$1.80	2.9%	10
Iron Mountain	IRM	$0.98	3.5%	$1.20	2.8%	4
United Parcel Service	UPS	$2.28	2.9%	$2.48	2.8%	10
Corning (*)	GLW			$0.40	2.7%	4
Kellogg	K	$1.74	3.3%	$1.76	2.7%	8
PepsiCo	PEP	$2.15	3.1%	$2.21	2.7%	10
Apple	AAPL	$2.65	1.8%	$11.65	2.6%	2
Bemis (*)	BMS			$1.04	2.6%	10
Coca-Cola	KO	$1.02	2.8%	$1.12	2.6%	10
International Paper	IP	$1.09	3.2%	$1.20	2.6%	3
Norfolk Southern	NSC	$1.88	2.8%	$2.00	2.6%	10
Automatic Data Processing	ADP	$1.55	2.9%	$1.70	2.5%	10
Campbell Soup	CPB	$1.16	3.5%	$1.16	2.5%	9
St. Jude Medical	STJ	$0.92	2.4%	$1.00	2.4%	2
Walmart (*)	WMT			$1.88	2.4%	10
Colgate-Palmolive	CL	$2.44	2.5%	$2.66	2.3%	10
Illinois Tool Works	ITW	$1.46	2.5%	$1.52	2.3%	10
United Technologies	UTX	$1.87	2.4%	$2.03	2.3%	10
Aqua America (*)	WTR			$0.70	2.2%	10
Archer Daniels Midland	ADM	$0.70	2.2%	$0.76	2.2%	10
Deere	DE	$1.79	2.3%	$1.84	2.2%	10
Medtronic	MDT	$1.04	2.6%	$1.12	2.2%	10
Honeywell	HON	$1.53	2.5%	$1.67	2.1%	9
Johnson Controls	JCI	$0.74	2.3%	$0.76	2.1%	9
Praxair	PX	$2.20	1.9%	$2.40	2.1%	10
Quest Diagnostics(*)	DGX			$1.20	2.1%	5
Valero	VLO	$0.65	2.4%	$0.80	2.1%	9

Company	Symbol	Dividend	Yield %	Dividend	Yield %	Dividend Raises, Past 10 Years
Becton, Dickinson	BDX	$1.80	2.1%	$1.98	2.0%	10
J. M. Smucker	SJM	$2.04	2.4%	$2.08	2.0%	10
Target Corporation	TGT	$1.32	2.1%	$1.50	2.0%	10
Whirlpool	WHR	$2.00	3.1%	$2.00	2.0%	3
IBM	IBM	$3.30	1.4%	$3.55	1.9%	10
McCormick & Co.	MKC	$1.24	2.3%	$1.36	1.9%	10
Time Warner Inc.	TWX	$1.04	2.9%	$1.08	1.9%	7
3M Company	MMM	$2.36	2.6%	$2.54	1.8%	10
Amgen	AMGN	$1.44	2.1%	$1.88	1.8%	2
Church & Dwight	CHD	$0.96	2.0%	$0.96	1.8%	7
Comcast	CMCSA	$0.60	2.2%	$0.78	1.8%	5
Eastman Chemical	EMN	$1.08	2.0%	$1.20	1.8%	2
Union Pacific	UNP	$2.49	2.2%	$2.78	1.8%	8
Kroger (*)	KR			$0.65	1.7%	7
Macy's	M	$0.70	2.0%	$0.85	1.7%	7
Patterson	PDCO	$0.58	1.7%	$0.66	1.7%	4
State Street (*)	STT			$1.04	1.7%	8
Tiffany	TIF	$1.25	1.7%	$1.28	1.7%	10
Mosaic	MOS	$0.50	1.0%	$1.00	1.6%	2
Schlumberger	SLB	$1.10	1.6%	$1.25	1.6%	7
Stryker	SYK	$0.85	1.2%	$1.06	1.6%	9
Abbott Laboratories	ABT	$2.01	3.4%	$0.56	1.5%	10
CVS Caremark	CVS	$0.65	1.5%	$0.90	1.5%	10
W. W. Grainger	GWW	$3.06	1.5%	$3.35	1.5%	10
Pall Corporation	PLL	$0.80	1.4%	$0.88	1.5%	8
Aetna	AET	$0.70	1.5%	$0.80	1.4%	4
Monsanto	MON	$1.20	1.6%	$1.50	1.4%	8
Starbucks	SBUX	$0.68	1.1%	$0.84	1.4%	3
UnitedHealth Group	UNH	$0.80	1.2%	$0.85	1.4%	5

Company	Symbol	Dividend	Yield %	Dividend	Yield %	Dividend Raises, Past 10 Years
Nike	NKE	$0.70	1.3%	$0.81	1.3%	10
Harman International	HAR	$0.30	0.6%	$0.60	1.2%	2
Costco Wholesale	COST	$1.00	1.2%	$1.14	1.1%	9
Sigma-Aldrich	SIAL	$0.80	1.1%	$0.86	1.1%	10
Fluor Corporation	FLR	$0.77	1.1%	$0.64	1.0%	2
Ross	ROST	$0.56	1.0%	$0.64	1.0%	10
FMC Corporation	FMC	$0.35	0.7%	$0.54	0.9%	5
Tractor Supply Company	TSCO	$0.72	0.5%	$0.92	0.9%	3
McKesson	MCK	$0.80	0.3%	$1.04	0.7%	4
Valmont Industries	VMI	$0.72	0.6%	$0.86	0.7%	10
Visa	V	$0.99	0.7%	$1.32	0.7%	5
FedEx	FDX	$0.52	0.6%	$0.56	0.6%	9
Perrigo	PRGO	$0.32	0.3%	$0.34	0.3%	10
Southwest Airlines	LUV	$0.03	0.2%	$0.04	0.3%	1
Allergan	AGN	$0.20	0.2%	$0.20	0.2%	1
Fair Isaac	FICO	$0.08	0.2%	$0.08	0.2%	2
CarMax	KMX					

About the Authors

PETER SANDER is an author, researcher, and consultant in the fields of personal finance, business, and location reference. He has written thirty-nine books, including *All about Low Volatility Investing, Value Investing for Dummies, The 100 Best Exchange-Traded Funds You Can Buy 2012, The 25 Habits of Highly Successful Investors, What Would Steve Jobs Do?, 101 Things Everyone Should Know about Economics,* and *Cities Ranked & Rated.* He is also the author of numerous articles and columns on investment strategies. He has an MBA from Indiana University, has completed Certified Financial Planner (CFP®) education and examination requirements, and lives in Granite Bay, CA.

SCOTT BOBO has a BS from Miami University in electrical engineering technology. After beginning his career in the defense electronics industry and teaching at the University of Cincinnati, he moved on to the computer and semiconductor industries in California, later specializing in audio and applications engineering in a twenty-plus-year career. He is now a full-time tax director for one of the world's largest software companies and continues to teach, write, and consult on technology issues for private and corporate clients. He resides in San Jose, CA.